THE DISSENTING
TRADITION

Professor Leland H. Carlson

ESSAYS FOR LELAND H. CARLSON

THE DISSENTING TRADITION

Edited by C. Robert Cole and Michael E. Moody

OHIO UNIVERSITY PRESS : ATHENS

Copyright © 1975 by C. Robert Cole and Michael E. Moody

Library of Congress Catalog Card Number: 74-27706
ISBN 8214-0176-9

Manufactured in the United States of America by
Oberlin Printing Company, Inc.
Designed by Harold M. Stevens

Table of Contents

Preface

THE TERM DISSENTING TRADITION was adopted for this volume of essays because there seemed no better description of its collective theme. Dissent in English history has been first a state of mind stemming from both the philosophy and practice of religious Nonconformity, and second a means by which to project an outlook that is regarded by its adherents as morally, ethically, and practically superior to the *status quo*. The fact and particular nature of the English church and state as by law established in the sixteenth and seventeenth centuries gave dissent a role to play which if not unique has been rare in western history. By examining particular examples of dissent, dissenters, and theories of dissent, the contributors to this collection have sought an explanation both for the continuity and breadth of that role.

The church remains established to the present day, as does royal government. Despite major alterations in the privileges and status of parliament, crown, and people that have come about specifically through parliamentary reform acts between 1689 and 1949, there has been no radical change in their constitutional relationship. The franchise and representation of parliament was reformed in favor of democracy, an aristocratic convocation ceased to exist outside of parliament, curiously increasing rather than diminishing the subjection of the church to an Erastian Establishment, and politics became a matter of secular parties, as did ideology. In the process the Establishment grew, even if changing somewhat in coloration. A Labour party leader may now belong, the same as a conservative. Nonetheless, the denotation of class through public school and university, the dominance of aristocracy in government, and a broad range of benevolent and paternalistic attitudes on the part of those who have governed, remain its manifestations. The charge often made by contemporary secular dissenters is that even under Labour governments there has been no diminution of the subtle aristocratic and paternalistic dominance of the Establishment. Legal repudiation of aristocracy, of class-consciousness, and of assumed privilege based on background seems to have had little real effect. Hence dissent continues even now to keep intact its original motivation. Perhaps in a curious way the secularization of government is responsible for this: bureaucracy, government services reaching ever deeper into the lives of the English people, and the replacement of the clergy's role in secular society by the civil servant who is already a secular agent. As once the clergy, now the civil service expresses the dominance of a social hierarchy with an aristocratic outlook. Even when the aristocracy had given way to new classes, its "governing class" mentality remained in government, in civil service, in university and public school, and especially in the church.

The undesired effect of this fact—undesired by those who were the Establishment—was to promote and encourage dissent, on-going in nature, and always connected by sentiment and tradition to the political and religious developments that had first created the Establishment. Nonconformity emerged in the sixteenth century, the result of both clerical and monarchial intransigence on matters of doctrine and organization in the established church. It came to lead out in objecting to Bishops, church rates, and eventually to the penal laws which proscribed its members' right to hold office and matriculate at university. Later, the tradition behind sectarian Nonconformity joined with radicalism to form a mood and an opposition that was germane more and more to dissent over social organization, economic inequity, foreign policy, and many other features of national life that continued to be governed by the Establishment. As dissent became mainly a secular phenomenon, its practitioners came to include all who opposed consensus in official doctrine. Radicals, liberals, socialists, and even conservatives were, on occasion, adherents to the dissenter's principal outlook. Party lines and ideological dogma were neither barriers nor guideposts for dissent: its point was repudiation of accepted views and practices. Originally a theory of religious organization—or lack of it—dissent had become by the late nineteenth century a theory of political, social, or intellectual resistance. It was distinguished chiefly by a libertarian strain, whether the dissenter was Tory, Liberal, Imperialist, Free Trader, Protectionist, or Socialist.

Always a part of dissent, the factor which above all separated it from other outlooks was the idea of liberty, however construed. Knollys denying the power of the bishops, Winstanley seeking a socialist utopia out of Christian brotherhood and equality, and A. J. P. Taylor advocating a radical foreign policy with libertarian socialist overtones, were only variations of this theme. A better world and a happier life was what the dissenter envisioned as the result of his resistance. The key to liberty was truth; no dissembler could find a comfortable or genuine place in the dissenter's pantheon. To be free was to know truth, and to know truth was to be free. From such a simple and classical formula the dissenter could draw the courage, steadfastness, and moral certitude requisite for opposing, in some cases at the risk of life and property, the official views of the Establishment.

This volume is dedicated to one of dissent's most distinguished historians, Leland H. Carlson. In his life he has been specifically a historian of Elizabethan separatists, the first dissenters, and presently the leading cataloguer and critic of their writings. In this role, he has been a devoted searcher after truth, conveying in his search the sense of true radicalism that underlines the dissenting frame of mind. As noted at length by Franklin Scott, whose tribute to Carlson opens this volume, his work has been careful, critical, and thorough, a search from beginning to end for an understanding of "Wie es eigentlich gewesen." The dissenter has been distinguished by the absolute nature of his viewpoint, an outlook always in opposition to some expression of the Establishment, which in turn has seemed to reflect that the principles of authority alone justify policy or belief. Authority as such in England has more often than not been pragmatic in nature. The dissenter, looking for the ultimate Right, has decried pragmatism in politics and religion—hence the inclusion of puritans in the dissenting tradition, even when they clung desperately to the established church. Historians with dedication to the pursuit of truth in the manner of Carlson are in this fashion absolute moralists, and thus are dissenters. Carlson did not begin so; but, as Scott notes further, fascination with uncovering historical mysteries led finally to seeking the truth behind the authorship of many dissenting tracts heretofore hazily or wrongly credited. Studying the separatists so closely brought him into a sympathy with them that in time made him virtually one of them. His search for truth thus expanded beyond the particular to the abstract, and he became in spirit a dissenter.

Dissent may be characterized best by noting its dedication to liberty of conscience, intellectual freedom, and the right of free expression. Behind this can be identified an exalted view of virtue, humanity, reason, and justice. These are the values to which Carlson's work has been single-mindedly devoted. However, as often as not dissenters have argued these values for themselves while denying them to others—never one of Carlson's faults. As frequently as its point of view was motivated by principle and belief, dissent was no less expressed by intolerance, narrow-mindedness, and demagoguery. Nonetheless, it has been the most exciting feature of English history, and, as A. J. P. Taylor argued, a force without which men would still be living in caves. I suspect that dissent will continue as long as there is in England both political freedom and social inequity, and an Establishment which pretends to form opinion and maintains class and privilege as a way of life. In this volume some of the dissenters' arguments have been laid out, along with descriptions of the essential qualities of repudiation, agitation, and sometimes violence that for good or ill has been the Dissenting Tradition.

Before acknowledging the contributions of various persons and institutions who helped make these essays possible, I should like to make this comment on the essays themselves. While few in number, they are distinguished in content and singularity of purpose. In arranging them I have sought to lay out both chronology and topic in order to underline the more profound dimensions of the problem. Part One deals with the manifestations of dissent in theological practice and doctrine: "Dissent from within," that is, both contemporary and later historical disputation over the nature of the earliest dissenters' religious views, as evaluated here by Professor Collinson; controversy in parish religious politics; change in the nature of dissenting doctrines in the context of philosophy, opinion, and policy, and the notation of its virtues and fallacies by contemporary critics. The second part carried dissent into the secular sphere: the reactions of an authoritarian Tudor government to dissident viewpoints, the transformation of a religious dissenter into a secular socialist, and the continuity of nonconformity into the perspective of a twentieth-century foreign policy radical. The final essay is a brief commentary on the justification of the historian as dissenter, described here as his obligation to be the penultimate critic. Through the arguments on historical criticism made by Lord Acton in his inaugural address at Cambridge, the role Professor Carlson has played is made clear.

To the following persons I wish to express appreciation for the role they have played in the preparation of this volume: Professor S. T. Bindoff, who was an enthusiastic supporter and adviser for the edition from the beginning, even though he was unable to contribute an essay; to the contributors themselves, many of whom burdened already with heavy schedules wrote in order to pay tribute not only to a noted scholar but a valued friend and teacher; to various members of the Claremont Graduate School history faculty whose cautions and advice smoothed many rough spots in the collecting and editing of this material; Elizabeth S. Wrigley, director of the Bacon Library in Claremont, and the Reverend William Johnson of Scarsdale, New York, for financial assistance in bringing this volume to publication; to the history faculty of Utah State University for providing travel funds in support of my work in editing the essays; and Ms. Chris Jeppeson, Ms. Ginny MacKee, and Ms. Ruby Shelton, whose time and energy was much expended in the performance of clerical service for the completed manuscript. On behalf of Professor Moody, I express our sincerest gratitude.

C. ROBERT COLE
Utah State University

MICHAEL E. MOODY
Denver University

Leland Henry Carlson: Man and Career

FRANKLIN SCOTT

Honnold Library, Claremont

LELAND CARLSON'S PERSONALITY and his attitude to history were well illustrated in the first lecture by him that I remember hearing. Jews and Arabs were not at the moment at each other's throats, but tension in the Middle East was high and western knowledge of the situation was low. Carlson had visited the Near East on his first trip abroad. He was concerned about the epic nature of the struggle in the Holy Land, especially concerned about the individual human lives that were poisoned by hatred and those, much fewer, who were ennobled by achievement and understanding. In a lecture carefully constructed to be both fair and enlightening he tried to explain to students and to adult forums what were the roots of conflict and the attitudes of the people involved.

He put it in the form of a debate in which he would argue first the cause of the Jews, then that of the Arabs, exposing the centuries of oppression of the Jews, the persistence of hope, the winning of a "homeland," the hard work and the intelligence applied in building the country of Israel. Then, on the position of the Arabs, he would analyze their condition of poverty, the deceits practiced against them by European exploiters, their sense of being robbed of their land, and their bitterness at the treatment meted out to the Palestinians. Carlson offered no solutions, but he left his listeners with an appreciation of the profound complexities of the situation and a realization that "right" was a very mixed-up matter.

Another lecture that revealed both Carlson and the vast extent of this world was on the joys of travel. The lecture was highly entertaining and the product of rich and changing experience, for he and his wife LaVerne share a passion for travel which they have been indulging for forty years. They have been three times around the world, by ship, by bus, and by plane; have stayed for extended periods in England, and at last count, have visited some seventy-five countries. They may not know all the ballrooms of the world-wide Hiltons or the fine salons of the Caribbean cruise ships. They prefer freighters and buses; they travel not only to see cathedrals and wild animals but also to meet people and find out what they think and how they live. They have journeyed with "das rollende Hotel" in North Africa and in northern-most Europe, sleeping in a trailer following the bus, eating "soup, soup, soup." One of their more ambitious ventures was a two-months bus trip from India across Asia and Europe to England. They have been up the Congo and the Yukon by boat; they have been to Spitzbergen and to the Kingdom of Swat, for 120 days around South America and through the Straits of Magellan. Most recently they have celebrated retirement and their fortieth wedding anniversary by a trip to Europe and down the African coast in a Yugoslav freighter. And this is only a sampling of the total. That lecture on travel has a rich background! But most of all Leland Carlson has been a teacher and a research scholar, and an inspiration for others to follow in his path.

Both Leland and his wife LaVerne come of Swedish Stock, but they make little of ancestry. Leland was born in the northern Illinois city of Rockford on March 25, 1908, and there he lived through his boyhood. He skipped through elementary school in seven years, meanwhile reading eagerly the Tom Swift series, Horatio Alger and other boys' books. He was active in the Swedish Mission Covenant Church and attended "Swede School" in summers. His confirmation class was the last to use both Swedish and English, and on recommendation of his parents he memorized the catechism in Swedish. It was at this time that he suffered a dangerous appendectomy. While in the hospital he was asked what he wanted most, and he said a gold watch. His folks bought it for him, but waited until he got well before having his initials inscribed!

In high school Leland was too small to try for athletics and could only envy the football and basketball stars. But he did participate in ROTC and became corporal, sergeant, and second lieutenant, and admits that he was unduly proud of the leather straps and leather leggings. He also earned money from the ages of six to sixteen years as a newspaper boy. A month before his graduation from high school in January, 1925 he began as a messenger boy in the Commercial National Bank; within the next two and a half years he became a bookkeeper and finally a teller, learning the while about deadbeats and business risks. He saved $1100 and put it in bank stock. A few years later the depression closed out the bank and his hoard, and made him a financial conservative. Through the high school and banking years he kept active in church affairs, as the pianist for the Sunday School and the Boys' Choir, and as the teacher of a class of ten-year-old boys where he "learned a few techniques of keeping students' attention." When the church split on the use of English or Swedish he went with the English faction, continuing his previous activities and becoming also the financial secretary of the new Bethesda Covenant Church.

Leland debated with himself about going to college or staying with his bright prospects at the bank. On the basis that college must come now or never and that he might yet return to the bank if disappointed in college, he made the decision to enter Beloit College nearby in southern Wisconsin, in the fall of 1927. He calls this the best decision he ever made, except for his marriage.

The college years were delightful and rewarding. A scholarship paid his tuition; board and room expenses were met by jobs such as managing two dining halls and summer work as a lifeguard and playground director back in Rockford. He joined Sigma Chi fraternity, made the basketball and tennis teams, but was not an athletic star. This fact he came to regret when in his senior year he lost out in the competition for student body president to one of the athletic heroes. He kept on with tennis throughout his active career, and according to one of his frequent partners he "played an almost errorless game, infuriating opponents." Course emphases in college began with speech (debating), history, Greek, philosophy, and botany, these narrowing down to botany and history, and finally to history alone because of the influence of three especially good teachers. The most notable among them was Professor Robert ("Dickie") Richardson. Grades averaged usually about *A*− except for one proud semester of straight *A*; his degree came in 1931 cum laude, and he was elected to Phi Beta Kappa, Sigma Xi and Phi Theta Kappa.

In the depression year 1931 there was little incentive, if indeed even any thought of it, to re-enter the banking field. Leland wanted to go on with studies in Greek and the Bible, religious and secular history. A good scholarship at The Chicago Theological Seminary offered just the right opportunity; but perhaps most important in the long run was the affiliation of the Seminary with the University of Chicago and its Divinity School. An unusual number of the great scholars in theology and history were still teaching and Leland was careful to study with most of them: Wilhelm Pauck, Edgar J. Goodspeed, J. M. P. Smith, and John T. McNeill in Seminary and Divinity School; T. V. Smith, Louis Gottschalk, Marshall Knappen, Tom Hutchinson, Bernadotte Schmitt (to mention but a few) in the University. The eager young graduate student had some contact also with the Greek scholar Paul Shorey, and with such historians as William E. Dodd, Andrew McLaughlin, and Ferdinand Schevill. These were exciting years at the University, the Hutchins period, filled with challenge and change.

In January, 1932, Leland met LaVerne Larson, a graduate student at the University in home economics, and this led to the "best decision" he ever made. The two were married in the Graham Taylor chapel of the Seminary in June, 1933. In 1934 they took their first trip to Europe, and in 1936 their second, this time on the maiden voyage of the *Queen Mary*, and with few exceptions all their travel since then has been together.

From 1932 for several years Leland combined study with teaching. As a result it was not until 1938 that he completed his work at The Chicago Theological Seminary for his B.D., *magna cum laude*; he had already earned a B.Th. at North Park Seminary, *summa cum laude*. At that time, he was commuting twenty miles between the North Side and the South Side of Chicago, to teach at North Park College, then a junior college. He was made chairman of the division of social sciences at North Park in 1936, and also dean of men, in 1938. His work at the University of Chicago continued until 1939 when he finished his dissertation on the opposition movement against Oliver Cromwell. It was during this period that Timothy was born (1938) and Kay (1939), the two prized children who in later years brought into the family also five prized grandchildren.

Since the combination of family, teaching, and administration (now that the dissertation was finished) could not utilize all his energies he happily responded to President Algoth Ohlson's request that he write the *History of North Park College* (432 + pages), published in 1941. He plowed through old minutes, six decades of Swedish newspapers, and interviewed 400 alumni and others for the "inside" history. Research for this volume opened up a mystery that tempted still further investigation, and three trips to Alaska (three more later, just for fun), resulted in a detective monograph, *An Alaskan Gold Mine: The Story of No. 9 Above* (1951), a tale of moonlighting missionaries and their conflict with their church over the question of who rightly owned the gold they found. Three of North Park's buildings were built with Alaskan gold, but after years of litigation most of the money was in the pockets of lawyers. Through the writing of this book the author learned his way around a dozen courts from County to Supreme Court level, and came to realize the great value of legal records in many kinds of historical research.

In the winter of 1942 Carlson was invited to join the department of history at Northwestern University in Evanston, where he quickly established himself as an outstanding teacher. He taught both graduate and undergraduate courses in English history, but his real fame came from the introductory course in European history. His lectures were well prepared and spiced with anecdotes from reading and travel; they made history personal and "relevant." The course attracted large enrollments and the students of the University honored him by choosing him as one of two "Ideal Professors" and dedicated to him the 1950 student yearbook, *The Syllabus*. A variety of other honors was showered upon him: the Beloit College Centennial Award in 1946, the Royal Swedish Medal in 1948, the Northwestern Centennial Award in 1951, honorary degrees from Beloit and Rockford, the gavel of "Great Teacher" for adult education and lecturing, Phi Beta Kappa presidencies of the Northwestern and later the Rockford chapter, and of the Phi Beta Kappa Association of Greater Chicago; he is a fellow of the Royal Historical Society of London and several times a fellow of the Folger Shakespeare Library.

Great success in teaching frequently brings temptations to quit teaching, especially to enter the "higher" ranks of administration. For a man like Carlson, enticing offers were inevitable. After twelve years at Northwestern University, and accompanied by soul-searching and doubt, he took on the presidency of Rockford College. It meant a return to his home town, though that was purely incidental. In five years at the helm President Carlson accomplished much: a new campus was acquired; Rockford Men's College (1955) and Rockford Evening College (1956) were founded; and the basis of full coeducation was established. But problems of finance and educational policy were demanding and wearisome. Carlson's own inclinations are clearly manifested in that during his five years as a college executive he took his vacations whenever possible in the Huntington Library or the British Museum. The life of teacher and scholar was more congenial to him than administrative dignity and power. Hence in 1959 he resigned and went as professor to the Southern California School of Theology.

The new location of this multidenominational seminary in Claremont provided opportunity also for appointment to a professorship in the Claremont Graduate School and for carrying on research not only in Claremont but in the nearby Huntington Library. Now he could devote himself fulltime to the things he wanted to do. He could teach, he could collect books and read them—and he loved books only slightly less than he loved people. On his retirement he was able to leave valuable collections to the Honnold Library and to the library of the School of Theology at Claremont. Toward the end of his salaried career an extra dividend was added when he was invited to serve for two years as the first Colin Rhys Lovell Professor of English History at the University of Southern California, another institution within commuting distance of Claremont.

Carlson's research achievements, his books and many articles, have been both recognized and promoted by numerous grants: several from the American Philosophical Society and the Folger Library, and in 1962-1963 a Rockefeller Fellowship. Beginning during his time at Northwestern and continuing for twenty-five years he contributed the quarterly bibliographical articles on English history for the *American Historical Review*. Since the late forties he has dedicated himself to the arduous task of compiling and editing what is to be a ten-volume series of the papers of Elizabethan Nonconformists.

Reminiscences of friends reach back through decades and point up the multifaceted proficiencies of the subject. He is a man of *virtu* almost in the Renaissance sense. His interest in tennis and other sports has already been mentioned. While in Chicago he loved to watch the Blackhawks play hockey. As a chess player he ranked high among the local amateurs: "He used to beat me at least five out of every six games," moaned one shrewd rival. Recently he has replayed by himself every game of the famous Spassky-Fischer series. His interests are universal, his curiosity all-encompassing and insatiable; "everything seemed to interest him and turn him on," whether it was books or people or an operation in the hospital at the Great Lakes Naval Training Station. He has been a highly popular lecturer not only on campus but on the public platform, and a fascinating conversationalist. Deeply convinced of the importance of history, he also possessed an enviable capacity to inculcate interest in others and to lead freshmen to specialize in the field.

His interest in people was sincere, but Carlson also worked consciously at the techniques of maintaining personal relationships. When he met a new acquaintance he was careful to learn how to spell the name correctly and how to pronounce it, and he questioned the person about his background and his job enough that he had knowledge to support memory. He made himself a close runner-up of the famous Jim Farley in the art of recalling names. Students even in classes of several hundred who had occasion to speak with their professor were impressed with his eagerness to know them personally as well as their immediate problems; he often took students to lunch or drank his mid-morning coffee with them.

An example of Leland's personal thoughtfulness is cited by Paul Schilpp, editor of the *Library of Living Philosophers*, a colleague and friend from Northwestern days. When Schilpp was working on his volume on Albert Einstein (his most admired subject) Carlson happened to take one of his repeated trips to England. In a London art shop he spotted a masterful portrait of Einstein and knew how his friend Paul would treasure it. Since he could not afford to buy it, when he got home he enlisted the aid of the Reverend Joe Thomas and together they persuaded the wife of a Northwestern trustee to purchase the painting and have it delivered at Schilpp's door. It was a combination of thoughtfulness and courtesy that will be long remembered.

His sympathy and kindness are referred to more frequently than anything else by those who speak of Carlson. "He never sent me away before I had time to lay my problem before him and solicit useful advice." "Leland was always generous in his dealings with me, willing to give me time even though he was always busy; [he was] considerate of his teaching assistants." "His kind, gentle treatment of students was one source of his success. . . . He showed his kindly personality even when being most exacting and critical. . . . He treated all students as individuals [with] a warmth, but still a formal relationship." "I have never known a person who surpassed him in human sympathy and understanding." But as Gray Boyce, his department chairman through several years, justly remarks, "He could demand much from [students] and a liking for [them] never meant that he catered to them intellectually or in his teaching."

With graduate students he was demanding. Martin Ridge, now editor of *The Journal of American History*, took a Carlson seminar at Northwestern and recalls having opened his paper with a colorful generalization: "Bonfires burned from Berwick-upon-Tweed to Lands End, when Charles returned to England." His stern mentor was not satisfied with documentation for Berwick, London, and Lands End—what about the places in between? More recent students in the Claremont Graduate School report the same demand for thoroughness of scholarship. Because of his own dedication and "knowledgeable, critical, illuminating and thorough scholarship and his rigorous requirements he vastly increased the skills by which we as professionals must live." "In seminars and in directing Ph.D. dissertations he devoted great time and care; no page written escaped his attention. His knowledge of source materials in England was wide, and he gave freely of this information." The present writer can attest that he gave the same painstaking scrutiny to manuscripts submitted for appraisal by his colleagues.

In his own life Leland could probably best be described as a Christian humanist. He did not, like many, eschew his pietist background, but he grew away from it through exposure to other influences in Beloit and Chicago, and now classifies himself as a liberal. Although he completed the theological curriculum both at North Park and at Chicago Theological Seminary he never sought a preaching ministry. Nevertheless it seemed quite fitting that his later years of teaching were based in a school of theology. All his teaching was permeated with a strong Christian ethic, and some of his students considered him a bit too religious. As one student put it, "In his mind history and a religious faith were firmly intertwined." A nonsectarian faith, it should be added.

His religious concerns combined with his interest in English history and church history to start him on the major research project of his life, the editing of the ten volumes of tracts of the "Elizabethan Nonconformists." This monumental and painstaking task has indeed required real dedication. Ray Billington, now of the Huntington Library where Leland has spent many days of investigation, judges that: "No one else could do what he has done, for no one would have the patience—let alone the skill." Carlson has obviously discovered a certain identification with the separatists of the six-teenth and seventeenth centuries. He sympathizes with and understands that their concepts of freedom of worship, of assembly, of the press, and of elect-ing clergy were steps toward democracy. For example, if clergy could be elected, why not magistrates? Therefore, James I "rightly saw the danger: no bishop, no king." Carlson has gone through line by line, word by word, the writings of Thomas Cartwright, Robert Harrison, Robert Browne, Henry Barrow, John Greenwood; when in 1966 Donald McGinn came out with a book arguing that John Penry was the real Martin Marprelate, Carlson was driven to still more intricate procedures to prove that this could not be true. He took courses in computer technology and finally had to become his own computer, ". . . for these electronic geniuses were mechanical idiots." By two years of intensive study of Martin Marprelate, his idioms, proverbs, legal phrases, anecdotes, stylistic devices, Carlson was able to assign some twenty books and manuscripts, anonymous or pseudonymous, to Martin. But clearly they were not Penry's writing. This search was another and more complicated detective job than the *Story of No. 9 Above*, and it took intui-tion as well as computer technology. The indefatigable researcher thinks he has pinned down that Penry with his heavy and frustrated style could not have been Martin, who is light, fluffy, sarcastic, clever. Rather, the most likely candidate is Job Throkmorton. But this is a tale to be read from Carl-son himself who, in a seminar paper for the William Andrews Clark Memo-rial Library in 1972, cast aside his kindly nature and made a slashing attack on McGinn and his book which, "in my judgment, is the most misleading book ever to have been written on the Martinist controversy. It is tenden-tious, illogical, biased, poorly researched, and unfair." Calm Carlson had almost been touched by the invective style of his separatists! He has traced their writings and their thoughts into every nook and cranny, and has allowed nothing to deflect him. Also, thanks be, he has thoroughly enjoyed the work itself and the trips it has required him to take to London and the British Museum, and elsewhere in England.

The deep satisfactions of Leland Carlson's life (beyond family) come from the reading and making of books. He has been especially devoted to English history from the accession of Elizabeth to the death of Cromwell. He enjoys the beautiful writing of James Anthony Froude and Thomas Bab-ington Macaulay, and the research of such scholars as Sir Charles Harding Firth and Samuel Rawson Gardiner; in his own Tudor field he admires the work of such scholars as Sir John Neale, A. L. Rowse, T. S. Bindoff, Joel Hurstfield, Patrick Collinson, Conyers Read, William Haller, Marshall M. Knappen, Paul S. Seaver, and Wallace T. MacCaffrey; he also appreciates the broader approaches of men like Arnold Toynbee and Will Durant. Per-haps even more he revels in the sense of creativity in his own research. He likes to see a pattern emerge from the study of sources, and he enjoys the development from rough notes to first draft, from completed draft to fair copy and on to galley proof and finished book. He is even proud of his proof-reading and still looks forward to the day when he may see a book of his without printing errors.

The joys he finds in reading, in detective research, and in watching his creative work grow into book form he never found in administration. Rockford College, when he took over, was in a downswing; enrollment was off and finances were precarious. As a private college for women it had no special call on the loyalties of Rockford, but its fine traditions in education for women were just what made the strongest appeal to alumnae and special friends. Carlson accepted the Rockford position on condition that the trustees would at least consider transformation of the college into a coeducational institution. They made the first step in 1955 with the founding of Rockford Men's College a year later (and this became the largest division of the school). But the new president had visions of something more. He had seen academies disappear as public high schools began to flourish, and he was watching as institutions such as the nearby teachers' college in De-Kalb burgeoned into large state universities. For Rockford he saw the need of a municipal university that might eventually become state-supported, like Wayne in Detroit, for example. However, he ran into three insurmountable obstacles: conservatism, timidity, and sentiment. The trustees and other supporters of the college considered the idea of a public institution inimical to the concept of "rugged individualism:" others were fearful of tackling big change; and the alumnae wept at the thought of sweeping away the basis of treasured memories. The time was not ripe.

Hence the president and his deputy Edward W. Mill buckled down to doing what they could. It meant lecturing and appealing for students and funds before high schools, factory and civic groups, to whomever would listen. It was strenuous, and worries about faculty salaries and other matters followed the president's head to the pillow. He accomplished much: he checked the decline of the college, created two new college units and laid the basis for full coeducation, and managed the removal of the site of the college from its crowded position inside the city to a handsome new 300-acre campus east of town. Financial support was doubled and quadrupled. It was pleasant to see a man come into the office and lay down a check for $5000, the next year a check for $15,000, next $25,000, and the following year $200,000. But all the academic side of things had to be left in the hands of a dean; the business and promotional side demanded ever-increasing attention and just didn't have that much appeal. The Rockford quinquennium in the Carlson career thus came to an end in 1959 when he resigned, with good feeling all around, to resume the scholar's career.

We need not make too much of it, but it is interesting that in thinking of Leland two of his former colleagues at Northwestern think also of the Greek philosophers: Earl J. Hamilton concludes paragraphs of praise by saying, "His attitude is always constructive. . . . His morale is always high. He could raise my morale when it was down; and when it was all right to begin with, he could make me feel like taking on Aristotle." Paul Schilpp regretted Leland's departure from scholarship for the Rockford presidency: "Almost any businessman can administer. But there are few who can be Socrates. Carlson has been one. Fortunately he had the good sense to return to his first love."

In sum, we can accept the judgment of an English publisher that "Carlson is a quiet, courteous and diligent scholar," especially if we add the old but irresistible characterization of the Clerk of Oxenford—"And gladly wolde he lerne, and gladly teche." For he too has trod the road to Canterbury and many more besides in his inextinguishable lust for travel and his constant searching of the minds of men. His innumerable acquaintanceships, many of them warm but limited by time and place, are more notable for their breadth than for their depth. Natural enough, because his life has been largely that of the classroom and the library cubicle, except for the fleeting contacts of world-wide travel.

One of his friends has listed aptly the adjectives most applicable to Leland Carlson: gentle, humane, patient, deeply intellectual, concerned, thoughtful, selfless. Robert Cole and Michael Moody and their collaborators in this volume of essays can take real satisfaction in thus honoring a man worthy of the honor.

Leland H. Carlson:
A Select List of Writings*

VERNON CARNER
Loma Linda University

MICHAEL E. MOODY
University of Denver

Books

An Alaskan Gold Mine: The Story of No. 9 Above. Northwestern University Studies. Social Science Series, no. 7. (Evanston: Northwestern University Press, 1951.)

Barrow, Henry. *The Writings of Henry Barrow, 1587-1590.* Sir Halley Stewart Trust Publications. Elizabethan Nonconformist Texts, edited with introductions by Leland H. Carlson, vol. 3. (London: George Allen and Unwin, 1962.)

Barrow, Henry. *The Writings of Henry Barrow, 1590-1591.* Sir Halley Stewart Trust Publications. Elizabethan Nonconformist Texts, edited with

---

* Dr. Carlson is engaged in completing his "Elizabethan Nonconformist Texts" series. The remaining volumes in it are to be *The Writings of John Penry* (2 vols.) and *A Parte of a Register* (2 vols.) (vols. 7, 8, 9, and 10 in the series). See Leland H. Carlson, "A Corpus of Elizabethan Nonconformist Writings," in *Studies in Church History: Volume 2, Papers Read at the Second Winter and Summer Meetings of the Ecclesiastical History Society* [1963], ed. G. J. Cuming (London: Thomas Nelson and Sons, 1965), 297-309.

In connection with his work on the "Elizabethan Nonconformist Texts" project, Dr. Carlson is also concluding work on a monograph concerning the authorship of the Martin Marprelate tracts. This book will be entitled *Martin Marprelate Gentleman, or, Master Job Throkmorton Laid Open in His Coulers.* It is scheduled for publication in the near future.

introductions by Leland H. Carlson, vol. 5. (London: George Allen and Unwin, 1966.)

Cartwright, Thomas. *Cartwrightiana*. Sir Halley Stewart Trust Publications. Elizabethan Nonconformist Texts, edited with introductions by Albert Peel and Leland H. Carlson, vol. 1. (London: George Allen and Unwin, 1951.)

Greenwood, John, and Barrow, Henry. *The Writings of John Greenwood, 1587-1590, Together with the Joint Writings of Henry Barrow and John Greenwood, 1587-1590.* Sir Halley Stewart Trust Publications. Elizabethan Nonconformist Texts, edited with introductions by Leland H. Carlson, vol. 4. (London: George Allen and Unwin, 1962.)

Greenwood, John, and Barrow, Henry. *The Writings of John Greenwood and Henry Barrow, 1591-1593.* Sir Halley Stewart Trust Publications. Elizabethan Nonconformist Texts, edited with introductions by Leland H. Carlson, vol. 6. (London: George Allen and Unwin, 1970.)

Harrison, Robert, and Browne, Robert. *The Writings of Robert Harrison and Robert Browne.* Sir Halley Stewart Trust Publications. Elizabethan Nonconformist Texts, edited with introductions by Albert Peel and Leland H. Carlson, vol. 2. (London: George Allen and Unwin, 1953.)

A History of North Park College, Commemorating the Fiftieth Anniversary, 1891-1941. (Chicago: North Park College, 1941.)

Articles and Pamphlets

"A Corpus of Elizabethan Nonconformist Writings." In *Studies in Church History: Volume 2, Papers Read at the Second Winter and Summer Meetings of the Ecclesiastical History Society* [1963], edited by G. J. Cuming. (London: Thomas Nelson and Sons, 1965.)

"The Discovery of Gold at Nome, Alaska." *Pacific Historical Review* 15 (1946): 259-278. [The authorship of this article is erroneously attributed to "T. H. Carlson" in *The Pacific Historical Review*.]

"European History." In *College Reading and Religion: A Survey of College Reading Materials, Sponsored by the Edward W. Hazen Foundation and the Committee on Religion and Education of the American Council on Education.* (New Haven: Yale University Press, 1948.)

"The First Mining Season at Nome, Alaska—1899." *Pacific Historical Review* 16 (1947): 163-175.

"A History of the Presbyterian Party from Pride's Purge to the Dissolution of the Long Parliament." *Church History* 11 (1942): 83-122.

"Judge George E. Q. Johnson." *American Swedish Historical Foundation Year Book 1949* (1949): 57-70.

"Martin Marprelate: His Identity and His Satire." In *English Satire: Papers Read at a* [William Andrews] *Clark* [Memorial] *Library Seminar, January 15, 1972.* (Los Angeles: William Andrews Clark Memorial Library, 1972.)

"Nome: From Mining Camp to Civilized Community." *Pacific Northwest Quarterly* 38 (1947): 233-242.

"Part I, 1898-1901; The Story of No. 9 Above." *Covenant Quarterly* 7 (1947): 195-237.

"Part II, The Eskimo Lawsuit." *Covenant Quarterly* 7 (1947): 238-269. [This article and the article listed immediately above have been combined and reprinted as a pamphlet for private circulation (n. p., n. d.).]

"Part III, The Arbitration Commission of 1904." *Covenant Quarterly* 8 (1948): 21-47.

"Part IV, The Appeal to the Courts." *Covenant Quarterly* 8 (1948): 157-185.

"Part V, Ramifications and Conclusion." *Covenant Quarterly* 8 (1948): 229-255.

"The Rise of Elizabethan Separatism." *Rice Institute Pamphlet. Papers Presented at the Eighth Annual South-Central Renaissance Conference, March 13-14, 1959* 46 (1960): 15-40.

"The Role of the Women's Colleges in the Next Ten Years." *Association of American Colleges Bulletin* 44 (1958): 78-88.

"Swedish Pioneers and the Discovery of Gold in Alaska." *American Swedish Historical Foundation Year Book 1948* (1948): 63-81.

"The Things That Are Excellent, or, Objectives of Rockford College. Inauguration Address of Leland H. Carlson . . . February 27, 1955." [Rockford, Ill.:] Rockford College, [1955].

Bibliographical Work and Book Reviews

Dr. Carlson, as section editor, compiled approximately ninety-five "British Commonwealth and Ireland" bibliographical articles for the *American Historical Review* between 1949 and 1974. In addition, he has written approximately 110 book reviews.

PART I

Towards a Broader Understanding of the Early Dissenting Tradition

PATRICK COLLINSON

THE STRATEGY OF THIS ESSAY[1] can be expressed in geometrical terms, as one of dimension. The origins of the dissenting tradition have received from religious, denominationally committed historians (and also, although this lies beyond the scope of this paper, from historians of early American culture) an excessively vertical, or linear treatment. Questions of genealogy, concerning the descent of religious bodies and systems, have prevailed. *A Genetic Study*, the subtitle of the late Professor Perry Miller's book *Orthodoxy in Massachusetts*,[2] is a label which can be widely applied to the literature. The present study is set in another dimension and explores some of the horizontal and lateral relationships of early protestant dissent. It treats the eighty years from the Elizabethan Settlement to the Long Parliament for this purpose, as historians often do for other legitimate purposes, as if they were a unity, and with more respect for regularities and consistent features than for events and developments. Politics are not forgotten but for reasons of economy disregarded, and so is the earthquake which immediately followed the period under review. Sometimes it may be helpful to share the ignorance of the early seventeenth century, few of whose inhabitants could have suspected that they were living in "Pre-Revolutionary England."[3]

The genealogical approach so apparent in much of the historiography of early Dissent owes something to the nature of the task, something to the way in which it has been tackled. If the story is told on a chronological plan, the historian is driven down a tunnel which shuts out any expansive views on either side. This tunnel is the separatist tradition, nearly continuous from the second or third decade of the reign of Queen Elizabeth I, a tradition of renouncing all communion with the Church of England in order to form, as might be said in the 1970s, an alternative church. Something may be said

3

about the first generation of Protestants, and even about their Lollard antecedents, but the story is assumed to have its proper beginnings with Elizabethan Puritanism, treated as the matrix of Dissent and migration. A recent writer remarks: "The English Reformation and Elizabethan Puritanism belong to the prehistory of Dissent; its own history begins with the Separatists."[4] The story detaches itself from the matrix with the earliest episodes of Separatism and Near-Separatism in London in the 1560s, and ten years later with the gathered church and the writings of Robert Browne and Robert Harrison. Separatism is now stuck with the brand name of Brownism, because of Browne's later defection a cause of grave embarrassment; as John Waddington wrote in 1869: "No educated Congregationalist can feel flattered by the ecclesiastical genealogy that takes its rise from Robert Browne."[5] The next two decades bring the reorganization of London Separatism under the leadership of Henry Barrow and John Greenwood, the martyrdom of Barrow and Greenwood and also of John Penry, the exodus to Holland, the long and controversial rule of Francis Johnson. The scene is now set for three or four decades in Amsterdam, Leyden and Rotterdam, and the themes are the troubled affairs of the Amsterdam church and its offshoots, the new elements entering from the East Midlands under Robinson and Smith, the rancorous relations between these groups and other nonseparated churches serving the needs of Englishmen overseas on, so to speak, legitimate business: an ecclesiastical Balkans of baffling diversity. Later still the story moves again, to New England, and to the search for true church principles by brethren in three countries. And all this is but the curtain-raiser to the properly denominational history which begins in the 1640s. Inevitably, the historian who follows this course closely and with an eye to every turn of persuasion or argument makes his own separation from the mainstream of English religious life in these decades. It is the contention of what follows that the broader context is as much a part of the early dissenting tradition as the annals of the Separatists.

It is not the purpose of this essay to enter into denunciation of denominational history, least of all at a time when the past as a system of values and in the shape of denominational and connexional archives is at serious risk from modern indifference. The soundness of the best denominational scholarship, as well as its inestimable value for the life of the churches, needs no emphasis. Nor do its more perverse characteristics.[6] It may be taken as read that denominational history, indeed ecclesiastical history itself, derives from martyrology and has been given to robust apologetic (as Benjamin Brook told his readers in 1813: ". . . the contents of these volumes tend to expose the evils of bigotry and persecution"[7]); that it is engaged history, committed to the buttressing of contested positions in the internal or external affairs of the churches; and that it has tended to foster an illusion of continuity between the past and the historian's present, so that the nineteenth century is assumed in the seventeenth, and the millenarianism which conditioned so much seventeenth-century perception becomes an embarrassment, rarely mentioned and perhaps not even noticed.

But a further critical point connects more directly with the present argument and will stand some elaboration. As the writing of denominational history became more professional and critical, from the late nineteenth century onwards, so its angle of vision was narrowed rather than extended. Waddington had written exuberantly of the *Track of the Hidden Church,* and of the light of congregational principles gleaming forth in unexpected ways.[8] He managed to write 700 pages of his *Congregational History* before he reached the reign of Elizabeth, expansive history on the scale of John Foxe's Book of Martyrs, adapting indeed a perspective and vision which were Foxe's to a denominational purpose. But the American scholar H. M. Dexter, who inaugurated the modern, critical study of congregationalist history, was not tempted to predate Independency. He derived it from its perceptible historical roots, which for him were literary roots: it was *The Congregationalism of the Last Three Hundred Years As Seen In Its Literature.*[9] (The astonishing Bibliography of 7250 items remains indispensable.) The process of scholarly contraction continued with another American classic, Williston Walker's *Creeds and Platforms of Congregationalism* (1893), which handled its subject as an intellectual system, pure and simple: in effect, "a Congregationalist is one who accepts the tenets of Congregationalism."[10]

In the first half of this century, the religious historians of early dissent continued with increasing sophistication and precision to investigate the descent of their church principles. Their writings reflect on the one hand a heightened denominational awareness and the formalising of inter-church relations, and, on the other, the prevailing and, as someone has said, still "majestically narrow" ways of Anglo-Saxon historians, the sovereignty of constitutional studies, dealing with the descent of political institutions on a basis of the rigorous study of the public records. Champlin Burrage and Albert Peel, the two leading scholars in this field, were at home in the great manuscript collections, compensating for Dexter's pronounced literary bias,[11] and Peel was one who knew the Elizabethan religious scene from the inside. But Peel was also a devoted servant of his church, who paid due attention to the somewhat scholastic question: "Who were the first Congregationalists?"[12] His bequest was the great series of Elizabethan Nonconformist Texts which Professor Carlson carries on his shoulders, and which we honor in this volume.[13] By establishing the complete canon of the earliest separatist printed literature, these volumes have brought refinement and reinforcement to an established historical school: witness the distinct advances registered in Dr B. R. White's recent review of the whole question.[14]

Meanwhile, in the United States, the great Perry Miller had complicated the genealogy by denying that the New England way of Congregationalism, the orthodoxy of Massachusetts, stemmed from the separatist tradition, as mediated through the New Plymouth Colony. It was John Cotton who first wrote, in 1648, of "the line of the Pedigree of the Independents in New-England,"[15] and Miller returned to something close to Cotton's account of the matter in deriving the pedigree from a distinct body of thought which, as he believed, proved of crucial importance among the various streams converging on the "single pool of New England orthodoxy," a source in its turn of English Independency. This, according to Miller, was the philosophy of "Non-Separating Congregationalism", of which more presently. This thesis, stated in *Orthodoxy in Massachusetts*, was contributory to the grander design of the book called *The New England Mind*, which asserted the majestic coherence of American puritan thought.[16] Miller never doubted that the early history of American culture was implicit in its literature, and it has taken a later generation of New England historians to point out (in the words of one of them) that "the history of the New England mind is not the history of New England."[17]

Evidently much of the scholarship we have considered, including the best of it, runs the risk of incurring strictures of the kind expressed by Lucien Fèbvre in a famous article of 1929 on the origins of the French Reformation, entitled "Une question mal posée."[18] In that article Fèbvre attacked a century of historians for their fixation on questions of a highly specific nature, while neglecting the deeper springs of cultural change. He ended with the demand that the words "specificité, priorité, nationalité" be erased from the historian's vocabulary. Transferred to the history of early English Dissent, such a programme would be too drastic, and would lead to some slipshod history.[19] Nor is it clear that questions of this order are necessarily "mal posée." But they are not the only questions. Dr. White evidently aspires to encompass "the whole story," and the final chapter of his book is called "The Significance of the English Separatist Tradition."[20] But 'significance' means its significance for the further evolution of nonconformist churchmanship. It is as if the historian of the fashionable subject of witchcraft in Tudor and Stuart England were to discuss its significance exclusively in terms of what the witchcraft tradition and the subsequent practice of witchcraft may owe to the witches of the seventeenth century. (No doubt such a work is even now in progress.)[21] The sociologist Dr. Bryan Wilson, who specializes in religious sects, regards them as isolated, model structures which may prove relevant to our understanding of the wider society to which they relate.[22] But the sects of the seventeenth century are approached by some denominational historians, not for what they may tell us about the Church and the society from which they came out, nor even, in that deceptive phrase, "for their own sake," or in the mountaineer's words, "because they are there," but for their value for denominational posterity, an entirely legitimate, but restricted motive.[23]

The escape-hatch from the critical prolegomenon to the main body of this essay is provided by Perry Miller's famous Non-Separating Congregationalists. These were a number of writers, William Bradshaw, William Ames, Paul Baynes, Robert Parker, and also, in his own distinctive vein, Henry Jacob, all flourishing in the first two or three decades of the seventeenth century, all ambiguously and eclectically related to the Church of England on the one hand, and to the churches of the separation overseas on the other.[24] Our knowledge of their opinions comes partly from manifestoes calling for further reformation as they conceived of it, such as Bradshaw's celebrated pamphlet *English Puritanisme containeing the maine opinions of the rigidest sort of those that are called puritans in the realme of England*;[25] partly from works of systematic divinity or casuistry, aimed at a European audience, notably from the pen of the internationally recognised Ames;[26] partly from polemical exchanges with John Robinson of Leyden and other Separatists.[27] Secondarily, in the 1630s, with the apparent conversion of John Cotton to these views at about the time of his emigration and that of Thomas Hooker, the line of non-separatist thought broadened to nourish the polity of the New England churches: the work of "a sort of second generation to the Ames-Bradshaw group" according to Miller.[28]

The Non-Separating Congregationalists apparently participated in many essential positions of Independency which had been discovered by the Separatists or which would be disclosed in the future by those of the Congregational Way. As Bradshaw wrote in *English Puritanisme*: "They hould and maintaine that every Companie, Congregation or Assemblie of men,[29] ordinarilie ioyning together in[30] the true worship of God, is a true visible church of Christ, and that the same title is improperlie attributed to any other Convocations,[31] Synods, Societies, combinations, or assemblies whatsoever."[32] ("Touching the outward forme," wrote Ames, there were "so many visible Churches as there are distinct congregations.")[33] "Joyning together" implied "a special bond among themselves . . . a covenant, either expresse or implicite, wherby believers doe particularly bind themselves to performe all those duties, both toward God and one towards another, which pertain to the respect and edification of the Church."[34] In most of these writings, the germ of a major principle of Independency appears, which in the future would distinguish those of the Congregational Way as much from Presbyterianism as from Prelacy: there may be and even ought to be synods, "convocations . . . voluntarily confederate," able to assist the local congregation with "counsel," "advice", "support." But synods can have no power to overrule or "rule imperiously" the churches, which must not suffer a "subordination," says Jacob, "or surely not a subjection."[35] Significantly, *English Puritanisme* has nothing to say on the subject of synods.

In spite of notions apparently incompatible with a national and hierarchical religious establishment, these writers condemned the path taken by the Separatists. As a casuist, Ames granted the rationality of choosing as between true churches "the purest as farre as we are able," but he found "grievous discommodities" in any "rash departure" from the English Church, which was a true church by the only valid criterion: true faith.[36] His close friend Bradshaw wrote on *The unreasonablenesse of the separation*.[37] Jacob's position was more rigid, since by 1616 when he formed at Southwark what is traditionally claimed as the first properly congregational church on English soil[38] (genealogy again!) he taught that Christians were bound in conscience to join themselves to "Christ's true, visible, political Church" in the form of "a free congregation of visible Christians," and to forsake other bodies which were "polities of men's mere devising." But Jacob and his congregation were willing to communicate with the English parish congregations so long as no assent was implied to human traditions and abuses, and to acknowledge that among these congregations were "many true, visible, yea politicall churches in some degree and in some respect," although their validity could be said to rest curiously and perhaps transiently on their ignorance of these truths.[39]

Some of Jacob's tracts and Ames against Robinson rest the case for non-separation not on the Church of England as an undifferentiated whole but on those godly elements in the Church and on the more "forward" preachers, "the true members of our best assemblies,"[40] in John Winthrop's words, "the faithfull in England (whom we account the Churches)";[41] and specifically on the agreement that was held to exist among these undoubtedly sound Christians to assemble and worship without constraint. This was what Ames had in mind when he wrote that a church covenant might be implicit rather than explicit. In subsequent New England writing it was taken for granted that although the covenant was a necessary ground for the Church's existence, such a covenant could and often did exist implicitly in England.[42] Ames had reminded Robinson of the "many exercises of religion in England" where none were present by constraint, and where the Prayer Book did "not so much as appeare."[43] Similarly, it could be alleged that wherever there was some element of agreement and mutual consent between the minister and his people, a valid ministry was present which was not prejudiced by the "accidents" of episcopal ordination and institution, or by the patron's rights in presentation, an argument with extensive background in the counsels of Elizabethan Puritanism;[44] as Bradshaw put it: "Soe that they are onely in aequivocation, and name, or Metaphorically, Priestes and Deacons: But really Pastors and Teachers."[45] If all ecclesiastical organization outside the congregation was merely civil, it could be acknowledged civilly, without harm to essentials. The English parishes were "entyre spirituall bodies though civilly combined into a diocesan government."[46] The majority of ministers migrating to Massachusetts after 1630 appear to have been impressed with such arguments as these. To their own satisfaction, they were making not "a separation (rigidly taken) but a lawfull secession, or a heavenly translation from corrupt to more pure churches." The Laudian regime had now made it, in terms of Ames's casuistry, less inconvenient to go than to stay. But this was a considered alternative to setting up "private separated churches" inside England, while "to make the *English* Churches, and their Ministries, and their Worship, and their Professors, either nullities or Anti-Christian" was said by Cotton from New England to be "a witnesse not onely beyond the truth, but against the Truth of the Lord Jesus and his word of Truth."[47]

The argument of *Orthodoxy in Massachusetts*, and for that matter the whole of Perry Miller's stately intellectual edifice, has taken some hard knocks. Since his death, the New England Way has been disassembled by a generation of revisionists for whom the acceptable word is "pluralistic," the damning word "monolithic."[48] Some time ago now, from the other side of the Atlantic, Dr. Geoffrey Nuttall, in the manner of Voltaire on the Holy Roman Empire, doubted whether the Non-Separating Congregationalist group was a "group," or truly "congregationalist," or "nonseparating," pointing out that "semiseparatist" was a preferable term, used by contemporaries.[49] Moreover it can be shown that Perry Miller's understanding, or rather misunderstanding, of puritan ecclesiology, whether separatist, or semiseparatist or nonseparatist, was vitiated (the word is hardly too strong) by a radical misapprehension of the puritan doctrine of covenanted grace, so that he imagined, against all the evidence, that the purpose of a church covenant was to restrict membership of the visible church to a minority of the proven elect, in order to achieve physical identity with the church invisible; whereas the true intention was to confine membership to the visibly worthy, that is, to "saints visible to the eyes of rational charity."[50]

Given that mistake near the heart of the matter, the Non-Separating Congregationalists (so-called) were bound to appeal perversely ingenious, so that Miller rejected their argument, except as a piece of casuistry, never ceasing to denigrate the "glaring inconsistency" of this "prize bit of circumlocution," this "abstruse point," this "adroit subterfuge," the fruit of a "labyrinthine process of . . . reasoning"—which, however, deceived no one. Of course, Miller was concerned only with the value of the argument as intellectual currency, and even so it is odd that such a "cobweb of sophistry" should have been credited with parentage of what he otherwise calls "the majesty and coherence of Puritan thinking."[51] It did not occur to him that affairs within the Church of England could have remotely resembled the account of them given or implied by Jacob and Ames. This essay seeks to rehabilitate the apparently shaky mainstay of a discredited thesis, and to put flesh and blood on the nonseparatist case as not merely intellectually consistent but corresponding in some degree to the experience of Puritans remaining unseparated in the Church of England. That a scholar of Perry Miller's stature should find such a proposition incredible points in the first place to the neglect of the grass-roots, manuscript evidence, and in the second to some inappropriate perspectives in relation to the Elizabethan and Jacobean Church and to the place of Puritanism within it.

These perspectives, widely shared, include some misunderstanding of how the Puritans related to the established church structures, coupled with a tendency to underestimate the extent to which the Church and society were affected by puritan practice and influence; failure to recognize the strong inbuilt tendency towards Independency in puritan circles; and reluctance to acknowledge the strength and forcefulness of Puritanism as a lay and popular movement. These complaints apply to much of the literature, but not, it must be said, to the books of the Master of Balliol, Christopher Hill,[52] which neglect none of these points, although they are turned by Hill to purposes rather different from those of the religious historian.

On the issue of definition and relationship, Puritanism is too often treated in contradistinction to Anglicanism or conformism as Nonconformity and minority opposition, which is to say that it is defined negatively, with respect to supposed norms, and peripherally, in relation to a supposed center. Of course Puritanism often embraced a nonconformist resistance to some Anglican ceremonies, or even a more general rejection of Anglican worship and polity, and there could be little point in denying that it was as a protest against the policy of the Elizabethan Church that it acquired identity in the first place. But it is also possible, and by the early decades of the seventeenth century preferable, to consider Puritanism as embodying the mainstream of English Protestantism, to which some of the distinctive institutions and ordinances of the established Church (loyalty to which was widely and usefully characterized as "formalism") were not so much opposed as irrelevant.[53] Some Jacobean and Caroline Puritans were not nonconformists at all in their response to what one of them called "things of small matter, not touching matter but manner, not substance but Ceremonyes, not piety but pollity, not devocton (*sic*) but decency, not conscience but Comelynesse,"[54] and yet as in Richard Baxter's youthful experience, contemporaries called them Puritans and had no doubt what they meant by it: a "singular" style of life.[55] Baxter's family were alienated from their neighbors, and the fact that they were called Puritans expressed their alienation, but it is nevertheless a mistake to interpret Puritanism too exclusively in terms of *anomie*.[56] At least it is necessary to decide what the Puritans were alienated from. In towns dominated by puritan oligarchs and in a Church widely infiltrated with puritan religion, often with the connivance of those in authority, it is not clear that Puritanism could always be equated with rejection of the *status quo*.

It is above all necessary to recognize that Puritanism expressed an evolved but still in some vital respects primitive and fresh Protestantism which, perhaps because of the peculiar conditions obtaining in the English Church, retained its free, popular and expansive impulse for longer than might otherwise have been expected. With the Puritans we are still in the full flush of the Reformation, not in some post-Reformation atmosphere of orthodoxy or unorthodoxy, and we are seeing the first fruits of a protestant preaching which was an appealing novelty in some regions as much as a century after the Reformation, nationally, is held in the textbooks to have occurred.[57] At no point is it possible to distinguish absolutely between Puritanism and, so to speak, mere Protestantism. This is not to deny that much of what we can recognize as Anglicanism was equally emergent in these decades, and was also legitimately derived from the Reformation. But as Dr. Tyacke has rightly insisted,[58] it was the high Anglicanism of the time, Arminian doctrine and Laudian formalism, which appeared strange and novel in the 1630s, whereas what we take for Puritanism would have been widely equated with orthodoxy. In 1641 a clerical writer remarked that he had been a minister for thirty years "when innovations were not thought of," and there can be no doubt that the innovations he had in mind were "innovations savouring of popery," for his experience had been in places "branded with the odious reproch of Puritanical rather than of Popish or formall." This was said in the context of a tract on the administration of the Communion which cites and approves "the ancient practice of the Church of England" of receiving in the chancel, seated around the table, and speaks of another very general custom to which the author takes exception only on practical grounds, of taking the bread and wine down to the people sitting in their pews.[59]

There is no satisfactory way in a single essay to justify claims for the widespread social entrenchment of Puritanism (in these senses) in Jacobean England. To some extent they must be taken on trust, as the impression of an extensive forager in the sources. In my *Elizabethan Puritan Movement* I tried to convey something of the gathering and expansive influence of a Puritanism which amounted to the continuing Reformation, clerical, popular and political, and I illustrated its progress particularly in East Anglia,

Essex and the Midlands.[60] For the early decades of the seventeenth century, the studies of Yorkshire by Dr. Newton and Dr. Marchant and of the other side of the Pennines by Dr. Richardson have demonstrated the great inroads made by puritan religion in regions which were not much affected before the end of the sixteenth century.[61] There is no need to go beyond the accessible biographies of puritan saints collected in the 1660s and 1670s by Samuel Clarke[62] to be impressed and widely informed about the religious lives and habits of those who called themselves sincere professors of religion and were spitefully called Puritans, and who grew up in the early years of the century. Like all improving and exemplary literature, these lives of divines and of eminent "private christians" must be read with discrimination.[63] They paint a rosy picture and are written within conventions of topic and language. The many implications of a mass movement are not to be trusted. The proportion of the total population which was Nonconformist in the late seventeenth century was small,[64] and earnest saints were perhaps never very numerous. Like John Foxe's martyrology, the stylized and specialized vocabulary must gloss over much variety of opinion and experience, as well as disguising a steady evolution towards a more spiritual and interior religion. Moreover the language of some of the biographies belongs to the fifties and sixties rather than to the twenties or thirties, which produces some subtle distortions. But when literary form criticism has done its worst, these narratives still contain invaluable information, especially on the corporate religious activities of the Puritans, which the manuscript sources tend to confirm and enrich. In skeletal essentials at least, an impressively homogeneous religious world is disclosed, suggesting that historians have been more imprecise in their delineations than is necessary.[65]

When Richard Baxter gave an account of his pastoral experience at Kidderminster in the 1650s,[66] most of the institutional forms which he described had been known in many parts of England for decades. It was these which structured the religious experience of the "choicest preachers and professors." A summary account of these well-established proceedings can be readily given. The professors, whose profession is frequently said to have arisen from some process of conversion (and it is in relation to conversion, in particular, that the conventions of the *Lives* may stand between us and reality), depended upon the ministrations of a godly preaching minister. Their lives revolved around the Sabbath, when the whole day was given up to religious exercises, normally with a sermon in the morning, after an abbreviated morning prayer, and a sermon linked with catechizing in the afternoon, with the interstices filled with other "exercises"; and around other sermons heard on at least one other day of the week. Where there was no acceptable preaching in their parish of residence, the godly went elsewhere, and this "gadding to sermons" in the Elizabethan phrase, "as doves to

the(ir) windows,"[67] which is the Biblical cliché of the biographies, was practised even when the people had their own preacher, "young and old together," "in companies" or "troops," "wet and dry," "summer and winter,"
"came from far and went home late," are phrases which reverberate.
Monthly communions also gathered the faithful from a wide catchment area,
and when disciplinary tests were applied to exclude scandalous or ignorant
parishioners from the sacrament the communion service itself became a
powerful solvent of parochial religion and a symbol of a differently ordered
Christian community.[68] When the godly enjoyed a preaching minister of
their own, whether he held the benefice or occupied a salaried lectureship
or a private position in some household, a close bond between pastor and
people was often established. Even in the case of beneficed clergy, episcopal
ordination and institution were sometimes regarded as mere civil procedures
to be passed through, or even obstacles to be circumvented. The puritan
patron often colluded in a measure of congregational election, sometimes
inviting the assistance if not the actual presbyterian laying on of hands of
other preaching ministers. Not infrequently the minister was directly supported, in whole or part, from the voluntary offerings of the flock, or by the
patron's generosity.

The sermons which the godly heard were rehearsed afterwards in exercises of "repetition," when the notes made by schoolboys and others were
brought into play. Repetition, conference, prayer and psalms occupied the
interval between public exercises on the Sabbath, and metrical psalm-
singing was employed on all occasions, even whilst walking or riding to
church, which in itself was not a casual but a studied social and religious
activity. In some places there were regular days of conference, held in the
houses of "the chief godly" or more "eminent Christians." These "conventicles" (in the eyes of authority or of hostile neighbors) were apparently the
groups from which open separation might, and on rare occasions and in
unusual circumstances did, arise.[69] Repetition could take place in church,
immediately after the sermon, or more privately in the minister's house or
in some other household, where it would approximate to the normal family
exercise of catechizing. It involved not only the answering of questions but
the offering of "conceived" prayer by members of the group encouraged to
"try their gift." It was a question whether women (often extraordinarily influential in these circles) might or might not offer prayer in these semi-public
circumstances.[70]

In addition, the preaching ministers met on regular occasions, most typically to support the "lectures by combination" or (in a specialized use of
the term) "exercises" maintained in market towns, or to attend regular
courses of lectures given by some celebrated divine in his own church,
these being often sermons *ad clerum*. A list of all the places where combi-

nation lectures were a regular institution would probably prove to be a gazeteer of prosperous market towns.[71] These exercises were descended from the learned but public preaching conferences of Elizabethan days known as "prophesyings."[72] Normally there would be no more than one sermon (in this way circumventing Queen Elizabeth's celebrated order inhibiting the prophesyings), but the whole company of preachers would be present, and they would afterwards dine together, by public expense at an inn or at one of the principal magistrate's houses, and would discuss with formality a question of divinity or some other matter of professional clerical concern. It does not take much imagination to conclude that these arrangements, rather than any formal diocesan and synodal machinery, represented the wider world of the Church beyond the parish for hundreds of clergy in the Calvinist tradition, although there were no rigid lines of segregation between these societies and the Church at large, and those who took part were not necessarily possessed of a divisively sectarian spirit. "Wee are noe waye encombred with buisie boddies to sowe the seedes of scisme emonge us to the unioynting of the peace of the ecclesiasticall boddie," wrote a Norfolk minister to the bishop of Norwich in requesting his allowance for an exercise at Swaffham, adding that the inhabitants of that town were "more rude than easilie will bee believed to be of those that have bene brought up in more civill places, the greater parte of them utterlie destitute of teaching ministers."[73]

The godly seem to have accompanied their own preachers to these exercises, and perhaps their own subsidiary meetings were dovetailed with those of the ministers, as in Baxter's Kidderminster. Already these comings and goings were regulated by a weekly and monthly calendar, in the manner of Free Churchmen and members of the Society of Friends ever since, a total departure from the saints' days and other holy days of the Church's year. Besides the familiar Sabbath, historians should take note of the fact that the exercise at Bury St. Edmunds was held weekly, on a Monday, from the time of Bishop Parkhurst in the 1560s until the coming of Bishop Wren in the 1630s led to its better "regulation." The exercise at Burton-on-Trent, for some reason known as a "famous" exercise, was also held on Mondays.[74] This looks more like the coming Nonconformity than Anglicanism, and so do the churchyards "barricaded with horses tyed to the outward rayles," as one writer puts it,[75] while their owners were at the lecture, a scene which points forward to the way of life of Strict Baptists in rural Suffolk (for example), where the chapels still provide accomodation for the horses and traps of the country people who would spend all Sunday there and bring their dinners, a hundred years ago and less.

In addition to these ordinary exercises, there would be extraordinary occasions for gathering: days of solemn humiliation and fasting, and days of thanksgiving. There were also funerals. In 1605 the funeral of Robert Walsh, a noted minister at Little Waldingfield in Suffolk, was a major event, with John Knewstub, doyen of the Suffolk preachers, delivering the sermon and heading the ministers who bore the coffin on their shoulders. John Winthrop noted the anniversary of the event in his almanac, immediately before the anniversary of the coronation of the king and queen.[76]

And that is really all that needs to be said, so far as concerns the external, corporate structures. As for the corresponding inner story, on the theological and spiritual plane, much more could be and has been written: the modern literature is copious. It remains only to add that whereas from time to time preaching exercises and especially market town lectures might be "suspected" and even "put down," they were as regularly raised up again,[77] and that it was only with the ascendancy of the Laudian bishops in the 1630s that this way of life was seriously disrupted. Before that it received some episcopal encouragement, most notably in Yorkshire and Nottinghamshire from Archbishop Tobie Mathew.[78] This and the security of puritan religion in many localities under the protection of landed gentry and urban oligarchs complicates any analysis of Puritanism in terms of opposition and *anomie*.

That this was a religion tending towards Independency and involuntary voluntarism is another suggestion to be offered on trust in an abbreviated discussion.[79] No doubt many of the clergy were in a general and no exclusive sense presbyterian in outlook, and whether presbyterian or moderate episcopalian or Erastian or indeterminate (all, with the exception of the last, more or less anachronistic labels before 1640), they would take the view that in a properly ordered Church there should be a parish ministry, supported from tithes and ministering to and exercising discipline over the entire population of resident and professed Christians. So much was assumed in the beginning, by the Elizabethan Puritans, and wherever local conditions were favorable a general reformation would be attempted on, so to speak, Genevan lines. As the Separatists repeatedly complained, the Puritans would still have the whole land to be the Church, and in the revolutionary circumstances of the 1640s, the old vision of a godly commonwealth was still bright and clear. But in the intervening years, as the expectation of further reform by public authority receded, and as puritan piety became progressively an interior matter, aspirations were inevitably introverted.[80] Everything attempted and accomplished was of a voluntary character, the result of a free collaboration of the godly. The theological achievement of the Puritans, from William Perkins onwards, can be roughly interpreted as the adaptation and domestication of Calvinism to fit the condition of voluntary Christians, whose independence of the ordered, disciplined life of the Church Calvin would have found strange and disturbing.

These points have often been noted as a late development, for example by Christopher Hill. But it could be argued that inasmuch as the godly were in some degree from the beginning a people apart, their situation had always been one of *de facto* Independency, even if their conscious and deliberate aims were at variance. As for matters of polity, the Elizabethan Puritans may have tended towards Presbyterianism, offering to erect in the place of bishops a hierarchy of synods on the French or Scottish or Dutch model. The national leaders, Cartwright, Travers and Field, were no doubt full-blooded Presbyterians, who advocated and even attempted to set up classical and synodal structures. But some of the theoretical literature of the period was reticent on the delicate question of how these structures were to be related to local churches, and it may be that whenever their own interests were involved, most Elizabethan Puritans would have been reluctant to concede to synods anything beyond the power to "counsel" and "advise" allowed in later years by the Independents. They would have derived such powers upwards, from the constituent congregations, and not downwards, from a true ministerial and synodical hierarchy.[81]

These suggestions are supported by the unique records of the conference of ministers which met in the 1580s in the Stour valley on the borders of Essex and Suffolk, the so-called Dedham *classis*, although the importance of these papers in this connection has been obscured by the wretched edition made by R. G. Usher for the Royal Historical Society in 1905, which omits some important documents and falsifies others. This conference (as it knew itself), or some members of it, aspired to exercise a properly presbyterian discipline over common church affairs, but signally failed to do so. They were obliged to record differences and to shelve decisions on important matters of doctrine and polity. The conference could not prevent the departure from some churches of ministers whom it thought should stay, and it could do nothing to restrain another congregation from arbitrary behavior towards its minister, beyond recording impotent words about "the people's course in rejecting and receiving their pastors without counsel of others." When instructed by a higher and representative assembly in London concerning its own membership, Dedham as a body failed to respond. "We reverence our faithfull brethren at London with their gratyous advises . . . yet being best privy in our conference, what inconveniences we see likely to ensue . . . in our consultation we finde not motives sufficient to perswade us . . . ," and so on. This letter was written six months after receipt of the letter to which it was an answer.[82]

The Dedham papers suggest that the bond between pastor and people was considered to be the firmest of all ecclesiastical ties. One member thought the conjunction so near that "thone shuld not forsake thother no more then man and wieff shuld", and another said: "Blame not the people for being lothe to part with their pastor, for if I were of that church, I had as lieve they shuldest pluck out myne eie as take from me my paster." This same brother, Richard Crick, no rustic but a Doctor of Divinity, uttered passionate words when the validity of his calling by his own people came into question, "being become now at length as jealous for the honor of the church [that is, for the honour of his own congregation] as any of you are for your owne."[83] This is evidence in itself for the forceful independence of the "professors" of the Stour valley, many of whom were substantial clothiers with business connections with Antwerp and other commercial centers. That the puritan laity, sometimes condescendingly called "simple gospellers" by the puritan clergy, were not a submissive following or captive audience but a vigorous source of initiative should cause no surprise. It was implicit in the Reformation itself, in its anticlericalism, which seems to have been a persistent force in English life, and in the direct access to unmediated religious knowledge and experience, offered by the English Bible in the popular Geneva version, which the godly carried with them to sermons.

Elizabethan anticlericalism assumed the form of sustained agitation against the nonpreaching, often scandalous clergy, in which the laity enthusiastically joined, both at the parliamentary level and locally, where the particular failings of particular clerics were lovingly "registered" to form part of a country-wide Survey of the Ministry.[84] There are many indications that it was the "simple gospellers" who objected most uncompromisingly to the surplice, the cross in baptism, and other celebrated dregs of Antichrist still entertained in the English Church.[85] Evidently antivestiarianism was the typical English form of that iconoclasm which students of the Continental Reformation recognize as a particularly significant expression of radical popular sentiment. When the puritan clergy spoke of the "offence" caused by such ceremonies they must be understood to speak precisely, in terms of the Pauline *topos* of the offense to the weaker brethren occasioned by the eating of meats offered to idols.[86] Sometimes the offense was taken beyond hope of satisfaction, and schism ensued. It was in this way, as likely as not, that Separatism was provoked in London in 1567 and in Norfolk in 1581, and threatened in other places. When Mr. Fletcher, vicar of Cranbrook in the Kentish Weald (grandfather of the dramatist) preached in defense of the ceremonies it was said that his credit was "almost broken in sunder." Some assigned their conversion to his teaching, "but these very parties do now also affirme" that he had "run headlong, to the eversion of many consciences, unlesse Gods spirite prevent them." "Eversion of conscience" implied nothing less than schism.[87]

It is probably a mistake to adopt a perspective which allows for the slow gestation of the religious capacity of lay Protestants, until its potential was at last realized after 1640. That potential was already perceptible a full century earlier, at least in parts of the South-East of England where Lollardy, that older dissenting tradition, still persisted.[88] In a county like Essex, or in the Weald, it is more plausible to suppose that the puritan clergy achieved success in bringing self-assertive lay religion under control, and in reducing to submissive and orthodox responses the strongly innate tendency to sectarianism and the heresy of free will. In the exceptionally rich archdeaconry records covering the county of Essex there are indications of the ferment beneath the surface: open-air preaching in the woods in one village, in another a conventicle gathered around the schoolmaster, its members keeping their children from baptism.[89] How lay initiative was simultaneously stimulated and tamed is suggested in a hostile account of Cranbrook in the 1570s: "It is a commone thing now for every pragmaticall prentise to have in his head and mouth the government and reformation of the Churche. And he that in exercise can speak thereoff, that is the man. Every artificer must be a reformer and teacher . . . ." An opponent corrects the record. For "artificers and pragmaticall prentises," read Cranbrook clothiers, men of substance.[90] One of these Cranbrook clothiers would become brother-in-law to Paul Baynes, who as a "Non-Separating Congregationalist" has already figured in this discussion.[19] (And Dr. Edmund Chapman, the leading figure in the Dedham Conference, was brother-in-law to a prominent clothier of the Stour valley.)[92]

Decades later another generation of artificers, the early Ranters and Quakers, recorded in their spiritual autobiographies the deadening effect of a routinised puritan religion which they had sought out in their youth, but which had brought them no nearer to valid experience. Laurence Clarkson aspired to pray in the exercise ("fain would I have been judged a professor with them, but wanted parts") and at length he succeeded, but his religious conceptions remained primitive and outside what pertained to his own condition. "My God was a grave, ancient, holy, old man, as I supposed, sat in Heaven in a chair of gold, but as for his nature I knew no more than a childe."[93] But this should be read as no more than a corrective to the evidence on the other side of the success of the preachers in arousing and nourishing a piety which was content to know and express itself in the categories of puritan orthodoxy, the type characterized in the mid-seventeenth-century sources as "plain godly," "solid old Christian." No doubt these successes were scored among the clothiers and their social equals and betters, with their dependents, rather than in the ranks of the "pragmaticall prentises" and "restless itinerant artisans," inhabitants of Christopher Hill's *World Turned Upside Down* and A. L. Morton's *World of the Ranters.*

Separatism, to return full circle, is normally understood as a rejection of the Church of England as a national and comprehensive establishment of religion, whereas the Puritans who did not separate are said to have been moved by veneration for the principle of the indivisible Church, conterminous with the Commonwealth, part of the Church Universal. This is not false, but it misses the point that the Separatists cut themselves off, not from some legal abstraction, but from fellowship with like-minded brethren within and yet not wholly of the Church of England. The literary controversies which served to define Separatism were conducted, not with the bishops or other official spokesmen for the establishment, but with fellow-puritans. What the Non-Separatists objected to on their side was not so much desertion of the national Church as the schism perpetrated against the best assemblies of England, the true Christians, the most forward preachers. Consequently the most prominent single issue was that of hearing, or not hearing, the godly and non-separated preachers, so that when John Robinson "came backe indeed the one halfe of the way" from Separatism,[94] the nature of his recantation was posthumously disclosed in a *Treatise on the lawfulnes of hearing of the ministers in the Church of England*.[95] The question on the side of the Separatists was whether the godly, by adhering to a Church which was a confused heap of good and bad, and by submitting themselves to the corrupt power of the bishops, had put themselves beyond public communion and even private fellowship. But on both sides there was reluctance to repudiate those suspected to be, as one writer puts it, "sound in the vitals of Christian religion."[96] So the debate was not primarily about the Church of England but about the status and credentials of the godly elements in the Church of England so long as they remained within it. Robinson was not at all incredulous in the face of the evidence cited by Ames of the practical possibility of realizing a kind of voluntary church life in the Church of England, short of separation. The Separatists had always acknowledged the "graces" enjoyed by the godly in the English church assemblies, and even their capacity to arouse faith.[97] The issue between Ames and Robinson was that Robinson insisted that all such voluntary undertakings were not public but private in nature, understanding "public" as meaning "by public authority," whereas Ames understood "public" to refer to any proceedings in a public place, involving more than individuals or single households, a highly significant distinction. Ames's argument, said Robinson, was "pretending to prove public communion upon private, . . . consisting of a continued equivocation in the terms, 'public licence,' 'government,' 'ministry,' and the like."[98]

So there was agreement between Separatists and Non-Separatists on the presence of substantial godly elements in the English Church which were characterised by apartness. That this godly party was socially apart is suggested by the "odious name" of puritan itself, and by a long tradition of vernacular antipuritan sentiment which is epitomized in Richard Baxter's autobiographical reflections, for example, in the resounding statement that "the warre was begun in our streets before the King and Parliament had any armies."[99] We have seen that the common life of the godly was to a great extent structured by the religious exercises which were distinctive of Puritanism, and which exerted a strong if unintended separatist pull. It was a way of life which contained within itself much casual and disorderly separatism, as the professors deserted their own ministers for other, more popular preachers, so that it was a recurrent cause for concern "that a pastor might have his own people."[100] When people trooped to John Rogers at Dedham saying "let's go to Dedham to get a little fire,"[101] church order of the most basic kind was at risk.

The theological rationale of this situation is clearer since the publication of John S. Coolidge's important study, *The Pauline Renaissance in England*. Penetrating the rich language pertaining to "edification" in St. Paul's understanding of the Church, and detecting the crucial connection between this concept and the theme of Christian liberty (for Coolidge this connection constitutes the key to "the whole mystery of Elizabethan Puritanism"), the Puritans thought of the Church as composed of lively stones, ever in building and constantly maintaining its life, as members of the body grew up in Christ by communicating their strength from one to the other. By contrast, and thanks to the Elizabethan polity, it was characteristic of Anglicanism to limit the meaning of edification to the imparting of instruction within an already established and completed, nonliving structure. Coolidge suggests that "it is not too much to say that the whole subtle but radical difference between the Puritan cast of mind and the conformist appears in their different way of understanding the verb 'to edify'." "The social order which results from the operation of the spirit of life is opposed not merely to disorder but, more significantly, to a non-living kind of order." Consequently it was no "abstruse point" for the Non-Separating Congregationalists to find the essence of the Church, not in the diocesan and parochial structures which outwardly and apparently constituted the Church of England, but in the instinctive resourcefulness of the godly in their free and willing coming together.[102]

Admittedly the Separatists were more consistent in their practical application of the Pauline theology, and Coolidge considers that "the vision of a living Church, planted and visible in England" in the course of time passed to them.[103] The Separatists could say with total confidence: "The matter of the building is people, joined together in the profession of the Gospel," and: "Neither lies our exception against any personal, or accidentary profanation of the temple, but against the faulty frame of it."[104] But the Non-Separatists did what they could to make the saints visible, and to give some tangible form to their private Christian experience, while not actually repudiating the public communion of national Church and parish. The form was inevitably the intensely fashionable form of a covenant, "covenanting," to quote Henry Jacob, "to live as members of a holy society together."[105]

It is well known that Richard Bernard, who drew back from the separation of the Scrooby-Gainsborough Pilgrims, entered into a "particular covenant" with about a hundred "voluntary professors" from a number of parishes around Worksop, "to watch over one another, to admonish one another, . . . and thereupon to receive the Lord's Supper";[106] and that John Cotton, with "some scores of godly persons" in Boston, "entered into a covenant with the Lord, in the purity of his worship," which Cotton later said was "defective, yet it was more then the Old Non-conformity."[107] It is not so well known that in 1588 Richard Rogers of Wethersfield in Essex, keeper of an early puritan diary,[108] associated "divers well-minded Christians," all of his own parish, "well nigh twentie persons" in a covenant, mutually to amend their course of living, and that their action and the text of the covenant itself were held up as an example to others in Rogers's best-selling *Seven treatises*, which appeared in editions of 1603, 1604, 1605, 1607, 1610, 1616, 1627 and 1630.[109] On a certain Sunday in 1616 John Winthrop of Groton in Suffolk, later of Massachusetts, "arose betymes, and read over the covenant of certaine Christians sett downe in Mr. Rogers booke." Within a few days he was constrained to acknowledge his own unfaithfulness and to renew his own covenant "of walking with my God, and watchinge my heart and wayes." Winthrop and what he calls his "company" were already covenanted to meet with a number of Suffolk preachers and their wives annually on September 17th, and every Friday "to be mindefull one of another in desiring God to grante the petitions that were made to him" on the occasion of that meeting.[110] "With him I covenanted", wrote Captain Roger Clap of his relations with his master in an Exeter household "famous" for religion.[111]

These covenants were not church covenants but belonged to the puritan experience of covenanted grace, an area quite remote at this time from any overt ecclesiological reference. It could even be said that they represent a pietistic retreat from the robust vision of Elizabethan Puritanism of a reformed Church and a godly social order. But as Edmund S. Morgan has argued, the puritan morphology of grace would eventually underlie a more profound and searching Separatism, when the New England churches would demand as the condition of membership something never required by the earlier Separatists: evidence of the saving work of Christ in the heart.[112] The nub of William Ames's objection to the Separatists was that they despised clear tokens of saving faith at work in the Church of England and approached a new doctrine of salvation by works in gathering separated churches of the visibly worthy. Covenanted groups within the Church of England were devoted, as the Separatists apparently were not, to a shared examination of the heart. It is significant that Rogers reports of his brethren in covenant that they "did as farre exceed the common sort of those that professe the gospel, as the common professors do exceed them in religion which know not the Gospell";[113] super-saints, in fact, but not so much in performance and worthiness as in their sorrowful recognition of how unsatisfactory their Christian profession had been. If the Separatists held together in their separation that blend of Pauline teaching on edification and Christian liberty, which was of the essence of Puritanism, these Non-Separatists clung more securely to the principal Pauline anchor of Protestantism itself: Justification by Only Faith.

The path of this argument may by now have clarified what was said at the outset about the need for a lateral or horizontal approach to early Dissent. The act of separation was momentous, carrying the actors to the far side of a profound theological, social and psychological divide. But it could arise almost circumstantially, or so it appears if considered in a wider context than one of creeds and platforms. The schism of the Separatists served only to formalise a *de facto* situation of advanced near-Separatism, and it draws attention to that more extensive phenomenon as the tip of an iceberg draws attention to the bulk beneath the surface. Once the wide extent of forms and degrees of sectarianism is recognised, interest may shift somewhat away from the significance of Dissent for the future, as the prophetic cause of lonely pioneers, and towards its meaning in the world of the early seventeenth century itself. The sociologist Bryan Wilson calls sects "catalysts," sometimes "crystallising in acute form social discontents and aspirations, and marking the moments of social structural collapse, and sometimes heralding, or even promoting, social regeneration."[114] How are such intriguing possibilities of a "socially transformative role" to be explored and tested in the case of early Dissent? What did it mean in early Stuart times to be a "virtual dissenter"?[115]

Local researches may reveal who the Separatists and semiseparatists and Puritans were, and establish (or fail to establish) a correlation with social status and occupation, and with differing rural and urban economies and patterns of human settlement. Professor Alan Everitt and others are pointing the way.[116] Postgraduate work recently completed or in progress will certainly invest our knowledge of Puritanism with greater social precision.[117] However, Puritanism will never lend itself very readily to the essentially statistical method of religious sociography. We are dealing with groups whose relation to the established Church was untidy and ambiguous, groups fuzzy at the edges, not with organized nonconformist bodies with formal church records and registers. Another method, at once more universal and more particular, will be to explore among personal and literary sources the meaning of puritan and dissenting experience in the context of family and community relations: literature and anthropology, rather than economics and agronomy.[118]

If one looks, simplistically perhaps, no further than the written page of puritan literature, letters, biographies, sermons, one is bound to notice how incessantly it harps on themes and analogies of human affection, on the fervent love which is to be found in the society of the godly. The conventions of this ardent language can be traced back at least as far as the Marian persecution, when John Bradford wrote from prison to his "dear hearts and dearlings in the Lord, . . . mine owne sweet heart in the Lord."[119] Dr. Richard Crick told his Dedham brethren in the 1580s that he had looked upon their backs with greater joy than he beheld the eyes of any other company, and that their faces were "as if I had seen the face of God."[120] By the seventeenth century, the *Lives* gathered by Clarke resound with confident reports of the intimacy enjoyed by this or that company of Christians. "Holy affections . . . were exceedingly kindled and kept alive in them." John Angier's people at Ringley in Lancashire were "kind and every way helpful." Baxter and his flock "took great delight in the company of each other."[121] To an impressive extent, puritan saints appear to have proved their calling by the faithful performance of social virtues, towards wives, husbands, children, servants, and members of the religious group in general.[122] A notable act of a notable Christian would not be to fast but to provide ample refreshment for the godly on a religious occasion. One comes to recognize stock situations: the pious matron whose anxious spiritual life is guided by the pastoral casuist with ardent encouragement, and who nurses the preacher when he is sick and attends his deathbed; the adolescent who finds religion when boarded out in another family.

Friendships so demanding and exclusive must have upset all kinds of other, pre-existent relationships. A common piece of invective in antipuritan literature was the accusation that puritan preaching divides communities previously at peace and destroys neighborhood and good fellowship.[123] Sometimes the Puritans cry foul and insist that they too pursue and hopefully promote a general social harmony,[124] but often the charge is admitted, although the blame is shifted to the enemy. Christ came to bring not peace but a sword. "Can yee put fire and water together but they will rumble?"[125] While the Elizabethan Puritans had earnestly sought the reform of whole towns and parishes, with "discipline" their watchword, the improving literature of the next century significantly warns the godly to make friends among their own kind, and to mistrust traditional ties, Dod and Cleaver instructing their readers not to rely on "carnall friends" but on "godly men, for they will proove our surest friends. Vicinitie and neighbourhood will faile, and alliance and kindred will faile, but grace and religion will never faile."[126] More tangibly, it is quite clear that the religious exercises which filled the leisure hours of godly professors literally took the place of what Baxter called "the old feastings and gossipings."[127] The old obligations to keep house and entertain were far from neglected, but they suffered a transference. Evidently the godly supplied one another with the love and mutual support which they might otherwise have looked for among kindred and neighbors. Samuel Clarke described how his own people in the Wirral of Cheshire "though living ten or twelve miles asunder, were as intimate and familiar as if they had been all of one houshold."[128]

When Robert Browne wrote of being "wholy bent . . . to search and find out the matters of the church," it is notable that his search went on in conversation, among friends. The principle of the gathered church was not a ratiocinative matter only but a truth apprehended among other "forward" Christians, or so one gathers from his *True and short declaration*. Disillusionment for Browne, as for many later "Brownists," such as the lapsed and excommunicated members of Francis Johnson's Amsterdam congregation, may have been at root the disappointment of soured and mutually destructive human relationships, the family at war.[129] Should the historian be too cautious to find in the eager quest for the true Church and in the tergiversations of Separatism evidence of social as well as ecclesiological yearnings? Of the secret, "privy" church of Protestants which gathered in Marian London, and which was an abiding inspiration to Separatists and Puritans alike, it was said by an early Elizabethan sectary: "That persecution grew so fast as that it brought many a hundred to know one another that never knew before; and we joined all with one heart and mind to serve God with pure hearts and minds according to his word."[130]

There are, or may be, dimensions of meaning to social puritanism which would far outrun the scope of this exploratory essay. Ever since the appearance of Max Weber's famous *Protestant Ethic and the Spirit of Capitalism* in 1904-5, the saints of the seventeenth century have been invested with an almost cosmic significance as in some sense the mediators of nothing less than the transition from traditional to modern society, the agents of rationalization. The vast literature erected upon and branching out from Weber,[131] stands in relation to this modest paper as Rohan, Gondor and Mordor stand in relation to the Hobbit's cosy Shire. But let it be observed, Hobbit-like, that modern students of Puritanism who continue to be prompted by Weber and, behind Weber, by Marx, are nowadays interested as much in the intimacies of family relations as in the strenuous spiritual warfare of the inner-worldly ascetic.[132] "Puritan zeal," Professor Michael Walzer recognizes, "was not a private passion" but "a highly collective emotion," the emotion of "oppositional" "masterless men," whose response to the alienating experience of disorder and anxiety was to reject traditional order and to begin the construction of a new order.[133] Christopher Hill sees Puritanism as a social as much as a religious force, fragmenting a society religiously constituted by state church and parish only to remold it by voluntary action. Puritan sects and groups were "united by community of interest rather than by geographical propinquity or corporate worship," but the components were, so to speak, molecules rather than atoms, families rather than individuals. Household religion is a major theme,[134] and the household is said to be the "essential unit" of puritan piety. In a variety of ways, this fact is made to connect with "the economic tension of the community in process of breaking up," which is "focussed upon the household in transition from a patriarchal unit of communal production to a capitalist form."[135]

However, Dr. John Bossy wonders whether the "traditional community," at least at the parish level, ever really existed. The true social forms of late medieval religion seem to have been not parochial but tribal, connections of natural or contrived kindred, acquired through blood, baptism or marriage. The unity of the geographical parish in both Protestant and Catholic countries was something strictly nonexistent, but striven for as an ideal. The despised figure of the alebench vicar, composing quarrels and promoting good fellowship, becomes transcendental, beating the bounds of the parish at Rogationtide more than a folk survival, the church ale something more than a binge to boost church funds.[136] If this is right, then the Puritans were describing a circle, retreating from the forced bonds of mere co-residence and neighborhood in order to lose their *anomie* in new and more relevant forms of those old ties of kindred which had ceased to count for very much by the seventeenth century.[137] Nothing could more beautifully illustrate the co-existence and tension of conservative and innovative elements which both Weber and R. H. Tawney,[138] from differing standpoints, saw as the enigma of Calvinism.

Inevitably the social forms described in the puritan literature of the early seventeenth century were transitional in their novelty and spontaneity. John Cotton taught that "the faith of the parent doth bring the Children and household of a Christian . . . under a Covenant of salvation, as well as the faith of *Abraham* brought his houshold of old under the same covenant."[139] A religion which set so much store by family could scarcely become the permanent cause of division within families, still less the ideology for some alternative society to which family ties would be a matter of indifference. Rather it became a major and perhaps dominant concern of puritan parents that their children should be seen to inherit the promises and to share with them in the covenant, not least when experience proved that the parental home was the hardest place of all in which to find religion for oneself.[140] On the subject of New England, and in the general context of an argument about the supposed declension of the American puritan spirit which is as old as Cotton Mather, Edmund S. Morgan has written vividly of the triumph of a "tribalism" which dried up the springs of authentic Puritanism. When the Puritans "allowed their children to usurp a higher place than God in their affections," and "when theology became the handmaid of genealogy, puritanism no longer deserved its name."[141] Whether the passing of what a mid-seventeenth-century writer called "the character of an Old English Puritan"[142] was something equally within the logic of the domestication of the puritan religious experience is a question hardly put as yet by English historians. But it is a question which belongs to the middle age of the dissenting tradition, not to its origins.

A certain distinguished historian of the Reformation has been heard to say that religious history is too important a matter to be left to the theologians. But it is too important to be left to the secularists either. Those who write from within the tradition, with theological awareness and spiritual sensitivity, have much the better chance of getting it right.[143] Unfortunately, ecclesiastical history, not alone among the ecclesiastical endeavors of modern times, has too often been characterised by a kind of self-esteem, a concern with identity, even and perhaps most of all when seeking to lose that identity in a wider and ecumenical future. The burden of this essay has been to argue that the subject of the historical identity of churches and religious movements, while important, is not exhaustive; or better, to argue that the question of identity is much wider than has sometimes been suspected.

NOTES

1. Adapted from a Special University Lecture in Theology delivered in the University of London on February 19, 1974.
2. *Orthodoxy in Massachusetts 1630-1650: A Genetic Study* (Cambridge, Massachusetts, 1933).
3. Cf. G. R. Elton, "A High Road to Civil War?," in *From the Renaissance to the Counter-Reformation: Essays in Honour of Garrett Mattingly*, ed. C. H. Carter (1966), 325-47. (London is the place of publication of all books cited unless otherwise stated.)
4. Stephen Mayor, *The Lords Supper in Early English Dissent* (1972), 29.
5. *Congregational History*, i. (1869), vi.
6. *See* a useful succession of papers in the *Baptist Quarterly*: E. G. Rupp, "The Importance of Denominational History," n.s. vol. 17 (1957-8), 312-19; Christopher Hill, "History and Denominational History," n.s. vol. 22 (1967-8), 65-71; B. R. White, "The Task of a Baptist Historian," *ibid.*, 398-408.
7. *Lives of the Puritans*, I (1813), xii.
8. Waddington published in Boston, Massachusetts, in 1863 a series of lectures under the title *1559-1620: Track of the Hidden Church, or the Springs of the Pilgrim Movement*.
9. New York (1879).
10. *See* Douglas Horton's Introduction to the Pilgrim Press edition, Boston, Massachusetts (1960).
11. In this respect Burrage's *The Early English Dissenters in the Light of Recent Research (1550-1641)*, 2 vols. (Cambridge, 1912), is the next major

landmark after Dexter, followed closely by Peel's *The Second Parte of a Register, Being a Calendar of Manuscripts under that Title intended for publication by the Puritans about 1593, and now in Dr. Williams's Library, London,* 2 vols. (Cambridge, 1915).

12. Especially in *The First Congregational Churches: New Light on Separatist Congregations in London, 1567-81* (Cambridge, 1920), and *The Brownists in Norwich and Norfolk About 1580* (Cambridge, 1920); and other papers in *Transactions of the Congregational Historical Society* and *The Congregational Quarterly.* See Norman F. Sykes's appreciation of Peel in the *Transactions,* vol. 17 (1952-5), 4-7.

13. It would be superfluous in this volume of all places to list the six volumes which have so far appeared, containing the works of Cartwright, Browne and Harrison, and Barrow and Greenwood, or the further volumes projected, which will contain the works of Penry and *A Parte of a register.* See the prospective statements by Peel and Carlson in the first volume, *Cartwrigntiana* (1951), vi-x.

14. *The English Separatist Tradition: From the Marian Martyrs to the Pilgrim Fathers* (Oxford, 1971).

15. *The way of congregrational churches cleared: in two treatises,* Wing C 6469 (1648), pt. I, 12.

16. *Orthodoxy in Massachusetts, op. cit.; The New England Mind: The Seventeenth Century* (Cambridge, Massachusetts, 1939); and *see* also especially "The Marrow of Puritan Divinity," in *Errand into the Wilderness* (Cambridge, Massachusetts), 1956.

17. Robert G. Pope, *The Half-Way Covenant: Church Membership in Puritan New England* (Princeton, 1969), 9.

18. "Une question mal posée: les origines de la réforme française et le problème générale des causes de la réforme" *Revue historique,* vol. 160, 1-73; reprinted, *Au coeur religieux du XVIᵉ siècle* (Paris, 1957), 3-70.

19. As in I. B. Horst's *The Radical Brethren: Anabaptism and the English Reformation to 1558,* Bibliotheca Humanistica & Reformatorica ii (Nieuwkoop, 1972), which is critical of "the particularistic approach: an emphasis on the unique and the formulation of clear answers," while it is unable to provide convincing evidence for the existence and influence of a native Anabaptist movement in England. To be fair to Dr. Horst, who has not persuaded many of his reviewers, he shares with the present writer a desire to transfer attention from the separatist to the non-separatist tradition of Dissent, and would not perhaps quarrel with the judgment of John Cotton (*op. cit.,* pt. I, 3) who denied that there was "such correspondency between the *Germane* Anabaptism and the *English* Brownism, as to make Brownism a native branch of Anabaptism." This was in answer to the Scottish Presbyterian Robert Baylie who had found "the derivation of the one from the other . . . very rationall." (*A dissuasive from the errours of the time,* Wing B 456, 1645, 13.)

20. *Op. cit.,* xii, 160-9.

21. Cf. Donald Nugent, "The Renaissance And/of Witchcraft" *Church History,* vol. 40 (1971), 69-78.

22. *Religious Sects: A Sociological Study,* 1970; and *Sects and Society: A Sociological Study of Three Religious Groups in Britain* (1961), Introduction, 1-11.

23. *See* Perry Miller's remark that Dexter and Williston Walker saw the past

"primarily in reference to their own present." (*Orthodoxy in Massachusetts*, xv.) This is hardly true of Dr. White, but the shadow of the old tradition lingers.

24. *See* the *Dictionary of National Biography* for biographies of all five; and Samuel Clarke, *The lives of two and twenty English divines*, Wing C 4540, (1660), and *The lives of thirty-two English divines*, Wing C 4539 (1677), for lives of Bradshaw (by Thomas Gataker) and Baynes. On Ames see especially K. L. Sprunger, *The Learned Doctor William Ames: Dutch Backgrounds of English and American Puritanism* (Urbana, 1972).

25. STC 3516 ([Amsterdam?], 1605); translated and published by Ames in 1610 at Frankfurt as *Puritanismus Anglicanus* and consequently sometimes misattributed to Ames; the original version republished, but with significant textual variations, in 1640 (STC 3517) and 1641 (Wing B 4158); the 1605 and 1640 edns. reprinted in facsimile, with other works of Bradshaw and Introduction by R. C. Simmons, Gregg Int., Farnborough, 1972. *See* also Baynes, *The diocesans tryall*, STC 1640 (1621), also reprinted in facsimile, Gregg Int., (Farnborough, 1971); and Jacob, *Reasons taken out of Gods word and the best humane testimonies proving a necessitie of reforming our churches in England*, STC 14338 ([Middleburg?], 1604).

26. *Conscience with the power and cases thereof*, STC 552, n.p. (1639); *The marrow of sacred divinity*, (first English edn. 1638), Wing A 3000, (1642). See also Parker, *De politeia ecclesiastica Christi et hierarchica opposita libri tres*, (Frankfurt, 1616).

27. Bradshaw, *The unreasonablenesse of the separation made apparent*, STC 3532 (Dort, 1614), printed with and paginated in sequence with Ames, *A manuduction for Mr. Robinson, and such as consent with him in private communion, to lead them on to publick*; Ames, *A second manuduction for Mr. Robinson*, STC 556, n.p. (1615). Bradshaw reprinted in facsimile in *Puritanism and Separatism: A Collection of Works by William Bradshaw*, with Introduction by R. C. Simmons, Gregg Int., n.p. (1972). Ames's writings against Robinson are to be reprinted in facsimile in a volume of *Church Controversies* by Gregg Int.

28. *Orthodoxy in Massachusetts*, 105, generally supported by Cotton, *op. cit.*

29. 1640 edn. substitutes for "men" "true beleevers" and omits "ordinarilie."

30. 1640 inserts "according to the order of the Gospell" between "together" and "in."

31. 1640 has "Congregations."

32. 1605 edn., 5.

33. *Marrow of sacred divinity*, 157; cf. Jacob, *Reasons taken out of Gods word*, 22.

34. Ames, *Marrow of sacred divinity*, 157-9.

35. Jacob, *An attestation of many learned, godly and famous divines*, STC 14328 ([Middleburg], 1613), 100 seq.; Jacob, *A confession and protestation of the faith of certaine christians in England*, STC 14330, ([Middleburg?], 1616), Sig. B 2; Baynes, *op. cit.*, *passim*; Parker, *op. cit.*, 329. That English divines were generally suspect in foreign Reformed circles for such views is suggested by the history of the English *classis* in the Netherlands as recorded in the Boswell Papers in the British Library, MS. Add. 6394 (partly printed in Burrage, *op. cit.*, vol. 2, 260-91.) *See* R. P. Stearns, *Congregationalism in the Dutch Netherlands: The Rise and Fall of the English*

Congregational Classics, 1521-1535 (American Socy. of Church History Chicago, 1940) and Alice C. Carter, *The English Reformed Church in Amsterdam in the Seventeenth Century*, Pubns. of the Municipal Archives of Amsterdam, vol. 3 (1964).

36. *Conscience*, bk. IV, 61-4. Cf. Jacob, *A confession and protestation*, Sig. B 8: "Doubtless we ought to leave the worse societies and to enjoy one that is and may be sincere."

37. *See* above.

38. *See* Benjamin Stinton's "Repository of Divers Historical Matters" in the so-called "Gould Manuscript," printed, Burrage, *op. cit.*, vol. 2, 292-308, and critically discussed, *ibid.*, vol. 1. 336-56.

39. *Reasons taken out of Gods word*, 55; *A confession and protestation*; *A collection of sundry matters* ([Middleburg?], 1616); and the Gould MS. printed by Burrage, *op. cit.*, vol. 2, 292-308. Jacob's earlier writings, in which he is presumed (perhaps not altogether correctly) to be totally at odds with the Separatists, contain many anticipations of these positions. *See A defence of the churches and ministery of England*, STC 14335 (Middleburg, 1599), *A short treatise concerning the truenes of a pastorall calling in pastors made by praelates* (in continuous pagination with *A defence*), and the papers of 1603-5 printed by Burrage, *op. cit.*, vol. 2, 146-66; *see* also John van Rohr, "The Congregationalism of Henry Jacob," *Transactions of the Congregational Historical Society*, vol. 19, 107-22.

40. John Sprint, *Considerations*, quoted and refuted in Henry Ainsworth, *Counterpoyson*, STC 234 ([Amsterdam?], 1608), 54 seq. The Separatist Ainsworth engages with this argument as stated by Sprint, Richard Bernard and William Crashaw.

41. Quoted, Miller, *Orthodoxy in Massachusetts*, 151.

42. Thomas Hooker, *A survey of the summe of church-discipline*, Wing H 2658 (1648), pt. I, 47-8. Cf. John Allin and Thomas Shepard, *A defence of the answer*, Wing A 1036 (1648), 13: "Congregations in *England* are truly Churches having an implicite Covenant."

43. *A manuduction*, Sig. Q 4.

44. *See* "The Congregation and its Ministers," pt. VII chap. 1, 333-45 of my *The Elizabethan Puritan Movement*, (Berkeley, 1967); and *A collection of certain letters and conferences lately passed betwixt certaine preachers and two prisoners in the Fleet* (1590), in *The Writings of John Greenwood, 1587-1590*, ed. L. H. Carlson, Elizabethan Nonconformist Texts vol. 4 (1962), 175-262.

45. *Op. cit.*, Sig. B 1ᵛ.

46. Ames, *A second manuduction*, 34.

47. Quoted Miller, *Orthodoxy in Massachusetts*, 151. Cf. Cotton, *op. cit.*, pt. I, 14: "Neither was our departure from ['the Parishionall Congregations in *England*'] even in those evill times, a Separation from them as no Churches, but rather a Secession from the corruptions found amongst them, unto which also we must have been forced to conforme . . . unlesse wee had timely departed from them."

48. Michael McGiffert, "American Puritan Studies in the 1960s." *William & Mary Quarterly*, 3rd ser. vol. 27 (1970), 36-67, reviewing much of the literature of revision and reporting the private communications of scholars.

49. *Visible Saints: the Congregational Way, 1640-1660* (Oxford, 1957), 10-11.

50. Ames departs as far as can be imagined from Miller's assumptions when he writes: "It is also very probable that there is no such particular Church in which the profession of the true Faith flourisheth, but in the same also there are found some true believers . . . But those who are onely believers by profession, so long as they remaine in that society are members of that Church, as also of the catholick Church as touching the outward state, not touching the inward or essential state. I *John* 2:19. They went out from us, but they were not of us." (*Marrow of sacred divinity*, 158.) On Miller's misapprehensions in this area see especially John S. Coolidge, *The Pauline Renaissance in England: Puritanism and the Bible* (Oxford, 1970), 71-6, and this statement in particular: "The nature of [the semiseparatist] compromise has been misrepresented in after times because of the modern *idée fixe* concerning the place of the doctrine of predestination in radical Protestantism." On this issue of covenanted grace, *see* Jens G. Møller, "The Beginnings of Puritan Covenant Theology." *Journal of Ecclesiastical History*, vol. 14 (1963), 46-67, Richard L. Greaves, "The Origins and Development of English Covenant Thought." *The Historian*, vol. 31 (1968), 21-35 and references supplied, and the Introduction by Dr Ian Breward to his *The Work of Williams Perkins* (Courtenay Library of Reformation Classics, Abingdon, Berks., 1970).

51. *Orthodoxy in Massachusetts*, 83, 84, 88, 89, 92-6; Coolidge, *op. cit.*, 74 n.57.

52. Especially not to *Society and Puritanism in Pre-Revolutionary England* (1964).

53. Professor L. L. Schücking in his pioneering study *Die Puritanische Familie* (Leipzig, 1929) insisted with reason that a distinctive pattern of domestic piety became the common property of both "Anglicans" and "Puritans," that the essential dividing line was one between "saints" and the children of the world, and that "denominational" labels lacked significance. Yet he called his study *The Puritan Family*.

54. The will of Robert Moore of Guiseley, Yorkshire, a veteran Elizabethan Puritan (see *The Seconde Parte of a Register*, vol. 2, 234-8), proved in 1642, printed, R. A. Marchant, *Puritans and the Church Courts in the Diocese of York, 1560-1642* (1960), 212-14.

55. Richard Baxter, *Reliquiae Baxterianae*, Wing B 1370 (1696), 1-3.

56. The mistake is made, for example, by Professor Mark Curtis in his essay 'The Alienated Intellectuals of Early Stuart England', in *Crisis in Europe, 1560-1660*, ed. T. Aston (1965), 295-316; and in the broader context of Professor Michael Walzer's *The Revolution of the Saints: A Study in the Origins of Radical Politics* (Cambridge, Massachusetts, 1965). For a particular local example of the social realities argued for here, see Paul Slack, 'Religious Protest and Urban Authority: The Case of Henry Sherfield, Iconoclast, 1633' in *Schism, Heresy and Religious Protest, Studies in Church History*, vol. 9, ed. D. Baker (Cambridge, 1972), 295-302. The trial of Sherfield, puritan iconoclast but also Recorder of Salisbury, suggests that the puritan urban oligarchy was ground between upper and nether millstones in the years of Laud's ascendancy. 'But in his own local community, it was Sherfield who was the representative of authority and the guardian, so it seemed, of social order.' Cf. T. G. Barnes, 'County Politics and a Puritan Cause Célèbre: Somerset Churchales, 1633.' *Transactions of the Royal Historical Society*, 5th ser., vol. 9 (1959), 103-22.

57. Christopher Hill, 'Puritans and "the Dark Corners of the Land".' *Transactions of the Royal Historical Society*, 5th ser., vol. 13 (1963), 77-102.

58. N. Tyacke, 'Puritanism, Arminianism and Counter-Revolution,' in *The Origins of the English Civil War*, ed. Conrad Russell (1973).

59. Ephraim Udall, Το Πρέπιον εμχαριστιχὸν *i.e. Communion comlinesse. Wherein is discovered the conveniency of the peoples drawing neere to the table in the sight thereof when they recive the Lords Supper. With the great unfitnesse of receiving it in the pewes in London for the novelty of high and close pewes*, Wing U 13 (1641). Udall was the son of the celebrated Elizabethan puritan preacher and pamphleteer John Udall. He was curate of Teddington, Middlesex, from 1614, and rector of St Augustine's, Watling St., from 1634. Udall was known as a Puritan, but the argument of this tract, making a utilitarian case for greater 'comliness', signalled a shift towards moderation, made clearer in the anonymous publication of 1642, misattributed to Archbishop Ussher but apparently Udall's, *The bishop of Armaghes direction concerning the lyturgy, and episcopall government*, Wing U 4.

60. Jonathan Cape, London, and University of California Press, Berkeley, 1967. The case is more copiously stated in my unpublished University of London Ph.D. thesis of 1957, 'The Puritan Classical Movement in the Reign of Queen Elizabeth I'.

61. J. A. Newton, "Puritanism in the Diocese of York (Excluding Nottinghamshire) 1603-1640," unpublished London Ph.D. thesis, 1955; summarized, "The Yorkshire Puritan Movement, 1603-1640." *Transactions of the Congregational Historical Society*, vol. 19 (1960-64); Marchant, whose study includes Nottinghamshire, *op. cit.*; R. C. Richardson, *Puritanism in North-West England: A Regional Study of the Diocese of Chester to 1642* (Manchester, 1972).

62. *A generall martyrologie, containing a collection of all the greatest persecutions which have befallen the Church of Christ from the creation to our present times. Whereunto are added the lives of sundry modern divines* Wing C 4513 (1651); *The lives of two and twenty English divines*, Wing C 4540 (1660); *The lives of thirty-two English divines*, Wing C 4539 (1667); *The lives of sundry eminent persons in this later age*, Wing C 4538 (1683). To these add such other lives as William Hinde, *A faithful remonstrance of the holy life and happy death of John Bruen of Bruen-Stapleford in the County of Chester, Esquire*, Wing H 2063 (1641), the *Life of Adam Martindale Written by Himself*, ed. R. Parkinson, vol. 4 (Chetham Socy, 1845); *Oliver Heywood's Life of John Angier of Denton*, ed. E. Axon, (Chetham Socy., n.s. 97, 1937), and *The Rev. Oliver Heywood 1630-1702: His Autobiography, Diaries*, ed. J. H. Turner, 3 vols. (1882). Cotton Mather's biographies in *Magnalia Christi Americana* (Boston, Massachusetts, 1702), are another storehouse.

63. Professor William Haller's justly famous *The Rise of Puritanism* (New York, 1938), in its biographical portions a veritable *Clarke Revised*, is a little incautious in the extent to which it reflects its principal source.

64. Alan Everitt, "Nonconformity in Country Parishes," in *Land, Church, and People: Essays Presented to Professor H. P. R. Finberg*, ed. Joan Thirsk, *Agricultural History Review*, vol. 18, Supplement (Reading, 1970), 186-8.

65. "The essential pattern of the lives of the elect, the 'saints' or 'godly', was unmistakable." (L. L. Schücking, *The Puritan Family*, English edn. (1969),

57.) Clarke remains for these purposes a surprisingly neglected source. None of his collections appear in Schücking's Bibliography. However, Owen Watkins, *The Puritan Experience* (1972), is a distillation of Clarke and of the rich autobiographical literature of the age.

66. *Reliquiae Baxterianae*, 83-7.

67. Isaiah 60:8.

68. These phenomena are discussed on the basis of Elizabethan evidence in my *Elizabethan Puritan Movement*, pt. VII, chap. 4, "The Meetings of the Godly," 372-82, and in a paper contributed to the Past and Present Society Conference on Popular Religion, 1966, "The Godly: Aspects of Popular Protestantism in Elizabethan England" (privately circulated by Past and Present Society) which embodies many citations from the Act Books of the Archdeaconries of Colchester and Essex. The most striking and persistent case known to me of a parish split into puritan and antipuritan factions effectively out of communion with one another is provided by the Essex village of East Hanningfield. The evidence is in vols. 12-15 of the Act Books of the Archdeaconry of Essex, Essex Record Office, Chelmsford, and in British Library, MS. Add. 48064 (Yelverton 70), ff. 85-7.

69. Clearly established, for example, in the origins of Broadmead Baptist Church, Bristol. (*The Records of a Church of Christ Meeting in Broadmead Bristol, 1640-1687*, ed. E. B. Underhill, (Hanserd Knollys Socy., 1847.) The case has been most recently discussed by Dr. Claire Cross in "He-Goats Before the Flocks: A Note on the Part Played by Women in the Founding of Some Civil War Churches," in *Popular Belief and Practice, Studies in Church History*, vol. 8, ed. G. J. Cuming & D. Baker (Cambridge, 1972), 195-202.

70. The question was put in the Dedham Conference in 1584 "whether it were convenient a woman shuld pray having a better gift than her husband," but it was "omitted as not necessary to be handled." (*The Presbyterian Movement in the Reign of Queen Elizabeth*, ed. R. G. Usher, Camden Socy. 3rd ser. vol. 8 (1905), 35.) For the role of women, *see* Cross, *loc. cit.*, my "The Role of Women in the English Reformation Illustrated by the Life and Friendships of Anne Locke," *Studies in Church History*, ed. G. J. Cuming, vol. 2, 258-72 and Keith Thomas, "Women and the Civil War Sects" in *Crisis in Europe, op. cit.*, 317-40.

71. It is a pity that Dr. Paul S. Seaver provides no such list in his fundamental study *The Puritan Lectureships: The Politics of Religious Dissent, 1560-1662* (Stanford, 1970). Seaver is systematic only in relation to London and devotes no more than three pages (84-7) to the subject of lectures by combination. Among evidence still much neglected one may cite the correspondence with Bishop Jegon of Norwich relating to exercises in several Norfolk market towns (*The Registrum Vagum of Anthony Harrison*, pt. I, ed. T. F. Barton, Norfolk Record Socy, vol. 32 (1963), 96-103); the notes of many scores of sermons preached at the West Riding exercises held at Halifax and other centers (British Library, MSS. Add. 4933A, 4933B), discussed by Newton, *loc. cit.*, but not by Marchant, *op. cit.*, and apparently unknown to Seaver; and the Report made to Bishop Neile of the Primary Visitation of the diocese of Lincoln made on his behalf in 1614, which gives many details, including the panels of membership, of combination lectures in eleven centers (Aylesbury, Berkhamstead, Huntington,

Leicester, Grantham, Sleaford, Market Rasen, Lowth, Grimsby, Alford and Horncastle.) This last report exists in MS. copies in the Cambridge University Library (Baumgartner MS. 8, ff. 220-2), British Library (MS. Add. 5853, ff. 166^v-8) and in Lincoln (Dean & Chapter MS. A4/3/43) from where printed, *Associated Architectural Societies Reports & Papers*, vol. 16, pt. 1 (1881), 31-54. Seaver makes no reference to it, and Professor Curtis (*loc. cit.*, 310) mistakes the c.70 clergy associated with these lectures for professional, salaried lecturers, an error perpetuated by Hill, *Society and Puritanism*, 85. For information on exercises in the diocese of Chester, *see* Richardson, *op. cit.*, 65-9. *See Wiltshire Parish Registers: Marriages*, vol. 2, ed. W. P. W. Phillimore (1906), 72 for the names of the thirteen ministers who maintained "the Saturday lecture" at Marlborough, Wiltshire. (I am indebted for this last reference to my colleague Mrs Alison Wall.)

72. Collinson, *op. cit.*, 168-76.
73. *Registrum Vagum*, pt. I, 98-9.
74. Seaver, *op. cit.*, 86; Collinson, *op. cit.*, 438; and my "The Beginnings of English Sabbatarianism," *Studies in Church History*, vol. 1, ed. C. W. Dugmore & C. Duggan (1964), 219.
75. Clarke, *Lives of sundry eminent persons*, 187.
76. *Winthrop Papers*, vol. 1 *1498-1628* (Massachusetts Historical Socy., 1929), 89, 153.
77. The preface to Thomas Beard's famous *Theatre of gods iudgements* (1631) (3rd) edn., thanks the magistrates of Huntingdon for their support "in the late business of the Lecture." Anthony Cade of Leicester in 1618 published a sermon preached at the Ordinary Monthly Lecture, "intermitted" by Bishop Barlow in 1611 and revived in 1614. (G. J. Cuming, "The Life and Works of Anthony Cade, B.D., Vicar of Billesdon, 1599-1639," *Transactions of the Leicestershire Archaeological & Historical Socy.*, vol. 45 (1969-70), 39-56.) In Bishop Neil's Visitation of 1614 the Huntingdon Lecture was said to have been "put down" by Bishop Barlow, the Leicester Lecture "questioned" in Barlow's time. "The cause was some received disgrace in a conference they held after their lecture. But I take it it was restored again."
78. Newton, *loc. cit.*, and Marchant, *op. cit.*, *passim*. Archbishop Mathew's Diary (which is in the form of a record of the sermons preached by him from 1583 until 1622, 1992 in all) records that he preached at Barnard Castle in 1593 "at the Exercise," when still dean of Durham. In August, 1609, as archbishop of York, he preached "at Mansfield Exercise," and in 1613 he preached at the Mansfield Exercise in July, the Nottingham Exercise in August, and the Retford Exercise in September. (Thomas Wilson's transcript of Archbishop Mathew's Diary, Minster Library, York, 38, 85, 92, 105.)
79. Extensively canvassed by Hill however, especially in *Society and Puritanism*.
80. Among a rich variety of literature see especially Watkins, *op. cit.*
81. Collinson, *Elizabethan Puritan Movement*, 107-8, 318-29. Although the evidence is not very explicit, I suspect that the counsels of the Elizabethan Puritans were as much divided by this issue as those of the French Calvinists. (R. M. Kingdon, *Geneva and the Consolidation of the French*

Protestant Movement, Travaux d'humanisme et renaissance, vol. 92 (Geneva), 1967.)

82. John Rylands Library, Manchester, Rylands English MS. 874; in part published in *The Presbyterian Movement, op. cit. See* my *Elizabethan Puritan Movement,* 222-31, 318-21.

83. *Presbyterian Movement,* 43-6; Rylands English MS. 874, f. 56. Cf. a remark of Thomas Carew, curate of Hatfield Peverel, Essex, and later in Ipswich: "The knot between pastor and people is not easily loosed." (*Seconde Parte of a Register,* vol. 2, 33.)

84. *Seconde Parte of a Register,* vol. 2, 88-184.

85. Collinson, *Elizabethan Puritan Movement,* 92-7.

86. Coolidge, *op. cit.,* 41-3.

87. Dr. Williams's Library, London, MS. Morrice B.11, ff. 17-18. The entire Cranbrook controversy of 1573 as recorded in this "Seconde Parte of a Register" manuscript (calendared, *Seconde Parte,* vol. 1, 116-20) is instructive in connection with the points made here.

88. The most recent discussion of the continuity of Lollardy and early Protestantism in these areas is in Dr. J. F. Davis's Oxford D.Phil. thesis "Heresy and the Reformation in the South-East of England, 1520-1559." (1968). Dr Davis identifies two major heartlands of late Lollardy and incipient reform (apart from London): a broad corridor of North Essex running from Colchester inland to Thaxted and from the Suffolk border south to Witham and Colchester (the country later covered by the Dedham Conference and sister conferences) and the Kentish Weald. (I am grateful to Dr. Davis for access to his thesis.)

89. Essex Record Office, Archdeaconry of Colchester Act Books, ACA 10, ff. 66-7^r; Archdeaconry of Essex Act Books, AEA 14, f. 148^r, AEA 15, ff. 273^v-4^v.

90. Dr Williams's Library, MS. Morrice B.II, ff. 8, 17^v.

91. C. C. R. Pile, *Dissenting Congregations in Cranbook* (Cranbrook and Sissinghurst Local History Socy., n.p., 1953), 4. Professor Alan Everitt associates the later strength of dissent in the Weald and similar areas with a forest rather than arable economy, and questions the often-asserted connection between the manufacture of cloth and dissent. The evidence from the Stour valley of Essex and Suffolk and from the Weald seems to favor very strongly the traditional association without damage to Professor Everitt's wider speculations. (*Loc. cit.,* 188-97.)

92. Collinson, *Elizabethan Puritan Movement,* 223.

93. Laurence Clarkson (Claxon), *The lost sheep found,* Wing C 4580 (1660), 5-6. Cf. George Whitehead in *Jacob found in a desert land,* Wing W 1936 (1656), 4: "For I was alwayes learning there, and could not know the Truth"; and Richard Farnworth in *The heart opened by Christ,* Wing F 485 (1654), p. 4: "And so likewise their Preaching became but as the telling of a Tale, or a boy that saith over his weeks work at the School, that he had learned all the week"; and Arise (Rhys) Evans, *An eccho to the voice from heaven,* Wing E 3457 (1652), 17: "For afore I looked upon the Scriptures as a History of things that passed in other Countreys, pertaining to other persons, but now I looked upon it as a mysterie to be opened at this time belonging also to us." On "Quaker Testimonies," *see* Watkins, *op. cit.,* 160-81 and his article, "Some Early Quaker Autobiographies." *Journal of the Friends Historical Socy.,* vol. 45 (1953), 65-74. For Clark-

son, *see* also Christopher Hill, *The World Turned Upside Down: Radical Ideas During the Puritan Revolution* (1972), 171-4 and A. L. Morton, *The World of the Ranters: Religious Radicalism in the English Revolution* (1970), 115-42.

94. Cotton, *op. cit.*, 8.

95. *Works of John Robinson*, ed. R. Ashton, vol. 3 (1851), 343-78.

96. Clarke, *Lives of sundry eminent persons*, 170. In c. 1580, for example, Robert Browne found Robert Harrison inhibited in the path to Separatism with regard to "M. Robardes, M. More, M. Deering and others [puritan preachers] whome he then did greatlie like off." (*A true and short declaration, Writings of Robert Harrison and Robert Browne*, ed. A. Peel & L. H. Carlson, Elizabethan Nonconformist Texts, vol. 2 [1953], 407-11.)

97. Robinson, *A iustification of separation from the Church of England*, STC 21109 ([Leyden?], 1610), 259.

98. Ames, *A manuduction*; Robinson, *A manumission to a manuduction*, STC 2111, n.p. (1615); Ames, *A second manuduction for Mr Robinson*; Robinson, *A treatise on the lawfulnesse of hearing of the ministers*, in *Works*, vol. 3, 361.

99. Richard Baxter, *A holy commonwealth*, Wing B 1281 (1659), 456-7.

100. A tract published in 1589, *Sophronistes: a dialogue, perswading the people to reverence and attend the ordinance of God in the ministerie of their owne pastors* (STC 22930), was written within the internal economy of puritan churchmanship. Cf. the troubles of one member of the Dedham Conference who was forced to seek a ruling "that a pastor should have his own people." (*Presbyterian Movement*, 30, 62.)

101. *Heywood's Life of Angier*, 50.

102. Coolidge, *op. cit.*, chap. 1 "Scriptural Authority" and chap. 2, "Christian Liberty and Edification," *passim*.

103. *Ibid.*, chap. 3, "Separation."

104. Ainsworth, *op. cit.*, 60; Robinson, *Works*, vol. 3, 72.

105. *The divine beginning*, Sig. A1.

106. *The Works of John Smith*, vol. 2, ed. W. T. Whitney (Cambridge, 1915), 335; *Robinson, Works*, vol. 2, 101. Cf. Richard Bernard, *Plaine evidences: the Church of England is apostolicall, the seperation schismaticall*, STC 1958 (1610).

107. Cotton, *op. cit.*, pt. I, 20. Said in answer to Robert Baylie (*op. cit.*, 55), who had alleged that in England Cotton had "minded no more then the old non-conformity."

108. Printed by M. M. Knappen in *Two Elizabethan Puritan Diaries* (American Socy. of Church History, Chicago, 1933), 51-102.

109. *Seven treatises, containing such directions as is gathered out of the holie scriptures*, STC 21215 (1603), ff. 477-95. The covenant is some 13,000 words in length. Rogers explains that it was entered into at a meeting, common enough in Essex, held in a private house "after some bodily repast and refreshing," and he is at pains to prove that the participants were "no Brownists, for they were diligent and ordinarie frequenters of publicke assemblies with the people of God," and that their meetings were not "conventicles, for the disturbing of the state of the Church and peace thereof; as many imagine that there can be no private fellowship among Christians, but it is to such ends: the contrary may be seen by their conference."

110. *Winthrop Papers*, vol. 1, 169, 199-201.

111. *Memoirs of Roger Clap*, Collections of the Dorchester Antiquarian & Historical Socy., vol. 1 (Boston, Massachusetts, 1844), 17.

112. *Visible Saints: The History of a Puritan Idea* (Ithaca, 1963).

113. *Seven treatises*, f. 477.

114. *Religious Sects*, 7.

115. John Berridge wrote to the countess of Huntingdon on April 25, 1777; "You say the Lord is sending many gospel labourers into the Church. True; and with a view, I think, of calling his people out of it . . . What has become of Mr Venn's Yorkshire flock?—what will become of his Yelling flock, or of my flocks, at our decease? or what will become of your students at your removal? *They are virtual Dissenters* now, and will be settled Dissenters then. And the same will happen to many, perhaps most, of Mr. Wesley's preachers at his death." (Quoted, Charles Smyth, *Simeon and Church Order* [Cambridge, 1940], 238-9.)

116. Everitt, *loc. cit.*, and in his *The Pattern of Rural Dissent: the Nineteenth Century*, Leicester University Department of Local History, 2nd ser. vol. 4 (Leicester, 1972). *See* also some fruitful suggestions from Everitt and Dr Joan Thirsk in *The Agrarian History of England and Wales*, vol. 4, *1500-1640* (Cambridge, 1967), esp. 111-12, 562-3. *See* also the studies of the early Quakers by Alan Cole ("The Social Origins of the Early Friends," *Journal of the Friends' Historical Socy.*, 48. [1957], 99-118) and R. T. Vann ("Quakerism and the Social Structure in the Interregnum." *Past and Present*, no. 43, [1969], 71-91.) Cf. Margaret Spufford, "The Social Status of Some Seventeenth-Century Rural Dissenters," in *Popular Belief and Practice, op. cit.*, 203-11.

117. *See* Richardson, *op. cit.*, chap. 1, "The Context and Distribution of Puritanism" (scil. in the diocese of Chester.) The forthcoming (London) doctoral study of Northamptonshire by Mr. W. J. Sheils of the Borthwick Institute of Historical Research, University of York, will undoubtedly break significant new ground in this respect.

118. Compare Alan MacFarlane, *The Family Life of Ralph Josselin, A Seventeenth-Century Clergyman: An Essay in Historical Anthropology* (Cambridge, 1970), with the criticism of E. P. Thompson (demanding, among other things, more sensitivity to literature) in "Anthropology and the Discipline of Historical Context." *Midland History*, vol. 1 (1971-2), 41-55.

119. John Foxe, *Acts and Monuments of the Church*, vol. 7, ed. S. R. Cattley (1838), 207-253 and many other such references; and in *Writings of John Bradford*, ed. Aubrey Townsend (Parker Socy., Cambridge, 1853).

120. John Rylands Library, Manchester, Rylands English MS. 874, f. 56. The reference is to Genesis 33.8, words spoken by Jacob to Esau, an appropriate *topos* in view of Crick's strained relations with his brethren when this letter was written.

121. Clarke, *Lives of sundry eminent persons*, 4; *Heywood's Life of Angier*, 56; *Reliquiae Baxterianae*, 85.

122. The title page of John Bunyan's *Christian behaviour* (1663), refers to "the Fruit of true Christianity, shewing the ground from whence they flow, in their Godlike order in the Duty of *Relations*, as *Husbands, Wives, Parents, Children, Masters, Servants*, etc." (Quoted, Schücking, *op. cit.*, 56-7.)

123. This element seems to be missing from a standard work on the subject, W. P. Holden, *Anti-Puritan Satire, 1572-1642*, (Yale Studies in English,

vol. 26 [New Haven, 1954]. Two Elizabethan *loci classici* for the argument, as reported by puritan pamphleteers, are *A dialogue concerning the strife of our church*, STC 6801 (1584) and George Gifford's *A briefe discourse of certaine points of the religion which is among the common sort of christians, which may bee termed the countrie divinitie*, STC 11845 (1581). *See* also "The defence of the mynisters of Kent" (1584) in *The Seconde Parte of a Register*, vol. 1, 230-41, which addresses itself to the charge that various preachers who are named have brought "deadly hatred and bitter division," "broile and contention" to their towns.

124. Richard Greenham of Dry Drayton was said to be "a great friend to, and promoter of peace and concord amongst his Neighbours and acquaintance, insomuch that if any had come to him who were at variance, he would either have made them friends himself, or if he could not prevail, he would have made use of other friends to reconcile them together, thereby to prevent their going to Law." (Clarke, *Lives of two and twenty English divines*, 15.)

125. Gifford, *op. cit.*, f. 46ᵛ.

126. John Dod and Robert Cleaver, *A plain and familiar exposition of the thirteenth and fourteenth chapters of the Proverbs of Salomon*, STC 6960 (1609), 119.

127. *Reliquiae Baxterianae*, 83.

128. Clarke, *Lives of sundry eminent persons*, 4-5. Mrs. Elizabeth Wilkinson "valued no friends like to those who were friends to her soul." (Clarke, *Lives of thirty-two English divines*, 420.)

129. *Writings of Harrison and Browne*, 397-429; George Johnson, *A discours of some troubles in the banished English Church at Amsterdam*, STC 14664 (Amsterdam, 1603); Christopher Lawne et al., *The prophane schisme of the Brownists or Separatists . . . discovered*, STC 15324 (1612).

130. Peter Lorimer, *John Knox and the Church of England* (1875), 300.

131. For critical surveys of the literature, and of the question, *see* P. Besnard, *Protestantisme et capitalisme: la controverse post-weberienne* (Paris, 1970); E. Fischoff, "The Story of a Controversy." *Social Forces*, vol. 2 (1944); H. Luethy, "Once Again: Calvinism and Capitalism," *Encounter*, vol. 22 (1964), 26-38; H. R. Trevor-Roper, "Religion, the Reformation and Social Change" in the volume of that title (1967); David Little, *Religion, Order and Law: A Study in Pre-Revolutionary England* (1969).

132. In addition to the literature reviewed here, cf. an important and fruitful line of research pursued by historians of seventeenth-century New England: Edmund S. Morgan, *The Puritan Family: Essays on Religion and Domestic Relations in Seventeenth-Century New England* (Boston Massachusetts 1944, revised edn., Harper Torchbooks, New York, 1966); John Demos, *A Little Commonwealth: Family Life in Plymouth Colony* (New York, 1970); Philip J. Greven Jr., *Four Generations: Population, Land and Family in Colonial Andover, Massachusetts* (Ithaca, 1970); and, more theological than "anthropological," Robert G. Pope, *The Half-Way Covenant: Church Membership in Puritan New England* (Princeton, 1969).

133. *The Revolution of the Saints, op. cit.;* and cf. Little, *op. cit.*

134. As it was more than forty years ago with Professor Schücking, who wrote of "the family theocracy" as "the nucleus of the Puritan way of life." (*Op. cit.*, xii, 56.)

135. *Society and Puritanism*, esp. chap. 12, "The Secularization of the Parish," chap. 13, "The Spiritualization of the Household," chap. 14, "Individuals and Communities."

136. "Blood and Baptism: Kinship, Community and Christianity in Western Europe from the Fourteenth to the Seventeenth Centuries" in *Sanctity and Secularity: the Church and the World, Studies in Church History*, vol. 10, ed. D. Baker (Oxford 1973), 129-43. Dr. Bossy continues along the line of an argument begun with his "The Counter-Reformation and the People of Catholic Europe." *Past and Present* no. 47 (1970), 56-68.

137. Macfarlane, *op. cit.*, pt. III, "The Social World: Family, Kin and Neighbours." 105-60.

138. *Religion and the Rise of Capitalism*, Holland Memorial Lectures (1922), 1926.

139. Quoted, Morgan, *The Puritan Family* (1966 edn), 135.

140. Both Morgan, *The Puritan Family*, and Pope, *op. cit.*, imply that here was the rub.

141. *The Puritan Family*, 185-6 and chap. 7, "Puritan Tribalism," *passim*.

142. The title of a tract by John Geree, published in 1646, Wing G 589.

143. When the lecture on which this essay is based was delivered, some reference was made at this point to the Rev. Dr. G. F. Nuttall, doyen of historians of the mature age of Dissent, who was present on that occasion. It is both seemly and salutary that a tribute to Dr. Nuttall should appear in this printed text, since his work is a constant reminder that there is more than one horizontal dimension to the study of religious history. Spiritual rather than merely sociological breadth and understanding are surely the least dispensable qualities in the religious historian, and always will be.

Sir Francis Knollys' Campaign Against the *Jure Divino* Theory of Episcopacy

W. D. J. CARGILL THOMPSON
University of London King's College

"This Knight being bred a banished man in *Germany* during the Reign of Queen *Mary*, and conversing with Mr. *Calvin* at *Geneva*, was never after fond of Episcopacy."
Thomas Fuller, *The Church-History of Britain* (1655), Book IX, Section v, 152.

IN HIS DICTIONARY Dr. Johnson defined a Dissenter as "One who, for whatever reasons, refuses the communion of the English Church."[1] In this sense there were very few protestant dissenters in Elizabethan England. Only the numerically insignificant Brownists and Barrowists carried their opposition to the established order to the point of rejecting the Church of England altogether. The great majority of Elizabethan puritans were not only not Separatists, they viewed the very concept of separation with abhorrence.[2] Like all the sixteenth-century protestant reformers, they believed implicitly in the indivisible character of the Visible Church of Christ. While they accepted that for purposes of external organization the Visible Church was divided geographically into a series of local or 'particular' churches, each of which was autonomous, they regarded it as axiomatic that within each commonwealth or state there could be only one church which was the Church of Christ and that to separate from "those assemblyes which," in Cartwright's phrase, "have Christ for their head"[3] was to commit the sin of schism.

There is thus an important historical difference between the character of protestant dissent in the Elizabethan period and later forms of protestant nonconformity. In the late sixteenth century, in contrast to the period after the Restoration, the mainstream of protestant opposition to the established order came from within the established church, not from outside it. The object of most Elizabethan puritans was not to break away from the Church of England, or even to secure for themselves liberty of worship within it except as a temporary expedient, but rather to bring about a more radical reform of the Church of England, along the lines of the Swiss Reformed churches, than Elizabeth was prepared to allow. In this sense they were not dissenters at heart. Most Elizabethan puritans were as theologically committed to the idea of a comprehensive national church, embracing all professed Christians in England, as Whitgift or Hooker. What they objected to was not the idea of an established church, but the form which establishment took. Given the opportunity, they would have been as unyielding in imposing their own concepts of uniformity on the Church of England as Elizabeth was in imposing hers.

At the same time, the dividing line between Dissent and Establishment in the Elizabethan period is often hard to determine. Although for convenience historians tend to use the label 'Puritan' to describe all those on the protestant side who criticized the Elizabethan Church for whatever reason, in practice it is anachronistic to think in terms of a clear-cut dichotomy between 'Anglican' and 'Puritan' in the sixteenth century.[4] Not only did most English protestants, until the closing years of the century, share the same theological assumptions, but at the beginning of the reign there was little fundamental disagreement even on matters of worship. In the early 1560s criticism of the 1559 Prayer Book came not only from men like Lawrence Humphrey and Thomas Sampson but also from bishops like Jewel and Parkhurst, who would have preferred to see the worship of the Church of England brought closer into conformity with that of the Swiss churches, and in the Vestiarian controversy of the 1560s many of the bishops were at first reluctant to enforce the provisions of the Act of Uniformity against the Precisians. Later, in the 1570s and 1580s, the divisions began to harden with the rise of the presbyterian movement and the emergence of a new generation of churchmen such as Whitgift and Bancroft, who were prepared to defend the institutions of the Church of England on their own merits and not simply out of deference to the queen. But even in the 1580s the distinction between critics and supporters of the establishment is not always sharply defined. If the hardcore of opposition was represented by the Disciplinarian puritans whose aim was the presbyterianisation of the Church of England by constitutional means, there was also—besides the Separatists who rejected the Church of England altogether—a substantial body of moderate opinion which tended to be ambivalent in its attitude towards the established order. Whitgift's policies aroused widespread resentment among clergy and laity alike, but probably only a minority of those who objected to his measures to enforce uniformity wished to see the principles of the Book of Discipline put into practice or the Prayer Book replaced by the Genevan service order. Many puritan ministers, who had scruples about wearing the surplice or using the sign of the cross in baptism, would have been satisfied with the kind of changes which had been proposed in the Convocation of 1563 and which were to be revived in the Millenary Petition of 1603. Similarly there were Calvinist theologians like John Reynolds of Oxford or William Perkins of Cambridge, who were intellectually in sympathy with the presbyterians but who were prepared to accept episcopacy as a human institution. Equally among the laity, opposition to Whitgift's policies came not merely from presbyterian sympathizers but also from many conservative protestants who deplored Whitgift's treatment of the puritan ministers but who had no desire to see any radical revolution in the structure of the church.

One of the most outspoken lay critics of Whitgift's policies in the 1580s and early 1590s was Sir Francis Knollys.[5] Knollys' career illustrates the difficulties of trying to draw a hard and fast distinction between Puritan and Anglican, critics and supporters of the established church, in the reign of Elizabeth. Born about 1514, he belonged, like his near contemporary, Lord Burghley, to a generation whose religious and political attitudes had been formed in the reigns of Henry VIII and Edward VI. A staunch protestant, he was one of the few laymen of any prominence to have been an exile on the Continent in Mary's reign, although whether he ever visited Geneva, as Fuller claimed, is uncertain.[6] On his return to England at Elizabeth's accession, he was immediately appointed Vice-chamberlain of the Royal Household and a member of the Privy Council—appointments which he owed in large part to the fact that his wife was Elizabeth's first cousin[7]—and he continued to serve Elizabeth loyally in a succession of Household offices until his death in 1596. Throughout Elizabeth's reign Knollys stood out as one of the most forthright and persistent champions of the protestant cause on the Privy Council and, although his personal devotion to the queen was never in question, he was one of the few councillors who was prepared to risk incurring Elizabeth's displeasure for the sake of his principles. He was one of the recognized leaders of the protestant party in the House of Commons in 1559;[8] he supported the prophesyings movement in the 1570s and opposed the move to deprive Archbishop Grindal of his see on the grounds that it would give encouragement to the catholics;[9] he was a fanatical anti-catholic, like many of his colleagues on the Council, and he was continually pressing for the adoption of more stringent measures against Jesuits and recusants at home and for more active support of foreign protestants abroad.[10] On the other hand, to describe Knollys as a 'Puritan' without careful qualification, as is often done, is misleading.[11] In many respects he was an establishment figure who was deeply committed to what he regarded as the traditional order in church and state. Despite his running battles with the bishops, he was not opposed to episcopacy as such, only to the manner in which the bishops exercised their authority, and there is no evidence to support Fuller's innuendo that he had imbibed Calvinist ideas of church government from Calvin himself in Geneva.[12] Equally, though he was always ready to intervene on behalf of puritan ministers, there is no evidence that he was opposed in principle to the Prayer Book, which he had helped to pass into law,[13] and he saw nothing incongruous in speaking against puritan measures in the House of Commons when called upon to do so in his capacity as a privy councillor.[14] But above all—and nothing could mark him off more clearly from the Disciplinarian puritans of the 1580s—he was a fervent supporter of the Royal Supremacy. If his religious outlook was that of an Edwardian protestant, his political ideas had been shaped by the events of the 1530s. As he reminded the House of Commons in 1593, he had been present in Parliament sixty years earlier in the twenty-fifth year of Henry VIII's reign, when the main legislation of the Reformation Parliament was enacted,[15] and he remained a thorough-going Henrician in his attitude to the government of the church until the end of his life. It is this combination of protestantism and erastianism which provides the key to Knollys' outlook in his later years. Not only did he believe that protestantism and the Royal Supremacy were mutually interdependent, so that anything which endangered the one constituted a threat to the other, but to a large extent his hostility towards the bishops was inspired by the suspicion that they were secretly conspiring to undo the achievements of the Henrician Reformation.

As he grew older Knollys became increasingly alienated by developments within the Church of England, especially after the appointment of Whitgift as Archbishop of Canterbury in 1583. In 1584, when Whitgift launched his first attack on the puritan clergy, Knollys was one of the privy councillors who was most active in challenging the legality of Whitgift's measures and for several months he conducted a bitter personal campaign against the archbishop, accusing him of acting unconstitutionally in suspending preachers, "zealous in religion and sound in doctrine," for refusing to subscribe his articles, "whereunto they are not compellable by law," and of seeking "an absolute power" which "openeth the highway to the Pope, to her Majesty's utter overthrow."[16] Unlike the majority of his colleagues on the Privy Council, who gradually came to acquiesce in Whitgift's policies with the passage of time, Knollys never abandoned his hostility towards the archbishop and his repeated protests against Whitgift's treatment of puritan ministers eventually brought down on him the wrath of the queen, who at one point ordered him to desist from any further intervention on their behalf.[17] Elizabeth's reprimand failed to silence Knollys for long. For in the course of 1588 he embarked on a new campaign against the bishops, accusing them of seeking to undermine the Royal Supremacy by claiming that they derived their authority over the inferior clergy *jure divino*, and for the next three years he pursued the matter relentlessly, bombarding Lord Burghley with a succession of letters and memoranda in an effort to persuade him that the bishops should be compelled to acknowledge formally that they derived their authority solely from the queen, and not from any higher source.

Sir Francis Knollys' campaign against the *jure divino* theory of episcopacy is familiar to modern historians through the numerous references to it which occur in Strype's *Life of Whitgift* and his *Annals of the Reformation*, both of which contain important documentary material relating to the affair.[18] In general, Strype's account of the controversy has been accepted uncritically by later writers but a re-examination of the evidence suggests that it stands in need of substantial revision.[19] Strype's basic mistake, which explains much of the confusion in his account, was to assume that Knollys' campaign was chiefly directed against Richard Bancroft's Paul's Cross Sermon of February 9, 1589.[20] As a result he completely misinterpreted several of the documents which he prints, which he rashly concluded were connected with Bancroft's Sermon, when they were not, while he also postdated the beginnings of the controversy by several months.   In addition, his account contains numerous errors of detail; documents are misquoted and misattributed, or wrongly dated; in one instance, excerpts from two different letters are cited as if they occur in the same document;[21] in another, different parts of the same letter are quoted in separate places in a manner which suggests that they come from different letters.[22] Fortunately, enough evidence survives to make it possible to reconstruct the history of the controversy in some detail. With the exception of one important set of papers which Strype used in the *Life of Whitgift* and which he was lent in 1711 by Dr. Thomas Brett, the future Non-Juror bishop,[23] all the documents which he cites are still in existence, while these can be supplemented by other manuscripts relating to the controversy of which he was unaware. In one important respect, however, the surviving evidence is one-sided: for it consists very largely of letters and papers which were sent by Sir Francis Knollys to Lord Burghley and which are now among the Burghley papers in the Lansdowne collection in the British Museum,[24] or at Hatfield, whereas Burghley's replies to Knollys have long since disappeared. As a result any account of the controversy must reflect the fact that our knowledge of it comes chiefly from Knollys himself and that, whereas Knollys' activities are well documented, we know much less about the reactions of his opponents or even about the part played in the affair by Lord Burghley except for what can be gleaned from Knollys' correspondence.

What precisely triggered off Knollys' campaign is uncertain. Strype based his account on the supposition that it was provoked by Richard Bancroft's famous Paul's Cross Sermon of February 9, 1589, while he also suggested that Knollys was not acting on his own account but was simply a frontman for the Disciplinarian puritans who supplied him with arguments "to manage at Court for the party."[25] However, there is no evidence to support either of these assumptions. In the first place, it can be shown that Knollys had already embarked on his campaign several months before Bancroft delivered his Sermon and that, in fact, Bancroft's Sermon played a much smaller role in the controversy than Strype supposed. Secondly, it is clear from Knollys' correspondence with Lord Burghley that his campaign against the *jure divino* theory of episcopacy was an entirely independent venture in which the leaders of the presbyterian movement were in no way involved.

In part, Knollys' campaign has to be seen as a reaction against the changes which were taking place in the Anglican theory of episcopacy during the 1570s and 1580s.[26] Whereas at the beginning of the reign most Elizabethan churchmen had accepted St. Jerome's view that episcopacy was a purely human institution, which was not introduced into the Church until after the death of the Apostles, and that there was no essential difference between bishops and other ministers, after the outbreak of the Admonition controversy a number of anti-puritan writers began to lay increasing emphasis on the historical antiquity of bishops and to claim that episcopacy rather than presbyterianism represented the traditional form of government used in the Church. The beginnings of this development can be seen in Whitgift's *Answer to the Admonition* (1572) and his *Defence of the Answer* (1574) in which he defended the right of the Church of England to retain the use of bishops on two main grounds: first, that the external government of the Church was a "thing indifferent," which each particular church had the right to determine according to its own particular needs and circumstances, and secondly that—contrary to what Cartwright and his associates alleged—distinctions of authority had existed in the Church since the earliest times. In one passage, on which Knollys was later to seize, Whitgift even went so far as to assert that "this superiority of bishops is God's own institution."[27] However, the significance of this remark should not be exaggerated, since in general Whitgift based his main argument against the presbyterians on the claim that no set form of church government was prescribed in scripture[28] and he was prepared to concede that all ministers of God's word were equal "*quoad ministerium:* 'touching the ministry'," while insisting that "*quoad ordinem et politiam:* 'touching order and government,' there always hath been and must be degrees and superiority among them."[29] During the 1580s the historical arguments for episcopacy were developed by such writers as John Bridges, Dean of Salisbury, in his *Defence of the Government established in the Church of England for Ecclesiastical Matters* (1587) and Richard Bancroft who, in his Paul's Cross Sermon of 1589, maintained that the Church had been governed by bishops continuously since the time of the Apostles or their immediate successors, although it was not until the appearance of Hadrian de Saravia's *De Diversis Ministrorum Evangelii Gradibus* in 1590 that the claim began to be put forward that episcopacy was instituted directly by Christ. These developments naturally aroused the suspicions of Sir Francis Knollys who saw in them a threat not only to the traditional protestant view that episcopacy was a human institution, but also to the queen's claim to be the ultimate source of all ecclesiastical jurisdiction, and part of the purpose of his campaign was to alert Lord Burghley to the dangerous implications of the new theories.

However, it is significant that at the time when Knollys first launched his campaign the claim that episcopacy was a divine institution had only been advanced in the most tentative terms, and the publication of Saravia's seminal treatise, which was responsible for the rapid development of the *jure divino* theory in the 1590s, still lay in the future. It therefore seems probable that the origins of Knollys' campaign were connected with Elizabeth's refusal to allow him to continue his opposition to Whitgift's measures against the puritans and that, whatever its more general implications, it was primarily intended as a device to enable him to resume his attacks on the bishops without formally disobeying the queen. That this is so is suggested by a passage in a letter which he wrote to Lord Burghley in August, 1589, at the height of the controversy, in which he protested somewhat disingenuously that no one could accuse him of having failed to abide by the queen's injunction.

Yoᵉ Lp: shall fynde [he wrote] that none of them [the bishops] shalbe able to prove anye substancyall matter agaynste me, synce the tyme, that longe since her Matie at wynsore did commande me, that I shoulde not deale withe the purytanns, as then her Matie called them, because her Matie did commytt the governmente of Religion to her byshopps onlye, synce the which tyme I have delte no more withe matters of Religion, then dothe appertayne to her Maties saffetye, consistinge in the true preservacion of her Maties supreme governmente, the whiche maye best be called matter of her Maties pollicie, and not matter of Relygyon, althoughe the Jesuytes do call all their treasons matter of Relygyon.[30]

This passage would seem to imply that, after his confrontation with Elizabeth, Knollys deliberately changed his tactics and began to accuse the bishops of undermining the Royal Supremacy by claiming that they enjoyed their authority *jure divino*, since in this way he could maintain in all sincerity that he was not interfering in matters of religion, but was defending a basic principle of the constitution which it was his duty as a privy councillor to preserve.[31] If this interpretation is correct, it would also explain the fact that throughout the controversy, although Knollys did attack other supporters of episcopacy, including both Bridges and Bancroft, his most persistent criticisms were reserved for Whitgift, whom he repeatedly accused of maintaining the *jus divinum* of bishops in his writings against Cartwright, and why, somewhat surprisingly, in the later stages of the debate he failed to take any account of the much more radical works of Saravia, Bilson and others which appeared in 1590 and the following years.

The beginnings of Knollys' campaign can be dated to the autumn of 1588, several months before Bancroft's Sermon was delivered. For the first document to survive is a long memorandum, written on November 4, 1588 by Dr. John Hammond in answer to two questions which Knollys had put to him concerning the authority of bishops. The original of this letter is now at Hatfield, having been forwarded by Knollys to Lord Burghley.[32] A contemporary copy of it, which had apparently once been in the possession of Archbishop Whitgift, was among the manuscripts which Strype was lent by Thomas Brett in 1711, and Strype printed it in a much abridged form in his *Life of Whitgift*.[33] Brett's copy, however, appears to have had no date or indication of authorship. Strype therefore assumed erroneously that it was written in the autumn of 1589, while, in keeping with his belief that the Disciplinarian puritans were behind Knollys' campaign, he suggested— somewhat implausibly, in view of its arguments—that it was the work of either Cartwright or Travers.[34]

The true author, John Hammond, was a prominent civil and ecclesiastical lawyer, whom Knollys was to consult on several occasions during the coming months. Knollys' choice of advisers does, in fact, suggest a much greater degree of political acumen than he is usually credited with: for the two men whose advice he sought during the controversy—Hammond, the civil lawyer, and John Reynolds, the theologian—though strong protestants, were men of moderate views, who were not identified with the presbyterian wing of the puritan movement, and it seems probable that, as a matter of deliberate policy, he avoided any direct association with the Disciplinarians. Of the two, it was Hammond who was to play the more important role in the controversy and during its early stages Knollys appears to have relied very heavily on his advice. From Knollys' point of view Hammond was a particularly valuable ally. He was a person of considerable legal standing: one of the small number of professional civil lawyers, he was a member of the College of Civilians and the High Commission, and a former chancellor of the diocese of London; as an ecclesiastical commissioner, he had played a leading part in the examination of Campion and other Jesuits in the early 1580s; and he was regularly consulted by the Privy Council in the 1580s on matters relating to the Civil Law.[35] In consequence, his opinions could be expected to carry weight with Lord Burghley. On the other hand, despite the fact that he was a civilian, he was a long-standing critic of Whitgift's policies and he had openly attacked the legality of the archbishop's articles in 1584.[36] On the question of church government his views were remarkably similar to those of Knollys himself. Although he appears to have sympathized intellectually with Calvin's theories,[37] as a lawyer he was a firm believer in the Royal Supremacy and he held a strictly Henrician interpretation of the powers of the bishops.

Knollys had apparently requested Hammond's opinion on two issues— "First, whether the name of a bysshoppe, as of an office having superyorytie over many Churches, or over the pastors thereof, be knowne to the Holye Scryptures or not. Second, whether superyorytie commytted to a mynyster of the Worde and sacrements over many Churches and pastors be mayntenable [i.e. permissible] by the Worde of God, or not."[38] To the first question Hammond gave the standard sixteenth-century protestant reply

"that the name of bysshops importinge suche superyoritie is not to be founde in the Scryptures. For by the whole course thereof it appearethe that the names of *Episcopus* and *presbyter* imported one function, so as he that was a pastor or elder was also byshoppe, and the bysshope in lyke sorte called elder, and therefore the name of *episcopus*, being no name of dystynction in offyce from the elder, could not importe superyoritie over elders"

—a view which he proceeded to support with a detailed examination of the New Testament evidence.[39]

On the second issue Hammond was prepared to argue that, although episcopacy in its modern form was not to be found in the New Testament, it was not forbidden and was therefore permissible. For "the supreme civyll magystrate in every countrye may appoynte under offycers in the execution of that government which he hathe in ecclesyasticall causes, as well as he may doe in cyvile matters, for the reason is all one in them bothe." But he was careful to insist that any authority committed to bishops in this way "is but an humayne ordynance, and may not be intytled to any greater authorytie, nor otherwyse sayd to be God's ordynance, than the offyce of cyvill magistrates be." As far as England was concerned, he concluded, in a passage which was to supply Knollys with one of his stock arguments in the coming controversy,

The Bysshopps of our realme do not (so farre as I ever yet harde), nor may not, clayme to themselves any other authorytie then is geeven them by the Statute of the 25 of Kynge Henry the 8., recyted in the fyrst yeare of hir Majesty's raygne, or by other statutes of this lande, neither is it reasonable they should make other clayme, for if it had pleased her Majesty with the wysdome of the realme to

have used no bysshopps at all, we could not have complayned
justely of any defect in our Churche, or if it had lyked them to lymyte
the authorytie of bysshopps to shorter termes, they might not have
said they had any wronge. But sythe it hathe pleased her Majesty to
use the mynystery of Bysshopps, and to assigne them this authoryte,
it must be to me, that am a subjecte, as God's ordynance, and
therefore to be obeyed according to St.Paule's rule.[40]

Hammond's original letter to Knollys of November 4, 1588 ended at this
point. But the copy which Strype used included an addendum, or "A supply
to this former part," as Strype terms it, which is not in the manuscript at Hatfield and which may have been written at a slightly later date.[41] In this
"Supply," Hammond proceeded to discuss the question whether—even
though bishops derived their powers of jurisdiction from the crown—they
could be said to enjoy the superior spiritual powers which they possessed
in relation to excommunication and ordination by "Gods immediate institution", or whether this was "a matter rather so disposed of in their persons,
as the rest of their jurisdiction is." In Hammond's view "the case" was "al
one." For the powers which bishops enjoy in excommunication and ordination are powers which belong to the Church as a whole, and the fact that
they are assigned to bishops rests solely on human ordinance, not on divine
law. In England these powers are conferred on the bishops by "the laws and
policy of this realm." "Whereto," he concluded,

"forasmuch as her Majesty giveth life, they must consequently
maintain, they do it by her Majesties authority: and so derive it
from God: because she is the Lords immediate minister with us.
For, if it had pleased her Majesty to have assigned the imposition of
hands to the Deans of every cathedral church, or some other
number of Ministers, which in no sort were Bishops, but as they be
Pastors; there had been no wrong don to their persons, that I can
conceive."[42]

Hammond's letter is important both because it illustrates the extremely
erastian conception of episcopacy held by an Elizabethan ecclesiastical lawyer in the 1580s and also because it provided Knollys with the principal
argument which he was to use over the next few years. Throughout the controversy Knollys was to base his main case against the *jure divino* theory of
episcopacy on the claim that the English bishops derived their authority
from the so-called Ecclesiastical Appointments Act of 1534 (25 Henry
VIII c.20),[43] revived in the first year of Elizabeth's reign, and that any suggestion that the bishops received their powers from a higher source than
the crown was an infringement of the terms of the act, which rendered the
person so offending liable to the penalties of *praemunire*.

Shortly after receiving it, Knollys forwarded Hammond's letter to Lord Burghley. Burghley's reaction to it is not known, but it was evidently considered important enough for a copy of it to be made and passed on to Archbishop Whitgift. During the next few months Knollys continued to press his attack on a number of fronts, although the evidence of his activities is somewhat fragmentary and it is not always easy to fit the details of the story together.

Among the Burghley MSS in the Lansdowne collection is another paper on the subject of the superiority of bishops, dated "In Januarie 1588 [9]", which was also forwarded by Knollys to Lord Burghley.[44] This paper is unsigned and its precise significance in the controversy is obscure, since it consists merely of a list of references to authors, who maintained the view that episcopacy was a human institution, ranging from St. Jerome to such sixteenth-century protestant writers as Calvin, Musculus, Beza and Lambertus Danaeus.[45] However, there can be little doubt that Hammond was the author of this paper as well, since the authors named in it are virtually identical with those mentioned by Strype as having been quoted in the concluding part of the "Supply" to Hammond's letter of November 4, 1588, which he did not print.[46]

The date of this paper also suggests the possibility that it may have been connected with another controversy in which Knollys became involved at the beginning of 1589. Among the manuscripts which Strype was lent by Thomas Brett, and which have since disappeared, were copies of three other papers relating to the question of the superiority of bishops, which were stitched together with the text of Hammond's letter of November 4, 1588.[47] The first two of these were printed by Strype in the *Life of Whitgift* and consisted of a syllogism by Sir Francis Knollys attacking a sermon delivered by an unnamed preacher on January 12, 1588[9] together with a reply to it by the preacher concerned,[48] while the third, which Strype omitted—"being," as he put it, "too long, and interrupting the history if it were here inserted"—comprised an answer to the preacher's reply.[49] Because of its subject matter, Strype jumped to the conclusion that Knollys' syllogism was directed against Bancroft's famous Paul's Cross Sermon and he automatically attributed the preacher's reply to Bancroft.[50] In fact, Strype's account is entirely misleading: for, as he should have noted, Knollys' syllogism refers to a sermon preached on January 12, 1588/9, whereas Bancroft's sermon was delivered a month later on February 9, 1588/9.[51] By a fortunate chance a document survives among the Rawlinson MSS in the Bodleian which is either the original or a contemporary copy of the reply to the preacher's answer to Knollys' syllogism, which was included among the Brett manuscripts but which Strype forbore to print on account of its length; and from this it is possible to identify the name of the preacher on January 12, 1588/9 as well as to fill in some of the gaps in Strype's account. This paper is headed "Short observacions of the answeares, delivered by Do: Bridges, to [yor Honoures *deleted*] S^r ffr. Knowles syllogisme,"[52] from which it appears that the preacher was Dr. John Bridges, Dean of Salisbury, the author of the *Defence of the Government Established in the Church of England for Ecclesiastical Matters*.

The text of Bridges' sermon does not survive, but it is possible to deduce his general line of argument from his reply to Knollys' syllogism. In his syllogism Knollys had written:

Major. Whosoever doth maintain, that any subject of this realm
    hath superiority over the persons of the Clergy, otherwise than
    from and by her Majesty's authority, he doth injury to her
    Majesty's supremacy.
Minor. The preacher, upon Sunday the 12th of January, 1588,
    maintained, that the Bishops of this realm had superiority over
    the inferior Clergy, otherwise than by and from her Majesty's
    authority, namely, *jure divino*.
Conclus. *Ergo*, the preacher therein did injury to her Majesty's
    supremacy: unless he can better expound this saying than I can
    imagine.[53]

In his answer Bridges did not deny that he had claimed that bishops enjoyed their authority *jure divino*. Instead he attempted to defend himself against the charge that the views he had expressed in his sermon were in any way inimical to the Royal Supremacy. Both the major and the minor premise of Knollys' syllogism, he insisted, were "captiously set down; the cavil being hidden in the word *otherwise*." For it was quite possible for bishops to "hold in some superiority, both *jure divino* and *jure humano*." This could happen in either of two ways. Firstly, there were some powers which bishops possessed, "as in superiority of ordaining and consecrating Ministers, and excommunicating," where "*jus humanum* and her Majesty's supremacy do approve, maintain, and corroborate *jus divinum*. To which purpose *jus humanum* doth *subservire juri divino*, without any abasement at all thereunto." Secondly, there were other ecclesiastical matters, which were not purely spiritual but belonged to the sphere of human law, which nevertheless "so long as they are concordant with the general rule of St.Paul, of *edifying* in order and comeliness, *jus divinum* doth on the other side approve, maintain, and corroborate them. So that both ways they may well be said to be *jure divino*: but especially the former." At the same time, he vigorously repudiated the charge that in maintaining the view that the bishops' authority was in some sense *jure divino* he was thereby suggesting that they did not derive their superiority over the inferior clergy from the queen. "For I never avouched any such thing: which had been clean contrary to the chief scope of my sermon; and against all mine own writings, both against the Papists and against these inordinate brethren, impugning her Majesty's laws, and calling in question her Majesty's supreme authority in ecclesiastical matters." Finally, after declaring that those who had heard his sermon could testify that the charges made against him were entirely groundless, he attempted to turn Knollys' syllogism against the puritans by arguing that it was writers like Cartwright, Fenner, Travers, Penry and the rest who did injury to her Majesty's supremacy. For they "do maintain, that the Doctors, the Pastors, the seignory of governing Elders, and the Deacons, such as they pretend to be erected in every congregation throughout the realm, have superiority over the persons, either of the Clergy, or of the Laity, *otherwise than from and by her Majesty's authority*, namely, *jure divino*."[54]

The Rawlinson copy of the "Short observacions of the answeares, delivered by Do: Bridges, to Sʳ ffr. Knowles syllogisme" is unsigned, but again there can be little doubt that it was the work of Hammond. From such evidence as survives it is clear that Hammond was the person on whose advice Knollys relied principally during the spring and summer of 1589,[55] and it is therefore likely that he would have referred Bridges' answer to him for his comments. But, in addition, there is considerable internal evidence which points to Hammond's authorship. In the first place, the general line of argument in the "Short observations" bears a close resemblance to that of Hammond's letter of November 4, 1588 and the "Supply" to it printed in Strype. Secondly, there is a remarkable similarity between the list of authors cited in the "Short observations" and those cited in the "Supply" to Hammond's letter and the Lansdowne paper of January, 1588/9, which suggests very strongly that all three papers must have been written by the same person.[56]

In spite of its title the "Short observations" is a long document running to 3¼ closely written sides of foolscap. It is therefore only possible to summarise its arguments briefly.[57] In forwarding Bridges' answer to Hammond, Knollys had apparently raised the question whether Bridges' views might be considered treasonable. Hammond began his reply with lawyer-like caution by insisting that he was not competent to pronounce on "what is treason, or not treason, because it is a pointe of another skill[58] then I doe professe." At the same time he was careful to stress that, since he had not heard Bridges' sermon itself, he could only judge him by what he had written in his answer. However, on the basis of this he was prepared to conclude that Dr. Bridges "dealeth uniustly wᵗʰ hir Maᵗⁱᵉ. ffor, as I doe conceave, hee yeldeth not unto hir hir full right in hir supreme auctoritie" (f. 43).

Hammond then proceeded to attack Bridges' claim that bishops could enjoy their authority both *jure divino* and *jure humano* as being based on a misuse of language. "I knowe not, howe I may allowe the manner of this speache, nor what warrant hee hathe thus to confounde the termes . . . ffor

when question is of any matter, whether it be Juris divini, or Juris humani:
I always understoode the question to be made of too opposite kindes which
can not concurre in one matter, and that by theis wordes vz. Iuris divini, are
ment such as have theire immediate ordinance from God. And vz. Juris
humani, such as take theire immediate auctoritie and being from man."
Therefore, it is logically impossible to say that something is both *juris divini*
and *juris humani*, "insomuch as one thing canot proceede immediatly from
twoe such distinct auctories." Nor is it satisfactory to argue, as Bridges
does, that "by way of approbacion" something may be said to belong to
both laws. For normally the purpose of discussing whether something is
juris divini or *juris humani* is to discover "whether they be chaungable by
civil auctoritie, or not" .... "in wch case hee showld receave a sleevles an-
sweare that were tolde, that the matter in question were in respect of y^e
magistrates allowance Juris humani, for so were hee noe whit nearer the
resolucion wch hee sought, then he was before" (f.43).

However, in Hammond's view, Bridges' "abuse of termes" was "not the
thing, wch offendeth hir Maties auctoritie." The real point at issue was that
"hee maintaineth that a Bisshops superioritie is in some points de Jure divino,
meaning, as I suppose, the immediate ordinance of God, for other definition
I knowe not." Here again, he insisted, Bridges' case rested on dubious logic.
For his argument appeared to be that, because ordination and excommunication were divine institutions—"as in truth they bee"—it must follow that
"therefore this superioritie imployd in the execucion of them, is also de Jure
divino, & so consequently the immediate ordinance of God." Such an argument, Hammond contended, if this was what Bridges meant—for he complained with some justification of the obscurity of Bridges' language—involved an obvious logical fallacy. For whereas a practice may be prescribed
in general terms in divine law, the particular manner in which it is exercised
may be left to human laws to determine. As an example, Hammond cited
the maintenance of ministers of the Word and the payment of tithes. In his
view, it is "an immediate ordinance of God" that ministers should be provided with adequate maintenance. But it does not follow from this that the
payment of tithes to the clergy is therefore required by divine law, since
ministers may be provided for in other and better ways and tithes may be
said to have "theire ground in humane pollicie" only (f.43).

Hammond, therefore, suggested that logically Bridges would have been
on safer ground if he had maintained that it was "by the immediate ordinance of God" that bishops "doe alone ordaine ministers and doe excommunicate:" for he could then have argued that "their superioritie in some
functiones is Gods immediate ordinance." On the other hand, had he done
so, he would immediately have laid himself open to attack on historical
grounds:

For I think that the most learned doe agree that in the times of the apostles, these offices were performed by the pastors, and elders in everie church in common, and that the office of a bishops calling alone was not knowne to the scriptures. or if that will not be granted yet it cannot be denied that since the times of the apostles, and when this office began to gather strength, it extended first but to one church, and in one church had for a good space, nether ordinance, nor excommunicacion tyed unto it. At other times having ordinacion it wanted the other."

Rather than argue the point at length—"sith . . . I have no leasure to oppose better reasons of myne owne"—Hammond then proceeded to quote a long series of extracts from ancient and contemporary writers, ranging from Jerome and Augustine to Calvin, Musculus, Zanchius, Beza and others in the sixteenth century, in support of his contention "that bishopes are wholie her [Majesty's] creatures, and not the immedeate creatures of God at all" (ff. 43^v-44).

Finally, Hammond dismissed Bridges' attempt to turn Knollys' syllogism against the Disciplinarian puritans as "but a verie slender shift." The two cases, he insisted somewhat disingenuously, were not comparable and did "not offer lyke wrong to her ma^{ties} autoritie." For whereas "D.Bridges in an office merelie positive, flatlie excludeth her ma^{ties} authoritie," the puritans' claims related to offices which were "not of mans, but of Gods immediate creacion . . . wherein on their parte there is no more offence then if they should say that matrimonie in all persons were Gods ordinance, and tooke no part of force from positive lawe." However, Hammond must have realized that he was treading on dangerous ground, for he hastily proceeded to explain in his final paragraph that he was not in any way opposed to "Bishops receaved by her ma^{tie} in place of pastors & elders"—of whom he thought "reverentlie." For he was "of opinion, that if the condicion of our times, or the frame of our Realme cannott admitt that government wch was used in the times of the apostles . . . a moderate government committed to a bishop, wthout impeachment of the purpose of the holie ghost is well to be allowed." "That case of necessitie excepted," however, he shared the view of Zanchius that the closer the church approximated to the simplicity of the apostles the better (ff. 44-44^v).

Further light on Knollys' activities during the early months of 1589 is thrown by a letter which he wrote to Sir Francis Walsingham on March 20, 1588/9. From this letter it is clear that, following Hammond's letter of November 4, 1588, he had launched an open attack on Whitgift and the bishops at court, accusing them of maintaining that they enjoyed their authority *jure divino*, and that, at the same time as he was pursuing his controversy with Bridges, he was trying to persuade Lord Burghley that the bishops' interpretation of their authority constituted a threat to the Royal Supremacy which could only be resolved by formally requiring them to acknowledge that their powers were derived solely from the queen. Walsingham was away from court sick during the spring of 1589[59] and Knollys' letter was designed to inform him of the state of the controversy, in the hope, no doubt, that he would lend his weight to Knollys' campaign. Knollys states that on the previous day he had sent Walsingham a "wryting . . . concerning the superioritie of Bysshops," which may have been a copy either of Hammond's letter of November 4, 1588, or possibly of the "Short observations," if it had been written by that date. He then goes on to give Walsingham his version of the dispute. "My lorde archebysshopp & the reste," he writes, "do take a dangerous course agaynste hir Ma[ties] supreme government, ffor they do clayme a superioritie of government to be knytte to theyre byshopryckes Jure divino dyrectlye:" for, although they admit that "all the superioritie that they have as bysshops" is derived "by way of medyacion of hir Ma[tie]," in the sense that it is the queen who appoints them as bishops, nevertheless, once they have been made bishops by the queen, they claim that "theyre sayd superyoritie" is "due unto them as knytte unto theyre bysshoprycke dyrectly Jure divino." Unfortunately the Lord Treasurer is "partely perswadid" that they "do not denye y[t] theyre superioritie is houlden by them as a grawnte geeven unto them dyrectlye from hir Ma[tie]" and that hence they do not claim it *jure divino*. But in fact, Knollys insists, he has clear evidence to the contrary. "But I must needes saye y[t] my lord archebysshoppe of Canterburye, & mye lorde Bysshoppe of Wynchester[60] have protested, & playnely avowed unto me that the bysshops of England have a superioritie over theyre inferyor bretherne dyrectlye Jure divino," while the same claims are also to be found in "the Bysshoppe of Canterburyes booke agaynst Cartewryghte (when the sayd bysshoppe was but Doctor Whytegyfte)" which "dothe manyfestlye declare the sayd archebysshops opynion in y[t] behalffe in manye places of the sayd booke." However, Knollys suggests that if Burghley would demand of the bishops in the queen's name whether they claimed their authority *jure divino*, the matter could easily be resolved; for they would hardly dare to insist on their claims, "oneles it be upon hope y[t] hir Ma[tie] would yeelde unto them theyre claymed superioritie to the preiudice of hir owne supreme government, & to the lyghte regarde of the opening of the highewaye to poperye to be made by the Jesuites to followe upon the same."[61]

During the next two months Knollys continued to press his attack, apparently with some success; for, at the end of May, he succeeded in persuading Burghley to agree to a meeting with Hammond to enable the latter to present the case against the bishops. On May 22, Knollys wrote to Hammond to advise him on what course of action to adopt at his meeting with the Lord Treasurer. "To the end that you may understand mine advice gratis," he wrote,

> ... I do think it best for you, upon your conference, to persuade
> my Lord Treasurer that first, it will please him to make her Majesty
> privy of the state of the controversy between the claim of the
> bishops' superiority over their inferior clergy; that they do not claim
> it directly from her Majesty's grant, but they claim it as appertaining
> to their persons by God's own ordinance, as soon as her Majesty
> hath made them Bishops. And that my Lord Treasurer will inform
> her Majesty, also, how greatly this claim is prejudicial to her
> Majesty's supreme government.

He then went on to suggest that Hammond should try to persuade Burghley to urge the queen to make the bishops set down their case in writing and to allow Hammond to reply to it, that thereby the bishops might be driven to revoke their claims—"or else her Majesty by your answer to their pretended claim may plainly see how injuriously against her Majesty's supreme government the said Bishops do seek by secret means to defraud her Majesty of her supreme government, given her directly and plainly from God, as well over the clergy as over the laity." Two days later, on May 24, Knollys forwarded a copy of this letter to Burghley, since, as he put it,

> I do take it necessary to make your Lordship privy of all my doings
> that may concern her Majesty's safety. . . . For I do know that, if any
> good shall be done for the preservation of her Majesty's safety
> against the dangerous deprivation of her Majesty's supreme
> government, privily sought by the undermining ambition and
> covetousness of some of our Bishops, . . . it must be done by your
> Lordship's good mediation, through your wise and modest
> government.[62]

The outcome of Hammond's interview with Burghley is not known, but it is clear that, if Knollys believed that Hammond would succeed in convincing him of the need to take positive action against the bishops, he was disappointed. Burghley's attitude throughout the controversy seems to have been equivocal. On the one hand, he was probably in basic sympathy with Knollys' views on episcopacy and Knollys certainly interpreted some of his letters as giving him encouragement. On the other hand, Burghley's relationship with Whitgift had changed since 1584 and, whatever his personal feelings in the matter, he clearly had no desire to be drawn into an open conflict with the archbishop on the issue, which in any case he probably regarded as of no great importance. As a result his policy appears to have been to temporize. While he endured Knollys' endless tirades with remarkable patience, he seems to have taken as little action as he could beyond passing some of Knollys' memoranda on to Whitgift and he refused to raise the issue with the queen.

During the summer of 1589 Knollys was away from court,[63] but he continued to pour out a stream of letters to Burghley from the country which became increasingly plaintive as the summer progressed. The first of these was written on July 5 from Oxford, where he had been attending the assizes in his capacity as Lord Lieutenant of the county. It is a long letter, which was ostensibly concerned with various matters that had arisen during the course of his visit to Oxford, but it is clear that the question which was uppermost in his mind was that of the queen's supremacy and in his conclusion he returned once more to the subject of his campaign against the bishops. This time he appealed to Burghley and the Lord Chancellor, Sir Christopher Hatton, for their support, "uppon whose good allowaunce and backinge I must muche depende, because I know my great lacke of wisdome, to keep or to obtayne any credite with her Matie." He, therefore, requested Burghley to show his letter to the Lord Chancellor[64] that "theruppon it may please yow two, either to incorage me or to discorage me in my travell in this behalf." At the same time he reaffirmed his belief that if "by your two LLps: perswacions" Whitgift could be induced to make the bishops acknowledge publicly "that they have no superioritie over ther inferior brethren, but suche as is to be derived unto them directlye from her Maties supreame auctoritie and governmente," this would "greatly advaunce Her Maties due honor and saffetye, and . . . overthrow the trayterous praquetices of all Jesuytes and semynaryes, that now to prowdlye do come into this Realme."[65]

Burghley's reply was discouraging and it immediately evoked a long and aggrieved letter from Knollys, dated from his house at Ewelme on August 4, 1589. "I have receyved your Lps letter of the firste of Auguste," he began, "wherein I have received verie smale comforte, and smale hope of the good mayntenance of her Maties saffetye, consisting in the syncere mayntenance of her Maties supreme governmente agaynste the covetous ambicion of clergie rulers: for your Lp: sayeth, that the questyon is verie dysputable, wherof I wrote unto your Lp:." He then proceeded to reiterate his complaints at great length and in a rambling fashion, launching first into a bitter attack on "the nature of covetous ambicion in churche governors" in all ages, as typified by "the prowde ambicious governmente of the scribes and Pharises" in the time of Christ, before turning once more to the question of "the superioritie of byshopps," which he now insisted that Christ had settled once and for all when he forbade his apostles to contend for superiority among themselves. "But," he added, "here you muste not take me, that I do denye that byshopps maye have anye lordlye auctoritie or dignitie that they have inioyed, so that they clayme it not from a higher auctoritie, then directlye from her Ma[ites] grante." What had particularly stung Knollys in Burghley's letter was his remark that the question was disputable; and, after protesting that he had no wish "to contende withe your Lp:," he went on to suggest—almost certainly correctly—"that the cause of your Lps: writinge unto me, that the questyon is verie dysputable, is not for that your Lp: is of that opinion, but rather for that your Lp: woulde brydell and staye me, from runnynge to faste befor your Lp: in the matter of her Ma[ties] saffetie." Finally, he protested with some asperity that even if Burghley were "to sett all the byshopps and all their favorers agaynste me, to prove me a distourber of their governmente in their suppressinge of preachers or otherwyse," they would be unable—as has already been quoted—"to prove anye substancyall matter agaynste me, synce the tyme, that longe since her Ma[tie] at wynsore did commande me, that I shoulde not deale withe the purytanns, as then her Ma[tie] called them."[66]

Knollys' next letter, written from his estate at Rotherfield Grays on August 15, was more cheerful. In the interval Burghley had sent him a paper written by an unnamed divine at court in answer apparently to a paper by Hammond "touchinge superioritie of byshopps."[67] In an accompanying letter Burghley had made some critical comments on the views expressed by the divine and Knollys interpreted these as a mark of encouragement. "My verie good Lo:," he writes, "I have perusede yo[r] courtlye, learned devine his wrytinge, whiche you sente unto me, And I am glad that yo[r] Lp: did myslike his answer to the beginninge of my booke." In forwarding the paper to Knollys Burghley had apparently not disclosed the identity of its author, but Knollys was confident that he knew who it was.

And I do know but one chapleyne of her Ma[ties], that I can gesse,
that wolde write with suche audacitie, agaynste the playne truethe
of the scripture. ffor he sayethe by waye of collection, that because
S[t] Paule did apoynte Tymothie and Tytus to ordayne elders in
everie congregacion, that therefore he takes it proved, that they had
superioritie over other elders. Althoughe the scripture sett downe
by S[t] Paule dothe make no mencion, that either Tymothie or Tytus
were byshopps, or that they had superioritie over other elders.

If such proofs are allowed, it is no wonder, Knollys added scornfully, that the bishops' claim of superiority may be alleged to be disputable. He was therefore returning the divine's paper to Burghley with the request that he should send it to "the grave, learned man aforesayde"—i.e. Hammond—to be answered.[68]

Unfortunately, Knollys does not state in his letter whom he suspected the author of the paper to be. However, a possible clue to the writer's identity is provided by a letter written by Matthew Hutton, the newly appointed Bishop of Durham, to Archbishop Whitgift on October 10, 1589. In this letter Hutton gave Whitgift a report of a conversation that he had had some-time previously with Burghley and Walsingham at a private dinner in the Lord Treasurer's apartments at court, "where we three only did dine to-gether." At this meeting various topics were discussed, among them "the *antiquity* and *lawfulness* of a Bishop." According to Hutton, when he was asked about the authority of bishops, he had answered by citing Titus i and I Timothy v and he had argued that, although it was true that the terms *Episcopus* and *Presbyter* were sometimes used interchangeably in the New Testament, nevertheless it was "certain that there was an office in the Apos-tles time, which Titus and Timothy did exercise, which was distinct from the office of them who had only authority to preach and minister the sacra-ments, but not to appoint Priests, and censure offenders."[69] In view of Hut-ton's emphasis on the cases of Timothy and Titus and the fact that his meet-ing with Burghley and Walsingham had clearly taken place several weeks before the date of his letter to Whitgift, possibly about the time that Burghley forwarded "the courtly, learned divine's" paper to Knollys, it seems plaus-ible to assume that he was the divine in question.

If Knollys' letter of August 15 suggests a revival of confidence, the mood did not last. A fortnight later, on August 30, he concluded a long letter to Burghley and Walsingham, dealing with the capture of a catholic recusant, named Randall, with a bitter complaint about the lack of support he was receiving from Burghley and other members of the Privy Council in the matter of the queen's supremacy.

But my good lorde, to be playne withe you [he wrote after recounting
the details of Randall's arrest] I do stande almoste discoraged to
serve her Matie faythfullye agaynste these popishe traytors, and
trayterous recusantes, because I do not fynde myselfe well backed
nor countenaunced, in mye standinge in defence of her Maties
righte in her supreame governmente agaynste the fowle claymed
superioritie of byshopps, not as undergovernors to her Matie, but as
supreme governors from above her Matie, to the overthrowe of her
Maties supreame governmente: the which her Maties supreme
governmente, I do wonder and am abashed to see that cheif
councellors of this estate do not stande to the defence thereof,
agaynste the sayd byshopps.[70]

Burghley's reply was evidently intended to mollify Knollys: for in a short letter, dated from Ewelme on September 18, 1589, Knollys expressed him-self in general agreement with the arguments that Burghley had used:

I have receyved your Lps letter of the xv[th] hereof, and I muste
needes agree with yo[r] Lp: to thinke, that our byshopps and all
mynysters of the worde hav their auctoritie which is called, potestas
clavium, from the word of God: but to have superioritie one above
another, is a posytyve ordenance by wysdome of men to avoyde
confucion. And I do thinke also withe your Lp:, that none of our
byshopps can mayntayne the contrarie: althoe their claymed
superioritie, and their unlawfull uringe of subscription dothe shewe
their ambicion, and covetousnes, to the preiudice of her Ma[ties]
supreme governmente to manefestlye, whereof I will speake more
hereafter.[71]

However, the fact that Burghley was prepared to state categorically that the
bishops derived their superior authority from positive law does not mean
that he was any more willing than he had been to take action against the
bishops; and it seems probable that the main purpose of his letter was to try
to persuade Knollys that his fears were ungrounded, since the bishops did
not claim their authority *jure divino*, although Knollys obviously remained
unconvinced.

Although Bancroft's Paul's Cross Sermon played a much less significant
part in the controversy than Strype attributed to it, it did not entirely escape
Knollys' attention. Strype erroneously believed that Bancroft's Sermon was
a manifesto of the *jure divino* theory of episcopacy, but, in fact, this is not
the case. Although Bancroft himself was later to claim under the influence
of Saravia that episcopacy was instituted by Christ,[72] in his Sermon, which
was delivered the year before Saravia's tract was published, he confined
himself to arguing, as Whitgift and Bridges had done before him, that episcopacy was the traditional form of government which had been used in the
Church since the time of the Apostles, whereas the presbyterian system was
a newfangled invention.[73] Nevertheless, the general tenor of Bancroft's Sermon was calculated to arouse Knollys' suspicions and at some point in the
summer of 1589 he wrote to Dr. John Reynolds of Oxford for his comments
on two specific questions arising out of it—first, whether Bancroft could be
accused of maintaining the *jus divinum* of episcopacy indirectly, if not directly, and, secondly, whether he was justified in alleging that both Jerome
and Calvin appeared to admit that bishops had existed in the Church since
the time of St. Mark.[74] On September 19, 1589 Reynolds sent Knollys a
long and scholarly reply, which later came to be highly regarded as a defense of the traditional sixteenth-century view that episcopacy was a human
institution.[75] Though a Calvinist in theology, Reynolds, like Hammond, was
a moderate and his criticisms of Bancroft were cautiously expressed. On
the first point raised by Knollys, he was prepared to agree that Bancroft

"seemeth to avouch the superioritie, wch Bishops have among us over the clergie, to be of Gods owne ordinance; though not by expresse wordes, yet by necessarie consequence, in that he affirmeth their opinion, who impugne that superioritie, to be heresie." "Wherein," he continued, "I must confesse that he hath committed an oversight in my iudgement: and himselfe, I thinke, if he be advertised thereof, will acknowledge it."[76] He then proceeded to attack Bancroft's argument that episcopacy had existed since apostolic times with a wealth of learned references to the Fathers and to medieval and sixteenth-century writers. Reynolds' answer to Knollys' second question followed logically from this. Bancroft, he insisted, was completely unjustified when "he affirmeth, that S.Jerom saith, and Mr Calvin seemeth on his report to confesse, that Bishops have had the said superioritie ever since the tyme of S.Marke the Evangelist . . . sith nether Jerom saith it, nether doth Calvin seeme to confesse it on his report." And after a brief examination of the evidence he concluded "it is certaine that neither of them doth affirme, that Bishops have so long tyme had such superioritie, as D.Bancroft seemeth to father upon them."[77] As he had done with Hammond's memoranda, Knollys forwarded Reynolds' letter in due course to Lord Burghley, but again Burghley's response is not known.

Shortly after his letter to Burghley of September 18, 1589, Knollys returned to court and there are no more letters from him to Lord Burghley on the subject of episcopacy for several months. However, it would be wrong to interpret this as meaning that he had abandoned his campaign. At court Knollys would have been in a position to press his arguments on Burghley in person and, although the evidence is fragmentary, it is clear that throughout the whole of 1590 he continued to be preoccupied with the question of the *jure divino* theory of episcopacy and that he was still actively campaigning to have the bishops compelled to acknowledge that they derived their authority solely from the crown.

An indication of Knollys' continued concern with the problem is provided by a letter which he wrote to Lord Burghley in the spring of 1590 on behalf of a puritan minister, named William Hubbock, who had been cited before the High Commission for preaching an allegedly seditious sermon.[78] It is clear from an earlier letter from Knollys to Burghley, dated March 29, 1590, that they had both tried to intercede with Whitgift on Hubbock's behalf, but without success.[79] Two days later, on March 31, having in the meantime received from Burghley Whitgift's answer to Burghley's letter, together "wth the decree of the greate commyssioners agaynst Mr Hubbocke," Knollys wrote again to the Lord Treasurer to protest against Whitgift's treatment of Hubbock and he took the opportunity to launch a general attack on the archbishop's policies. After reminding Burghley how often Whitgift had opposed Parliament's requests for measures to encourage a learned ministry, and "how greatelye (if not tyrannouslye) the archebys-shoppe hathe urged subscription to his owne artycles wthout law," he returned once more to the theme of the bishops' claim to divine right:

And yor lordshyppe dothe also knowe how playnelye the sayd
archebysshoppe in his booke intytled, *Doctor Whytguift against
Cartwryght,* the sayd archbyssoppe hath claymed in the ryghte of all
bysshops a superyorytie belonging to them, over all the inferyor
clargye from godes owne ordynance, to the popyshe iniurye of hir
Maties supreme government. Now it is no suffycyent recompence for
the archebysshoppe to say barelye, y^t he dothe not clayme at this
present a superyorytie over the inferyor clargye from gods owne
ordynance, oneles the sayd archebysshoppe wyll also retracte his
clayme of superyorytie from godes owne ordynance sett downe in his
prynted booke . . . as before is sayd wthout the wch retractacion hir
Maties supreme government can neither be salved, nor preserved
(as I do thinke).

He, therefore, appealed to Burghley "to have a zealous care of hir Maties saffetye," and he urged him that the only way "to avoyde hir Maties extreme danger, so vyolentlye intended & labored by the pope & the kynge of Spayne & by theyre confederates now in this dangerous tyme," was "to abate the ambytion and covetousnes of bysshops" by making them acknowledge that they had no superiority over the inferior clergy except such as was granted to them from the queen, in accordance with the statute of 25 Henry VIII, revived in the first year of Elizabeth. "By wch statute the bysshopps are barred from offending of hir Maties prerogatyve royall, and from offending of the lawes & customes of the realme." "Whereby," he went on to assert— putting forward a novel constitutional doctrine, of which Elizabeth would have disapproved profoundly—"the sayd bysshops are not onelye subiecte to the supreme government of hir Matie: But also subiecte and answerable to the councellors of estate in y^t behalffe."[80]

There are interesting parallels between this letter and a paper which Knollys drew up a few weeks later, a copy of which survives among Robert Beal's papers in the Yelverton MSS. The paper, which is headed "A true Declaracion of some partes of the misgovernment of the Churche of England by the Bysshoppes at this day, written the.16.day of May. 1590," consists of two lengthy quotations—the first from the statute, 25 Henry VIII c.20 (the Ecclesiastical Appointments Act of 1534), to which he had referred so frequently in the course of the controversy, and the second from Whit-gift's *Defence of the Answer*—each of which is followed by brief comments by Knollys. In his comments on the first passage, Knollys argues that by this act it is manifest that the bishops have no superiority over the inferior clergy "otherwyse then is lymyted unto them by Statute," and that "whoso-ever offendethe in any parte of the sayd Statute" is liable to the penalties of *praemunire*. From which it follows, he maintains, that all bishops and their under-officers who have deprived preachers "by vertue of theire offyce as Bysshops, wthoute a good and lawfull commission from hir Matie are fallen into the penalty of the premunire, by offending of the prerogatyve royall of hir Matie, and by offending of the Lawes and Customes of this realme." The passage from Whitgift is of particular interest for the study of the contro-versy, since it contains the statement that "this superioritye of bysshops is gods owne instytucion," and it is clearly the passage that Knollys had chiefly in mind whenever he accused Whitgift of maintaining the *jus divinum* of bishops in his writings against Cartwright.[81] Not surprisingly, Knollys' com-ment on it is that "this Clayme of superioritye of Bysshops aforesayd to be gods owne instytucion, is dyrectlye agaynst hir Maties prerogatyve royall in hir supreme government," and therefore it "must necessarilye be retracted, as repugnant to hir Maties supreme government, and to hir Maties prerogatyve royall." However, he then went on to put forward the curiously Henrician suggestion that in order "to avoid this ambytious and covetous preiudice to kinges and princes" the latter should "appoynt a temporall magistrate to be his and theyre deputyes or vicegerent y^t may examyne and take accompte of all the decrees and doinges of bysshops, in theyre courtes, or otherwyse, whereby the prerogatyve royall and the supreme government of kinges and princes may be saffely preserved and mayntened."[82]

This paper presents something of a mystery, since the circumstances in which it was written are not known and there is no evidence to show what use, if any, Knollys made of it. From its contents it would appear to have been written while the issues raised by Hubbock's case were still very much in his mind, and it may represent an attempt by Knollys to marshall more clearly the arguments that he had used in his letter of March 31. At the same time, in view of its date, it is possible that it may be connected with a draft letter from Knollys to Queen Elizabeth, which is preserved among the Burghley papers in the Lansdowne MSS and which is endorsed "the. 22. of May. 1590."[83] This letter contains the well-known passage in which Knollys apologizes for "myne oulde error, to saye, that I have not hereto-fore (in wayghtye matters) used suche temperancye of speache as wyser men have done to your Matie, nether have I suppressed myne abundant affections (in so wayghtye cases) as wyser men have done & should doe." Strype consequently assumed that this letter was written by Knollys in order to make his peace with the queen and he interpreted it as evidence that "in the month of May, the Queen was displeased with him for meddling in this matter of the constitution of her Bishops; and, as it seems, commanded his absence."[84] But Strype's interpretation is almost certainly incorrect. In the first place, the letter is only a draft and there is no evidence that it was ever sent to the queen. Secondly, it contains no reference to Elizabeth's having commanded him to absent himself from court. Thirdly, an alternative reading of the text suggests that Knollys' primary purpose in writing the letter was not to apologize for his past errors but rather to try to persuade the queen to allow him to state his case against the bishops before her. For he goes on to write—admittedly, in the deferential language which Elizabeth expected from her courtiers—"Nowe to avoyde theise myne oulde errors, I do most humbly crave at your Maties handes at this present, that it wyll please you y^t my lorde Treasorer may be placed to be a faythefull reporter, & true dealer, betwene your Matie and me, and also betwene me and suche, as I shall accuse for iniuring of your Maties saffetye, and of your Maties supreme government." The last words suggest that far from apologizing for his attacks on the bishops, Knollys was still hopeful of persuading the queen that the bishops constituted a threat to the Royal Supremacy. It therefore seems likely that the letter was composed—possibly in conjunction with the paper of May 16—as a fresh move in his campaign against the bishops, Knollys' object on this occasion being to petition the queen directly for permission to lay his case before her, but that, following his usual practice, he took the precaution, before sending it, of submitting it to Burghley for his approval. If this interpretation is right, there can be little doubt that the letter was never dispatched, since Burghley would almost certainly have vetoed it.

That Strype was wrong in suggesting that Elizabeth had reprimanded Knollys in May, 1590, for meddling with the question of episcopal authority is shown by the fact that he continued to campaign actively against the *jure divino* theory during the later months of that year. In August he was provoked to a fresh outburst by the publication of a tract in defense of episcopacy, entitled *A Reconciliation of all the Pastors and Clergy of the Church of England*, by Anthony Marten, one of the Sewers of the Queen's Chamber.[85] Marten's pamphlet was not a work of great consequence in itself and it is doubtful whether in other circumstances it would have attracted Knollys' attention, especially as he seems to have completely ignored the much more important *De Diversis Ministrorum Evangelii Gradibus* of Hadrian de Saravia, which had appeared only a few weeks earlier and on which Marten drew in the concluding pages of his book. But it is clear that Knollys' anger was aroused by the fact that as a Sewer of the Queen's Chamber Marten was a member of the Royal Household and therefore, in a sense, one of his own subordinates.

On August 14, 1590, Knollys wrote an indignant letter to Lord Burghley in which he complained that "upon Wednysday last Mr Martyn the Sewer, presented to me a booke of his owne making, wherein he pretendethe a reconcyliacion of the clargie, but indeede the booke is none other, but a parrasytycall promoter of the ambytious & covetous government by the claimed superyorytye of bysshops." "Now I do fynde," he continued,

> y^t Mr Martyn hathe had craftyer councell in the penning of his
> booke, then is conteyned in his own heade, although I do thinke the
> penning thereof to be his owne doing: but when he dothe come to
> showe the reasons of the presbytery men, y^t are adversaryes to the
> bysshops claimed superyoryte, The answers y^t he makethe to these
> reasons, are the answeres, y^t Doctor Whytegyft dothe make agaynst
> Cartewryght.[86]

He then went on to accuse Marten of maintaining that the authority of bishops was "godes institucion first" and only "in a second degree . . . from the Queenes Maties authorytie & allowance"—a view which, Knollys insisted, "smellethe of treason agaynst hir Maties supreme govcrnment."[87] After repeating the familiar charges against the bishops, Knollys therefore put forward a new proposal—that Burghley should persuade the queen to allow the controversy to "be dyscussed by the common consent of the most learned unyversitye men, to whome the bysshops must needes geeve place for the matter of true learning: because" (he suggested somewhat naïvely) "the chieffe devynes of the unyversitye are not yet corrupted wth worldly promotions, nether are they parcyall as yet, nor towched wth ambytion & covetousnes, as the bysshops claymed superyorytie must needes be."[88]

Burghley appears to have ignored Knollys' letter of August 14, for on September 8 Knollys wrote again to protest against Marten's book. He began by reminding Burghley—as if any reminder were needed—how "my chieffest study hathe bene of longe tyme to seeke out the true preservacion of hir Maties saffety specyally towching the mayntenance of hir Maties supreme government." Then, after repeating yet again his claim that the bishops derived their authority from the statute of 25 Henry VIII and that anyone who offended against the terms of the statute was liable to the penalties of *praemunire*, he proceeded to argue that

> because Mr Martyn the Sewer, an ordynarye servant to hir Matie,
> hathe rashelye in his late prynted booke, dedycated by him unto
> hir Matie, in favoure of the superyorytie of bysshops, so foolysshlye
> advanced the sayd superyorytie of bysshops, That he dothe justyfye
> largelye & plentyfullye the sayd superyorytye of bysshops to be
> first from godes owne ordynance, & in a second degree hee claymethe
> the same superyorytie, (also for the bysshops,) from hir Maties
> grawnte and allowance, But by clayming of the sayd superyorytye
> of government fyrst & pryncypally from godes owne ordynance,

& not pryncypally & dyrectlye from hir Maties grawnte, nor from hir supreme government, Therfor Mr Martyn aforesayd is fallen into the penalty of the premunire, as also Doctor Whytegyfte is lykewyse, by clayming longe synce in his prynted booke agaynst Cartewryght, that the superyorytie of bysshops is godes owne instytucion, & not an humayne ordynance, whereof hir Matie is the supreme governor.

Finally, he informed Burghley in no uncertain terms, "I do thinke it highe tyme for the preservacion of hir Maties saffetye, that my sayd opynion may fourthew^th come to tryall whether it be true or false."[89]

If Knollys' letter was intended as an ultimatum to Burghley, it had little effect. For two months later he returned to the subject in a pessimistic letter, dated November 9, 1590. In the meantime he had written an answer to the arguments put forward in Marten's book and he now forwarded this to Burghley for his perusal, since, as he states, "I dare not presume to sett fourthe anythinge towchinge hir Maties saffetye w^thout yor lordshippes good consent to the same." He therefore begged Burghley "to take the paynes to reade over my sayd wryting before I proceede anye further therein, for w^thout yor lordshyps good allowance thereof, I do meane to surcease & stay from further wrytyng in that behalffe."[90] The tone of this letter suggests that he hardly expected Burghley to approve of what he had written and that he was becoming resigned to the abandonment of his campaign.

In fact, the end came shortly afterwards. Although the details are not clear, it is evident that at some point during the next few months Elizabeth finally lost patience with Knollys and ordered him to desist from pursuing the matter any further. By May, 1591, Knollys was in a state of despair. On May 14, he poured out his feelings in a long letter to Burghley. After describing how he had been present the previous day at a meeting of the Star Chamber, when the case of Cartwright and his fellow prisoners was discussed for the first time, he went on to relate how, when he was asked his opinion on a point of procedure, he had not dared to speak his mind freely, "bycawse I dowted, whether hir ma^tie wold allowe me to speyke my conscyence in hir ma^ties behalffe agaynst the uniust claymed superyorytye of bysshops, dyrectly ympunging of hir ma^ties supreme government as I do take it, and as I have offerd before hir ma^tie to prove it, and as I am not aferde in the starre chamber, by the help of lerned cownsayle to prove it (yf hir ma^tie woll gyve me leave)." "Indeed," he continued, "your Lp. dothe see what a strayte I am dryven into: for it is a deadly greaffe unto me to offend hir ma^tie, specially publyklye, and yet I had rather dye than to ympugne hir ma^ties safetye by anye pleasyng speache." He therefore begged Burghley to show his letter to the queen—

to the ende that hir ma^{tie} may gyve me leave to speyk myn owne
conscyence frelye in the behalffe of hir ma^{ties} safetye in this case
aforesayde, or els that yf so motche grace can not be obtayned of hir
ma^{tie} for me, Than my desyre is that to avoyd hir ma^{ties} offence
wth the offence of my conscyence also, that it woll please hir
ma^{tie} to make me a pryvate man, that I may so be scylent, and avoyd
hir ma^{ties} offence, the wch offence I am desyrous to flee even as
from a serpent.

The pathos of this letter is underlined by Knollys' final sentence—"Althoe
wrytyng dothe hinder my syghte, yet I durst not wryte otherwyse than wth
myn owne hand in this case."[91]
If Burghley showed this letter to the queen—which is perhaps unlikely—
Elizabeth took no notice of it, for Knollys remained in office until his death
five years later. But from this time on—to judge by his few surviving letters
to Burghley—he appears to have tried fairly scrupulously to observe Elizabeth's injunction not to attack the authority of the bishops; and, although
he continued to protest on occasion against the treatment of Cartwright and
his fellow ministers,[92] there are no further references to the *jure divino* theory
of episcopacy during the remainder of 1591 and the whole of 1592.
Knollys' suspicions of the bishops, however, remained unaltered and at
the beginning of 1593 he returned to the attack for the last time. The occasion was provided by a debate in the House of Commons on a motion by
James Morice, Attorney of the Court of Wards, for leave to introduce two
bills attacking the *ex officio* oath and other aspects of Whitgift's ecclesiastical government.[93] In the course of the debate Morice came under heavy attack from several of Whitgift's supporters in the House. Angered by these
attacks, Knollys intervened on Morice's behalf and delivered a long ha-
rangue, in which he repeated his familiar argument that the bishops derived
their authority from the statute of 25 Henry VIII and that anyone infringing this act was liable to the penalties of *praemunire*, while he also questioned the bishops' right to hold their courts in their own names, instead of
in the name of the queen.[94] The next day, February 28, Morice was sum-
moned before the Privy Council and ordered to be confined to the house of
Sir John Fortescue, the Chancellor of the Exchequer. Significantly, Knollys
was not one of the councilors present on this occasion but on the same day
he wrote to Burghley in Morice's support. The ostensible purpose of his
letter was to send Burghley "a booke of suche collections, as I have gathered,
spetyallye towchinge hir Maties supreme government," but he took the opportunity to defend Morice against his critics in the House of Commons.
The queen's supreme government, he complained, "begynnethe now to be
impungned in oure lower house of parlement by the cyvilians, and also spe-
tyallie by Mr Dalton, the lawier, and chieffelie impungninge a speeche y^{t}

Mr Morrys, the atturney of the courte of wardes, dyd use yesterdaye, agaynst certen abuses now used in the government of the clergie," and he accused the civilians of wishing to "have a kynde of monarchye in the sayd clergie government, as is in the temporaltye, The which clergie government they would have to be exempted from the temporall government, Saving they speake not agaynst the prynces government towching the supremacye." At the same time, he assured Burghley "that in myne opynyon Mr Morrys did speake bothe modestlie, & wyselye, & warylie, & trulye towching the abuses in the government of the clergie at this present." But, somewhat disingenuously, he omitted any reference to his own part in the debate.[95]

Reports of Knollys' speech, however, inevitably reached Burghley and at the end of April, shortly after the dissolution of parliament, Knollys wrote a long letter to the Lord Treasurer to explain his conduct. After thanking Burghley for his good offices in helping to obtain the award of the Garter for him from the queen, he proceeded to give him an account "of my dealinge in this parlemente tyme agaynst the undue claymed superyoryytie of Bysshops over theyre inferior bretherne." He explained at some length how in his speech, after reciting the statute of 25 Henry VIII, he had challenged the right of the bishops to hold their courts in their own names—"Whereunto I was answered, That the bysshops do keepe theyre courtes nowe by prescryption." Such an answer, he protested to Burghley, was unsatisfactory: for it was contrary to the royal prerogative for anyone to hold a court without a special license from the crown, and, in fact, the bishops "in Kynge Edwardes dayes" obtained an act of parliament to enable them to hold their courts in the king's name. But this statute was repealed under Mary and was not revived at Elizabeth's accession. The bishops would have done wisely, he insisted, if they had followed the example of their Edwardian predecessors and sought a similar statute to authorize them to hold their courts in the queen's name; but since they had not done so, and since it was unlawful for anyone to hold a court except by grant from the crown, he could not understand how they could claim to hold their courts in their own names by prescription. Finally, he returned for the last time to the issue which had obsessed him for so long. Reminding Burghley that "yor lordshyppe sayd unto me, that the Bysshops have forsaken theyre clayme of superyoryytie over theyre inferyor bretherne latelye, to be by godes owne ordynance, and y^t nowe they do onelye clayme superyoritie over theyre inferyor bretherne from hir Maties supreme government," he demanded: "If this be true, Then it is requysyte & necessarye, y^t my lorde Archebysshoppe of Canterburye y^t nowe is, do recante or retracte his saying in his booke of the great volume agaynst Cartewryghte, Where he sayeth in playne woordes (by the name of Doctor Whytgyfte) That the superyoritie of Bysshops is godes owne instytucion, wch saying dothe Impungne hir Maties supreme government dyrectlye, & therefore it is to bee retracted playnelye & trulye, ffor chryst playnely confessed y^t his kingdome was not of this worlde, and therefore he gave no worldlie rule or prehemynence unto his apostles."[96]

This letter represents Knollys' final outburst on the subject of the *jure divino* theory of episcopacy. He still had three more years to live. But he was now nearly eighty and in failing health; and, although it is clear from his two letters to Burghley in the spring of 1593 that he had abandoned none of his suspicions of the bishops, from this time on he appears to have reverted to his policy of silence, for no letters survive on the subject from the last three years of his life. From his later letters to Burghley, Knollys emerges as a sad and defeated old man. Although, as the award of the Garter showed, he had not lost Elizabeth's personal favour, his campaign to have the bishops compelled to acknowledge that they derived their authority solely from the crown had ended in complete failure. Elizabeth had forbidden him to pursue the matter any further; Burghley had failed to support him; Whitgift's position had been greatly enhanced by the exposure of the Classical movement and he was now virtually unassailable; while the *jure divino* theory of episcopacy itself, against which Knollys had argued so strenuously, was gaining ground rapidly in the early 1590s under the influence of Hadrian de Saravia's *De Diversis Ministrorum Evangelii Gradibus*, although paradoxically Knollys' later letters to Burghley contain no reference either to Saravia's work itself or to any of the tracts which followed it.

Knollys' lack of success has dogged him beyond the grave. Modern historians have, in general, refused to take his campaign seriously and they have tended to dismiss it as the obsession of a cantankerous old puritan, who, in Conyers Read's phrase, was "virtually in his dotage."[97] But such a judgment is not altogether fair. Although it is true that the question of the bishops' authority became something of a King Charles's head with Knollys and it is difficult not to feel a certain sympathy for Burghley, who must have found Knollys' endless stream of letters a constant source of embarrassment, nevertheless his campaign did touch on important theological and constitutional issues. Throughout the formative years of the English Reformation there had been a general consensus among English protestants that episcopacy was a purely human institution, while the same principle was embodied in the theory of the Royal Supremacy as it had been propounded in the reign of Henry VIII. Knollys could therefore claim considerable historical justification for his assertion that the *jure divino* theory of episcopacy constituted a threat not only to traditional protestantism, but also to the Royal Supremacy: for, if followed to its logical conclusion, it involved an implicit denial of the Henrician doctrine that the crown was the exclusive source of the jurisdictional authority of the bishops. In practice, so long as the crown and the episcopate remained as closely allied as they did throughout the greater part of the seventeenth century the threat was only hypothetical. But almost exactly a hundred years later the prophetic nature of Knollys' warnings was to be revealed at the time of the Non-Juring schism, when the Non-Jurors refused to recognize the right of crown and parliament to deprive Archbishop Sancroft and his colleagues of their sees on the ground that they held their authority in the church *jure divino*.

How far Knollys, with his Erastian views, can properly be classified as a puritan must remain a matter of debate; but there is a certain irony in the fact that it was Knollys, the so-called puritan, who was defending the traditional Tudor order in church and state, whereas it was Whitgift and his colleagues of the establishment who were the innovators with their claim that episcopacy was in some sense a divine institution. But such ironies are characteristic of the history of dissent.

NOTES

1. Samuel Johnson, *A Dictionary of the English Language*, 3rd ed. (London: W. Strahan, 1765), I, sig. 7F.
2. For a classic statement of this view, *see* "An Answere unto a Letter of Master Harrisons by Master Cartwright being at Middleborough" (1584) in Albert Peel and Leland H. Carlson, eds., *Cartwrightiana*, Elizabethan Nonconformist Texts, I (London: Allen and Unwin, 1951), 49-58.
3. Peel and Carlson, *Cartwrightiana*, 50.
4. Cf. Patrick Collinson, *The Elizabethan Puritan Movement* (London: Cape, 1967), 13.
5. There is no biography of Knollys. The fullest account of his career is still that written by Sir Sidney Lee for the *D.N.B.*, although it is inaccurate on many points of detail. For his early life down to 1559, see Christina Hallowell Garrett, *The Marian Exiles* (Cambridge: Cambridge Univ. Press, 1938; repr. 1966), 210-13.
6. Thomas Fuller, *The Church-History of Britain, From the Birth of Jesus Christ until the Year M.DC.XLVIII* (London: 1655), Book IX, 152, quoted before, 39. Miss Garrett suggests that Knollys visited Geneva briefly, along with his son Henry, in November, 1553, as an envoy sent by Cecil to Calvin "with the object of obtaining permission for the establishment of a colony of English religious emigrants within their borders," and she identifies the two Knollyses with the unnamed English gentleman and his son who were referred to by Calvin in a letter to Viret dated November 20, 1553 (*Marian Exiles*, 211-2). However, this theory, like Miss Garrett's general hypothesis regarding Cecil's role in organizing the emigration of English protestants at Mary's accession with which it is closely linked, must be regarded as purely speculative and there is no concrete evidence that Knollys left England before 1555. All that is known with certainty of Knollys' period of exile is that he was in Basle in the winter of 1556-7, when his name appears in the Matriculation Register of the university, and

that he subsequently moved to Frankfurt, where he was one of those who attempted to mediate between the two rival factions in the contentions of 1557, although he eventually subscribed the new Discipline in December, 1557; he also appears to have visited Strassburg as a delegate from the Frankfurt congregation (*Marian Exiles*, 212). Miss Garrett is almost certainly correct in arguing against the *D.N.B.* that he did not return to England until after Elizabeth's accession (*Marian Exiles*, 212).

7. Knollys' wife was Catharine Carey, daughter of Anne Boleyn's elder sister, Mary, and sister of Henry Carey, Lord Hunsdon. For the importance of the Boleyn connection in Elizabeth's Privy Council, see Michael Barraclough Pulman, *The Elizabethan Privy Council in the Fifteen-seventies* (Berkeley, Los Angeles, London: Univ. of California Press, 1971), esp. 37, 39-42.

8. J. E. Neale, *Elizabeth I and her Parliaments 1559-1581* (London: Cape, 1953), 57ff.

9. *See* the letter from Edwin Sandys, Bishop of London, Knollys, Sir Thomas Smith and Sir Walter Mildmay to John Parkhurst, Bishop of Norwich, May 6, 1574, printed in George Cornelius Gorham, *Gleanings of a Few Scattered Ears during the Period of the Reformation in England* (London: Bell and Daldy, 1857), 487-8, and the letter from Knollys to Sir Thomas Wilson, January 4, 1577/8, B. L. Harleian MS. 6992, no. 44, cited in John Strype, *The History of the Life and Acts of the Most Reverend Father in God, Edmund Grindal* (Oxford: Clarendon Press, 1821), 354.

10. Cf. the paper entitled "M[r] Tresorer of the howshold his opynyon towchyng hir ma[ties] safetye 6th. Julii. 1586," B. L. Lansdowne MS. 51, no. 12, printed in John Strype, *The Life and Acts of John Whitgift, D.D.*, 3 vols. (Oxford: Clarendon Press, 1822), III, Book III Appendix XXXIV, 199-200.

11. In general, most modern historians have tended to apply the label "Puritan" to Knollys automatically, e.g., Neale, *Elizabeth I and her Parliaments 1559-1581*, 57, "Sir Francis Knollys . . . who throughout his career—as we shall have occasion to note—proved a godly, outspoken Puritan;" Conyers Read, *Lord Burghley and Queen Elizabeth* (London: Cape, 1960), 465, "As for Knollys, he was first, last and all the time a belligerent Puritan;" A. G. Dickens, *The English Reformation* (London: Batsford, 1964), 299, "Knollys in particular was to figure for many years among the most ardent Puritan laymen of the reign;" G. R. Elton, *England under the Tudors* (London: Methuen, 1955), 293, "that staunch puritan, Sir Francis Knollys." A significant exception is Patrick Collinson, who for the most part avoids the use of the term "Puritan" in his frequent references to Knollys and instead prefers to describe him (I think, correctly) as "an old-fashioned protestant" (*Elizabethan Puritan Movement*, 386).

12. *See* Fuller, *Church-History of Britain*, Book IX, p. 152, cited before, 39. Neale suggests that Knollys, along with at least four of his colleagues on the Privy Council (Bedford, Mildmay, Warwick and Walsingham) "would all perhaps have welcomed some form of Presbyterian experiment" (*Elizabeth I and her Parliaments 1559-1581*, 292), but I can find no evidence that this is true of Knollys and it is questionable how far it is true of any of the others.

13. On at least one occasion, in 1572, he rebuked Elizabeth for permitting the Prayer Book order of service to be "daily broken as well in her own chapel

as in her closet," *see* Neale, *Elizabeth I and her Parliaments 1559-1581,* 303.

14. Cf. Neale, *Elizabeth I and her Parliaments 1559-1581,* 198-9, 201-2; J. E. Neale, *Elizabeth I and her Parliaments 1584-1601* (London: Cape, 1957), 62.

15. *See* his letter to Lord Burghley, April 29, 1593, reporting his speech in Parliament in February, 1593, B. L. Lansdowne MS. 75, no. 37, summarised in Strype, *Whitgift,* II, 124-7 (discussed later, 67-8). The *D.N.B.* states that Knollys entered Parliament for the first time in 1542 as member for Horsham. But it is clear from this letter that he was already a member in 1534. The editors of the *History of Parliament,* to whom I am indebted for information regarding Knollys' parliamentary career, think that he probably entered Parliament at a bye-election in 1533, as he would have been too young to have been elected in 1529, although this cannot be confirmed since no bye-election returns survive for this parliament.

16. *See* the letter from Knollys to Archbishop Whitgift, June 20, 1584, summarized in Historical Manuscripts Commission, *Calendar of the Manuscripts of the Most. Hcn. The Marquis of Salisbury, K. G., &c., preserved at Hatfield House, Hertfordshire,* in progress (London: H.M.S.O., 1883-), III, 35-6, and the related letter from Knollys to Lord Burghley, June 13, 1584, P.R.O. State Papers Domestic, Elizabeth, vol. 171, no. 23, summarized briefly in *Calendar of State Papers, Domestic Series, of the Reigns of Edward VI, Mary, Elizabeth,* ed. R. Lemon and M. A. E. Green (London: H.M.S.O., 1856-72), II (1581-90), 181. As Fuller observed, it is curious that Knollys was not one of the privy councillors who signed the joint letter from the Council to Whitgift of September 20, 1584, protesting against his treatment of the Essex ministers (Fuller, *Church-History of Britain,* Book IX, 152); but the probable explanation for this is that he was absent from court at the time. Knollys was still actively attacking Whitgift in January, 1585, when he drew up a libellous syllogism accusing the Archbishop of Canterbury of practising "poopyshe tyrannye to the indangeryng of hir ma[ties] safetye" (B. L. Lansdowne MS. 97, no. 15). Part of Whitgift's reply to this syllogism was printed by Strype in *Whitgift,* I, 563-5, under the year 1589, as if it was connected with the later controversy over the *jure divino* theory of episcopacy. But this is clearly a mistake, since the original manuscript of Knollys' paper, which is written in Knollys' own hand, bears the endorsement "the. 30. of Januarye. 1584 [i.e. 1585]." Strype also states incorrectly that the conclusion of Whitgift's reply is lost: in fact, the whole of his answer is to be found in B. L. Lansdowne MS. 396, ff.51-6.

17. *See* the letter from Knollys to Lord Burghley, August 4, 1589, B. L. Lansdowne MS. 61, no. 54, cited later, 45.

18. Strype, *Whitgift,* I, 558-65, 597-601, 614; II, 32-4, 50-5, 71-3, 121-7; III, Book III Appendices XLIII-IV, 220-8; John Strype, *Annals of the Reformation and Establishment of Religion . . . during Queen Elizabeth's Happy Reign,* 4 vols. in 7 (Oxford: Clarendon Press, 1824), III, ii, 97-102, Book II Appendix LXVII, 601-2; IV, Appendices IV-V, 6-9.

19. One of the few historians to recognize that Strype's account of the controversy was unsatisfactory was Roland G. Usher in a little known article, "The Supposed Origin of the Doctrine of the Divine Right of Bishops" in

Mélanges d'Histoire Offerts à M. Charles Bémont par ses Amis et ses Élèves (Paris: Alcan, 1913), 539-47, subsequently reprinted under the title "Bancroft and the Divine Right of Bishops" in *Theology*, 1 (1920), 28-34. However, though critical of Strype (see esp. *Mélanges*, 546, n.1), Usher was unable to shake off Strype's influence and his own account of the controversy is misleading. I am indebted to Dr. W. J. Baker of the University of Maine for drawing my attention to this article.

20. *See* esp. Strype, *Whitgift*, I, 558-63.

21. Strype, *Whitgift*, II, 50-2. Although Strype purports to be quoting here from a letter of Knollys to Burghley, dated March 31, 1590 (B. L. Lansdowne MS. 64, no. 32), the first part of the letter as quoted on 50 is, in fact, taken from Knollys' letter to Burghley of August 4, 1589 (B. L. Lansdowne MS. 61, no. 54).

22. Strype, *Whitgift*, I, 597-8, 603-5. Both these extracts come from the same letter from Knollys to Burghley, dated July 5, 1589 (B. L. Lansdowne MS. 61, no. 47).

23. These papers formed part of a group of manuscripts relating to puritan activities in the years 1588-90, which Thomas Brett sent to Strype in June, 1711, and which Strype quoted extensively in his *Whitgift*. In a letter to Strype, dated June 25, 1711, Brett stated that these papers "are descended to me from Sr *John Boys* who was Brother to my Mothers Great-Grandfather. He was a Lawyer with whom Archbishop *Whitgift* advised in matters of common Law, being ye Steward both of his Court at *Canterbury*, & that of ye Dean & Chapter. And I suppose these Papers were put into his Hands that he might give his Grace Advice how to deal with ye Puritans according to our Laws" (Cambridge Univ. Library Baumgartner MSS., Strype Papers, 6, no. 429). In this letter Brett asked Strype to return the papers when he had finished with them and Strype seems to have complied with this request, but they have since disappeared. They are not among Brett's correspondence in the Bodleian nor among the Brett family papers now in the Kent County Record Office at Maidstone, although it is possible that they may still survive elsewhere. In his letter of June 25, 1711, Brett enumerated the nine items that he was sending to Strype in some detail. The papers which relate to the controversy over the *jure divino* theory of episcopacy can be identified as Item 3, which Brett described as follows: "3. Is stitched in Paper, & contains a Controversy about ye Superiority of Bishops whether it be *Iure divino* or *humano*, occasioned by a Sermon preached at Court Jan. 12. 1588. The Title on ye outside Leaf is, *Touching Superiority of Bishops, wth a Syllogism, & an Answer to ye Same, & a Reply thereunto*."

24. These papers were at one time in Strype's own possession, having been lent to him by Sir William Hickes of Ruckholt, the grandson of Burghley's secretary, Sir Michael Hickes. After Sir William's death in 1703, they remained in Strype's custody until his own death in 1737, when they were sold by his representatives to the antiquary, James West, after whose death in 1772 they were purchased by Lord Shelburne, later first Marquess of Lansdowne (see *D.N.B.*, *sub* Strype). Strype does not appear to have made any use of the Burghley papers at Hatfield.

25. Strype, *Whitgift*, I, 558-9.

26. I have discussed the development of the theory of episcopacy in the Eliza-

bethan period more fully in an earlier essay, "Anthony Marten and the Elizabethan Debate on Episcopacy" in *Essays in Modern English Church History in Memory of Norman Sykes*, ed. G. V. Bennett and J. D. Walsh (London: A. & C. Black, 1966), esp. 47-60.

27. *The Works of John Whitgift, D.D.*, ed. John Ayre, Parker Society, 3 vols. (Cambridge: Cambridge Univ. Press, 1851-3), II, 378.

28. Cf. Whitgift, *Works*, I, 6.

29. Whitgift, *Works*, II, 265.

30. Letter of Sir Francis Knollys to Lord Burghley, August 4, 1589, B. L. Lansdowne MS. 61, no. 54, printed in Strype, *Annals*, IV, Appendix IV, 6-9. Unfortunately Knollys does not state when his interview with Elizabeth took place. But it presumably occurred between July, 1586, when he wrote the memorandum entitled "Mr Tresorer of the howshold his opynyon towchyng hir ma^{ties} safetye 6th. Julii. 1586" (*see* before, 70, n. 10), which includes a proposal that the bishops should be restrained from condemning "knone, zealous preachers agaynst the poopes supremacye, for refusing to subscrybe to unlawfull artykles," and the autumn of 1588.

31. Knollys had touched on the question of the bishops' authority in his letter to Burghley of June 13, 1584, in which he complained of "the absolute authoritie of Bisshoppes (specially over theyre brethern) that hathe no fowndation in the worde of god, nor otherwyse but by lawe posityve, specially in yngland" and accused the bishops of seeking to draw their authority "upp to a hyre fowndation w^{th}owt controlment of prynce or cownsayle" (P.R.O., S.P. Dom., Eliz. 171, no. 23). But at that stage he was primarily concerned with establishing the illegality of Whitgift's attempts to enforce subscription to his articles and it was not until 1588 that he began to make the *jure divino* theory of episcopacy his main target of attack.

32. It is printed in full in H.M.C., *Calendar of Salisbury MSS.*, III, 367-70, where it is wrongly calendared as "Dr. Hammond to Lord Burghley." The confusion is due to the fact that the original paper is endorsed "Mr Doctor Hammon to Mr Tresorer"—i.e. Knollys, who was Treasurer of the Household, not Burghley, who was Lord Treasurer.

33. Strype, *Whitgift*, III, Book III Appendix XLIII, 220-4. *See* also Strype, *Whitgift*, I, 600-1.

34. Strype, *Whitgift*, I, 601.

35. For Hammond, *see D.N.B.*, John Venn and J. A. Venn, *Alumni Cantabrigienses*, Part I (to 1751), (Cambridge: Cambridge Univ. Press, 1922-7), II, 294. Hammond was appointed chancellor of the diocese of London by Bishop Sandys in 1575 but was replaced by Edward Stanhope in 1577, when Aylmer succeeded Sandys as Bishop of London (*see* Collinson, *Elizabethan Puritan Movement*, 202). Collinson implies that Hammond was removed because he was regarded by Aylmer as too moderate in his attitude towards the puritans, but I have found no evidence to support this. At this period the chancellor of a diocese held office only during the tenure of the see by the bishop who had appointed him and it seems more likely that Aylmer was merely exercising the customary right of patronage of a new bishop when he appointed Stanhope, who had influential family connections, as chancellor in place of Hammond.

36. Collinson, *Elizabethan Puritan Movement*, 257-8, 488 n.15.

37. *See* later, 53.

38. H.M.C., *Calendar of Salisbury MSS.*, III, 367; Strype, *Whitgift*, III, 220-1.
39. H.M.C., *Calendar of Salisbury MSS.*, III, 367-9; Strype, *Whitgift*, III, 221. Strype does not print Hammond's discussion of the scriptural texts which extends to over two pages in the *Calendar of Salisbury MSS.*
40. H.M.C., *Calendar of Salisbury MSS.*, III, 369-70; Strype, *Whitgift*, III, 221-2.
41. The first part of the "Supply" is printed in Strype, *Whitgift*, III, 222-4, but Strype omitted the concluding section of the paper which consisted of citations from Jerome and other writers on the subject of episcopacy. The subject matter of the "Supply" suggests that it may have been composed a few weeks after Hammond's original letter, at the time of Knollys' attack on Bridges' sermon of January 12, 1589 (*see* later, 49 ff.).
42. Strype, *Whitgift*, III, 222-3. At the end of his extract Strype states, "Then the writer proceeds to alledge S. Hierom, and some modern writers, as Calvin, Musculus, Beza, Hemingius, Sanchy [i.e. Zanchius], and Sadelius, and Danaeus" (224).
43. This act, also known as the Act in Absolute Restraint of Annates, is printed in full in Henry Gee and William John Hardy, eds., *Documents Illustrative of English Church History Compiled from Original Sources* (London: Macmillan, 1896 repr. 1910), No. LII, 201-9.
44. B. L. Lansdowne MS. 59, no. 8. Printed in Strype, *Annals*, III, ii, Book II Appendix LXVII, 601-2.
45. The full list is as follows: Jerome, Cyprian, Marsilius of Padua, Calvin, Musculus, Beza, Hemingius, Zanchius, Antonius Sadelius, Lambertus Danaeus.
46. Strype, *Whitgift*, III, 224, cited before, n.42. Alternatively, it is possible that the Lansdowne document, which appears to be in the hand of Knollys' secretary, is not a new paper by Hammond but simply a selection of extracts from the "Supply," which Knollys had copied out and forwarded to Lord Burghley.
47. *See* before, 72 n.23.
48. Strype, *Whitgift*, I, 560-3.
49. Strype, *Whitgift*, I, 563.
50. Strype formed this impression on first reading the MSS. In a letter to Thomas Brett, written on July 14, 1711, to acknowledge the receipt of his papers, he commented, "In y⁶ 3ᵈ Paper, y⁶ Preacher there mentioned, for y⁶ Ius divinum of Bps, was (if I am not mistaken) Dʳ Bancroft & y⁶ privy Counsellor I know to be Sʳ Fra. Knolles. For I have several original Letters of his about yᵗ very Argument of y⁶ Bps Superiority infringing y⁶ Queens Supremacy. He was a mighty Patron of the Puritans" (Correspondence of Thomas Brett, Bodleian MS. Eng. Theol. C.24, f. 414). It is typical of Strype that, having once formed the opinion, on the basis of what can only have been a hasty first reading of the documents, that Bancroft was the preacher referred to, he never subsequently revised his views.
51. R. G. Usher noticed this discrepancy, but he concluded that the date mentioned in Knollys' syllogism was an error for February 9, 1588/9, due to a careless blunder on Strype's part, and he accepted Strype's assumption that the syllogism was directed against Bancroft's Sermon (*Mélanges Offerts à M. Charles Bémont*, 546 n.1).
52. Bodleian Rawlinson Ms. C. 167, ff. 43-44ᵛ. The fact that the phrase "yoʳ Honoures" is crossed out in the title and "Sʳ ffr. Knowles" is inserted instead

suggests that this must be either the original manuscript of the reply which was sent to Knollys or a copy made directly from it.

53. Strype, *Whitgift*, I, 560. Bridges, in his answer, suggested that Knollys was not the author of the syllogism—"the honour of the person that delivered it (but I think made it not) in all dutifulness always reserved" (562)— and Strype, presumably on the basis of this remark, stated that the reply to the preacher's answer was made "by him that framed the syllogism" (563). However, it is clear from certain comments made on the syllogism in the first paragraph of the "Short observations" that the author of the latter was not responsible for the syllogism and there is no reason to doubt that it was, in fact, the work of Knollys.

54. Strype, *Whitgift*, I, 560-3.

55. *See* also, 54-5, 57.

56. The authors cited in the "Short observations" are: Jerome, Augustine, Marsilius of Padua, Calvin, the Magdeburg Centuriators, Musculus, Zanchius, Beza, Hemingius, Danaeus, Sadelius. On this occasion Hammond amplified the references in the Lansdowne paper of January, 1588/9, by giving extensive quotations from most of the authors listed (Bodleian Rawlinson MS. C. 167, ff. 43^v-44).

57. References to the folio nos. in Rawlinson MS. C. 167 are given at the end of this and the following paragraphs.

58. I.e., the Common Law, not the Civil Law.

59. Read, *Lord Burghley and Queen Elizabeth*, 448.

60. Thomas Cooper. For his views on episcopacy, see *An Admonition to the People of England. 1589.*, ed. Edward Arber, The English Scholars Library, No. 15 (Birmingham: Arber, 1882), esp. 36, 61ff.

61. P.R.O. State Papers Domestic, Elizabeth, vol. 223, no. 23. Summarized briefly in *Cal. S.P. Dom., Elizabeth*, II (1581-90), 584.

62. Both these letters are printed in full in H.M.C., *Calendar of Salisbury MSS.*, III, 412-3.

63. No attendances at the Privy Council are recorded for Knollys between June 19 and November 28, 1589 (*Acts of the Privy Council of England*, New Series, ed. John Roche Dasent, London, H.M.S.O., 1890-1907, XVII (1588-9), 299; XVIII (1589-90), 241).

64. As an afterthought Knollys inserted the words "and to M^r secretarye [i.e. Walsingham]" at this point, but without altering the wording of the rest of the sentence.

65. B. L. Lansdowne MS. 61, no. 47. Extracts from this letter are given in Strype, *Whitgift*, I, 597-8, 603-5.

66. B. L. Lansdowne MS. 61, no. 54. Printed in Strype, *Annals*, IV, Appendix IV, 6-9. *See* also Strype, *Whitgift*, I, 598-600; II, 55.

67. Knollys' wording is ambiguous. At the beginning of his letter he refers to the divine's "answer to the beginninge of my booke"; later to "his answer to the wrytinge of the grave, learned man, whiche I nomynated unto you, touchinge superiorite of byshopps"—a clear reference to Hammond. Although it is possible that the first reference may be to a separate paper by Knollys, it is more likely that only one work is intended, a paper by Hammond which Knollys had forwarded to Burghley. Whether this was a new paper by Hammond drawn up after his meeting with Burghley at the end of May or one of his earlier papers, there is no means of telling.

68. B. L. Lansdowne MS. 61, no. 57.

69. Strype, *Whitgift*, III, Book III Appendix XLIV, 224-8. *See* also, *Whitgift*, I, 614. Strype's transcript of this letter, which he prints in full,was made from a contemporary copy in the Petyt MSS, now Inner Temple Petyt MS. 538, vol. 38, ff. 324-6.
70. B. L. Harleian MS. 6994, no. 106. At the end of the letter Knollys added a short postscript, written in his own hand: "I do not marvayle, that their be so manye martanysts, synce ower bysshopps doe incroche uppon hir ma^ties supreme government, & alone wold have the expowndyng of the scriptures, by theyre unlawfull urged subscriptions."
71. B. L. Lansdowne MS. 61, no. 66. Summarized in Strype, *Whitgift*, I, 600.
72. [Richard Bancroft], *A Survay of the Pretended Holy Discipline* (London, 1593), esp. 104-6, 142.
73. Richard Bancroft, *A Sermon Preached at Paules Crosse the 9. of Februarie, being the first Sunday in the Parleament, Anno. 1588*. (London: E. B. [Edward Bollifant] for Gregorie Seton, 1588, i.e. 1589), esp. 10ff., 69, 99. For a discussion of Bancroft's views, *see* W. D. J. Cargill Thompson, "A Reconsideration of Richard Bancroft's Paul's Cross Sermon of 9 February 1588/9" in *Journal of Ecclesiastical History*, 20 (1969), 253-66.
74. In *Whitgift*, I, 559-60, Strype gives what appears to be a quotation from Knollys' letter to Reynolds. In fact, Knollys' letter does not survive and the words Strype attributes to him in quotation marks are taken from Reynolds' reply. *See* Cargill Thompson, *Journal of Ecclesiastical History*, 20 (1969), 260 n.1.
75. Reynolds' original letter, which Strype used, is in B. L. Lansdowne MS. 61, no. 27. It was printed twice in the seventeenth century, first, in 1608, the year after Reynolds' death, in *Informations, or a Protestation, and a Treatise from Scotland. Seconded with D. Reignoldes his letter to Sir Francis Knollis. And Sir Francis Knollis his speach in Parliament. All suggesting the usurpation of Papal Bishops*, 73-87, and again in 1641 when it was issued separately under the title of *The Iudgement of Doctor Reignolds concerning Episcopacy whether it be Gods Ordinance. Expressed in a letter to Sir Francis Knowls, concerning Doctor Bancrofts Sermon at Pauls-crosse, the ninth of February, 1588. In the Parliament time*. Both these editions contain numerous inaccuracies. In addition, it appears to have circulated in manuscript in Reynolds' lifetime and at least two late sixteenth- or early seventeenth-century manuscript copies of it survive, B. L. Harleian MS. 3998, no. 2, and B. L. Sloane MS. 271, ff.41^v-43.
76. B. L. Lansdowne MS. 61, no. 27, fol. 78; *Informations, or a Protestation*, 73-4. The reference is to Bancroft, *Sermon*, 18-9, where Bancroft maintained that Aerius had been condemned as a heretic for holding that there was no distinction between a bishop and a presbyter.
77. B. L. Lansdowne MS. 61, no. 27, ff.79^v-80; *Informations, or a Protestation*, 84-7. The reference here is to Bancroft, *Sermon*, 14, 69.
78. For Hubbock, *see D.N.B.*; Strype, *Whitgift*, II, 32-4; Collinson, *Elizabethan Puritan Movement*, 405.
79. B. L. Lansdowne MS. 68, no. 77.
80. B. L. Lansdowne MS. 64, no. 32. Summarized in Strype, *Whitgift*, II, 33-4.
81. The whole passage quoted by Knollys will be found in Whitgift, *Works*, II, 378-9: "It is a marvellous matter that you delight to run so fast upon a false

string. . . . But such bold assertions without proof are meet principles for such a ruinous and tottering platform as you dream of."

82. B.L. Additional MS. 48064 (Yelverton MS. 70), ff.94-5.
83. B. L. Lansdowne MS. 64, no. 46. Strype printed it twice, in *Whitgift*, II, 54-5, and *Annals*, IV, Appendix V, 9.
84. Strype, *Whitgift*, II, 54.
85. For Marten's tract, *see* Cargill Thompson, "Anthony Marten and the Elizabethan Debate on Episcopacy" in Bennett and Walsh, *Essays in Modern English Church History*, 44-75.
86. Knollys was quite justified in making this accusation in that Marten's arguments were very largely taken from Whitgift's writings against Cartwright. On the other hand, although Marten claimed that distinctions of authority had existed in the Church since apostolic times, in the main part of the book (like Whitgift) he laid great weight on the argument that no set form of government was prescribed for the Church in Scripture and in places his conception of church government appears to be almost as Erastian as that of Knollys himself. It is only in the concluding pages of the book, written, as he admits in his preface, after he had read Saravia's *De Diversis Ministrorum Evangelii Gradibus*, that he suddenly shifted his ground and began to argue categorically that episcopacy was instituted by Christ and the Apostles and that it ought therefore "to remain in most places perpetual." (*See Essays in Modern English Church History*, 62-75).
87. Knollys' reference appears to be to Anthony Marten, *A Reconciliation of all the Pastors and Cleargy of the Church of England* (London, 1590), 31ᵛ, although the passage in question hardly justifies Knollys' attack (*see Essays in Modern English History*, 70).
88. B. L. Lansdowne MS. 64, no. 69. Summarized in Strype, *Whitgift*, II, 53-4.
89. P.R.O. State Papers Domestic, Elizabeth, vol. 233, no. 62. Summarized briefly in *Cal. S.P. Dom., Elizabeth*, II (1581-90), 687.
90. B. L. Lansdowne MS. 65, no. 60.
91. B. L. Lansdowne MS. 68, no. 84. Summarized in Strype, *Whitgift*, II, 71-3.
92. Cf. his letter to Lord Burghley, January 9, 1591/2, B. L. Lansdowne MS. 66, no. 52, printed in Thomas Wright, ed., *Queen Elizabeth and her Times* (London: Colburn, 1838), II, 417.
93. For an account of this debate and its aftermath, *see* Neale, *Elizabeth I and her Parliaments 1584-1601*, 267-79.
94. For Knollys' speech, *see* his letter to Lord Burghley, April 29, 1593, cited below.
95. B. L. Lansdowne MS. 73, no. 30. Printed in Sir Henry Ellis, ed., *Original Letters, Illustrative of English History*, Third Series (London: Bentley, 1846), IV, 111-2. *See* also Strype, *Whitgift*, II, 123-4.
96. B. L. Lansdowne MS. 75, no. 37, Knollys to Lord Burghley, April 29, 1593. This letter was printed in 1604 as an appendix to [William Stoughton], *An Assertion for true and Christian Church-Policie* (Middleburgh), n.p., and again in 1608, along with Reynold's letter on Bancroft's Sermon, in *Informations, or a Protestation* (*see* before, 76 n.75), 88-93. It is also summarized very fully in Strype, *Whitgift*, II, 124-7.
97. Read, *Lord Burghley and Queen Elizabeth*, 465.

The Trials of a Puritan in Jacobean Lancashire

MARK H. CURTIS

Scripps College

IN LANCASHIRE, three miles north of Warrington on the River Medway, a large medieval church dedicated to St. Oswald crowns a gently rising hill. It stands at the divide of two ancient roads, one of which is now a heavily traveled modern highway. Its graceful fourteenth-century spire, springing from an embattled tower, still dominates, as it has for generations, the countryside round. A short distance to the west—less than a quarter of a mile— is the rectory, a handsome hall which a traveler in the days of William III called "a princely building." Together church and hall are the center of Winwick parish, which until the nineteenth century was one of the richest church livings in England.[1]

In the midst of this bucolic setting there occurred on Good Friday, 1616, an outburst of violence that both disrupted the reverent worship of the devout and broke the peace of the village and countryside. The scene of this outrage was Winwick parish church itself; the occasion, the induction of a new rector, Josiah Horne, the deprived vicar of Orwell, Cambridgeshire, who had played a minor role in the Puritan propaganda campaign of the years 1604-1609.[2] The participants on the one side were Horne and an official party to carry out the ceremonies of induction; on the other, Thomas Bold, M. A., a claimant to the rectory of Winwick, superinstituted by the presentation of the Earl of Worcester, the clerk and churchwardens of the parish, and several members of the local gentry. For more than two weeks clashes between these two groups, involving bodily assault and the brandishing of arms, kept the whole community in an uproar and for nearly a decade thereafter the consequences still set neighbor against neighbor and furnished frequent occasions for bitter legal disputes.

78

The outburst of violence signified far more than the pastoral comedy that appeared on the surface. It occurred in a closely knit rural society still deeply attached to its local gentry and magnates and resentful of outsiders with new ideas and attitudes. The members of this society, including the gentry, were largely Catholic recusants. Over the years they had buttressed their religious position by gaining a firm hold on the economic affairs of the church in this large, rich parish. The intruders on this scene were representatives of the established church and the royal government who were trying to complete the work of the Reformation in Lancashire—a labor long demanded by ardent Protestants and long acknowledged as desirable by the authorities. They had enlisted the assistance of Josiah Horne, whose known adherence and dedication to Puritan causes assured them of a reliable, steadfast agent for their purposes. Finally both the Lancashire men and the intruders had strong champions in the court of James I who were engaged in a struggle for power within the Privy Council and were not above carrying their conflicts into local affairs, especially when local affairs involved matters of national policy as well as personal influence.

The rioting that so irreverently shattered the Holy Week observances of Winwick parish began soon after 10:00 A.M. on Good Friday. Bold, who was officiating at a service in the parish church, claimed that just at the moment when he was administering "the holy sacrament of the body and blood of our Savior Jesus Christ," Horne and his confederates, twenty "riotous, routous, wilful and disordered persons, and all of them disguised, weaponed, armed, and arrayed with divers kinds of unlawful weapons, . . . as well invasive as defensive"—assembled in the church and in accord with a premeditated conspiracy blasphemously interrupted the service, assaulted Bold, and "endeavored by force and strong hand to have thrown him out of the church." Bold added that these acts had filled him with fear for his life.[3]

Thus the essentials of the story from one side. Here was no indication of purpose or motive; merely a denunciation of the malice, jealousy, and disorderliness of Bold's assailants. This account leaves the impression that the informant obviously wanted to convey: a band of barbarous, bloody-minded villains, heedless of their duty to God and man, had violently interfered with the normal life of harmless unsuspecting people at the most solemn moment of the Christian year.

The other side of the story gives an entirely different picture. Horne categorically denied that Bold was the lawful parson of Winwick parish, claiming that the rectorship of Winwick was rightfully his own, a claim buttressed with a recital of facts supporting it: he had been legally presented by the King and properly admitted and instituted, not by the Bishop of Chester because that diocese was vacant, but by the Archbishop of York. Having feared trouble at his induction, he had come to take possession of his new parish armed, not with weapons "as well invasive as defensive," but with an archbishop's mandate of induction, reinforced by a special warrant from the Court of High Commission. The disorderly persons who attended him were a notary public, a rector of a neighboring parish who was also a Justice of the Peace, a messenger from the Court of High Commission, and several respectable gentlemen of Lancashire and Cheshire.[4]

As for the riot itself, Horne, rather than being the attacker, was the attacked. He had suffered indignities and injuries inflicted by Bold and his friends. It all began when the clergyman accompanying Horne, Richard Eaton, vicar of Great Budworth in Cheshire, was helping him carry out the formalities of induction. They read the mandate of induction in public and had tacked up a true copy of the High Commission warrant on the south door of the church. Then as Horne, in accordance with legal procedures, was reading the Thirty-nine Articles in the church, he was assaulted by Bold, the churchwardens, and the parish clerk. Horne's assailants announced "with great rage and fury, contempt and audacity" that they little regarded the Archbishop and the Court of High Commission, and that they would not obey the warrant and mandate of induction. Bold and one of his confederates allegedly asserted "that there should be much bloodshed afore any mandate of induction were executed." They wrested the Book of Articles from Horne's hands and threw it on the ground. Going then to the chancel, Horne tried once more to read the Articles and a second time he was interrupted and despitefully used. One of the churchwardens struck him, threatened to remove him from the church by force, forbade the clerk to give him the keys to the church, and in contempt of lawful authority tore down the warrant Horne had posted on the church door. On the church porch, Horne tried a third time to read the Articles and a third time the supporters of Bold attacked him. Thomas Dakin, a churchwarden, pulled off his cloak and again threw the Book of Articles on the ground. Finally when Horne retreated to the churchyard and tried for a fourth time to do his duty, the churchwarden laid violent hands on him, threw him to the ground, and "with his hands upon his sword threatened and offered to assault him and pulled the said Book of Articles out of his hand and scornfully threw it into the highway." Only then did Horne and his party, defeated for the time being, depart from the church.[5]

Horne's opponents were not, however, content with such an inconclusive victory. When the new rector and his companions retired to the village inn, Bold and his confederates tried to seal their triumph by terrorism. They followed Horne to the inn, threatened the proprietor for giving Horne refuge, and then burst into the room occupied by Horne and his company. Richard Bold, brother of Thomas, "did then and there presumptuously, preemptorily, and audaciously in his majesty's name command" all present except Horne and himself to depart. Horne, having heard how "popish recusants" like Bold had violently mistreated other good religious men in Lancashire, demanded that his companions stand by him. Bold then questioned him about the authority by which he acted and showed utter contempt for his replies. He then served on Horne an injunction issued by the Court of Duchy Chamber to forbid Horne and the former incumbent, John Rider, now Bishop of Killaloe, from seizing the church of Winwick.[6]

For the moment Bold and his confederates had the upper hand; but only for the moment. If they thought that their violence and threats had permanently rid them of Horne, they were badly informed about his character and the determination of his supporters. A retreat from Lancashire to Cheshire was only a tactical move to prepare for another and more successful attack. In less than two weeks Horne and his company returned with reinforcements. They had received from the Court of High Commission a warrant for the arrest of Thomas Bold, his brother Richard, the two church-wardens, Thomas Dakin, and Gregory Freind, and the parish clerk William Taylor. They brought with them John Brunt, "one of the sworn messengers of his majesty's Chamber," who was to make the arrests; Edward Yarworth, bearer of a special mandate from the Archbishop of Canterbury directed to the curate and churchwardens of Winwick and commanding that Horne be allowed to have peaceful possession of his rectory; William Leigh, rector of the parish of Standish and justice of the peace for Lancashire; Sir Richard Brooke of Norton, Cheshire; and two other prominent gentlemen of the same county.[7]

On April 9, when they made their entry into Winwick, they searched diligently for Thomas Bold, but in vain. That gentleman later testified that he had shut himself up in his house because he feared for his life. Failing to find Bold, they tried to gain entrance to the locked church. But again they were frustrated. It was not, therefore, until Sunday, April 14 that amid tumult and uproar, Horne finally took possession of his living and performed the acts that completed his induction to his benefice. The Bolds and their friends, most prominent among whom was Henry Stanley, illegitimate son of Henry Stanley, 4th Earl of Derby, used every trick to prevent the act from being consummated.[8] In the morning they locked both parishioners and royal messengers inside the church and Horne and Leigh outside. In the afternoon, when Leigh and Horne returned with some parishioners whom they had won to their side, the Bolds and their party created an uproar to disturb Horne as he read the Articles. They would neither let Leigh preach a sermon nor consent to having Bold himself preach on this occasion. When Horne undertook to give a sermon in the churchyard, his adversaries rang the church bells until Leigh as justice ordered them to cease such outrageous behavior. At the conclusion of this ceremony those few persons who stayed

in wind and rain to hear Horne preach petitioned the Archbishop of Canterbury and the High Commission. They declared that they had obeyed the
mandate to induct Horne and urgently requested that Horne remain as their
pastor.[9]

Horne's persistence had paid off. He had not only been legally inducted
to his new living but had won a measure of support for himself among his
new parishioners. As yet, however, he enjoyed nothing more than a foothold
in the parish. The disorders that greeted his coming were but the outward
sign of an opposition that had deep roots in Lancashire. Furthermore the
antagonists on both sides had weeks before begun legal actions that would
continue for nearly a decade.

The legal battles had opened almost immediately after Horne had been
presented and instituted to the parish of Winwick in January. Immediately
after his presentation, he and John Rider, the former incumbent, began a
suit in King's Bench to recover some tithe corn that had been "inned" or
gathered by the Earl of Worcester, John Fortescue, and the latter's wife
Frances. The three defendants in this case immediately complained in the
Court of Duchy Chamber that such proceedings before King's Bench deprived them of their ancient rights and violated the liberties of the County
Palatine of Lancaster. On February 9 the Court of Duchy Chamber granted
them an injunction that ordered John Rider to drop the suit in King's Bench
and forbade both Rider and Horne, or any person to whom they might lease
the rectory of Winwick or any part of it, to commence any other such suits
in common law courts until the case could be heard in the Palatine Court
of Duchy Chamber.[10]

Worcester's action in superinstituting Thomas Bold to Winwick parish
and the resistance of the churchwardens to Horne's induction on Good Friday were both efforts to protect the leaseholders of the rectory against
Horne's claims to the glebelands and tithes of the parish. In answer to a Bill
of Information brought by the King's Attorney-General in Star Chamber,
Thomas Dakin and Gregory Freind, the churchwardens, asserted that Horne
on March 29 "did make title and claim unto all the glebelands, tithes and
other profits belonging to the rectory and church of Winwick aforesaid."[11]
They further charged that he impeached the right of the Earl of Worcester
to such property and income and "did . . . publicly and openly discharge
the parishioners then and there present from the payments of any tithes to
the said Earl . . . or to any other but to himself only and withal threatened
to commence suit against all such as would do otherwise and promised to
save harmless those that would pay their tithes unto him, alleging, affirming
and arrogating to himself that his bond was as good in that place as the said
Earl. . . . ."[12] Induction was a key matter in challenging the validity of the
old lease and in confirming Horne's claim to the temporalities of the parish.

Institution gave him a certain title to the glebe and the tithes but only induction gave him the right to bring legal suits to secure them.[13]

The violence during Easter Week itself immediately gave rise to further suits—this time in the Court of Star Chamber. These are of special interest because they reveal the depths of feeling stirred by the struggle over the rectory of Winwick. The cases in King's Bench and Duchy Chamber involved fundamental legal issues regarding title to property rights that belonged to the rectory. It was in Star Chamber, however, that the political and religious issues underlying the whole controversy came into the open.

Thomas Bold was first in the lists. On April 25, he entered a Bill of Complaint against Horne, Bishop John Rider, Richard Eaton, Sir Richard Brooke, and others which alleged that they had conspired to perpetrate all the disorders described before.[14] Horne, on his side, moved onto the field more slowly, but made up with force what he lacked in speed. By May 6 when he replied to Bold's charges, he had enlisted the King's Attorney-General on his side. Instead of bringing a counter suit on his own behalf, Horne managed to have Sir Francis Bacon, the Attorney-General, exhibit not a Bill of Complaint but an official indictment or Bill of Information against Thomas Bold and his confederates, Richard Bold, Henry Stanley, Thomas Dakin, Gregory Freind, Richard Taylor, and others.[15] Nor did Horne rely solely on the civil authority of the realm. Sometime after the Easter outrages he brought Bold's claim to the rectory before one of the spiritual courts of the realm—probably the Court of High Commission. Here he quickly got satisfaction, for on June 6, 1616 at Lambeth a sentence of deprivation for simony was passed against Thomas Bold, parson of Winwick.[16]

The ready support that authorities in Church and State gave Horne in his troubles indicates that his conflict with Bold was something more than an unsavory quarrel over preferment and the profits thereof. Why should the Archbishop of Canterbury and the Court of High Commission be so liberal with favors on behalf of a Puritan minister who had formerly been suspended and deprived and who had once been deeply involved in a campaign of Puritan agitation against the ritual, vestments, and discipline of the Church? Why should the Attorney-General champion his cause and transform what seems a private quarrel into a public affair? What interests did Bold represent and how did they come in conflict with the purposes and policies of the officials who backed Horne? How did it happen that Winwick lay at the convergence of all these personal interests and public causes? To be able to raise these questions shows of itself that this incident has overtones that make it more than a sordid tale of rustic greed and private ambition.

To turn first, however, to mundane things, the living of Winwick was a juicy bone of contention. Church and hall bore silent witness to the wealth of the parish. Generously endowed in the early Middle Ages, the rectory of Winwick steadily grew in value despite the stresses and strains of economic and religious changes. Rated in Henry VIII's *Valor Ecclesiasticus* at £102 9s 8d, the revenues provided an actual return in 1615 of more than £460. Thirty-five years later, they had risen even higher and the Commonwealth visitors estimated them at slightly more than £664. In a day when a majority of parish livings were worth less than £50 per annum, such an income was not just ample; it was opulent.[17]

Such magnificent endowments, of course, made the rectory of Winwick a coveted prize for anyone who by one means or another could lay claim to a part or all of its profits. The people behind Thomas Bold had possessed such a claim since the first years of Elizabeth I's reign. One cause, therefore, of the riots of 1616 was fear that long-standing rights were threatened, if they were not indeed being violated. For more than fifty years only a fraction of the revenues of Winwick parish had been used for spiritual and ecclesiastical purposes. In 1563 Thomas Stanley, then rector of the parish as well as Bishop of Sodor and Man, leased the rectory for ninety-nine years to his kinsman Sir Thomas Stanley, second son of the then Earl of Derby, for a payment of £120 a year. The agreement, which had the approval of the patron of the living, Edward Stanley, 3rd Earl of Derby, and William Downham, Bishop of Chester, contained the conditions that the incumbent and his successors should pay from their £120 a year all the costs of repairing and maintaining the chancel and hall and "all duties temporal and spiritual" that might be levied on the rectory. In other words, Sir Thomas Stanley as farmer of the rectory, and his successors and assigns, were to receive the rents, profits of mills, tithes, and other revenues free of all encumbrances except for the £120 rental charge.[18] By 1615 interest in this lease had passed to Edward Somerset, Earl of Worcester, who was holding it in trust for two of Sir Thomas Stanley's grandchildren, Petronella Stanley and Frances Fortescue née Stanley, the daughters of Sir Edward Stanley of Winwick Hall, Tonge Castle, Shrewsbury, and Eynsham, Oxfordshire. Their more famous, or notorious, sister, the celebrated beauty Venetia, did not apparently share in this bounty.[19]

Besides the revenues of the rectory there was another right which men of the day considered of material value and guarded jealously—the "advowson" or the right to present at the death or resignation of an incumbent the man who should be installed as his successor. Since the fifteenth century the Earls of Derby had possessed the advowson of Winwick and in 1595 William Stanley, the sixth Earl, had presented John Rider to this living, presumably with an understanding that he would observe the terms of the lease made in 1563. Sometime subsequently, however, Derby had also granted the advowson to the Earl of Worcester as trustee for Petronella and Frances Stanley.[20]

Horne's threat to the long-standing customs of Winwick arose from the unusual way in which the rectory became vacant in 1615. Three years before, the King had created John Rider Bishop of Killaloe.[21] Thereby, as Rider and Horne put the matter in their reply to Bold's accusations, ". . . the said advowson of the . . . parish church of Winwick . . . became void and so continued void until or about the month of September in the year of our Lord God one thousand six hundred and fifteen."[22] What they meant was that the Earl of Derby's right of presentation was for the time being suspended, for the King had by ancient ecclesiastical custom a right, which superseded all others, to present to vacancies resulting from promotions to bishoprics. Although the King's elevation of Rider voided the advowson of Winwick, Rider kept the living itself in commendam, and therefore it did not become vacant until the summer of 1615 when he resigned in favor of Horne.[23]

The decision to use this vacancy for the advantage of the Protestant cause was in keeping with a long-standing but sporadically applied policy of Church and State. The persistent loyalty of the people of the North and West to the old religion was the source of much concern to the English authorities. From Lancashire as much as from any other region the royal government had received alarming reports in the reigns of both Elizabeth I and James I. Typical of these were the ones made in the years 1590-91 to the Privy Council. Among "the manifold enormities" evident in Lancashire were the freedom with which Jesuits and seminary priests circulated among the people; the boldness they were permitted to show in offering to debate publicly about the validity of their beliefs and rituals; daily celebration of Mass, oftentimes with little attempt to conceal what was happening; secret performance of marriages and christenings without asking banns or proper registration of the rites; the frequent rebaptizing of infants already baptized according to the Book of Common Prayer; inadequate supervision of schools and schoolmasters so that many children were nurtured there in popery; disturbance of worship services in a multitude of ways but most offensively by use of private prayers, crossing, knocking of breasts, and even close handling of rosaries; observance of fasts and festivals no longer kept in the Church of England, and refusal to attend catechizings or Evensong, and the use of Roman rites in the burial of the dead.[24]

The audacity with which recusants in many parts of Lancashire carried themselves still appears in various documents of the period. In 1605, for instance, John Ashton, although denying charges that he had denounced the King's supremacy and called James I a heretic, proudly admitted before the

Quarter Sessions held at Wigan that he was "a recusant and so hath been all his lifetime." He went on to assert that his conscience would not allow him "to reform himself."[25] Another steadfast papist, Sir Alexander Barlow, boasted in his will dated April 14, 1617 that he died "a true and perfect recusant Catholic." He was buried on April 21, 1620 by torchlight in the collegiate church of Manchester.[26]

Occasionally, if pushed too hard, Lancashire recusants would use violence to resist and to intimidate their persecutors. None of these incidents was anything like a widespread concerted rising against authority, but they did involve armed men who tried to terrorize opponents by the use of physical force. At Garstang, for instance, the vicar and a guest, the Queen's preacher, were awakened on the night of August 20, 1600 by musket fire and the sound of a bullet striking the vicarage. When the vicar went to the window to investigate, the marauders shot at him. Drawing back in alarm, he sent his servant to do what he could to drive them off. That faithful man, as he left the house, drew the fire upon himself, though by good fortune was not hit. Because the assailants were firing from concealed positions, no one could see or identify any of them. Probably if they had been seen, the observer would have been little the wiser. A man who had met them on the way to the vicarage reported that they were twenty or more in number, armed with javelins, horse staves, guns, and bows and arrows. Several wore visors, and most of the others had red caps and painted faces. The vicar never learned why they had attacked him, but he felt certain they came because a pursuivant of the Bishop of Chester had that night arrested some recusants near Kirkland.[27]

Nothing can better illustrate the attitude of the community toward the disturbers of the peace than the testimony taken by the justices of the peace who made an inquiry into the attack. None of the ninety or more witnesses examined could identify any person who had assaulted the vicarage or would name anyone suspected of having done so. The answers of a trained soldier of a nearby village demonstrates the evasiveness of them all. Even though he was testifying only three weeks after the event, he could not remember where he was on the night of August 20. He asserted, however, that he had taken no part in the affair. Further, he could not say whether Stephen Sager, a goldsmith strongly suspected of being the ringleader in the outrage, had had anything to do with it. Finally, he was obviously most irregular in his religious duties, for he could not recall when he had last gone to church.[28]

By far the most widespread outburst of violence in Lancashire occurred in the spring of 1603. At the death of Elizabeth and the accession of James I Lancashire experienced "a short cessation of law and justice." Some recusants laid in a stock of arms on the chance that circumstances would make it possible for them to strike a blow for their cause. Although later investigation showed that rumor had exaggerated what had taken place, still those officials who were trying faithfully to enforce the law needed to have their commissions renewed or their authority would not have been respected.[29]

Local support for recusancy in Lancashire went far up the social ladder. All through Elizabeth's reign a large proportion of the gentry remained loyal to the old faith. In 1564, when the justices of the peace in England as a whole were split nearly evenly between those who accepted the Elizabethan settlement and those who were indifferent or opposed to it, the Lancashire justices were overwhelmingly papist: only six were reported "favorable" to the Established Church; nineteen were "unfavorable." In accounting for the religious condition of Lancashire in the 1590s, observers accused justices, bailiffs, and other officials, not of deliberately conniving to circumvent the law but of failing to do their duties. Fourteen justices, three of whom were also ecclesiastical commissioners, were still suspected at the end of Elizabeth's reign of being papists. Justices and sheriffs levied only small fines on persons outlawed for recusancy and seldom arrested them or impounded their goods. Spies in the confidence of the High Commissioners got word of any contemplated moves against recusants and warned the suspected persons so that they might avoid arrest and questioning. Persons who farmed the fines and forfeitures of recusants—i.e., who made an agreement with the government to collect these penalties—worked out very easy terms with the guilty parties.[30] Occasionally, to be sure, a family whose chief members became involved in treasonable activities of national importance, for instance, that of John Travers of Ridgate in the Babington Plot of 1586, lost heavily through fine and forfeiture. But the remarkable feature of Lancashire life was the continued well-being of persons who were bold and subtle enough to defy changes in policy and law.

In the 1590s, when England was at war with Spain, the religious condition of outlying counties like Lancashire began to cause real concern to the Queen and her council. Special commissions were issued to the president of the Council of the North, the bishop of Chester, and the Earl of Derby as lord lieutenant of Lancashire to suppress Catholic recusancy, to arrest priests, and to build up support for the government. Recusant wives of men who seemingly conformed received special attention. The resistance and unco-operative attitude of the gentry and the community at large was fully acknowledged. Late in the decade the government supplemented its repressive measures with others designed to deal with the problem in a positive way. Noting that many church livings in Lancashire were of little value because as in Winwick parish revenues had fallen into the hands of private persons and that consequently the number of competent pastors and preachers, "men of learning and credit," were too few to have any great effect on the society of Lancashire, the Queen appropriated £200 per annum out of "profits of recusants' lands" to establish stipends of £50 apiece for four preachers to strengthen the hands of the well-affected clergy of the county. The Bishop of Chester, who was allowed to appoint at his own discretion two of these missionary-preachers, also had the responsibility for assigning them to those parts of the county that had the heaviest concentrations of popish recusants.[31]

James I continued to give royal support to such efforts for overcoming the hold of Catholicism on the people of Lancashire. Before and during the Hampton Court Conference he made known his agreement with the policy of planting a preaching ministry in the strongholds of recusancy, especially in Ireland, the borders, and Lancashire. At the Conference, he promised the Puritan spokesmen, particularly Laurence Chaderton, master of Emmanuel College, Cambridge and a Lancashire man, that in order to combat the Roman adversaries in Lancashire special concessions be extended for the time being to the nonconforming Puritan clergymen of that county.[32]

But James's purposes were rarely carried out with the same firmness that he showed in propounding them. Furthermore, James's great ambition was to bring all his people into a compact of loyalty to himself. Hence he was disposed to indulge Catholic subjects who acknowledged his supremacy. Even the fear and passion aroused by the Gunpowder Plot did not inaugurate a systematic official persecution of the Catholics. James proclaimed to Parliament five days after the unveiling of the plot that he distinguished between the few fanatics who planned such devilish practices and the many Catholics who were good and loyal men.[33] Especially during Archbishop Bancroft's primacy in the Church, such ambivalence in policy and practice was not likely to produce significant effects. Bancroft, into whose hands initiative in ecclesiastical matters fell after the Hampton Court Conference, was more concerned with reducing the Puritan critics of the Church of England to uniformity than he was in converting the hinterlands to Protestantism. Therefore, despite the preaching of a small number of conscientious ministers and lecturers, few recusants were turned from their unlawful ways or dislodged from their entrenched positions.

The way in which Catholic recusants with strong local and national connections could become entrenched is well illustrated by the state of affairs of Winwick parish in 1615. Horne accused his opponents the Bolds, the churchwardens, and all their supporters of being papists.[34] An inquiry into their background largely substantiates Horne's allegations and reveals not only how they neutralized the power of the Church to convert the people to Protestantism but how they took advantage of the complex legal and economic relations of the Church to divert most of the revenues of a wealthy parish to their own use.

Thomas and Richard Bold, though they probably belonged to a cadet branch of a prominent Lancashire family, the Bolds of Bold, were little more than pawns.[35] Thomas Bold was superinstituted to Winwick parish by the Earl of Worcester as the latter made an effort to retain the advowson entrusted to him. Richard Bold was a solicitor in the service of the local magnates.[36] The real powers opposed to Horne were the Earl of Worcester, John Fortescue, his wife Frances née Stanley, and Petronella Stanley. These persons were closely related and all strongly attached to the ancient faith.

Worcester and the two Stanley sisters were first cousins once removed. Worcester's aunt, Anne Somerset, wife of Thomas Percy, 7th Earl of Northumberland, was the mother of Lucy Percy, wife of Sir Edward Stanley of Winwick, and mother of Petronella and Frances. Northumberland was the chief conspirator in the Northern Rebellion of 1569-70 and was executed at York in 1572. He died professing his loyalty to Rome. His wife, Worcester's aunt, became an exile and an intriguer among English Catholics in the Low Countries. She died in a convent at Namur and one of her daughters was prioress of a Benedictine convent for English exiles in Brussels. Her third daughter, who, with her husband Sir Edward Stanley, lived for some years at Winwick Hall, was reported in 1590 to be a popish recusant. John Fortescue, whose grandfather was Sir John Fortescue, Chancellor of the Exchequer at the end of Elizabeth's reign and Chancellor of the Duchy of Lancaster under both Elizabeth and James, belonged to a family that had reverted from the lukewarm Protestantism of an Elizabethan politique to Roman Catholicism. He had a sister who became an Augustinian canoness of an English monastery in Louvain. In 1616 he and his wife made their residence in Winwick Hall and were obviously the local representatives and custodians of the Worcester-Stanley interest in that area. Little is known about Petronella Stanley but there is no evidence to suggest that she did not share her sister's and cousin's religious convictions as well as some of their material possessions.[37]

Behind the Worcester-Stanley connection stood the weighty political, social, and economic power of the local magnate, William Stanley, 6th Earl of Derby, another of the Stanley sisters' first cousins once removed. Even though Derby's finances had been sorely strained by the settlement forced on him by his brother Ferdinando's widow and her three daughters and despite his instability of mind and erratic temperament, he was the most important landowner in the county and during the years 1607 to 1626 he also bore the King's commission as lord lieutenant of Lancashire and Cheshire. Derby and his father and grandfather before him had always been faithful royal servants and, though showing no enthusiasm for the Protestant establishment of the Church, they had never aroused suspicion as persons ill-disposed to the changes of 1559. Like many of their contemporaries, however, and perhaps more than most, they had to live with the tensions of

conflicting loyalties. The center of their power and influence lay in one of
the most conservative counties of the realm. Among their close relatives and
other dependents was a great number of persons who ardently clung to the
old faith. To promote the cause of the Pope they dared not do, but to protect
the interests of their kinsmen and followers they must do, almost as a matter
of self-preservation. Thus William, Earl of Derby, wrote in 1600 to his
wife's uncle, Sir Robert Cecil, interceding for his cousin Edward Stanley,
the father of Frances and Petronella, who had been kept waiting over two
months for a chance to answer charges brought against him before the Privy
Council. Thus he had disposed of the next presentation to Winwick rectory
to Worcester. And thus Derby's chief legal adviser, Sir Thomas Ireland,
was also the learned counsel for Worcester, Fortescue, and the Stanley sisters in their various suits at law with Horne.[38]

Local sentiment, provincial suspicion, and dislike of interlopers also of
course went hand-in-hand with the Derby connection in strengthening the
Worcester-Stanley cause. In making his complaint against Horne and his
cohorts, Bold took pains to point out that several of Horne's supporters, and
even some who were allied by marriage with Lancashire families, were outsiders and intruders from another county.[39] Likewise in pleading before the
Court of Duchy Chamber, Worcester and his associates denounced cases
begun against them by Rider and Horne as an infringement of local privileges and liberties and a contempt of the palatine system of justice.[40]

Beyond the local loyalties and interests brought into play by this incident
were influential persons and factions at the royal court itself. Behind the
Bolds, the Fortescues and the Stanleys stood Edward Somerset, Earl of
Worcester, Privy Councillor since Elizabeth's reign, commissioner for the
Treasury since the Earl of Salisbury's death, and Lord Privy Seal by royal
appointment dated January 2, 1616. On Horne's side was George Abbot,
Archbishop of Canterbury, who had succeeded Bancroft and who brought
to his position a strong anti-Catholic sentiment and a reputation for sympa-
thizing with the Puritan cause. Worcester and Archbishop Abbot were antagonists in much more than this comparatively obscure struggle. They belonged to two factions of the Privy Council that were contending for influence with the King and pre-eminence within the government. Abbot was a
leader of the anti-Spanish Protestant faction and Worcester was an ally of
the Howards and a staunch supporter of their policies for an alliance with
Spain and an indulgence for the King's Roman Catholic subjects. Worcester
himself was a Catholic, though he had of course always shown himself steadfast in his allegiance to Elizabeth and James.

In early 1616, at the time of Horne's arrival in Winwick, Abbot and his
anti-Spanish Protestant party were anticipating the sweet taste of victory.

Henry Howard, Earl of Northampton, the craftiest of their opponents, was dead. Although his brother Thomas, Earl of Suffolk, had been made Lord Treasurer, the whole structure of Howard influence was tottering. Nearly a year earlier George Villiers, the handsome young man whom Abbot himself had helped introduce at court, had become a gentleman of the bedchamber, despite the jealousy of the reigning favorite, Robert Carr, Earl of Somerset, a member of the Howard faction. Somerset himself and his notorious wife, Lady Frances Howard, were in fact in disgrace and were standing trial for the poisoning of Sir Thomas Overbury in the Tower. To cap the whole situation the negotiations for a marriage treaty with Spain were floundering and James in impatience had agreed to release Sir Walter Raleigh from the Tower to make a diversionary, if not threatening, move in the Caribbean. It was at such a conjunction of circumstances, unfavorable to the pro-Spanish and pro-Catholic faction, that Bishop John Rider decided to resign his Winwick benefice in favor of Josiah Horne.

It hardly seems possible that it was only coincidence that the machinery of Church and State was engaged in the effort to induct Horne as rector of Winwick parish. It is also of exceptional interest to note that the Archbishop of Canterbury and an Irish bishop had selected a deprived Puritan vicar of Orwell, Cambridgeshire, as their preferred candidate for this position. Despite all the anti-Puritanism of Bancroft's system, all the equivocations of James I's foreign and religious policies, and the rising influence of a new theological position among some of the intellectual leaders who would later support William Laud, Church and State in the second decade of the century still had need of the ardor, dedication, and capacity for self-sacrifice of the moderate Puritans. On the other hand, Puritans such as Horne could in serving the Church still see opportunities to spread their attitudes and ideals and bring about a right reformed church in England.

As events developed between April, 1616, and Horne's death in 1626, the situation in Winwick required all the dogged determination and disregard for personal ease that a dedicated Puritan could muster. To stay the course he had to have courage, some personal charm to win a few supporters in the local community, and the patience to seek a settlement through the tortuous course of a multitude of legal actions. In the ten years that remained to Josiah Horne he fought at least eleven cases at law in King's Bench, Duchy Chamber, the Assize Courts, and Star Chamber.[41]

The most important of these cases were the ones tried in Duchy Chamber and the Lancashire Assizes, for these were the ones that decided the validity of Horne's title to Winwick parish and its revenues. Bold's claim to Winwick was called into question by the Attorney-General's Bill of Information and found defective because of simony by a judgment in the Court of High Commission.[42] Such impeachments of an opponent's claim did not, however, establish the legality of Horne's. Only long, drawn out litigation finally settled the issue.

The lengthy series of legal disputes began with the suit brought in Duchy Chamber by Worcester, the Fortescues and Petronella Stanley. An injunction awarded to these plaintiffs ordered Rider and Horne to stay their suit in King's Bench and not to bring any other action concerning Winwick rectory in that or any other court until the cause could be heard in Duchy Chamber.[43] On May 7, after hearing legal arguments by counsel for both parties, the judge concluded that the case should be tried in Duchy Chamber, yet granted Horne permission to take possession of one field of the glebe twenty days before the next assizes. He should, if he chose to pursue that course of action, then notify Bold of his deed. The latter was immediately to bring "an action of trespass against the said Horne at the next assizes at Lancaster . . . who shall plead therein that the said close is his freehold whereunto the plaintiff shall reply that it is his freehold, ... And that neither of them shall therein take any advantage that the rectory is in lease neither shall the said lease be given in evidence or the validity thereof come in question in that action, but both parties to stand upon the lawfulness of their incumbencies and inductions."[44]

Needless to say Horne declined this means of settling the dispute between him and his opponents. Not only did it exclude from controversy the important issues of the lease but it presumed that Bold had a claim to the living and gave him whatever advantage might arise from his appearing before a local jury as an aggrieved party. By this date Horne had already received the support of the Attorney-General in exhibiting a bill against Bold in Star Chamber and had hopes that the Court of High Commission would find Bold's superinstitution invalid under any circumstances. Hence, instead of joining in a collusive action at the assizes, he brought on June 14, a counter-suit in Duchy Chamber against Worcester and his allies.[45] Three days later his legal counsel, a Mr. Crewe, probably either Randolph or Thomas Crewe, submitted a double-headed motion to the Court. First, reciting the facts that Horne had entered a sufficient answer to his opponents' bill and that Bold had been deprived of Winwick parsonage because of a simoniacal agreement made for his presentation, he asked that the injunction be dissolved. Next he wanted a commission immediately granted to authorize examiners to take depositions of witnesses in both the suit and countersuit.[46] The Court, upon hearing arguments on this motion two days later, refused to lift the injunction but agreed to join the two cases as one and sent out a writ of *dedimus potestatem* requiring four examiners to take depositions and return them to the Court by the next Michaelmas term.[47]

Although all of the depositions, after several delays, were submitted before the end of Michaelmas term, 1616, the final hearings could not conveniently be held during that term. They were therefore postponed until Thursday, January 30, in the next or Hilary term.[48] When the opposing arguments were finally presented, they took two full court days because of "the length and many points in the . . . cause."[49] Indeed so complex and difficult were these questions that the Duchy Chamber finally decided that "the same causes are more fit to receive trial at the common law than in this court." It was therefore ordered that the case "be referred to a trial at the common law and the whole matter to be found by special verdict by action to be brought by the said Josiah Horne . . . against all or some of the plaintiffs in the first bill . . . before the justices of assize at Lancaster at the next assizes . . . whereunto they shall appear gratis and plead without delay and confess entre and oustre so as the same may receive trial at the next assizes. And as the verdict and judgment shall pass so the possession shall be established by this Court." Meanwhile Worcester and his allies were to continue to enjoy the profits of the rectory, though they were required to give security to cover "the mean profits of the said parsonage to the said Josiah Horne, if judgment fall out for the said Josiah Horne . . ., and they were to pay Horne the back rent due on the lease of the rectory."[50] A supplementary order of the Court, made on February 12, directed the sheriff of Lancaster to draw up a list of 48 names of freeholders, "not allied nor tenants to the earl of Derby nor the plaintiffs, from which the judges of assize might pick an indifferent jury . . . for finding of the special verdict."[51]

The "law's delay" kept this special case from coming to a decision in the next assizes. It did not in fact come to a judgment until Michaelmas term in 1618, more than eighteen months later. In the end, however, the verdict rewarded Horne's patience.

As it was argued, the case turned on two points: first whether Thomas Stanley, bishop of Sodor and Man, was the lawful incumbent of Winwick parish when in 1563 he leased the rectory for 99 years and secondly whether Josiah Horne was a good incumbent who had the right to bring suit for trespass. On both issues judgment was given in Horne's favor. Stanley was found to have been no incumbent for several reasons, but chiefly because he had before 1563 accepted a second living with cure of souls without procuring a sufficient dispensation from the provisions of a Henrician statute against pluralism. Horne was judged to be a good incumbent because Rider had resigned to him and because Bold had secured his presentation through a simoniacal agreement to continue the lease. "Thus," the report concluded, "the lease is void [and] Mr. Horne is a good incumbent at least to bring the action, and if the lease be void, the plaintiff is first in possession. And so the court was of that opinion and accordingly gave judgment for the plaintiff."[52]

In that litigious and quarrelsome age victory in one legal battle—even though a major one—did not end the war. Horne's adversaries were irrepressible. Before this verdict was made in Horne's favor, they had already begun another suit. That too, when it was submitted to the arbitration of Justice Finch and Baron Denham, resulted in February, 1620, in a settlement upholding Horne's title to the Winwick parish but not awarding him all its revenues.[53] Undismayed, they continued through the rest of Horne's life to trouble his ministry. In 1620 they made a second unsuccessful attempt to present and superinstitute another man to this living, this time John Mere, canon of Chester. And finally they attempted in the years 1621 to 1623 to have Horne deprived. For this purpose they found a willing tool in John Gee, curate of Newton in Makersfield, then a chapel-of-ease in Winwick parish. This man was, according to his later confession, at that time "warping toward the popish side and infected with that sour sharp and cruel leaven."[54] Horne, in suing Gee and his confederates, among whom the chief persons were John Fortescue and Lady Frances his wife, Petronella Stanley, Roger Bradshaw, John Ince, and Thomas Dakin, charged that they sought to slander him so that he would be deprived and so that Gee, who was pledged to authorize the farm of the parsonage at the old rate, might be put in his place. They circulated their libelous statements in the form of articles for exhibition against Horne in the Court of High Commission.[55]

Both Horne's continuing favor with the ecclesiastical authorities and fate worked in combination to save him one last time from his enemies. In 1623 Gee rather than Horne ran afoul of High Commission. On April 23 of that year he was fined £10 for contempt of that court, perhaps because he failed to make an appearance upon a summons issued at the request of Horne. Five months later, on October 26, Gee, who had by this time become a convert to Rome, was present at the "Fatal Vespers" in Blackfriars when the collapse of a floor plunged most of a Jesuit preacher's auditors to their death. While still in shock from this tragedy, Gee came into the hands of Archbishop Abbot and his chaplains Goad and Featly. Under their ministrations, he renounced his conversion to Rome and returned to the Church of England. To prove the sincerity of his recantation he wrote *The Foot out of the Snare, with a Detection of Sundry Late Practices and Impostures of the Priests and Jesuits in England* (1624). The fourth edition of this popular tract, also published in 1624, contains an acknowledgment of, and an apology for, the wrong which he had inflicted on Horne. It opens with these words:

I must needs do public right unto one whom I have publicly wronged,
I mean my neighbor minister, *Master Josiah Horne, Parson of
Winwick in Lancashire*: at whose great danger, if not ruin, I cannot
deny, but that I was induced to aim, by suggested surmises and

groundless criminations. I will not seek to shift off my fault, and lay it on those of the popish faction, who were my inciters, abettors, or confederates; though some of them know, and cannot (without double dealing) deny, that they offered both the proof of the crimination, and price of my charges, for his conviction in those heavy and unjust articles which I exhibited and pursued against him. /56/

In the spring of 1626 death released Horne from the anxieties and troubles that had been his lot in Lancashire. His triumphs over his opponents did not, however, immediately guarantee a peaceful incumbency for his successor, Charles Herle. Horne's widow, who was in possession of Winwick Hall at his death, was immediately served with an order from the Court of Duchy Chamber to restore that property to the Earl of Worcester, the Fortescues and Petronella Stanley. Instead, she surrendered it to Herle, who was presented on June 26. He apparently managed to get the injunction dissolved and then came to a compromise settlement with the Stanley interests. For the remaining period of the lease, i.e., for approximately thirty-five years, the revenues of the rectory were to be administered by trustees. Herle as rector would receive from them an annual stipend of £225 and the remainder, estimated to be approximately £500 would go to the other claimants, the heirs of Sir Thomas Stanley.[57]

It is ironic that Horne's struggle came to an end just as William Laud was beginning to rise to an ascendancy that would aim at the final eradication from the Church of England of Puritans like the beleaguered rector of Winwick. Yet the accomplishments of Horne in Lancashire, achieved despite the entrenched interests and loyalties of a close-knit society, helped assure that Laud's efforts would not be crowned with complete success. Horne's staunch and steadfast defense of his rights guaranteed in large measure that a Puritan would succeed him. Furthermore in the midst of his legal battles, he found time to carry out his calling and was reputed to be "a learned preacher and bountiful housekeeper."[58] He also set up a monthly exercise or prophesying at which assembled ministers of Puritan disposition exhorted one another and took counsel together.[59] In all he did, he and his cause were fortunate that in the middle of the second decade of the seventeenth century divisions in the Privy Council made it possible for the sympathetic support of Archbishop Abbot to enlist the force of Church and State on his side.

NOTES

1. Victoria County History, *Lancaster*, vol. 4, 123, 126; Sir S. Glynne, *Churches of Lancashire*, Chetham Society, vol. 27, 91; Edward Baines, *History of the County Palatine and Duchy of Lancaster* (London, 1936), vol. 3, 629 ff.
2. Mark H. Curtis, "William Jones: Puritan Printer and Propagandist," *The Library*, Fifth Series, vol. 19 (1964), 59; Albert Venn, *Alumni Cantabrigiensis*, (Cambridge, Eng., 1922).
3. P[ublic]. R[ecord]. O[ffice]., St[ar]. Ch[amber]. Proc[eedings]. 8/53/3, Complaint of Thomas Bould [Bold] vs. Josiah Horne, *et al.*, fol. 2.
4. P.R.O., St. Ch. Proc. 8/53/3, Answer of Horne, *et al.* to Complaint of Bold, fol. 1; P.R.O., St. Ch. Proc. 8/21/8, Bill of Information of Sir Francis Bacon, Attorney General vs. Thomas Bold, *et al.*, fol. 3.
5. *Ibid.*; P.R.O., St. Ch. Proc. 8/53/3, fol. 1.
6. *Ibid.*
7. P.R.O., St. Ch. Proc. 8/21/8, fol. 3; St. Ch. Proc. 8/53/3, fol. 1.
8. The mother of Henry Stanley, the confederate of Thomas Bold and the illegitimate son of Henry Stanley, 4th Earl of Derby, was Joan Halsall of Knowsley. By a will dated April 27, 1594, Edward Halsall of Halsall gave "to my godson Master Henry Stanley . . . one angel of gold." This will also contains the following words: "First I commit myself wholly to the mercy of Almighty God by whose grace I trust to die a member of his Catholic church." G. J. Piccope, ed., *Lancashire and Cheshire Wills and Inventories. . . , Second Portion*, Chetham Society, vol. 51 (1860), 216-7.
9. P. R. O. St. Ch. Proc. 8/21/8, fol. 3 and 8/53/3, fol. 1.
10. Bishop John Rider and Josiah Horne had sometime before February, 1616, brought suit in the County of Middlesex in the Court of King's Bench against a retainer of Worcester and the Fortescues for trespass. It was alledged that this individual had committed trespass by harvesting grain that belonged to the rectory of Winwick. Obviously, Rider and Horne, in defiance of the lease of the rectory, were claiming this for themselves as rightful incumbents. This "action of trespass" in King's Bench is referred to in a case brought in the Court of Duchy Chamber by the Earl of Worcester and the Fortescues. P.R.O., D.[uchy of] L.[ancaster] 5, vol. 27, 510-1; 522-3.
11. P.R.O., St. Ch. Proc. 8/21/8, fol. 1.
12. *Ibid.*
13. Sir Walter Henry Frank and Sir Robert Phillimore, *The Ecclesiastical Law of the Church of England*, 2nd ed., vol. 1, (London, 1895), 357.
14. P.R.O., St. Ch. Proc. 8/53/3, fol. 2.
15. P.R.O., St. Ch. Proc. 8/21/8, fol. 3.
16. C[alendar]. [of] S[tate]. P[apers]. D[omestic]., James I, 1611-1618, 372.
17. *Valor Ecclesiasticus, Henry VII*, vol. 5, 220; *Lancashire and Cheshire Church Surveys*, 1649-1655, ed. Henry Fishwick, *The Record Society* for . . . *Lancashire and Cheshire*, 1879, Part I, 46. In the nineteenth century, before the parish was divided, the revenues were said to be worth £7,000 and Winwick was described as the richest parish living in England.
18. Brit[ish]. Lib[rary]., Harl[eian]. MS 738, fol. 83 ff.; Bodl[eian]. Libr[ary]., Coll[egium]. Exon[iencis]. MS 150, fol. 1; Victoria County History, *Lancashire*, vol. 4 127-8 n.

19. Bodl. Libr., Coll. Exon. MS 150, fol. 1.
20. *Ibid.*
21. Sir F. Maurice Powicke and E. B. Fryde, eds., *Handbook of British Chronology*, 2nd ed. (London, 1961), 366.
22. P.R.O., St. Ch. Proc. 8/53/3, fol. 1; Bodl. Libr., Coll. Exon. MS 150, fol. 1.
23. On August 11, 1615, Bishop Rider renounced his commendam before a Master of Chancery and on August 30, 1615, when this renunciation was enrolled in Chancery, he strongly supported the King's presentation of Horne with these words: "I am willing to resign to Josiah Horne." Bodl. Libr., Coll. Exon. MS 150, fol. 1.
24. C.S.P.D., Eliz. I, 1591-1594, 158-9; F. R. Raines, ed., "A Description of the State, Civil and Ecclesiastical, of the County of Lancaster about the Year 1590," *Chetham Miscellanies V*, Chetham Society, vol. 96, (1875), 1-48.
25. James Tait, ed., *Lancashire Quarter Sessions Rolls*, Chetham Society, New Series, vol. 77, 282-3.
26. Thomas William King, ed., *Lancashire Funeral Certificates*, (Chetham Society, vol. 75, 1869), 46.
27. C.S.P.D., Eliz. I, 1598-1601, 466.
28. *Ibid.*, 467.
29. Letter from the Bishop of Chester to Sir Robert Cecil, May 16, 1603, H[istorical]. M[anuscript]. C[ommission]. R[eports]., Salisbury MSS, vol. 15, 92-3.
30. C.S.P.D., Eliz. I, 1591-94, 158-9 and 288; C.S.P.D., Eliz. I, 1598-1601, 7, 15.
31. *Ibid.*, 153; letters of the Bishop of Chester to Sir Robert Cecil, March 6, 1599 and February 20, 1600, H.M.C.R., Salisbury MSS, vol. 9, 91-2 and vol. 10, 41.
32. "Anonymous Account of Hampton Court Conference" in R. G. Usher, *The Reconstruction of the English Church*, London and New York, 1910, vol. 2, 353; William Barlow, *The Summe and Substance of the Conference*, 1604, repr. in Edw. Cardwell, *A History of Conferences . . .* , (Oxford, 1849), 210-11; "A memoriall of some principall matters . . . concerning an order to be taken in some causes ecclesiasticall, Ianuar. 18, 1603," P.R.O., S[tate]. P[apers]. 14/6/19; cf. S. P. 14/6/18, 20 and Brit. Mus., MS Cott. Cleo. F. II, fols. 120-120v.
33. David H. Willson, *James VI and I.* (New York, 1956), 226.
34. P.R.O., St. Ch. Proc. 8/53/3, fol. 1.
35. I have been unsuccessful in identifying Thomas and Richard Bold. They are described as brothers in Star Chamber Proceedings, P.R.O., St. Ch. Proc. 8/53/8 and 8/21/8, but none of the Bolds of Bold had two sons bearing these names, although a son with one or the other of them frequently appears. There were several other Bold families in Lancashire who had sons with these names who attended Oxford or one of the Inns of Court.
36. P.R.O., St. Ch. Proc. 8/21/8, fol. 1.
37. D[ictionary]. [of] N[ational]. B[iography].; C.S.P.D., James I, 1603-1610, 6; *Calendar of Commissions for Compounding*, vol. 4, 2539; Edward Baines, *History of Lancashire*, 4 vols., (London, 1836), vol. 4, 10-11; Thomas Fortescue, Lord Clermont, *A History of the Family of Fortescue*, (London, 1869).
38. D.N.B.; H.M.C.R., Salisbury MSS, vol. 5, 305; vol. 10, 246; vol. 17, 198;

G. J. Piccope, ed., *Lancashire and Cheshire Wills and Inventories from the Ecclesiastical Court Cheshire, Second Portion*, Chetham Society, vol. 51, 216-7.

39. P.R.O., St. Ch. Proc. 8/21/8, fol. 2.

40. P.R.O., D.L. 5, vol. 27, 510-11.

41. Listed in Chronological order, the cases were:

    (a) On or before January, 1616. King's Bench. Rider and Horne vs. A servant of Worcester, John and Frances Fortescue, and Petronella Stanley. Issue: Ownership of tithe corn in Winwick Parish. Cited in P.R.O., D.L. 5, vol. 27, 510-11.

    (b) January, 1616. Duchy Chamber. Worcester, *et al.* vs. Rider and Horne. Issue: Injunction to stay the suit in King's Bench and to bring the case before Duchy Chamber with the defendants in the King's Bench case becoming the plaintiffs in Duchy Chamber. P.R.O., D.L. 5, col. 27, 510-11, 522-3, 556, 567, 577, 591, 642-3, 654-5, 662, 664, 677, 688, 705, 718, 762, 770-1, 779, 790, and 796.

    (c) April 25, 1616. Star Chamber. Thomas Bold vs. Josiah Horne, *et al.* Issue: Conspiracy, armed riot, and disturbances of divine service. P.R.O., St. Ch. Proc. 8/53/3.

    (d) May 6, 1616. Star Chamber, Attorney-General vs. Thomas Bold, *et al.* Issue: Assault and violent resistance to lawful authority. P.R.O., St. Ch. Proc. 5/21/8.

    (e) Before June 6, 1616. Court of High Commission for Ecclesiastical Causes (?). Horne vs. Thomas Bold. Issue: Simony in procuring presentment to Winwick rectory, C.S.P.D., Jas. I, 1611-1618, 372.

    (f) June 14, 1616. Duchy Chamber. Horne and Rider vs. Worcester, *et al.* Issue: Counter-suit to have injunction that was granted in case (b) voided. P.R.O., D.L. 5, vol. 27, 625.

        (1) June 19, 1616. Duchy Chamber. An order was issued to merge this case with case (b) P.R.O., D.L. 5, vol. XXVII, 654-5.

    (g) Lent, 1617. Assizes at Lancaster. Horne vs. John Fortescue, *et al.* Issue: Trespass on the case involving title to the glebe of Winwick parish. This case came about because the judge in Duchy Chamber found that the causes in question between the two parties "are more fit to receive trial at the Common Law than in this Court" and ordered Horne to bring action against some or all of his opponents at the next Assizes. Reports of this case are in Bodl. Libr., Coll. Exon. MS 150, fols. 1-43 and Brit. Lib., Harl. MS 738, fols. 83-132v.

    (h) July 9, 1622. Star Chamber. Horne vs. Thomas Dakin, *et al.* Issue: Libel. P.R.O., St. Ch. Proc. 8/175/18.

    (i) 1623. High Commission. Josiah Horne [?] vs. John Gee. Issue: Catholic Recusancy. P.R.O. Exch. K.R. Eccl. Docs. E 135/13/4, fol. 105.

    (j) December 10, 1623. Star Chamber. Horne vs. John Gee, John Fortescue and his wife Frances, Petronella Stanley, *et al.* Issue: Libel and multiplication of vexatious suits. P.R.O., St. Ch. Proc. 8/175/19.

    (k) November 4, 1624. Star Chamber. Horne vs. John Bretherton of Hey Hall, Lancashire, *et al.* Issue: Forcible trespass and assault. P.R.O., St. Ch. Proc. 8/175/20.

42. P.R.O., St. Ch. Proc. 8/21/8, fol. 3; C.S.P.D., Jas. I, 1611-1618, 372.

43. P.R.O., D.L. 5, vol. 27, 522-3

44. *Ibid.*, 577.
45. *Ibid.*, 625.
46. *Ibid.*, 629.
47. *Ibid.*, 642-3 and 654-5.
48. *Ibid.*, 718.
49. *Ibid.*, 762.
50. *Ibid.*, 770-1.
51. *Ibid.*, 796.
52. Bodl. Libr., Coll. Exon. MS 150, fols. 1-43; Brit. Lib., Harl. MS 738, fols. 83-132v.
53. The arbiters decided that during Horne's lifetime "the capital messuage and manor of Winwick with other parts of the rectory should remain to him and the rest of the benefice to the Earl of Worcester, Sir John and Dame Frances Fortescue, and Petronella Stanley. . . ." William Beaumont, *Winwick: Its History and Antiquities*, Warrington, 2nd ed. (1878), 37.
54. P.R.O., St. Ch. Proc. 8/175/19, fol. 6.
55. *Ibid.*, fol. 7.
56. John Gee, *The Foot out of the Snare*, 4th ed. (1624), 95.
57. Beaumont, *Winwick*, 40-1.
58. P.R.O., St. Ch. Proc. 8/175/19, fol. 6.
59. John Ley, *Defensive Doubts, Hopes and Reasons for Refusall of the Oath, imposed by the Sixth Canon of the Late Synod*, 1641, sig. A4; Beaumont identifies the location for this meeting, designated in the text only by the letter W, as Winwick. Beaumont, *Winwick*, 42.

The Idea of Liberty in the Theological Writings of Sir Henry Vane the Younger

J. MAX PATRICK

The University of Wisconsin-Milwaukee

IF THE POLITICAL and other secular papers of Sir Henry Vane the Younger were extant, historians' accounts of the Puritan Revolution would be far fuller and more accurate than they are. For he was a major figure in the events of his times: Governor of Massachusetts in 1636 at the age of 23, one of the chief leaders of the Long Parliament from 1640 to 1653 and again when it was revived in 1659, an energetic member of the Commonwealth Councils of State in 1649-53, and, in the 1650s, an active opponent both of the Protectorate and of restoring the monarchy. In various capacities he exacerbated the Antinomian Controversy in America, contributed to the impeachment of Strafford, strongly supported the Root and Branch Bill, helped to prosecute Laud, sat as a lay member of the Westminster Assembly, promoted the Solemn League and Covenant, abstained from politics during the period of the regicide but returned to Parliament and the Council of State after it, consistently worked for religious toleration and the separation of church and state, and objected to Cromwell's dissolution of the Long Parliament as "dishonest" and "immoral." Vane declined a seat in the Little Parliament, conspired against the Protectorate, was arbitrarily imprisoned by Cromwell, emerged after his death as leader of the Republican party, compromised with the army, and fiercely opposed the Restoration. In the 1660s he was imprisoned, excepted from the Bill of Indemnity, tried for treason, and sentenced to death despite both houses of Parliament's petition that he be spared.

From his public career and the surviving documents, his main positions on liberty are clear. He advocated a complete separation of church and state, and insisted that neither of them had any rightful authority over indi-

100

vidual spiritual freedom. Accordingly, he opposed religious tyranny whether exercised by Episcopacy or Presbyterianism, arguing that no government, whether ecclesiastical or political, could deny individual freedom of conscience and remain consistent with God's providence. For he saw the guidance of God in the events of the Puritan Revolution. These events pointed to a government based on Christian principles, one which would tolerate all religions and work for the glory of God rather than the worldly self-interests of men. Toleration was essential because men were at different stages of spiritual development: what one suppressed might be a higher stage than what one has yet achieved. Moreover, men need a climate of freedom in order to realize what is right for them and to discover God's plan for human government, a plan that is innate in the natural order of things. This they will do best by means of free debate, whereby they will arrive at laws by common consent, agreeing and associating with others who likewise renounce private interests for public welfare and who surrender to the group thus constituted government over the outward man.[1]

Though this much has been reasonably clear to students of Vane, his theological works, *The Retired Man's Meditations* (1655), *Two Treatises* (1661), and *A Pilgrimage into the Land of Promise* (1664) have generally eluded understanding both by his contemporaries and historians. Bishop Gilbert Burnet confessed that he "could never reach their meaning";[2] the Reverend Richard Baxter found them "cloudily formed";[3] Edward Hyde, earl of Clarendon, declared that Vane's religious inspiration "corrupted his reason";[4] and even Vane's disciple and earliest biographer, George Sikes complained that "'tis past the skill of human nature to interpret him."[5] Modern biographers have had the same difficulty. James E. Hosmer calls Vane's theology "confusion thrice over";[6] William W. Ireland states that "in reading Vane's theological writings, one believes that there is a meaning, yet it escapes";[7] and John Willcock refers to them as "the aberration of a great mind."[8] And in 1941 when I wrote to Lord Barnard, the twentieth-century descendant of Henry Vane, to enquire if any manuscripts had survived, and mentioned that I was investigating Vane's religious thought, he replied that there were no manuscripts and that, in any case, "his theology simply does not make sense."

It is not my purpose here to attempt to clarify all of Vane's intricacies but to elucidate his concept of true liberty. Behind it is the distinction between natural and supernatural which was a postulate of most seventeenth-century thinkers.[9] On the level of nature are natural law in science and ethics, natural religion as it exists among those to whom the Judaeo-Christian revelations are unavailable, natural philosophy—including the teachings of Plato and Aristotle—and natural institutions such as the state. Such is the world of paganism and non-Hebraic, non-Christian humanism. In the realm of the supernatural, known to theologians as the level of grace, are the revealed truths that derive from God: divine law, theological truths, divinely revealed ethics, divine philosophy (divinity), and the divinely ordained institution of the Church.

In Vane's thought Adam was created in a state of nature, subject to natural law—that is to the law of God inherent in man's own nature and in the whole creation.[10] In this condition Adam's liberty was limited and precarious: he was free either to persist in natural righteousness, using his natural faculties of reason and conscience, or he could disobey the law of God within him and yield to his equally natural impulse "to direct his own steps."[11] But a third choice was open to him. Spiritual or supernatural truths were not directly revealed to him: that would be impossible in a state of nature. However, the means of his reaching to the level of grace were indicated to him in various typifications.[12] For example, the Forbidden Fruit was, among other things, a type. If Adam, using his natural reason, meditated on the fact that the fruit tempted him and the fact that he had a capacity for hardening his nature so that he could disobey the law of God, he would have to come to the conclusion that his freedom was risky. Sooner or later he would probably weaken of his own free choice, freely rejecting the dictates of God and his own reason. Adam's meditating could thus have led him to give up his mutable natural freedom and natural righteousness. If he made the reasonable choice, he would surrender his natural freedom and subordinate his will to that of God.

By this renunciation of self-will and mutable natural freedom, Adam would move into the realm of the supernatural, the level of grace and spirit. He would no longer be in a state of nature. Moreover, he would gain that perfect immutable freedom which God, Christ, and the elect angels enjoy. For God, though possessed of perfect freedom, "cannot but will good, as of his own nature bound up to it." "Such freedom does import a powerful binding up and restraining of the mind from all possibility of doing evil . . . and as powerful a bent . . . to do what is good."[13] God could have given man such a fixed nature, incapable of evil; but he would not bind his servants immutably to their duty without their own consent.[14]

In other words, for Vane, true freedom meant the attainment of a condition in which one would not want to make anything but the best choice: a man is truly free only when he has freely given up his capacity for making wrong choices. The means thereto is willing subordination to the will of God.

All this is perhaps more easily understood today if it is translated into secular terms. When we say that John has "character" and is "dependable," we mean that his behavior and choices in particular situations are predictable: we can count on him to tell the truth, to carry a job to completion without supervision, or the like. But this does not mean that John is a robot or lacks freedom. It merely means that in the past he has freely made certain choices between good and evil, or practical and impractical, and has made these permanent decisions. He has freely conditioned his character. He still chooses between good and evil, practical and impractical, but does so in accordance with his past experience and decisions. He has, as it were, fixed himself in righteousness and practicality. And what I have here called "character" is what in the seventeenth-century Milton called "virtue"—not the untested kind of inexperienced innocence that he termed a "cloistered virtue," but the achieved power or *virtus* of an inner strength built up from past experience and choices. The virtuous man is he who has learned from past mistakes and sound decisions what is right and who has freely fixed his nature so that, almost automatically, he chooses what is right and reasonable. And, to return to Vane, what is right and reasonable *IS* the will of God.

Vane gives further development to this insight in theological terms. He notes that Adam mistakenly preferred to "direct his own steps" and disobeyed the law of God that was inherent in his nature and in the whole creation. Then the Word or Second Person of the Trinity descended to the level of nature, was sacrificed, and satisfied God's justice, whereupon "common salvation" was extended to all mankind; i.e. men were restored, though in varying degrees, to their primitive, mutable, natural righteousness.[15]

To some men God gave the Holy Scriptures, first the Old Testament, then the New. These writings made the original threefold choice more explicit: disobey and be damned; or persist in mere natural righteousness and its precarious, dangerous freedom; or resign natural righteousness and freedom and become a willing servant of God, thereby rising to the level of grace. The law of God as laid down in *both* the Old and the New testaments was, in Vane's view, still essentially that same natural law except that it was made more explicit by them.[16] Men who obeyed the letter of the New Testament often thought that they were rising to the level of grace and attaining the immutable higher freedom. But they were mistaken: their delusion was that restored natural righteousness was the attainment of immutable salvation. They were still in a state of nature—acceptable to God and therefore not to be condemned or persecuted—but still in a dangerous and mutable state of natural freedom. To move beyond that state they had to rise above adherence to the letter of the New Testament.[17]

It will be remembered that typifications were available to pre-fall Adam indicating to him that he could reach the level of grace by making the third choice—resigning his natural liberty and freely subordinating his will to the will of God. The Old Testament more explicitly indicated to men this means of reaching the level of grace; and the New Testament made the means clearer still. But the process was the same: to gain the level of grace and knowledge of the Father which is the journey's end of a Christian, a man must resign his natural will and freedom and become a willing servant of God.[18] In other words, such a man must repudiate the level of nature; and he must depart from naturalistic or legalistic interpretation of the Bible, searching for its higher significances.

It is a standard doctrine of Christianity that God accommodated the Bible to human intellects. Since men's understandings and vocabulary are limited, He fitted or simplified His great truths so that they could be, in some measure at least, apprehended by imperfect man on a level of nature. As Milton remarked in his *Christian Doctrine*: ". . . he has brought himself down to our level expressly to prevent our being carried beyond the reach of human comprehension, and outside the written authority of scripture, into vague subtleties of speculation."[19] However, Vane's position was closer in this matter to that of Erasmus, who praised those interpreters of Scriptures "who depart as far as possible from literal meaning."[20] For him and for Vane, incompleteness and obscurity in biblical passages did not mark limits to legitimate speculation but were the means to additional light. Allegorical, typical, mystical, and spiritual interpretations based on such passages were God's means to progressive revelation. They were ladders up from the level of nature to the sublime level of supernatural grace. This was the significance of the title of Vane's last major work, *A Pilgrimage into the Land of Promise by the Light of the Vision of Jacob's Ladder and Faith, or a Serious Prospect into Life Eternal.*

How is one to know when such interpretations are true? Vane's answer is paradoxically simple yet characteristic of the complexity of his thought. He saw the triplicity of the Trinity patterned throughout the universe. It was present in the threefold choice and was as reiterant throughout nature as quincunxes were for Sir Thomas Browne. Even Vane's Trinity, like Peter Sterry's, consisted of three persons, each of whom mirrored the triplicity of their unity. Similarly there were three sources of truth: the inner voice is the first; Scriptures are the second. Neither of these is valid unless the one confirms the other. But when such a confirmation takes place, the two sources fuse to become a new source of truth. Their impact extends meaning into mystical significance and new insights.[21] Again the line between natural and supernatural has been crossed; for such a mystical experience is on the level of grace.

Vane would have said that Milton in *Christian Doctrine* was righteous in strict obedience to the "plaine Text" of Scripture but had not yet reached the higher truth. When Milton wrote that treatise he had but the "form of knowledge and truth in the letter and written word." The letter *testified* to the coming of Christ; but it was not Christ.[22] In *Christian Doctrine*, Milton was mistaking the testimony for reality.

It was against such legalisms that Vane had struggled when he was Governor of Massachusetts in 1636. There he agreed with Mrs. Hutchinson that the preachers Cotton and Wheelwright were under the covenant of grace; but the other preachers, such as Hugh Peters, were under a covenant of works: they were hardened legalists who mistook common salvation—the restoration of man to primitive righteousness after the Fall—for immutable or final salvation. Similarly one reason for Vane's opposition to Cromwell, from 1653 on, was that, in his opinion, Cromwell had hardened into mere legal righteousness.

According to Vane those who decide to resign their natural will and freedom and thus to fulfill the command of the gospel (whether typified in nature, or made more explicit in the Bible, or apprehended directly when a fusion of Scriptures and the inner voice enables an immediate mystical apprehension of the gospel command) become absolute servants of God; for this decision means that they have to sacrifice everything, scorning all worldly and fleshly goods, allowing their bodies to be sacrificed and their natural wills to be crucified.[23]

The Word Incarnate went through this process. However, the sacrifice of Jesus upon the Cross was but a particular instance on the level of nature of a process that is eternal. For Vane subscribes to the doctrine of the perpetual sacrifice of the Logos: it takes place from the beginning; it still continues; and, on the level of nature, it is known specifically to human beings not only in the sacrifice of Christ but in the martyrdoms of many saintly persons.[24] According to George Sikes' biography of Vane, it took place in Vane himself.[25] For Vane willingly chose to die a martyr's death along with the regicides: he could almost certainly have obtained a pardon had he sought it. As it turned out historically, his was the cruelest martyrdom of all—the emptiness of a man's suffering bravely for a cause that was dying with him, and of being hanged, drawn, and quartered for religious beliefs that baffled even his own followers.

He believed that the pattern for the sacrifice of self was given by the crucifixion of the Word.[26] Man's own sacrifice allows him to obtain the benefit of the sacrifice of the Word and enables him to quit his fleshly self—the level of nature and the law—and to be received into the spirit of the Word. There, on the level of grace, he attains conjunction of spirit with God; and in that conjunction there is perfect freedom, a "unity and simplicity of the motion of our will with his will."[27]

True freedom then, is the power to will immutably that which is good, to do it not only without any resistance from within him that wills and does it, but against all . . . tempting. . . . Thus God is most free, who tempts none nor can Himself be tempted to or by evil. And thus is he free who is fully born of God into a likeness and conformity with His divine freedom of will.

The spring of all this is not only in the use of reason but in the experience of love for God. "This is the love that with a holy and delightful efficacy, attractiveness, and persuasiveness carries the regenerate soul captive to the obedience and faith, constraining it with the greatest readiness and delight to run the race of God's commandment."[28]

There is much nobility and grandeur in Vane's conception of the true Christian life. He escapes from the idolatry of the Book which froze other Puritans into uncompromising rigidity and harshness; he does so by liberalizing biblical interpretation. He provided a means whereby Puritanism might have transcended its narrowness. His system necessitates toleration, permits manifold-mindedness, and allows for a wide range of religious experiences and practices. Yet his doctrines end in the impractical: they are hardly for this world. In some ways they are the *reductio ad absurdum* of one extreme of Puritan thought. Nevertheless, as regards their heavenly end, they are practical. They might almost be called a handbook for travelers to heaven. Vane thus reveals some of the defects as well as some of the virtues of Puritanism. His main discovery was to point out a means which could relieve Puritanism of its tendency to rigid legalism, which translated its static standards into dynamic norms, and which rationalized its gropings toward mysticism.

NOTES

1. Vane's ideas are variously expounded in Margaret A. Judson, *The Political Thought of Sir Henry Vane the Younger* (Philadelphia, 1969); John Willcock, *Life of Sir Henry Vane the Younger, Statesman and Mystic, 1613-1662* (London, 1913); John Forster, *Life of Sir Henry Vane. Eminent British Statesman* (London, 1838); F. J. C. Hearnshaw, *Sir Henry Vane the Younger, Puritan Idealist*, Congregational Worthies Series, No. 2 (London, 1910); James R. Hosmer, *The Life of Young Sir Henry Vane* (London, 1888); William W. Ireland, *The Life of Sir Henry Vane the Younger* (London, 1905), and C. W. Upham, *Life of Sir Henry Vane* (Boston, 1838). In *Milton and the Puritan Dilemma, 1641-1660* (Toronto, 1942), Arthur Barker discriminatingly explores Vane's possible influence on Milton.
2. *History of His Own Time*. vol. 1, 7 vols. (Oxford, 1823-33), 295.
3. *Reliquiae Baxterianae* (London, 1696), 75.
4. *History of the Great Rebellion*, Book XVI, section 88.
5. *The Life and Death of Sir Henry Vane Kt.* (London, 1662), 3.
6. *Ibid.*, 429.

7. *Ibid.*, 447.

8. *Ibid.*, 256.

9. Cf. A. S. P. Woodhouse, "The Argument of Milton's *Comus*," *University of Toronto Quarterly*, 11 (October, 1941), 46-71.

10. Vane, *Pilgrimage*, 19-20.

11. *Ibid.*, 26-27; *The Retired Mans Meditations*, sig. A3.

12. *Ibid.*, 10-20.

13. *Ibid.*, 27.

14. *Ibid.*, 28.

15. *Meditations*, 100; *Pilgrimage*, 32, 43, 51.

16. *Pilgrimage*, 40.

17. *Ibid.*, 60.

18. This doctrine is amplified by Vane's disciple, Joshua Sprigge, in *A Testimony to an Approaching Glory* (2nd ed., London, 1659), 49.

19. John Milton, *Christian Doctrine*, ed. Maurice Kelley, trans. John Carey, in *Complete Prose Works of John Milton*, ed. Don M. Wolfe, *et al.*, vol. 6 (New Haven, 1973), 133-34.

20. Desiderius Erasmus, *Enchiridion*, V.29, B, C, D.

21. *Meditations*, 14. *Pilgrimage, passim.*

22. *Pilgrimage*, 70.

23. *Meditations*, 219.

24. *Ibid.*, 220.

25. *The Life and Death of Sir Henry Vane, Kt.*, 1.

26. *Pilgrimage*, 64.

27. *Ibid.*, 77.

28. *Ibid.*, 66.

The Transformation of Dissent:
a Review of the Change from the Seventeenth to the Eighteenth Centuries[1]

JOHN W. WILKES
New York University

THE PURITAN DISSENTER of the early and middle seventeenth century was motivated by many economic, political, and social forces, but it is safe to say that a fervent religious faith drove him above all else. The radical religious groups of the mid-century—the Levellers, the Diggers, the Millenarians, the Fifth Monarchy Men, and even the Anabaptists—were probably even more conscious of the socio-economic and political forces that controlled their lives. Yet they, too, were driven by a profound, if not fanatical, religious belief. All these had as a prime purpose the change of existing religious beliefs into different patterns which satisfied their particular desires and ideas. This zeal for religious reform in England was even older; it went back to medieval times. The Lollard movement of the fourteenth century and the church reforms of the sixteenth century are only the best known. With this long tradition of dissent from established forms and urge for religious reform which reached its climax of open bloody warfare between 1643 and 1648, how can we explain the sudden collapse of such forceful movements during the latter part of the seventeenth and early part of the eighteenth centuries?

Common questions have arisen. It is almost trite to say the movements were spent in the fanaticism of civil war and a decade of irregular rule—people were tired and turned away from religion.[2] Is this true? Is there only this negative reason for the decline of dissent? Are there no possible positive reasons for the change in religious attitudes? Another aspect of the question is the degree to which dissent did disappear. Again it is commonplace to mention the Wesleys and the rise of Methodism in the last sixty years of the eighteenth century as a rather mild revival of dissenting ideas.[3] But is this all? Was Methodism religious dissent in the same sense as the earlier movements?

Dissent and dissenters did change, of that there can be no doubt. The essential question remains: did the causes for change come from within religious ideas and groups, or did the causes for change come from external pressures? It is the thesis of this essay that religious dissatisfaction remained, but that external forces caused fundamental changes in the modes of expressing that dissent.

The premise that people were tired of religious enthusiasm, and thus dissent quickly died, is a simple matter to refute. One need mention only the development of the Quakers.[4] George Fox had founded his sect during the chaotic years of the interregnum, but it was after 1660 that the movement really grew. Of all the small religious groups in England, these Quakers would be the most devout and obstinate. They pursued their quiet, unorthodox ways with a tenacity that defied any authority. They held to their simple life despite all opposition.

The Anabaptists continued their beliefs in spite of active and often severe persecution.[5] Prison terms were long and harsh. Perhaps because their membership came largely from the lower socio-economic levels of society and they had no recognized leadership, they remained small in numbers; however they lasted as a separate body throughout the period of "religious decline." They offered something that the more vocal groups at mid-century did not: a concentration on their religious ideals and the role of the individual within that context. The Levellers, Diggers, Fifth Monarchy Men, and the other similar groups had wandered from their religious moorings and become involved in too many other issues. Rather quickly they did disappear into the mist of history because they lost their long-term religious appeal.

However it was not only in the small groups of the strictly devout that dissent continued. The Anglican Church, established by law, returned in 1660. For two years it was, of course, a divided house, for Anglicans, Presbyterians, and even Puritans struggled to control it.[6] The latter denominations had not yet given up the struggle. Within the political framework of the Restoration it was almost inherent that the Anglicans would win.[7] They did achieve official control. Some Presbyterians and Puritan Independents capitulated and joined the ranks of the victor, but others retreated into their own worlds and protested their political reliability and religious drama. They largely accepted minority status.[8]

If the Anglicans won the tactical battle in 1662, they did not achieve a monolithic unity. Past Puritans retained some old beliefs in spite of their acceptance of the Anglican institutions. The force of their arguments was often

supported by entirely external pressures. Before going on to the new dissenters of the eighteenth century, the Methodists, it is necessary to turn aside
and examine these external pressures which were so influential.

It is an established fact that the Protestant Reformation of the sixteenth
century was the final blow to the old medieval concept of a united Christen-
dom with its religiously sanctioned views of a well-ordered society.[9] The
fanaticism on all sides, which was the result, intensified religious fervour.
It makes little difference whether the religious changes were directed and
controlled by kings, as in England, or not; the masses of people gradually
developed the sense of participation and action. The more extreme people
and groups in Protestant countries moved to demand greater and greater
individualism, and in Catholic countries the more extreme people often
founded or joined new, strict, and active religious orders. The intensity of
the feeling carried on into the great religious wars of the first half of the
seventeenth century—the Thirty Years War on the continent and the Civil
War in England. Both may have had strong religious origins, but both were
eventually diverted from a large measure of their ideological and theological
beginnings.[10] Masses of common people suffered and lost their illusions of a
new world order.

One result of the military acts of the Reformation was to lead peoples and
governments to accept multiplicity and division in a religious as well as in
a political sense. The nation-state with its established religion became the
accepted norm. If one accepted this arrangement, one accepted the existence
of different religions in the world if not in one's own country. At first this
may have intensified national rivalries, but in the long term it made harder
denunciation and attack against people of differing sects within a country as
long as each was regarded as politically loyal. *De facto* or qualified religious
toleration appeared in the later seventeenth century—first in the United
Netherlands and then in England. Even the revocation of the Edict of Nantes
by Louis XIV in 1685 was motivated more by political factors than by religious ones.[11] If even informal toleration was growing, noisy and active dissent was bound to lose adherents because moderates could see their way
ahead.

Another outside force which deeply affected religious life came out of the
new ideas concerning the physical nature of the world and universe which
were being put forth by scientists and explorers from all over Europe. In
one sense the great voyages of discovery by Vasco da Gama, Columbus, and
Magellan at the end of the fifteenth and during the sixteenth centuries began
the process. It was not so much that these spectacular trips proved the earth
was round, for many educated people had long accepted that; rather it was
the information about many strange lands and peoples, peculiar social customs and ways of life, and differing religions which the seamen brought back

that was important.[12] Even common people began to realize that Europe was not the entire world—to say nothing of one's own country, province, or locality. Again the sense of a single unique way of life was shattered. People might cling to a belief in their own superiority, but they no longer can deny the existence of others.

Even more devastating was the series of astronomical and physical discoveries and theories which began to be put forth around the middle of the sixteenth century and continued through the whole of the seventeenth.[13] Copernicus, Tycho Brahe, Kepler, Galileo, Newton, and many lesser known figures went far beyond the explorers. They destroyed the ancient and religiously sanctioned idea that the earth was the center of the God-created universe. Necessarily this meant that man, especially European man, was not the central creation of God. Many men from many states contributed new proofs about the world and the universe. These all seemed to be conveniently summed up in Isaac Newton's three laws on the physical nature of the universe published in 1687.[14] If the world acted on the basis of natural laws which were immutable, invariable, and discoverable, what was the role of religion? Indeed, what was the importance of the disagreements among Christian sects? Thus explorers in a general way and scientific discoveries of natural, universal laws in exact ways undermined religious fervor and thus dissent.

The scientific discoveries had other indirect effects. The acceptance of the physical laws of the universe led many to enquire into the existence of other kinds of laws: laws on the relationship of man to his fellow man, laws on the relationship of man to himself, or laws on the nature of the relationship of man to God. Clearly the implication of all was a greater interest in the individual. John Locke, building partly on these ideas of natural laws, in his *Essay Concerning Human Understanding*, put forth a philosophical and psychological series of theories which seemed to explain these relationships for many people.[15] His followers in the eighteenth century had more difficulty, especially Bishop George Berkeley who had to use intellectual gymnastics to insure a role for God in the world of law. David Hume gave up this struggle and lapsed into a bland agnosticism.

Even earlier in the seventeenth century a long series of philosophical writers such as Descartes and Spinoza had questioned old theological ideas. Rene Descartes' little tract *Essay on Method* was surely an expression of how to arrive at secular proof. Spinoza was a polite atheist. Both men were really safe only in the Netherlands.[16] Locke and his English followers were indirectly influenced by these men and their development of rational thought. Through Locke and others their ideas contributed to the decline in religious argument.

At the end of the sixteenth century another type of writing, concerning political government, poured forth. Even earlier Sir Thomas More had used a favorite Renaissance form when he presented his ideal world in *Utopia*. However it was with men like Jean Bodin and Francisco Suarez that consistent and at least quasi-scientific systems were drawn up.[17] In seventeenth-century England such political theories were particularly popular. Even King James I in his *True Law of Free Monarchy* and *Basilicon Doron* and his Lord Chancellor, Francis Bacon, tried their hands. These early works all tended to approve some form of divine origin and authorization for government. Thus they fitted the religious-centered world of the day as much as the religious leaders Luther, Calvin, and Loyola.

The real change came in mid-century. With the Cromwellian destruction of the ancient monarchy and execution of the anointed king, the God-ordained authoritarian government was gone;[18] yet if God could be flouted in this way, something was wrong with previous theories. Either God had not been the supreme lawgiver or men were violating God's law. The successive failures of the Puritan elite to promulgate and implement an effective constitution and government seemed to indicate that men had violated God's law. That, indeed, was the tacit position of the Restoration government in 1660.[19] However the Puritans believed themselves to be God's chosen people; thus they could not, nor would not, have broken God's law. The answer must be the alternative—God had not established government but left that to man. It is out of this dilemma that Thomas Hobbes arose. He was a firm believer in strong royal government, but a moral calvinist even though officially an Anglican. He solved his problem in *The Leviathan* by basing government on a man-made social contract and not on divine will, but it was a contract in the English legal sense and thus inviolate by one party.[20] The specifics of the contract do not matter here, rather it is the emergence of a new theory. Robert Filmer in *Patriarcha* and James Harrington in *Oceana* presented other theories, but they did not achieve the response of the social-contract theory. Finally, John Locke took up the challenge.

Locke accepted the social contract theory but not the basic Hobbesian assumptions about the nature of man. Again the details of the system are not important here, but the conclusions are. *The Second Treatise on Civil Government* finds sovereign power to rest in the people. It is, thus, the individuals who are important. Also the prince is the figure of the sovereign people; and if he does not rule according to their will, he can be removed.[21] It is not a far step from these political ideas to religious toleration at least, in the English case, for all protestants. Locke's *Letters on Toleration* of 1694 supports such a view and bolsters the Toleration Act of 1689. Many who earlier would have been fervent dissenters found the more tolerant political and religious attitudes to be agreeable.

A last important outside influence was the emergence of the idea of the "great creator" God who transcended all earthly matters. He created the universe and all its natural laws, but man and his world lived and were controlled by these laws of nature. God did not intervene. This deistic approach to religion was particularly strong among the French aristocracy and the educated elite, but it had many English adherents from the same classes.[22] However, in England, deism was more important in a very peculiar form known as "latitudinarianism" or "broad church" views. The class structure of English society meant that most of the aristocracy and the educated were members of the established Anglican church by the end of the seventeenth century for political reasons if no other. These were also the groups that controlled or were appointed to the higher offices of the church. They were also the groups likely to be affected by deistic or latitudinarian ideas. Thus the prelates and other high church officials tended to be very tolerant of dissent, at least protestant dissent.[23] The famous Bangorian Controversy, provoked by Bishop Hoadly's supposed view that salvation could be attained outside the church, illustrates how far some bishops were willing to compromise their official doctrines.[24] So far as many possible dissenters were concerned, the attitudes of the prelates made it easier to remain quietly within the church.

The case is not so simple among the lower clergy: the vicars and curates. Their ranks were split, and a majority probably opposed the deistic influences and latitudinarian views of their superiors.[25] The long fight in the Convocation of Canterbury between the upper House of Bishops and the lower House of Clergy from 1712 to 1717 illustrates the conflict.[26] The more tolerant bishops ignored many specific problems (such as more parishes for growing London areas) which the lower clergy recognized. The many procedural quarrels were often mere excuses to gain control of convocation and thereby its substantive enactments. The result was actually a victory for the bishops, for the crown prorogued Convocation in 1717. It was not to meet again in business session for about 150 years. The official attitude of the church as expressed by its bishops provided a home for a wide spectrum of views throughout the eighteenth century. Most potential dissenters were satisfied with their place.

Some lesser forces from outside the dissenting circles may merely be mentioned here. One of these in England was surely the growing number of people by 1700 who could read and even had some small amount of other education.[27] Another was the rapid expansion in the number of broadsides, pamphlets, newspapers, and other popular publications in early eighteenth-century England. Both education and communication tended to broaden the views of the public, and in one way they helped to reduce fanaticism even if often increasing sectarianism or some other special interest. In 1707 the Act of Union between England and Scotland, among other things, legally recognized the continuation of the Presbyterian Church as the established church of Scotland. Therefore within the new Kingdom of Great Britain some legal diversity existed, and this compromise tended to keep English Presbyterians out of active dissent. To some degree the War of the League of Augsburg and the War of the Spanish Succession from 1689 to 1713 greatly increased nationalistic enthusiasm which was sustained and re-enforced by later wars of the eighteenth century.[29] This nationalism encompassed the national church—the Anglican Church—and people were less willing to criticize its institutions as long as wide latitude was allowed within it. Many other minor forces played roles, but these seem to indicate how varied and intense were the pressures at work to influence men toward religious peace and quiet.

One should also note that the quickening pace of economic, especially commercial, life provided expanded and varied avenues of activity for the gentry and townsmen.[30] Banking and other financial dealings provided still other outlets for other men with special abilities.[31] Many who earlier might have channeled their energies into religion-centered movements found it more stimulating and rewarding to engage their talents in these economic arenas. Also the rapidly growing colonial empire opened new possibilities for the energetic or dissatisfied. The chances for successes seemed enormous; the chances for failure seemed small.[32]

What has been said can essentially be summed up in one word: secularization. All of these external forces provided important pressures which turned the thoughts of men away from religion and the church. They could be economic, intellectual, or political forces, but they were all secular in nature. They opened up the horizons of men in both an intellectual and geographical sense, but the direction of all was toward *this* world as it existed. The religiously oriented medieval world with its emphasis on oneness, order, and moral truth had been unable to meet successfully this many-sided attack. The world of variety, laws, and the individual moved ahead. Religious answers to the questions of the world became insufficient for many people; the proponents of the cause of religion, both established and dissenting, fought losing battles as long as they held to old ideas and outmoded methods.[33]

Nevertheless religious dissent did not succumb entirely, in England, to secularization during the eighteenth century. Its outward form may not even have undergone much change, but its purposes and aims did. Perhaps the chief reason was an essential failure of the secularizing forces to generate any recognizable standards of values or deep moral commitments.[34] Whatever the failings of the old religion-dominated world, it had provided clear values by which men could live. Individuals and groups may not have agreed with the values, but they were plain, simple, and fulfilling. The secular world may have released the individual energies of men to produce economic, intellectual, and political advantages undreamed of under the old order of things, but secularization was particularly void of moral guidelines and social responsibility.

By 1700 the increasingly tolerant Anglican Church, dominated by its bishops of largely secular attitudes, found little time for its pastoral work. The prelates and other high clergy joined their voices in pious praise of "faith, hope, and charity," but then most of them turned to the more exciting world of secular activity.[35] The lower clergy, often dedicated men, were poorly trained, poorly paid, with slim prospects of advancement. They often did not understand the problems of their rapidly changing world and, thus, could not help their parishioners.[36] No moral standards or any sense of social mission was likely to emerge from such a situation.

Thus while the theological and liturgical tensions, which had produced dissenters in the sixteenth and early seventeenth centuries, declined by 1700 in the face of secularization, new moral and social tensions were being created. The great questions were not so much detailed theology but rather how and what people the church should serve. Secularization had focused attention on the people, even the individual, but the church of the early eighteenth century was in large part failing to meet the needs of the mass of individuals, if not ignoring them entirely.

To the ruling class of England and their wealthy allies, the established church provided exactly the right kind of religion.[37] It was tolerant with wide latitude for beliefs; it was not overly demanding in a spiritual or financial way; it was not moralistic and only mildly reproved those who committed sins; it provided polite security for younger sons and relatives; and it kept services short except for special occasions when it provided great pomp and beauty. It was comfortable for them.[38]

To the lower classes, and especially the poor, the established church provided little. They could not understand the academic sermons, when a sermon was given at all. They were expected to pay to support the church. They received little personal comfort or advice from the local vicar much less from their bishop. The Anglican Church of the early eighteenth century, in most cases, failed to provide warmth and solace to the unfortunates especially in the cities.[39]

Furthermore, the church was not alone in this failure. Neither the government, nor the landlords, nor wealthy merchants and bankers had any time for the mass of people. We are generally well acquainted with the conditions in which the poor, sick, orphans, and debtors lived in London; many excellent histories prove the facts, and many brilliant works of fiction evoke the senses.[40] It is enough to note that dirt and disease, drunkenness and immorality, crime and starvation, death and brutality were ever present. Density of population was heavy in London even in 1700, so each characteristic was intensified. Still much the same was true in the smaller cities and towns.[41] Only in the small villages was there a chance for decent housing for the poor, and often even that was not true. Sunlight and a slightly better diet were the main advantages of rural living.[42] Into this squalid world few of the upper classes cared or dared to go. The Established Church was the same as the rest of the Establishment.[43]

Yet there were individuals from the upper classes who were exceptions. As early as the 1720s voices began to be raised concerning the inhuman conditions in which certain defined groups lived: orphans, the sick, insane, poor, debtors, and others.[44] By 1729 the Solicitor-General and the Attorney-General had been asked to give an opinion on the legality of slavery.[45] From what origin these pleas came, we cannot know. Indeed, the emotions may have different sources in each individual involved. What we do know is that the cries and pleas grew throughout the century. They would eventually conquer the English conscience in the nineteenth century.[46]

It is clear that from the beginning the Quakers were prominent in the humanitarian movements.[47] However we find few signs that the Anabaptists (Baptists they were beginning to be called) were prominent; perhaps they were all too poor. We know that some Presbyterians and Independent Congregationalists (the remaining Puritans) were important especially in the areas of education.[48] Yet none of these nonconformists and dissenters could supply great numbers of critical voices. Numbers could come only from within the Anglican Church, and there we must look.

Note has already been taken of the fact that the lower clergy were usually more orthodox than the bishops. Nevertheless among the parish priests and rectors there were some who had conformed to Anglican rites after 1662 but still retained many of their puritan and dissenting ideas. Such a person was Samuel Wesley, Rector of Epworth.[49] Moreover he was married to an avowed nonconformist. This elder Wesley was a successful and apparently popular clergyman. He and his wife had several children—among them John and Charles.[50] Both were sent to Oxford. When John returned for advanced work, he found Charles had just organized a religious study group. In a short time John became the leader. Both Wesleys were devout and rather orthodox Anglicans, but they deplored the blandness of the church in 1730. Their purpose, therefore, was to introduce new intellectual fervor into the church. They were certainly not popular dissenters of the old type. In 1735 John Wesley joined General Oglethorpe on his trip to the new colony of Georgia. Charles Wesley went along as bookkeeper and secretary; however, before leaving London he was ordained a priest of the Anglican Church so he could assist his brother. Charles' health broke down, and he returned to London before the end of 1735; John remained until 1737. Even at this stage, by all outward signs, they were an unlikely pair to lead a religious revival and become the outstanding nonconformists of the eighteenth century.

Something, nevertheless, had convinced John Wesley that his church had failed to communicate with the people. He began to preach whenever he could find a pulpit. He continued to study the Bible, was inspired by a visit to a community of Moravian Brethren, and experienced a spiritual conversion which confirmed his views toward the common man. Charles Wesley eventually joined with his brother after finding scriptural proof and undergoing his own conversion. They began their ministry: John over all of England and Charles mostly in the London and Bristol areas. They preached the old Protestant lesson of salvation by faith alone to the ever growing audiences; yet neither wished to leave their Anglican Church.[51] Charles, in particular, rejected any open break. It was and remained a strange kind of dissent throughout the eighteenth century.

The mass audiences and popular appeal of the Wesleys and their clerical friends upset the placid and rational Anglican establishment; however, the increasing resistance of the regular churchmen only made the Wesleyans, or Methodists as they were coming to be called, more attractive to the mass of the population.[52] By the 1760s even a few upper-class people joined the enthusiasts. The fervent sermons, the simple language, the appeal to individual faith, the willingness to go among the poor and deprived, all contrasted vividly with the ways and ideas of the Anglican authorities. Moreover, the expression of emotion in prayer, preaching, and hymn singing brought to religion what it had lost in the excessive intellectualization of the late seventeenth century.[53] This emotional reaction was plain in other areas of life: the spread of the romantic and gothic forms and substance in literature and the arts, the study of myths and legends, the changes in music by the end of the eighteenth century, and the growth of a reaction against empiricism in philosophy.

The reappearance of emotion in religious life was not confined to Methodism in England. It had counterparts in Pietism in Germany, the "Great Awakening" in the American colonies, even in Jansenism within the Catholic faith of France. Each of these was a protest against the state of rationality and intellectual toleration in religion. Each brought the heart back into religion to counterbalance the mind.[54] And each appealed mainly to the lower classes.

Methodism, however, went further than most. It wholeheartedly joined with the secular humanitarian movements in England. It provided many of the leaders and workers in the hospital and orphan care movements, educational and school development, prison reform and legal changes, and the anti-slavery drives.[55] Its members could join with others, including many Anglicans, in these "good works." The enthusiasm generated by evangelical religion could find its way into many reform movements which were becoming socially acceptable to most Englishmen. The enthusiasm was not directed primarily against the established church institutions such as dissent had done in the sixteenth and seventeenth centuries. John and Charles Wesley always claimed that they were good Anglicans trying to give their church meaning for all the people. Many who were influenced by the Methodist preachers never left the Anglican church, but instead they became a leaven within that church which would come to fruition many years later.[56] Those who did leave the Anglicans to establish the formal Methodist Church founded an institution whose ways, means, and emotions were different, but whose theology was not strikingly different.[57]

Dissent, which had meant violence and bitter discord in the sixteenth and early seventeenth centuries, faced a whole new series of external situations, ideas, and forces by the end of the seventeenth and early eighteenth centuries. Most of the factors had to do with secular events, ideas, and developments. The old religious-centered world was destroyed and with it the old theologically oriented and rigid churches and their critics. In its place there grew a new secular-centered world, and churches had to adjust or wither away. In France the Catholic Church failed to adjust, and it paid a high price in the French Revolution. In England the reaction was the emergence of the rather lackluster Anglican Church of 1720—largely tolerant, mainly unenthusiastic, and unfulfilling to the masses. Dissent, therefore, also changed: critics found fault with the aims, methods, and scope rather than with the tolerant theology. In a sense both the Established Church and its critics had been secularized. Both claimed to exist for the people and to work to save and improve the individual. One used form and established procedures; it failed in the eighteenth century. The other used emotion and attention to immediate problems of this life; Methodists, Quakers, and other smaller groups succeeded.

Dissenters had fought, bled, and died in the sixteenth and early seventeenth centuries. Those who remained retreated into compromise or sullen isolation in the late seventeenth century. However, they charged back in new forms and against new evils in the eighteenth century. Particular kinds of dissent died in the ebb and flow of history, but the dissenting spirit remained in nonconformity of all kinds. That spirit in its secularized form ultimately would triumph. As Peter Cartwright, Oliver Cromwell, George Fox, John Wesley, or Thomas Clarkson might have believed and said: "His truth goes marching on." The existence of dissent is what gave life and vitality to religious institutions. It meant that someone cared enough to struggle. Without that struggle religious institutions, or any others, would have atrophied. The religious life of England was remarkable because the dissenting spirit never really died. The transformation of dissent to meet changed conditions was an unusual sign of vitality and life in the early years of the eighteenth century.

NOTES

1. This essay is based on the researches of many authors. They have examined their specific areas of study far better and in much greater detail than I can. Instead this is an effort to draw together the many ideas and facts into some kind of coherent whole which will help explain the events and attitudes of the eighteenth century.
2. "Lethargic" is the word used by G. N. Clark, *The Later Stuarts*, 156.
3. See: Elie Halevy, *England in 1815*, especially 410-417, and Basil Williams, *The Whig Supremacy* for the standard views.
4. W. C. Braithwaite, *The Beginnings of Quakerism* and *The Second Period of Quakerism*; Godfrey Davies, *The Earlier Stuarts*, 196-197; Clark, *The Later Stuarts*, 18, 22-23; Halvey, *England in 1815*, 438.
5. W. T. Whitley, *A History of British Baptists* and A. C. Underwood, *A History of the English Baptists*.
6. A. Whiteman, "The Re-establishment of the Church of England," *Royal Historical Society Transactions*, 5th Series vol. 6 (1955), 111-131; G. R. Cragg, *From Puritanism to the Age of Reason*; Norman Sykes, *The Church of England and Non-Episcopal Churches in the 16th and 17th Centuries*.
7. Norman Sykes, *Church and State in England in the Eighteenth Century* and David Ogg, *England in the Reign of Charles II*.
8. R. S. Bosher, *The Making of the Restoration Settlement: the Influence of the Laudians, 1549-1662*; G. R. Abernathy, Jr., *The English Presbyterians and the Stuart Restoration, 1648-1662*; G. R. Cragg, *Puritanism in the Period of the Great Persecution, 1660-88*; Charles F. Mullett, "The Legal Position of English Protestant Dissenters, 1689-1767," *Virginia Law Review* 22 (1936) 495-526; *ibid.*, 23 (1937), 389-418.
9. The Peace of Augsburg in 1555 accepted the principle of *cuius regio, eius religio*; this may have been a reluctant compromise on the part of all concerned, but it did recognize the existence of both Catholics and Lutherans. The Treaty of Westphalia in 1648 officially extended this recognition to Calvinists, though in practice Calvinists had had recognition before. Anglicanism never received such specific international recognition, but all European states recognized England which of necessity meant the English Established Church.
10. C. V. Wedgwood, *The Thirty Years War*; *ibid.*, *The King's War*; Christopher Hill, *Intellectual Origins of the English Revolution* and *Puritanism and Revolution: Studies in Interpretation of the English Revolution of the 17th Century*; Richard B. Schlatter, *The Social Ideas of Religious Leaders, 1660-1688*.
11. W. F. Church (ed.), *The Greatness of Louis XIV: Myth or Reality*; W. H. Lewis, *Louis XIV*.

12. Louis B. Wright, *Religion and Empire, 1558-1625*; K. E. Knorr, *British Colonial Theories 1570-1850*; Charles R. Boxer, *The Dutch Seaborne Empire, 1600-1800* and *The Portuguese Seaborne Empire, 1415-1825*.

13. Herbert Butterfield, *The Origins of Modern Science*; W. C. Dampier, *A History of Science and Its Relations with Philosophy and Religion*; A. R. Hall, *The Scientific Revolution*; A. Wolf, *History of Science, Technology, and Philosophy in the 16th and 17th Centuries*.

14. R. S. Westfall, *Science and Religion in 17th Century England*; A. Koyre, "The Significance of the Newtonian Synthesis," *Journal of General Education*, 4 (1950), 256-268; E. N. daC. Andrade, *Sir Isaac Newton*.

15. J. Gibson, *Locke's Theory of Knowledge and Its Historical Relations*; M. Cranston, *John Locke: A Biography*.

16. S. P. Lamprecht, *The Role of Descartes in Seventeenth Century England, Studies in the History of Ideas*, Vol. 3.

17. G. H. Sabine, *A History of Political Theory*; Beatrice Reynolds, *Proponents of Limited Monarchy in Sixteenth Century France: Francis Hotman and Jean Bodin*; Julian H. Franklin, *Jean Bodin and the Sixteenth Century Revolution of Law and History*; Joseph H. Fitcher, *Man of Spain: Francisco Suarez*.

18. C. V. Wedgwood, *A Coffin for King Charles*.

19. The general assumption of the Restoration rulers was that all laws to be accepted must be in ancient form, that is, signed by the king. All other acts of parliament were nonexistent and therefore void. In practice no laws from 1642 to 1660 were in effect. *See* B. Behrens, "The Whig Theory of the Constitution in the Reign of Charles II," *Cambridge Historical Journal* 7 (1941), 42-71.

20. Peter Zagorin, *A History of Political Thought in the English Revolution*; J. Bowle, *Hobbes and His Critics*; H. Warrender, *The Political Philosophy of Hobbes*.

21. S. P. Lamprecht, *The Moral and Political Philosophy of John Locke*; W. Kendall, *John Locke and the Doctrine of Majority Rule*.

22. Basil Willey, *The Seventeenth Century Background*.

23. C. F. Mullett, "Toleration and Persecution in England." *Church History* 18 (1949), 18-43; Clyde L. Grose, "Religion of Restoration England." *Church History* 6 (1937), 3-12 Sykes, *Church and State in England in the Eighteenth Century*.

24. Benjamin Hoadly was successively Bishop of Bangor (1716), Hereford (1721), Salisbury (1723), and Winchester (1734). His "Reasonableness of Conformity to the Church of England" (1703) and "Preservative Against Non-jurors both in the Church and State" (1716) precipitated the pamphlet war known as the Bangorian Controversy. His "Nature of the Kingdom or Church of Christ" (1717) brought the quarrel to a climax.

25. G. Every, *The High Church Party, 1688-1718*; G. M. Straka, *Anglican Reaction to the Revolution of 1688*.

26. Pedro T. Meza, "The Controversy in Convocation 1701-1717: A Study of the Church and Politics in Early Eighteenth Century England," Unpublished Ph.D. dissertation, New York University, 1968.

27. J. W. Adamson, *Pioneers in Modern Education, 1600-1700*; H. McLachlan, *English Education Under the Test Acts, Being a History of the Nonconformist Academies 1622-1820*; J. W. A. Smith, *The Birth of Modern Education: The Contribution of Dissenting Academies, 1660-1800*.

28. L. W. Hanson, *Government and the Press, 1695-1763*; R. P. Bond, (ed.), *Studies in the Early English Periodical (1700-1760)*; D. H. Stevens *Party Politics and English Journalism.*

29. G. M. Trevelyan, *England in the Reign of Queen Anne*; Stephen Baxter, *William III*: David Green, *Queen Anne.*

30. G. N. Clark, *The Wealth of England 1496-1760*; John H. Clapham, *Concise Economic History of Britain (to 1750)*; R. Davis, *The Rise of the English Shipping Industry in the Seventeenth and Eighteenth Centuries*; G. D. Ramsey, *English Overseas Trade During the Centuries of Emergence.*

31. The Bank of England was founded in 1694; the great Joint Stock Companies expanded greatly; and insurance became important for the first time.

32. Frank W. Pitman, *The Development of the British West Indies, 1700-63*; Richard Pares, *War and Trade in The West Indies 1739-1763*; Bal Krishna, *Commercial Relations Between India and England (1601-1757)*; C. M. Andrews, *The Colonial Period of American History*, vol. 4.

33. John Orr, *English Deism: Its Roots and Its Fruits*; Leonard Elliott Binns, *The Evangelical Movement in the English Church*; Sykes, *Church and State in Eighteenth Century England*; Basil Willey, *The Eighteenth Century Background.*

34. Willey, *The Seventeenth Century Background* tries to present a coherent pattern, but if it ever existed it was far too intellectualized for all but a few. J. B. Bury, *The Idea of Progress* attempted to present a unifying ideal generated by the secular movements, but even if such did occur, it was mostly French, mostly after 1750, and mostly beyond the grasp of ordinary people. Carl Becker, *The Heavenly City of the Eighteenth Century Philosophers* similarly fails to discover a wide, popular, unifying theme. The moral values of English literature of the period reflect no acceptable standards; Dryden, Pope, Swift, Defoe, Restoration drama and poetry are mainly for the knowing elite.

35. One should not criticize the bishops too severely because it was expected by law and custom that they attend parliament and other political functions. Moreover, more than half the English sees did not provide a salary adequate to pay the just expenses of the bishops; several bishops, therefore, held a second or even third church post in *commendam* to gain a living wage. Obviously a bishop could not attend to all his duties. Furthermore many dioceses were too large for proper control by one bishop. Nevertheless, it is fair to say that the eighteenth century bishops were particularly sterile when any question of reform arose.

36. One essential problem was that there were too many clergy for the number of jobs available. Thus an uncommitted vicar, who had probably received his appointment through patronage or influence, found it easy to delegate his responsibilities to a miserably paid curate and live an easy life. The curate could do little but survive.

37. John Stoughton, *Religion in England Under Queen Anne and the Georges, 1702-1800*; J. H. Overton and Frederic Relton, *The English Church from the Accession of George I to the End of the Eighteenth Century*; Sykes, *Church and State in England in the Eighteenth Century.*

38. *Ibid.*

39. *Ibid.*; Evelyn D. Bebb, *Nonconformity and Social and Economic Life 1660-1800*; Dorothy Marshall, *English People in the Eighteenth Century.*

40. G. M. Trevelyan, *English Social History*, vol. 3; Dorothy George, *London*

Life in the Eighteenth Century; Dorothy George, *England in Transition*; Marshall, *English People in the Eighteenth Century*. For fiction we need only refer to such writers as Defoe, Fielding, Gay and Smollett.

41. George, *England in Transition*; more biased views are in J. L. and B. Hammond, *The Town Labourer*.

42. *Ibid.*

43. George, *England in Transition*; Marshall, *English People in the Eighteenth Century*, Sykes, *Church and State in England in the Eighteenth Century.*

44. General James Oglethorpe for the debtors, Captain Thomas Coram for the orphans, the many contributors to the founding of Bethlehem Hospital (Bedlam) are widely known examples.

45. On January 14, 1729, Philip Yorke, Attorney-General, and Charles Talbot, Solicitor-General, were asked. They agreed slavery was legal: *see* Philip Yorke, *The Life of Lord Chancellor Hardwicke* . . .

46. The vast amount of social reform legislation put on the statute books during the nineteenth century (from the abolition of the slave trade in 1807 to the Lloyd George Reforms of 1906-1911) owed much of its existence to the humanitarians. Even the rise of socialist movements in England included a strong element of humanitarian ideas and impulses.

47. William C. Braithwaite, *The Second Period of Quakerism*; Rufus M. Jones, *The Later Periods of Quakerism*; Richard H. Fox, *Dr. John Fothergill and His Friends: Chapters in 18th Century Life.*

48. These dissenting academies provided much the best education during the eighteenth century.

49. Mabel R. Brailsford, *A Tale of Two Brothers: John and Charles Wesley*; see also: Luke Tyerman, *Life and Times of the Rev. Samuel Wesley* and John Kirk, *Mother of the Wesleys: A Biography.*

50. *Ibid.*

51. Brailsford, *A Tale of Two Brothers*. All biographies of the Wesleys agree on this point.

52. E. Gibson, "Observations upon the Conduct and Behaviour of a Certain Sect usually distinguished by the Name of Methodists" (1744), quoted by E. Neville Williams, *The Eighteenth Century Constitution 1688-1815.*

53. Brailsford, *A Tale of Two Brothers.*

54. David Belden, *George Whitefield, the Awakener: A Modern Study of the Evangelical Revival. . . .* ; Umphrey Lee, *The Historical Backgrounds of Early Methodism Enthusiasm*; Leonard Elliott Binns, *The Evangelical Movement in the English Church.*

55. Brailsford, *A Tale of Two Brothers*; Halevy, *England in 1815.*

56. "Fruition" in the sense of the growing social action of the Anglican Church in the nineteenth and twentieth centuries. This might be exemplified by the election of Frederick Temple as Archbishop of Canterbury in 1896.

57. In the twentieth century ecumenical movements—Anglicans and Methodists—have had little trouble reconciling dogma; it is in other areas that differences persist.

The Usable Dissenting Past:
John Strype and Elizabethan Puritanism

CECILE ZINBERG

California State University, Fullerton

A VISITOR to the parsonage of Low Leyton, Essex, in March, 1733, found an old man, busily at work in his study, "turned ninety, yet very brisk and well, with only a decay of sight and memory."[1] The old man was John Strype whose work for the past forty years had been the writing of scholarly accounts of sixteenth century men and events. During these years he had refought the controversies of the Reformation century in the hope that the same light and brightness which he thought had triumphed then would emerge victorious in his own time. Casting one eye on religious and political events of the late seventeenth and early eighteenth centuries and the other on documents related to the political and religious history of the sixteenth century, Strype produced work after work as a bastion against the imminent and potential dangers capable of subverting his religion and that of his contemporaries.

Fifty-one years old when, in 1694, his first Tudor biography—that of Archbishop Thomas Cranmer—was published, Strype, for the next four decades, limited his historical narratives and biographies to the Tudor period. His works followed in rapid succession. By 1727, ten years before his death, they included biographies of Sir Thomas Smith, Bishop John Aylmer, Sir John Cheke as well as Archbishops Matthew Parker, Edmund Grindal and John Whitgift. In his *Ecclesiastical Memorials* Strype related the history of the reigns of Henry VIII, Edward VI and Mary Tudor and in his *Annals of the Reformation* he dealt with the reign of Queen Elizabeth. He also edited John Stow's *Survey of London*, annotated the section on Mary Tudor for White Kennett's *Complete History of England* and published six of his own sermons.[2]

Strype's scholarship has had an enormous impact on the historiography of the English Reformation. His works (replete with reprints of sixteenth-century documents) have been cited perhaps more than any other monographic series dealing with Tudor ecclesiastical history. Only recently, but still infrequently, have historians coupled their admiration for Strype's efforts with some suggestion that his works might not be as valuable as once supposed. In an appendix to his classic volume *Tudor Puritanism: A Chapter in the History of Idealism* (1939), M. M. Knappen pointed out that Strype neglected chronology, had little critical sense and was inaccurate in his transcription of sources, yet Knappen also claimed that "for all his faults he must be loved because, after his fashion, he put in print materials which otherwise must have been virtually inaccessible, though in time many of them found their way into the Harleian and Lansdowne collections and so into the British Museum." Moreover, Knappen characterized Strype as only "mildly Anglican in his point of view" and contended that his "lack of style and devotion to the sources kept his personal opinion from obtruding itself to any great extent."[3] More recently, in 1970, Professor Leland H. Carlson, in his estimable volume on *The Writings of John Greenwood and Henry Barrow, 1591-1593*, after citing more than twenty-three errors in a document reprinted by Strype, wryly concluded: "Good old Strype—he accomplished an enormous task for which we are grateful—but he too is human and fallible."[4]

When criticizing Strype's efforts, therefore, modern historians have emphasized inaccuracies in documents appended to his works. But in order to assess the pragmatic value of Strype's volumes and to understand fully his interpretation of Elizabethan Puritanism, it is necessary to examine his writings in the context of the ecclesiastical controversies of his own time. Emerging from such an examination is a portrait of Strype as a protagonist in the conflicts of the late seventeenth and early eighteenth centuries who intended that his works serve an instructive function in his own day. To promote unity within the Augustan Church[5] Strype, in his historical and biographical studies, assailed the emergence and growth of the Puritan movement, exaggerated the degree of ecclesiastical consent in Elizabethan Anglicanism and glorified the efforts of those Churchmen combating dissent and fostering accord.

Strype was born in 1643, attended first St. Paul's School, London, and then Cambridge University where he earned his B.A. degree in 1665 and M.A. degree in 1669.[6] In November, 1669, he accepted the position of vicar at Low Leyton where he was to remain until shortly before his death in 1737. Strype's responsibilities brought him into contact with influential public figures, especially Whig Churchmen, and thus involved him in the political and ecclesiastical controversies of his time.

Like many Englishmen, Strype had welcomed in 1660 the return of the monarchy and Charles II.[7] Under James II, however, Strype was confronted with a difficult decision. In 1687 when instructions to acquaint his parishioners with James' Declaration of Indulgence were sent him, he refused to comply.[8] It was the Glorious Revolution, however, which compelled many clergymen, including John Strype, to make truly major decisions. The ecclesiastical arrangements brought about by the Revolution reflected more precisely the issues and allegiances prefiguring the main features of the eighteenth century Church and, at the same time, encouraging the persistence of earlier controversies and loyalties. The fortunes of the Toleration and Comprehension Bills illustrated graphically how existing partisanships and convictions began a chain of challenges and responses determining the complexion of eighteenth-century Anglicanism. The connecting links were the various images, real or imagined, conjured up by the traditional, yet still meaningful cry, "The Church in Danger!" The images, brought into focus by more precise definitions of the threat and by more specific identifications of the enemy, resulted in attempts to ward off and, in some instances, to destroy the enemy. The prime forger of the chain was the Revolution Settlement; the choice of images resulted from the failure of the Settlement's architects to prevent the secession of Non-Jurors and to provide for the inclusion of Dissenters.

The presence of Non-Jurors as a group distinct from the Anglican community reminded the lower clergy of the political issue of 1689 and their attachment to the doctrines of passive resistance, divine right and sanctity of oaths. The response of many, therefore, was strengthened adherence to these doctrines and, in less abstract terms, dislike of the Toleration Act, dissatisfaction with the Revolution Settlement—ranging from vague discomfiture to active Jacobitism—and abhorrence of Dissenters. Regarding themselves as defenders of continuity within the Church, these clergymen employed a High Church vocabulary emphasizing their allegiance to the Tory political interest.

Their opponents were also reminded of 1689. Low Churchmen, especially those within the episcopate, were committed to the staunch defense of the Settlement, particularly the legality of William's regal status, the support of the Toleration Act and the accommodation of differences between Anglicans and Dissenters. Translated into the vocabulary of politics, Low Churchmen's convictions made them potentially valuable allies for Whigs. In 1733, Edmund Gibson, Bishop of London, could still define a Whig as one adhering to "the settled principle of maintaining the Protestant succession, the church establishment and the Toleration."[9] Ecclesiastical and political rhetoric, often indistinguishable, therefore served as definitional guidelines for allegiance both in Church and State.

Strype's allegiances were indeed more clearly delineated by the change of monarchs in 1689. The Glorious Revolution, according to Strype, was an example of divine deliverance. In a sermon preached on July 8, 1689, he hailed God who, delivering England from her domestic and foreign enemies, had blessed her with a Protestant King and a Protestant Religion. His elation, however, was marred somewhat by the awareness of possible schismatic effects for the Anglican Church of differences in opinion, especially among clergymen, regarding the Revolution Settlement. Although the Toleration Act had received royal approval two months earlier, the Comprehension Bill and the fate of the Non-Jurors still remained sources of dissension. Issuing a warning to his listeners, Strype advised them to sacrifice their personal biases in the interest of ecclesiastical harmony and consent. Peace, he suggested, was essential for the survival of Christianity; differences of opinion which destroyed peace were detrimental to religion. Strype, therefore, urged his audience to remedy this "partly by concealing our different Judgments . . . partly by complying with and submitting to the Customs of the National Church, as far as we can possibly so that we may live peaceably with all men."[10]

Despite his warning that decisions based on party considerations would be detrimental to Christianity, Anglicanism and England, Strype, by his resolutions between 1687 and 1689, firmly committed himself to the Low Church Whig position and to the concept of consent within the Anglican Church. Strype was rewarded for his loyalty. In 1689 he received and retained until 1724 the position of lecturer at Hackney, London,[11] and in 1711, possibly as a reward for his allegiance during the Sacheverell affair,[12] he was presented with the position of sinecure rector at West Tarring, Sussex.[13] But of Strype's ecclesiastical positions, the one which brought him into closest contact with the episcopate and which most directly involved him in the religious and political controversies of his day was that of Rural Dean of Barking. Strype was expected to acquaint clergymen of the Deanery with the Bishop of London's orders and briefs; supervise, on occasion, the enforcement of the prelate's directives; and instruct clergymen within his jurisdiction to exert their influence so that designated candidates would be elected to the House of Commons for the county of Essex.[14]

Strype's historical pursuits, however, provided him with the best opportunity to express his allegiance and loyalty to the Church and Government and to emphasize the need for consent and unity within Anglicanism. His interest in writing and publishing histories dealing with the sixteenth century was facilitated by his vicarage's proximity to the home of Sir William Hickes, whose grandfather Sir Michael Hickes had served as secretary to Queen Elizabeth's minister, William Cecil, Lord Burghley. William Hickes had inherited the majority of the family manuscripts; through a combination of circumstance and chicanery, Strype obtained and kept the entire collection. He also acquired papers of John Foxe, the sixteenth-century martyrologist.[15] To this core of sources he added documents obtained from England's most distinguished families, leading ecclesiastics, and fellow antiquarians and historians.[16]

Strype's desire to exchange material with his fellow antiquarians and historians generally transcended his opinion of their political and religious positions. At times, however, his willingness to aid them was confined to those sharing his Low Church convictions. For example, in 1714 the friends of Thomas Hearne, the Non-Juring medieval historian, complained bitterly to him that upon visiting Low Leyton to see Strype's manuscript collection they had been turned away without a glimpse.[17]

Strype's attitude toward his manuscripts was far more than that of a mere collector. Repeatedly he stated that his Tudor documents should be preserved for the sake of posterity. Thus, at the age of eighty-eight when Strype found that he was unable to write the fourth and final volume of his *Annals of the Reformation*, covering Elizabeth's reign from 1588 to 1603, he instead published a volume consisting entirely of reprinted documents. Of transcending importance, however, was Strype's firm belief regarding the usefulness of his sources and their importance to the historian fortunate enough to have acquired them.

Strype regarded historical inquiry as a useful weapon in contemporary controversies. For him, sixteenth-century ecclesiastical history and biography, particularly of Elizabeth's reign, were the worthiest subjects since they would most probably have an immediate, practical effect. "Of the use of such an history," Strype declared in the first volume of his *Annals of the Reformation*, "there is none, I believe, but is sensible." After reading about the "reasonable, just, and wise methods" used in the reforming of the Church under Elizabeth, clergymen and laymen alike would learn "upon what firm ground of scripture and antiquity our reformation stands, and will help us to direct and enlighten us in our controversies about it."[18]

Strype's biographies of Elizabethan ecclesiastics similarly were intended to be didactic. By relating the careers and emphasizing the virtues of Elizabethan prelates, he sought to enhance the reputation of the Church of England and to inspire his readers' emulation. In his biography of Archbishop Matthew Parker, for example, Strype contended that, because of the vigilance, patience and learning of the Elizabethan hierarchy, ". . . our reformed Church was happily settled and maintained." He also suggested that his account of Parker should produce in the "observing reader . . . a high respect and esteem both to the Church of England and its hierarchy of Archbishops and Bishops."[19] And in 1710 Strype had an opportunity to use ecclesiastical biography to aid the Low Church cause. A year earlier the

Tory High Churchman, Henry Sacheverell, in an attack on the policy of toleration for dissenters, asserted that Puritanism had been established in England "by the intercession of that False Son of the Church, Bishop Grindal."[20] The weapon Strype chose was the publication of his biography of Archbishop Edmund Grindal.[21] He hoped that his vindication of Grindal would "direct us better to judge of our modern controversies, and be a means to reconcile an honourable esteem towards it; and perhaps to unite Protestants in a better understanding together, both at home and abroad."[22]

Strype was thus confident that by detailing the ecclesiastical history of the Elizabethan period he could promote unity and consent within the Augustan Church. After reading his works, his contemporaries would be less likely and, more important, less willing to quarrel among themselves about issues confronting the Church. Discontented individuals and groups would take heed, look back, as he had, to the late sixteenth century and realize that that era had been marked by the triumph of virtue and piety. His publications were intended effectively to employ the power of the word to persuade or influence others. They were to provide the means by which his generation could fight both the forces within society capable of undermining the inherited sixteenth-century ecclesiastical traditions and those within each individual tending to lower the exemplary standard of conduct governing the lives of his Elizabethan heroes.

In light of Strype's conviction of history's utility, not surprisingly his interpretation of the Elizabethan age emphasized whenever possible the theme of consent and accord. For him, Elizabeth's greatest accomplishment was the religious settlement embodied within the Act of Supremacy of 1559. "By this single act of supremacy," extolled Strype, "a great and notable step was made towards the restoring of religion."[23] He likewise lauded the enactments of Elizabeth's first parliament through which the "ancient supreme authority of the kings of this realm was vindicated from the papal encroachments and usurpations upon it, popery overthrown, [and] true religion, founded upon the word of God." That the Parliament of 1559 had acted expeditiously occasioned further celebration: while "all the bishops, zealous creatures of Rome, and many other popish lords, sat in the parliament house, and had free votes there, and bestirred themselves as much as they could," Parliament still managed to accomplish its task in scarcely more than three months.[24] By the following year, moreover, the Anglican Church was firmly established. "After this change of government," Strype rhapsodized, "how easy and happy a condition did both the church and state of England feel themselves! The people were abundantly sensible of it, and many of the best and wisest sort could not but acknowledge it openly."[25]

In his zeal to impose harmony and unity, i.e., consent, upon his historical material, Strype overstated the average Elizabethan's awareness of the theological changes and the unanimity of public opinion. Of the potential threat represented by those who had not conformed to the newly established settlement, Strype was certainly not unmindful. But since the Augustan Church found it necessary to cope with real or potential dangers posed by Non-Jurors and Dissenters, he portrayed the Elizabethan Church's major concern as that of warding off dangers from Roman Catholics and Puritans.

Strype devoted substantial portions of his historical narratives and biographies to Puritan activities. Assessing the movement as of 1565, Strype commented that the Puritans labored to show "their utter dislike and resistance of that conformity . . . , that when the superiors should observe how irksome these matters were, they might be discouraged any further to press them."[26]

As characterized by Strype, however, Puritanism of the 1560's was not monolithic. Clearly by 1567 the "refusers of the orders of the Church . . . were grown now into two factions." The first was "of a more quiet and peaceable demeanour." Although criticizing prescribed clerical vestments and specific ecclesiastical ceremonies,[27] they took Communion and "willingly and devoutly" used the Book of Common Prayer. On the other hand, the second faction was potentially more disruptive—and hence more dangerous—to the Church of England. Going beyond ritualistic and ceremonial objections, they "disliked the whole constitution of the church lately reformed," met in private homes instead of churches, had their own ministers and, substituting the Genevan Prayer Book, rejected "wholly" the Book of Common Prayer. And to Strype's chagrin, at these "clancular and separate" congregations, they had "not only prayers and sermons, but the Lord's Supper also sometimes administered."[28]

In his treatment of the late 1560's, Strype reiterated his concern about the two Puritan types. The first type, piqued by the clerical vestments issue, still wanted to "unsettle many things lately established in the church and to bring others in their stead." But more alarming was the type of Puritan who was dissatisfied with the reformed Church and who "would have it reformed again *by the word of God*" according to the Genevan model.[29] For Strype the latter group consisted of men with "more zeal than knowledge"[30] who resorted to "weak arguments and examples from the word of God."[31] It was these men who throughout the Elizabethan period caused "great differences and discords among the queen's protestant subjects."[32]

Appraising the Puritan movement for the first three decades of Elizabeth's reign, Strype repeatedly expressed dismay about its inexorable growth. They had by 1571 "daily got ground, and increased more and more, being favoured and countenanced by many in Court and City."[33] Five years later Puritans had begun to devise substitutes for the episcopalian system. Many "now were very zealous," complained Strype, "for the new way of discipline in the Church, conformable to that practised at Geneva by *Elders*" which was "quite different from the ancient and present government by *Bishops* and their officers." Moreover, by this time, Puritans, attempting to establish their discipline in parish churches, had infiltrated Northamptonshire and Warwickshire and thereby created "great hubbubs and disturbances."[34] By 1581, "averse" to the episcopalian form of church government, Puritans were scorning the Anglican Church as "unchristian" and as corrupted by "idolatry and superstition as the Jewish Church was when Jehoshaphat first entered upon the reformation of it."[35]

If in 1583 the condition of the Anglican Church was "tottering," declared Strype, this was attributable not only to Roman Catholics but also to disaffected Protestants. Many ministers had undermined the Church's constitution "by disaffecting the people's minds" against the Book of Common Prayer and by holding meetings in private houses "upon a pretended religious account . . . to read the Scriptures and good books, to catechize and instruct youth, and to pray and confer together." Strype was particularly critical of those ministers who had either been improperly ordained or who had not subscribed to the principles of the Act of Supremacy of 1559, the Book of Common Prayer and the Thirty-Nine Articles. These ministers preached but refused to read the Liturgy and administer the Sacraments because they disliked the "manner and form thereof prescribed in our Communion Book."[36] Notwithstanding Archbishop John Whitgift's conviction that Puritan tenets "must be the ruin of the State as well as the Church" and his attendant efforts "to crush these Disciplinarians who dictated all this malice," the movement continued to grow. Strype lamented that by 1588 the Puritans had "set up their discipline, and had their *classical* and *provincial* assemblies" where they "proposed questions, in matters of religion and conscience, . . . resolved them and made orders and decrees for the government of their churches."[37]

Strype reserved his greatest concern and most abusive statements for those Puritans who had attacked the system of episcopacy. Condemning the calling of Bishops as "Antichristian" and viewing them as a "remnant of the Antichristian brood," Puritans favored "throwing down the whole constitution of the Church of England, and setting up another different discipline . . . , under pretence of restoring the right Gospel government."[38] In their many publications, the "refusers of the ecclesiastical discipline" attempted to portray the Bishops as "odious," assailed them as "*persecutors*" and charged that what the Bishops did was less for the Church than for "securing their own credits."[39] Strype dismissed as disingenuous the alleged reasons behind Puritan dissatisfaction with the episcopal hierarchy. If Puritans vented their spleen at the Bishops, it was because the Bishops had been their chief opponents. Consequently, the Puritans strove "to pull up this hierarchy by the roots," decrying it as "Antichristian, and utterly unlawful to be exercised in a Christian Church."[40]

Strype believed that Queen Elizabeth had exercised sufficient diligence toward thwarting the movement's progress. Although the Queen "bore no kindness" for Puritans, still the movement continued to mushroom.[41] Alerted to increased Puritan activity in 1571, Elizabeth determined "to put a stop to it." She therefore ordered that churchwardens, using "all diligence at their peril," prevent the performance of ecclesiastical functions in any places of worship or private residences by those who did not have licenses from the Queen, the Archbishop or the Bishop of the diocese.[42] Moreover, when in 1572 the Puritans introduced two Parliamentary bills aimed at the "whole overthrow" of established rites and ceremonies,[43] the Queen, "highly displeased with these attempts of laymen in matters of religion,"[44] successfully repelled them.

In 1573 Elizabeth again resolved to suppress Puritanism. Strype argued that the Queen vigorously prosecuted the Puritans because they had "too openly depraved the orders established by law."[45] Elizabeth's "anger was awakened against them" after the publication of various Puritan tracts, and she issued "fresh commands to see after the regulation of these evils."[46] This situation "awakened the State to take some more diligent cognizance of it."[47] The Queen's proclamation of October 20, 1573, "against the despisers and breakers of the orders prescribed in the Book of Common Prayer" was followed by instructions to "make inquiry after any breaches of her ecclesiastical laws," to cite those who broke them, and to inflict punishment accordingly.[48]

A month later Elizabeth still felt it necessary to enforce her proclamation. In a letter to the Bishops, transmitted through the Council, she faulted them for their laxity in dealing with Puritans. Strype explained that the Queen "blamed" the Bishops for having taken "no more care for preventing these disorders" and instructed them to identify violators of the prescribed rites and to punish them according to ecclesiastical law.[49] Although allowing that the Bishops were "not then so forward to take punishment upon these defaulters," Strype rationalized that they were subjected to considerable Puritan "reproach and hatred."[50] Greatly troubled by the charge, the Bishops thought it "hard" that responsibility for these disorders should be "laid upon them without difference," that the "labour and drudgery" of punishing Puritans was "irksome," would make them "odious" and brand them as "persecutors." The task, commiserated Strype, was more than could be expected of them and should have been implemented by the temporal authority which, according to the Bishops, was "only able to restrain those practices."[51] The Bishops had been "broadly accused to have minded little else . . . than their own covetous ends," and Strype suggested that the letter had been signed by some of their "greatest enemies" including the Earl of Leicester and Sir Francis Knollys who were "well enough affected towards those persons against whom this letter was written."[52]

Strype's defense of the Bishops' diligence typifies his attitude toward various episcopal efforts to confront the Puritan challenge. To an even greater extent than her competence and perseverance, Strype attributed Elizabeth's success to her selection of prelates. The men chosen had been instrumental in the survival and strengthening of the late sixteenth-century Anglican Church. It is thus the Archbishops and Bishops of the Elizabethan Church who emerge as the true heroes in Strype's account of how State and Church dealt with the Puritan movement.

Strype maintained that by 1561 Elizabeth had appointed a sufficient number of bishops who, by virtue of their inner qualities, became energetic in the task of preserving the reformation of religion. In this way the Church was "replenished with a new set of bishops, professors of the gospel, and most of them sufferers for it."[53] Elizabeth was certainly aware of the attributes of her appointed ecclesiastics. Describing the Queen's nomination in 1576 of John Whitgift to succeed Nicholas Bullingham as Bishop of Worcester, Strype claimed that she knew "his great deserts toward this Church, and excellent abilities in learning and government" which were "things nowadays specially regarded in appointing Bishops over the churches."[54]

Not surprisingly, Strype emphasized in the Elizabethan Archbishops and Bishops precisely those qualities—piety, dedication to the Church and scholarship—which he thought characterized the Latitudinarian-Low Church Whig ecclesiastics of his own day. In his biographies and narrative histories, Strype repeatedly stressed the virtues of the Elizabethan Churchmen. Bishop John Aylmer, charitable and humble, lived "contentedly and thankfully with what he had" and never "repined nor envied."[55] The dedication of his biography of Whitgift emphasized the "several singular Christian virtues shining in Queen Elizabeth's three Archbishops, right worthy to be followed by all their successors, as very profitable for *their* conduct especially." Matthew Parker was a man "above the world, contemning all the faint and fading glories of it." His "high place and dignity did not puff him up, nor hinder him aspiring to, and earnest expectation of, the more substantial satisfactions of another world." The soul of Edmund Grindal, Parker's successor as Archbishop of Canterbury, had a "firm and comfortable affiance and trust in God, necessary for his high and holy calling and office." Finally, "invincible patience" was "conspicuous" in Elizabeth's last Archbishop of Canterbury, John Whitgift, despite the many "oppositions, taunts, reproaches, calumnies, clamours, lies, and unsufferable abuses he underwent in Parliaments, in Court, in city, in country" while preserving the Reformed Church.[56]

More admirable for Strype was the Elizabethan ecclesiastics' loyalty and service to the Church, as reflected in their policy toward Puritan dissidents. His works abound with accounts of their determination to stifle the Puritan threat. Aylmer, for example, was "industrious" in opposing the Puritans[57] and insisted on "due conformity" to the Anglican Church.[58] He believed that enforcement of laws against Puritans was the "best bulwark" against Roman Catholicism and for this reason "spared neither Papist nor Puritan."[59] As a result, he incurred the wrath of both Roman Catholics and Puritans—but that of the latter "appeared most visible against him." Because Aylmer had "roundly executed his office in reclaiming or suppressing them," the Puritans did not hesitate to "defame and show their ill-will to him."[60]

Archbishop Matthew Parker was equally forthright in the enforcement of the ecclesiastical discipline. In 1566 Parker, complying with the Queen's instructions to end the Puritan agitation, became discouraged because of the Council's reluctance to support him and because of the dissenting clergy's "clamour and rage" and "hard names they gave him."[61] Although Parker found compliance distasteful, he persisted through "obedience" to the Queen and even asked that the Council "stand up by him with their authority." He was unsuccessful, however, in obtaining this desired support. While wondering about the "great neglect" of the Council, Parker understandably but temporarily "grew more languid" in his efforts against the Puritans.[62]

At the same time Strype cautioned the reader against the interpretation that Parker had been remiss in discharging his responsibility and reiterated that his main concerns were loyalty to the Queen and order within the Church. "Sedulous" that Elizabeth's "will and pleasure" be honored, Parker enforced conformity because it led to ecclesiastical unity and peace.[63] Well aware of the potential danger of the Puritans, their activities and ideas caused him "great grief" because they portended the "ruin of religion and learning" and threatened "confusion to the country."[64]

If Strype was interested in defending Parker against a possible charge of laxity in his dealings with Puritans, he was still more concerned about Edmund Grindal's reputation in this regard. Indeed, one of Strype's intentions in writing his biography of Grindal was to dispel erroneous notions about his deportment when Bishop of London. "Since the good Archbishop hath been so much, and yet so darkly talked of," Strype averred, "justice and religion require that right be done to his name."[65]

Henry Sacheverell's 1709 sermon *The Perils of False Brethren, Both in Church and State* had proclaimed that a man must be "very weak, or something worse, that thinks or pretends the Dissenters are to be gained or won over by any other grants and indulgences than giving up our whole Constitution." More specifically, Sacheverell asked "have they not ever since their unhappy plantation in this kingdom, by the intercession of that false son of the Church, Bishop Grindal, always improved and rose upon their demands in the permission of the Government?" And had not "Queen Elizabeth, . . . deluded by that perfidious Prelate to the toleration of the Genevan discipline, found it such a headstrong and encroaching monster that in eight years she foresaw that it would endanger the monarchy as well as the hierarchy."[66]

Strype acknowledged that Grindal is "commonly now-a-days thought to have held the reins too loose" and for his "slackness" is "vulgarly blamed."[67] More precisely, Grindal's reputation had suffered because of specific identification with the Puritan exercises of Elizabeth's reign. "Nothing," complained Strype, "to this day sticks upon the Archbishop but the matter of the Exercises, and his suspension" which is the "stumbling block and the rock of offense."[68] But the accusation was "unjust"[69] and Grindal's honor had been denigrated because of later historians' failure to view his policy toward the Puritans in the context of his own time when his "episcopal abilities and admirable endowments for spiritual government" were "much celebrated."[70] Grindal "best knew what courses were fittest to be used, . . . observed how things then stood in the State and Church" and then acted accordingly.[71] Moreover, his "zeal and affection" for the Anglican Church were evidenced by his efforts to "reclaim those they styled *Precisians and Puritans.*" Although Grindal's temperament was "easy and complaisant," when "he saw that no other means would bring them to obedience," he resorted to stronger measures—especially for the puritan leaders whom he "styled *fanatical* and *incurable.*"[72] Finally, while Grindal was condemned "for this gentle usage," his successor Whitgift was commended for the same tactics by the biographer George Paul who, Strype pointed out, had declared "happy . . . it was for that crazy state of the Church, not to meet with too rough and boisterous a physician" for he "preserved it with conserves and electuaries, and some gentle purges" whereas "with strong purges in all likelihood [the Church] might have been much more in danger."[73]

Strype was considerably more emphatic than Paul regarding Whitgift's energetic efforts and tactics. As early as 1574—nine years before he became Archbishop of Canterbury—Whitgift preached a sermon before the Queen assailing those "controversies now so hotly exercising the peace of the Church, and undermining the principles of the Reformation." In his "great and solemn auditory" Whitgift denounced the Puritans for making "such disturbances" and for rendering themselves "very agreeable to, and admired by, the common people" through their "plausible behaviour and doctrines." Whitgift's motivation in later publishing this sermon was "to undeceive the people" and "to show, . . . what dangerous persons these new reformers were, and how much evil lay under their goodly pretences."[74]

Upon his elevation to the Archbishopric of Canterbury, Whitgift began to enforce strict conformity and the "vigilant and industrious Prelate"[75] continued this policy throughout his tenure. By 1595 Whitgift's "patience, watchfulness, and interest, had pretty well appeased the great stirs raised by the *new reformers.*"[76] Within the following year the Archbishop's efforts had forced the dissidents to resort to other measures: "namely, the casting out devils from persons pretendedly possessed by them . . . so the amazed multitude, having a great veneration for these exorcisers of devils by the power of their prayers and fastings, might the more readily and awfully submit to their opinions and ways, which likewise was a practice borrowed from the Papists, to make their Priests revered, and to confirm the laity in their superstitions."[77] Strype's account of 1598 boasted that "we may look back upon our Archbishop's past labours, pensive cares, incessant painfulness and watchfulness, against the insults of the enemies of the Established Church; and observe, how by this time he had gotten in good measure the victory over them."[78]

In his voluminous accounts of how the Elizabethan prelates expressed their loyalty and devotion, Strype was particularly impressed by their responses to the profusion of Puritan writings. Just as Strype believed his historical scholarship serviceable to the Augustan Church, so too was he convinced that the Elizabethan hierarchy's allegiance could not have been expressed more effectively than in writing books. Therefore, Strype's works abound with references to those ecclesiastical writers who celebrated consensus within the Elizabethan Church or who refuted dissent. Accordingly, Strype treated in minute detail the efforts of Bishop John Jewel, Richard Hooker, Matthew Parker and Edmund Grindal as well as those of hundreds of lesser known apologists. An apt exemplification of his interpretation of how Elizabethan Churchmen used the printed word to demonstrate loyalty to the Church and opposition to Puritanism is Strype's depiction of John Whitgift's role.

In 1572 the Puritans published a treatise which was "written with much bitterness, and designed quite to overthrow the present state and government of it." This treatise, "openly and insolently against the Church, reformed and established by law," was entitled *An Admonition to the Parliament*. Strype maintained that it had been written during the period of the vestiarian controversy and was actually "more dangerous [than the controversy] in that it utterly condemned the present Church and the ministry of it." Whitgift was then Master of Trinity College, Cambridge, but the Church, avowed Strype, "had need of his . . . learning." Matthew Parker, Archbishop of Canterbury, therefore chose him "of all the learned men in the realm" for the "answering" of the dangerous book.[79] The refutation envisioned by Parker was to be a "more complete vindication of this Church, and the cavils of the averse party most satisfactorily answered."[80] Strype applauded Whitgift's *Answer* as "excellent": in it "may be seen all the arguments and pleas used in those times, for laying Episcopacy and the Liturgy aside, and all the exceptions to them drawn up to the best advantage; and herein also are subjoined a full and particular answer and refutation of the one, and vindication of the other: together with the favourable sense of the learned men in the reformed Churches abroad, . . . and their approbation of this Church's form and discipline, and the government of it by Bishops."[81] Strype thus concluded that Whitgift's *Answer* should be "justly esteemed and applied to, as one of the public books of the Church of England, containing her profession and principles;" it was a definitive answer to the Puritans comparable to Bishop John Jewel's defense of the Church against Roman Catholics.[82]

Whitgift's high regard for *apologiae* extended beyond the Admonition controversy. During his tenure as Archbishop of Canterbury he not only refuted slanderous attacks on the Church of England but enlisted the aid of others for the same purpose. "By the Archbishop's vigilance and advice," Strype enthused, "not a petition, pamphlet, or book escaped without a speedy and effectual answer."[83]

Thus the heroism of the Elizabethan period for Strype focused upon the inseparable areas of religion and scholarship. His heroes were those who combined piety, service to the Church and erudition. Strype himself combined these virtues in his own career, emulating his Elizabethan models by steadfastly and painstakingly performing his ministerial and scholarly duties. During his lifetime Strype repeatedly disclaimed involvement in political and religious controversies, insisting that he was "no party man, but would be a good Christian and a sincere son of the Church of England."[84] But John Strype was no less a protagonist in the conflicts of the late seventeenth and early eighteenth centuries than those who more openly combated the tendencies endangering the welfare of the Anglican Church. Through his historical works, Strype was an active adversary. The battleground on which he waged his struggle was the century of the Reformation in England; the arms used were the manuscripts, records and documents upon which he based his interpretations of sixteenth century men and events.

NOTES

1. Letter, Samuel Knight to Zachariah Grey, March 24, 1733, reprinted in John B. Nichols, *Illustrations of the Literary History of the Eighteenth Century* (8 vols.; London: John B. Nichols & Son, 1817-58), vol. 4, 327.
2. *BIOGRAPHICAL AND HISTORICAL WORKS*: Memorials of Thomas Cranmer (1694); Life of . . . Sir Thomas Smith (1698); Historical Collections of the Life . . . of John Aylmer (1701); Life of . . . Sir John Cheke (1705); Annals of the Reformation, 4 vols. (1709-31); History of the Life . . . of Edmund Grindal (1710); Life . . . of Matthew Parker (1711); Life . . . of John Whitgift (1718); Ecclesiastical Memorials, 3 vols. (1721).

EDITIONS, PREFACES, ETC.: *Works of John Lightfoot*, vol. II (1684) [edited by Strype]; *Some Genuine Remains of John Lightfoot* (1700) [edited and prefaced by Strype]; James Bonnell, *Harmony of the Holy Gospels* (1705) [edited and prefaced by Strype]; Richard Hooker, *Laws of Ecclesiastical Polity* (1705) [Interpolations to Izaak Walton's Life of Hooker by Strype]; Francis Godwin, "Annals of the Reign of Queen Mary" in White Kennett, *Complete History of England*, trans. by John Hughes (1706, 1719) [annotated by Strype]; John Stow, *Survey of London*, 2 vols. (1720) ["now lastly corrected, improved and very much enlarged and . . . brought up to the present time by John Strype. To which is prefixed the life of the author, writ by the editor."] *PUBLISHED SERMONS*: *Sermon Preached at the Assizes at Hertford* (1689); *David and Saul: A Sermon Preached on the Day of National Thanksgiving* (1696); *Lessons Moral and Christian, For Youth and Old Age* (1699); *Lessons Proper for Fallible Man* (1708); *Thankful Samaritan* (1711); *End of the Upright Man* (1729).

Strype's biographical and historical works were reissued by The Clarendon Press, Oxford, 1812-24, 26 vols. Subsequent references in this essay will be to this edition.

3. M. M. Knappen, *Tudor Puritanism: A Chapter in the History of Idealism* (Chicago: University of Chicago Press, 1939), 503.

4. Leland H. Carlson, *The Writings of John Greenwood and Henry Barrow, 1591-1593* (London: George Allen and Unwin, Ltd., 1970), 451. For a penetrating critique of Strype, see W. D. J. Cargill Thompson, "A Reconsideration of Richard Bancroft's Paul's Cross sermon of 9 February 1588/9," *Journal of Ecclesiastical History*, 20 (October, 1969), 253-66. I wish to thank Dr. Cargill Thompson for reading this essay and providing valuable suggestions.

5. Although "Augustan Church" has been used in a broader sense, for the present purpose it will denote the Anglican Church during the first third of the eighteenth century.

6. For an account of Strype's life, see Cecile Zinberg, "John Strype and the Sixteenth Century: Portrait of an Anglican Historian" (unpublished Ph.D. dissertation, University of Chicago, 1968), 100-184.

7. C. Litton Falkiner, "Some Letters of Toby and James Bonnell," *English Historical Review*, 19 (January, 1904), 123.

8. Letter, Joshua Stanley to John Strype, 1687, Cambridge University Library, Strype Correspondence, Baumgartner Papers, vol. I, No. 123. Hereafter cited as *S.C.*

9. As quoted in Norman Sykes, *Church and State in England in the XVIIIth Century* (Cambridge: Cambridge University Press, 1934), 33.

10. John Strype, *A Sermon Preached at the Assizes at Hertford, July VIII, 1689* (London: Printed for Richard Chiswell, 1689), 27-29.

11. Letter, Benjamin Hoadly to John Strype, Easter Tuesday, 1689, *S.C.*, vol. 5, No. 236.

12. See *infra*, 127-28 and 133-34.

13. Letter, Benjamin Ibbot to John Strype, May 23, 1711, *S.C.*, vol. 6, No. 415; Letter, Thomas Baker to John Strype, August 22, 1711, *S.C.*, vol. 10, No. 51.

14. Letter, Henry Compton to John Strype, November 20, 1701, *S.C.*, vol. 5, No. 219.

15. For Strype's version of how he acquired the Burghley papers, see his will, Great Britain, Public Record Office, Prob. 11/686. For an account of Strype's acquisition of both the Foxe and Burghley collections, see W.D.J. Cargill Thompson, "John Strype as a Source for the Study of Sixteenth Century English Church History" in *Studies in Church History*, vol. 11 (London: Blackwell, 1975), 239-40.

16. The value of Strype's collection became so well known that in 1708 Robert Harley purchased a portion of it. Harley regarded Strype's price as exorbitant, calling it the "dearest bargain I ever bought." Letter, Humphrey Wanly to John Strype, July 25, 1708, *S.C.*, vol. 6, No. 336.

17. Charles E. Deble, ed., *Remarks and Collections of Thomas Hearne* (11 vols.; Oxford: The Clarendon Press, 1885-1921) vol. 4, 337.

18. John Strype, *Annals of the Reformation and Establishment of Religion and Other Various Occurrences in the Church of England, During Queen Elizabeth's Happy Reign* (4 vols., 2d ed.; Oxford: The Clarendon Press, 1824), vol. I, Part I, vi.

19. John Strype, *The Life and Acts of Matthew Parker, the first Archbishop of Canterbury in the Reign of Queen Elizabeth* (3 vols., 2d ed.; Oxford: The Clarendon Press, 1821), vol. I, xiv.

20. Henry Sacheverell, *The Perils of False Brethren, Both in Church and State* (London: Henry Clements, 1709), 19.

21. Because of a felt urgency to vindicate Grindal's reputation, Strype decided to publish his biography of Grindal earlier than anticipated.

22. John Strype, *The History of the Life and Acts of the Most Reverend Father in God Edmund Grindal, the First Bishop of London and the Second Archbishop of York and Canterbury Successively in the Reign of Queen Elizabeth* (2d ed.; Oxford: The Clarendon Press, 1821), iv.

23. Strype, *Annals of the Reformation*, vol. I, Part I, 104.

24. *Ibid.*, vol. I, Part I, 105.

25. *Ibid.*, vol. I, Part I, 305.

26. Strype, *Parker*, vol. I, 382.

27. These ceremonies included "kneeling at the Sacrament" and the use of "the Cross in Baptism [and] the ring in marriage." Strype, *Grindal*, 169.

28. *Ibid.*, 168-69.

29. Strype, *Annals of the Reformation*, vol. I, Part II, 349-50.

30. *Ibid.*, vol. I, Part II, 350.

31. *Ibid.*, vol. I, Part II, 352.

32. *Ibid.*, vol. I, Part II, 350.

33. Strype, *Parker*, vol. 2, 191.

34. Strype, *Grindal*, 320.

35. Strype, *Annals of the Reformation*, vol. 3, Part I, 66-67.

36. John Strype, *The Life and Acts of the Most Reverend Father in God, John Whitgift, D.D., the Third and Last Archbishop of Canterbury in the Reign of Queen Elizabeth* (3 vols., 2d ed.; Oxford: The Clarendon Press, 1822), vol. I, 228.

37. *Ibid.*, vol. I, 554.

38. Strype, *Parker*, vol. 2, 109-110.

39. *Ibid.*, vol. 2, 191.
40. *Ibid.*, vol. 2, 285.
41. *Ibid.*, vol. 2, 345.
42. *Ibid.*, vol. 2, 65.
43. *Ibid.*, vol. 2, 201-202.
44. *Ibid.*, vol. 2, 203.
45. *Ibid.*, vol. 2, 238-39.
46. *Ibid.*, vol. 2, 255.
47. *Ibid.*, vol. 2, 320.
48. *Ibid.*, vol. 2, 320-22.
49. *Ibid.*, vol. 2, 345.
50. *Ibid.*
51. *Ibid.*, vol. 2, 347.
52. *Ibid.*
53. Strype, *Annals of the Reformation*, vol. I, Part I, 372.
54. Strype, *Whitgift*, vol. I, 152.
55. John Strype, *Historical Collections Relating to the Life and Acts of the Right Reverend Father in God, John Aylmer, Lord Bishop of London in the Reign of Queen Elizabeth* (2d ed.; Oxford: The Clarendon Press, 1821), 119.
56. Strype, *Whitgift*, vol. I, iv-v.
57. Strype, *Aylmer*, 36.
58. *Ibid.*, 184.
59. *Ibid.*
60. *Ibid.*, 39.
61. Strype, *Parker*, vol. I, 451-52.
62. *Ibid.*, vol. I, 452.
63. *Ibid.*
64. *Ibid.*, vol. 2, 258.
65. Strype, *Grindal*, iv-v.
66. Sacheverell, *Perils of False Brethren*, 19.
67. Strype, *Grindal*, 447.
68. *Ibid.*, vi.
69. *Ibid.*, 447.
70. *Ibid.*, v.
71. *Ibid.*, 447.
72. *Ibid.*, 448.
73. *Ibid.*, 447.
74. Strype, *Whitgift*, vol. I, 120-21.
75. *Ibid.*, vol. I, 227.
76. *Ibid.*, vol. 2, 226.
77. *Ibid.*, vol. 2, 340.
78. *Ibid.*, vol. 2, 395.
79. *Ibid.*, vol. I, 54-55.
80. *Ibid.*, vol. I, 85.
81. *Ibid.*, vol. I, 86.
82. *Ibid.*, vol. I, 86-87.
83. *Ibid.*, vol. 2, 482.
84. Letter, John Strype to Ralph Thoresby, March 21, 1710, reprinted in Joseph Hunter, ed., *Letters of Eminent Men Addressed to Ralph Thoresby* (2 vols., London: H. Colbourn and R. Bentley, 1832), vol. 2, 234-35.

Religion in the Life of Charles Middleton, First Baron Barham*

MICHAEL E. MOODY

University of Denver

ADHERENTS OF THE EVANGELICAL MOVEMENT within the eighteenth-century Anglican church would have rejected the label of "Dissenters" if anyone had applied it to them.[1] They considered themselves good communicants of the Church of England; yet there is no doubt that their active objections to the frivolity and corruption of society and to the inadequate theology and open worldliness of the Hanoverian Church[2] placed them in opposition to much of the Anglican establishment of their day.[3] Indeed, Evangelicalism came to be a distinct movement within the Church, and it displayed distinctive characteristics of its own.[4] Historically it is especially significant for its ability to permeate the lives of those who embraced its outlook at a time when many Anglicans lacked religious inspiration.

Charles Middleton, the best British naval administrator since Samuel Pepys,[5] had become involved with Evangelicalism by 1761, and the resulting influence of his spiritual convictions on his secular activities suggests the force of Evangelical doctrines in deepening the earlier religious concerns of his life. Historians have largely failed to explore religion as a factor in Middleton's life. Many have stated that he had strong Evangelical beliefs,[6] but none have tried to trace the possible effects of such convictions. This essay will attempt to fill this void. Its conclusions must be tentative, because all of Middleton's papers have not yet been analyzed. Nevertheless, it may be illuminating to define his religious beliefs, to consider the relationship of religion to his activities both inside and outside the British navy, and to speculate concerning the effect of his religious convictions on his achievements.

140

I

Middleton's religious beliefs probably developed early in his life. No evidence is available to indicate where he was first exposed to pious influences. It is possible that such ideas were strong in his family, for his paternal grandfather was a doctor of divinity.[7] In any event, it is clear that by 1761 he was associated with the Evangelical movement within the Church of England.[8] This group was composed of middle-class Anglicans who shared a common bond of belief in the total depravity of human nature; in the doctrine of grace, or God's free and undeserved mercy as the sole originating cause of man's salvation; in the need of a conscious conversion in all men; and in the witness of the Holy Spirit, whereby a man had an inner consciousness of being in a state of grace.[9] To these beliefs, the Evangelicals added a modified doctrine of election. They interpreted this to mean that those who did not share their moderate Calvinist ideas were "nominal Christians." In Evangelical thinking, these "nominal Christians" could not be saved until they experienced a conscious conversion to God and espoused Evangelical ideas.[10]

Finally, the Evangelicals believed in the concept of the immanence of God. They saw Him as intervening so directly in human affairs that there was no room at all for the elements of chance, fortune, or luck. From their point of view, even the smallest daily events had religious significance.[11]

Such teachings as these were chiefly responsible for making the Evangelicals strict moralists.[12] From their point of view, Britain in the eighteenth century was "a festering heap of corruption." Specifically, they were discontented with the degeneration of British religion and the decline of British morals.[13]

To correct this situation, the Evangelicals launched a campaign to restore the nation to a truly religious and moral state.[14] Their reform crusade reached its most active phase from approximately 1787 to 1825.[15] During these years, they made a concentrated effort to achieve their purposes by founding many societies to reform morality and to spread their views among the British people. They also led the agitation for the abolition of the British slave trade as a means of acquainting other pious Englishmen with their cause.[16]

The Evangelicals accomplished much. They helped to raise the tone of morality and religion among all classes.[17] In addition, they were instrumental in ending the British slave trade and in organizing many charitable and vice prevention associations. These groups helped to instruct the lower classes in piety and self-help by educational programs which sought to inculcate cleanliness, thrift, and Bible reading.[18] Lastly, the Evangelicals aided the Church of England's foreign missionary efforts by founding the Church Missionary Society for Africa and the East in 1799.[19]

These Evangelical endeavors, however, did not totally erase impiety, vice, and immorality in Britain. While the Victorian era of British history did see substantial improvement, these advances should not obscure either the Evangelical failure to produce a truly moral and religious nation[20] or the difficulties of the Evangelical character. Just as Victorian Britain was not as free of vice as the Evangelicals wished it to be, so the Evangelicals were not as free of personal problems as they thought themselves to be.

Two flaws were evident in the Evangelical outlook, both reflecting their elitist spirit. The first was pride, which caused self-righteousness.[21] F. K. Brown stated this point when he observed that

. . . in their knowledge that the truth had made them through grace acceptable for salvation while others who were not Evangelicals were not acceptable, in their knowledge of the kind of religion and morality that England had to have, there was a certainty, and a consequent exaltation, that together with their manifest and exclusive closeness to [the] Deity served them for a righteousness and led them to trust themselves and despise others.[22]

The second was "a conviction that the converted are allowed and even commanded to employ ways and means, when in their judgment necessary, that are not virtuous in ordinary people."[23] These flaws as well as the constructive aspects of Evangelical thought should be borne in mind in an examination of how Middleton's religious views affected the rest of his life.

II

Only a few facts are known about Middleton's life and religion during his early years, but a sketch of his youth by Sir John Knox Laughton reveals some significant information.[24] Charles Middleton was born on 14 October 1726,[25] son of Robert Middleton, collector of customs at Borrowstoness, Scotland. His mother was Helen Dundas, daughter of Charles Dundas and cousin of Henry Dundas (later, Lord Melville), who became one of Middleton's close friends and political allies.[26] This alliance of the Dundas and the Middleton families produced an interesting fusion of qualities in Middleton. On his father's side, his great-grandfather, Alexander Middleton, had been a doctor of divinity at King's College, Aberdeen. George Middleton, Charles' paternal grandfather, had later held the same position.[27] His relatives on his father's side were known for legal expertise and political manipulation.[28] Robert Dundas, his maternal great-grandfather, was a judge, and his grand-uncle, also named Robert Dundas, was on the bench of the Scottish court of session.[29] This cursory sketch of Middleton's forbears shows clearly how both business and religion were represented in his background.[30] Both were important factors in his later life as an Evangelical reformer.

With these legal and religious ancestors, one might expect that Middleton would become a lawyer or a clergyman. Such was not the case. Following a short period of education, he entered the navy as a captain's servant on the ship *Sandwich* in April 1741.[31] After seven months, he was made a midshipman aboard the *Flamborough*.[32] Four years later, in November 1745, he attained the rank of lieutenant and went to the *Chesterfield*.[33] Middleton served on this ship and on several other vessels until 1756.[34] Then, in February 1757, he sailed to the West Indies aboard the *Anson*. While he was there, a ship command opened for him in March 1757. He was promoted to the rank of commander, and for a brief period he had charge of the *Speaker*, a small twelve-gun sloop which was ordered to protect British commerce in the Caribbean. On 22 May 1758, he advanced to the rank of post captain and took command of the *Barbados*, another small sloop.[35] The next four years saw Middleton still serving in the West Indies commanding various vessels.[36] In October 1761, he returned to England in the twenty-eight gun ship *Emerald*.[37] The rest of Middleton's sea duty between 1761 and 1778 was brief. He served short, routine terms as captain of a few other ships, but he spent most of this period away from the navy on half-pay. Not until he became comptroller of the navy on 22 July 1778, did he again take up his naval career for a prolonged period on a full-time basis.[38]

These years of sea service furnish the first available evidence of religious influence in Middleton's life. He knew that the naval instructions provided for

... divine service ... to be performed morning and evening, on
board of every king's ship, according to the liturgy of the Church of
England; and a sermon [to be] preached on Sundays, unless bad
weather or other extraordinary accidents prevent it. [They also
forbade] ... all dissolute, immoral, and disorderly practices. ...[39]

The naval code further prohibited swearing, drunkenness, and fornication aboard naval vessels.[40] While all these rules were in the naval regulations, Middleton reported that

... the truth is that they are practicable, though seldom practised. I
was sixteen years in the sea service before I was made a captain
[1741-1757], and never, during that time, heard prayers or divine
service performed a-board of ship, nor any pains taken to check

vice or immorality, further than they interfered with the common
duty of the ship. . . .

. . . I never knew an instance of . . . [communion] being
administered on board of any ship, and I see no reason whatever for
not giving it, but that the chaplains are seldom in priest's orders. . . .
[He also observed that] Sufficient attention was not always paid
to the character of [the chaplain's] person; and in many, very many
instances, the name of the chaplain was kept upon the books, when
he himself was either serving his own living or as a curate to some
other person.[41]

Middleton found the situation that these abuses caused intolerable, for
he was convinced that true virtue must be founded upon Christianity.[42] Furthermore, he was sure that the sea officers, especially the ship captains, must
take the initiative in remedying these problems. He emphasized this point in
the following statement:

. . . I have selected him [the ship's captain] as the instrument under
God by which the morals of seamen are to be corrected and
established.
. . . if the admiralty would furnish the means, and the captain
execute his instructions, no set of men in the community can be
better placed for religious instruction than seamen. . . .
. . . if he [the chaplain whom Middleton wished to have placed on
board all ships of more than twenty guns to assist the captain] had
the power of distributing bibles and other good books amongst the
seamen . . . to be paid for by themselves at pay day—I have little
doubt but our seamen would be amongst the foremost of the lower
classes of the people in examples of piety and good conduct. Much—
very much will depend on the character of the captain.[43]

Since Middleton placed so much emphasis on the role of individual com-
manders in reforming morality and inculcating religion, it is not surprising
that he himself took vigorous action to put his ideas into practice when he
received a ship of his own. He later remarked that

. . . as soon as I became a captain [in 1758] I began reading prayers
myself to the ship's company of a Sunday, and also a sermon. I
continued this practice as long as I was in commission and without
a chaplain, and it never was omitted when I had one. I did not indeed
venture to carry it further than Sundays, because the practice was
confined to those days by the very few ships who had chaplains,
when followed at all; and I should have only acquired the name of
methodist or enthusiast if I attempted it.[44]

Middleton may have shrunk from fully carrying out his religious wishes, but he enforced the regulations against vice to the letter. Drunkenness and swearing were strictly forbidden, and no women were ever admitted aboard the ship unless they were known to be wives of the seamen.[45] Subordinate officers on Middleton's ships were expected to aid him in controlling immorality. In fact, Middleton seems to have had a low opinion of officers who did not co-operate with his reforming endeavors. He stated in his "Captain's Order Book" in 1775 that "whoever is known to countenance or pass over either of these vices [drunkenness and swearing], will be looked upon as unfit for executing the duties of his station and be discharged from walking the quarter deck."[46]

Providing for the spiritual and moral lives of his men was not the only task that Middleton's religious views caused him to undertake while he was a ship captain. Evangelicals had long been interested in helping the lower classes to better their lot by teaching them the virtues of cleanliness and frugality as well as godliness.[47] Middleton also tried to teach these lessons to his crews.[48] Indeed, he showed an almost paternalistic regard in instructing them about how to care for themselves properly. "Such [persons] as are found careless about their clothes or dirty in their persons, [his "Captain's Order Book" read, are] to be punished . . . as far as a few strokes [with a whip]. If [they are] habitually so, [they are] to be scrubbed in a tub . . . ."[49]

The men were to have adequate clothing as well as clean bodies. The "Order Book" specified that the lieutenants were to inspect the men's clothes regularly to make sure that they possessed all required naval garments. Care was to be taken, however, to keep them from buying needed apparel and other articles from unscrupulous pursers and from selling items to each other at inflated prices.[50]

Although he had already required his men to keep themselves and their garments clean, Middleton made additional efforts to insure the healthful environment that he desired. He ordered that some sleeping hammocks be washed each morning in rotation, and that the sides of the ship be scrubbed down each day.[51] Even officers' interests were sacrificed when they conflicted with the welfare of the men. For instance, Middleton wrote in his "Order Book" that oversized "[officers' cabins (were) to be reduced to the size allowed by the navy board] . . . so that the seamen may not be deprived of the space allowed them, which at best is found full insufficient."[52]

Middleton's religious convictions, which made such a strong impact on his administration of his vessels, were strengthened when he married Margaret Gambier on 22 December 1761.[53] She was the granddaughter of Nicholas Gambier, a Huguenot who had escaped from France when the Edict of Nantes was revoked, and the daughter of James Gambier, warden of the Fleet prison.[54] In addition, she was a friend of many Evangelicals.[55]

The closest of the new Mrs. Middleton's Evangelical comrades was Miss Elizabeth Bouverie.[56] These two women had been lifelong companions, and the Middletons spent much of their time after their marriage with Miss Bouverie at her estate of Barham Court at Teston, Kent.[57]

Both women were interested in Evangelical charitable and philanthropic projects, and soon after his wedding Middleton entered into their work. The three of them joined with other Evangelicals to concentrate upon educating "truly religious" young men for holy orders in the Church of England and purchasing church livings in as many prominent places as possible for "religious clergymen."[58] Initially, however, they lacked a cause and an organization to unite them and to enlist more pious Englishmen.[59] The Middletons, along with several other Evangelicals, overcame these problems when they stumbled across the issue of the British slave trade and persuaded William Wilberforce to lead a parliamentary battle to abolish it.

The catalyst which caused the Middletons to become concerned about the slave trade was the Rev. James Ramsay.[60] Ramsay was an Evangelical minister who had formerly served as a surgeon on the ship *Arundel* when Middleton had commanded her in 1759-60.[61] One day he boarded a slave ship to care for a sick slaver. He was shocked by the condition of the Negroes in the vessel,[62] and he never forgot what he had seen. In later years, he took holy orders and returned to the West Indies where he collected much first-hand information on the atrocities of the slave traffic, for he was determined to stir up agitation to abolish it. The movement that he started in the West Indies brought him so much opposition that he was obliged to leave the islands for Britain.[63] Upon reaching England, he looked for a place from which to carry on his campaign. His opportunity came in 1781 when Middleton and Miss Bouverie offered him the living of Teston and Nettlestead.[64] He accepted the position, and he was soon writing a pamphlet to awaken the British public to the Negroes' plight.[65] Middleton and his wife read his work. Both of them were horrified, and they asked Ramsay to tell them more.[66]

Mrs. Middleton was especially disturbed. After considering the slave trade's horrors for some time, she finally suggested to her husband and others that they should "urge the necessity of bringing the proposed Abolition of the Slave Trade before parliament, as a measure in which the whole nation was concerned."[67] Her spouse replied that he wished to do so, but he could not because he had never spoken in Parliament before.[68] Instead, he promised that he would write to William Wilberforce and ask him to champion the cause in the House of Commons.[69]

Since Wilberforce had already thought about the issue of the slave trade and met with Ramsay in November 1783, he welcomed Middleton's proposal. He wrote a long letter to Middleton and followed it up with a visit to Barham Court in the autumn of 1786.[70] The cumulative effects of this meeting, his own earlier impulses, and the urging of his other friends persuaded Wilberforce to take up the campaign for slave trade abolition in Parliament in 1787.[71] Now many Evangelicals had a goal to unite them: the abolition of the slave traffic.[72] They also acquired an organization; in fact, they had been holding meetings at Barham Court and at Clapham since 1786 to lay strategy and to gather information for the coming contention.[73]

Middleton's contributions to the struggle against the slave trade continued long after the first Barham Court meeting. Once he and Wilberforce met, a mutual interest in Evangelical undertakings and abolitionist schemes made them close friends.[74] The first consequence of this friendship was that Middleton supplied part of the information which Wilberforce needed to open his parliamentary debate on the slave traffic. Many persons whom Middleton knew had lived in the West Indies, and some of them had personal knowledge of the trade.[75] These people joined him and Wilberforce at Barham Court to inform them about the Negroes' condition. Strategy meetings were also held there with other prominent Evangelicals in attendance.[76] From these early discussions, and later ones at Clapham, came the agitation that brought the slave trade to an end in 1807.[77]

Middleton consistently supported the anti-slave trade movement,[78] but he also participated in other Evangelical moral and humanitarian projects. From 1787 until his death in 1813, he was involved in twenty-two Evangelical societies.[79] He was an officer as well as a member in some of these groups. By 1813, he had served as president of the London Jew Society and the Sunday School Society (1812); and as vice-president of the Lock Hospital, the Church Missionary Society (1812), and the Society for the Relief of Persons Imprisoned for Small Debt (1799). In addition, he was a charter member of Wilberforce's Proclamation Society (founded in 1788), an early subscriber to the Evangelical Stranger's Friend Society, and a member of the Evangelical Philanthropic Society.[80]

Although Middleton was an active figure in Evangelical moral, humanitarian, and anti-slave trade circles, he still found time to continue to work for the improvement of the common naval seaman's lot after he became comptroller of the navy on 22 July 1778.[81] The post of comptroller carried with it the unofficial chairmanship of the Navy Board. This board had a broad range of responsibilities which included building and fitting out of ships, purchasing shipbuilding supplies, managing the naval dockyards throughout the world, and transporting men and supplies. Moreover, it had a freer hand in its work than the subordinate boards of other governmental departments. The comptroller was thus able to claim a status which was second only to that of the first lord of the Admiralty.[82]

From the office of the comptroller, Middleton pressed advice on the first lord,[83] although this sometimes meant stepping outside of his immediate sphere of authority.[84] Middleton also used his influence to attempt to put some of the measures which he had instituted aboard his ships into practice throughout the entire fleet. In 1783, he submitted a memorandum to the Admiralty entitled "Duty of Captains in the Navy."[85] This document stressed the need for religious services and moral conduct on British naval vessels, and it placed the main responsibility for carrying out the regulations cited on the shoulders of the captain of each ship.[86] The effect on the navy of Middleton's ideas is difficult to gauge. They probably had some impact, for, as time passed, more and more officers began to run their ships along the lines that he had proposed.[87]

Middleton's concern for the common seaman did not end with one memorandum. He also instituted an effective measure to improve health conditions aboard British men-of-war. After noticing the alarming rate of sickness on naval vessels from 1778 to 1781, he and his board acted.[88] They knew that the crux of the problem was the procedure for processing and distributing new men to their permanent ship assignments. Instead of leaving newly raised men crowded together on small boats and receiving ships for a lengthy period before they were transferred to their respective ships, they organized a system of "slop ships."[89] New men were taken to these ships to undergo inspection and cleaning, and to receive new clothing before they went to join their assigned vessels.[90] They were also conveyed to their ships in healthier and less crowded boats.[91] These changes had a marked effect upon the health of the seamen. Dr. Gilbert Blane even went so far as to maintain that between 1779 and 1794 these alterations were responsible for a substantial reduction in sickness on naval craft.[92]

While Middleton's Evangelical commitments seem to have prompted him to originate and to support constructive reforms both inside and outside the navy, it is also probable that they had two constricting effects on his character. Indeed, these were common failings of many Evangelicals. In the first instance, their presumption of their own salvation and subsequent closeness to God led many to assume the correctness of all their ideas and actions. Secondly, the Evangelicals justified the use of methods to attain their ends which they would not have found acceptable in ordinary people.[93] In Middleton's case, these phenomena appear to have been combined with a high sense of his abilities, an ambitious nature, and a sincere belief that he was acting in the best interest of his country.[94] These qualities in his personality can be documented from the time when he became comptroller, and they continued to play a traceable part in his career until his retirement as first lord of the Admiralty in early 1806.[95]

If these factors were a part of Middleton's character, how did they affect his life? In the first place, they could partially account for his difficulty in working with or under men whose ideas differed from his own. John Norris characterized him as a "fanatic for efficient administration whose professional sensibilities were supplemented by strong evangelical religious principles . . . ."[96] Even Henry Dundas, Middleton's close friend and kinsman, apparently recognized this failing in his relative. ". . . [Charles] has very great official talents and merit," he wrote in 1794, "but he is a little difficult to act with from an anxiety, I had almost said an irritability of temper, and he requires to have a great deal of his own way of doing business in order to do it well."[97] Possibly Middleton's conviction that his ideas and methods were right and others' opinions were wrong intensified his "irritability of temper."

Furthermore, Middleton's convictions evidently gave him a self-righteous outlook which, when coupled with his lofty sense of his personal knowledge and experience,[98] permitted him to denounce certain practices that he found unacceptable in others. At the same time, however, he often indulged in many of the same activities himself. The best examples of this behavior lie in his attitudes and actions regarding the influence of politics in the navy, the use of patronage and nepotism in the making of naval appointments, and the factor of personal ambition in his own career.

Patronage, or "Interest," was an integral part of eighteenth-century British naval procedures. To begin with, a young officer candidate needed influence to obtain a post aboard a ship in almost all cases. As time passed, "Interest" was necessary for every transfer to a new ship, for promotion to any higher rank, and for securing a position at the bottom of the post captain list. It could also provide the best supplies, the best sailors, and all kinds of desirable perquisites.[99] Moreover, nepotism was practiced; indeed, it was almost inseparable from the patronage system.[100]

Much evidence suggests that Middleton was an opponent of political influence in the navy.[101] He referred to the spirit of partisan politics which existed among naval officers from 1778 to 1782 as "abominable," and he repeatedly criticized the Earl of Sandwich (first lord of the Admiralty, 1771 to 1782) for his "political manipulation" of dockyard appointments. After he failed to persuade Sandwich and his successors at the Admiralty to stop using their "political system" for filling these positions,[102] he wrote in 1786, that ". . . I find politics have got too great a hold on this [the civil] branch of the navy for me to withstand it. God knows what is best; but I shall contend no more for the public . . . . I trust those who follow me will have more weight than I have had, and influence ministers to correct these evils."[103]

It later turned out that Middleton was able to strike a blow against politics in the navy himself. In 1805, as first lord of the Admiralty, he effectively discouraged the tradition of allowing naval officers to sit in Parliament by refusing leaves of absence to ship captains who wished to attend to parliamentary duties.[104]

Despite Middleton's aversion to those who mixed political and naval careers, his views did not prevent him from sitting in Parliament himself while he served as comptroller. He stood for election to the House of Commons from the borough of Rochester as a Tory supporter of the younger William Pitt in 1784.[105] Rochester was considered an Admiralty borough, for many of its approximately five hundred voters were employed in the naval dockyards,[106] but there was also a strong independent group in its electorate. Middleton was thus apparently willing to prevent any potential competition by obtaining £1,330 of King George III's secret service money for election use.[107] The Rochester constituency elected him, and he sat for it from 1784 to 1790.[108] These were interesting actions for a man who opposed the combination of politics and naval service.

Equally evident was the discrepancy between Middleton's professed attitude toward patronage and his actions. Middleton did not object to the patronage system, but he thought that it was sadly abused [109] by influential men who often harmed the public interest either by practicing nepotism or by paying no attention to the merits of the people whose claims they supported. He often stated that he was above such dealings. In 1805, while he was first lord of the Admiralty, he wrote to Admiral Cornwallis:

. . . With regard to patronage the service has become too extensive
to make it any longer an object; and I declare to you that since my
coming to this [the Admiralty] board, I have made but one master
and commander; and when I read over the claims before me,—from
admirals and captains for their children, from the king's ministers,
members of parliament, peers . . . I do not see when I am to make
another. Under these circumstances it is impossible that any person
in my situation should give satisfaction. If I steer clear of injustice
I shall think myself fortunate. To conclude, in all matters of
patronage, I execute it as I would any other duty belonging to the
office [of first lord], I hope with impartiality.[110]

While Middleton asserted his impartiality, the truth seems to have been nearer to the sentiments expressed in a conversation that took place between William Wilberforce and the younger William Pitt. Wilberforce reported the dialogue as follows: "Sir Charles," said Pitt, "is the best man of business I know, but he will do any thing for a[n Evangelical]." "He has the good sense," was my reply, "to know that he cannot be secure of the due execution of his measures, unless he can depend upon his instruments."[111] In fact, traceable instances of Middleton's patronage activities reveal that he may well have often favored men with religious tendencies like his own.[112]

If Middleton was not wholly objective in his patronage actions, he was also not immune to practicing nepotism. He repeatedly sought naval employment for his brother, George Middleton.[113] Moreover, he was extremely interested in furthering the career of his nephew, James Gambier. Middleton had raised Gambier in his home until he was eleven years old, and the boy developed a strong Evangelical faith which later earned him the nickname of "Preaching Jemmy" in the fleet.[114] These circumstances caused Middleton to take an active part in James's advancement.[115] So effective was Middleton's intervention on Gambier's behalf that Gambier not only became a post captain at the age of twenty-one[116] but he received the best seamen and subordinate officers available to man his ship.[117]

There is little doubt that Middleton's favors to Gambier could have been better bestowed elsewhere. Gambier turned out to be a mediocre ship and fleet commander whose major assets were only personal courage and integrity. To make matters worse, his strict religious feelings colored his judgment of men, for they led him to favor sailors with real or feigned religious convictions, while his treatment of other members of his crews caused great disaffection among them.[118] His conduct in battle was fearless, but often controversial. At Basque Roads in 1809, his handling of the fleet resulted in a court-martial. He was acquitted; yet modern historical opinion is still divided on this and other issues concerning him.[119] Despite this controversy, however, his uncle's favors to him never faltered.[120]

Middleton's declarations that he had no personal ambitions to satisfy were as persistent as his statements that he did not indulge in patronage and nepotism. In 1782, he wrote to Lord Shelburne:

Having no views to gratify but what regards [the] public good, I
feel no difficulty of divesting myself [of] that narrow Idea which
subsists in most officer[s], of concealing the Secrets belonging to
them. . . .
    Under the last Administration, I was offered every thing that could
be called a gratification of Ambition and Emolument but declined
all on public ground.[121]

Does this statement conform more closely to Middleton's actions than his pronouncements about his principles regarding politics, patronage, and nepotism? The answer is apparently no. Piers Mackesy notes in *The War for America 1775-1783* that he was "a forerunner of the administrators who were soon to convert the archaic racket called government into the efficient instrument which transformed Victorian England."[122] But he was also

exceedingly ambitious and by no means as free from connections
as he liked to imply. Before he became Comptroller he was not
above promising the First Lord [Sandwich] his vote and influence in
East India Company affairs. He was related to those Scottish political

manipulators, the Dundases; and before discussing his appointment to the Navy Board with Sandwich he told him he wished to talk the matter over with "some confidential friends. . . ." Nor was his connection with [the Earl of] Shelburne a wholly disinterested, though it was a devious one.[123]

In addition, although Middleton couched his proposals for naval reform in terms of the public good (and there is no denying that most of them *were* in the public interest), some of them bore the stamp of personal ambition.[124] His wish for a new office of sea ordnance, presumably under Navy Board control, bore the mark of this search for power,[125] and so did his desire that the comptroller should be an admiral with a seat at the Admiralty Board.[126] But another effort manifested these contradictions even more strongly.

Throughout 1781, Middleton conducted a campaign to gain control of the dockyard patronage for the Navy Board, which he headed.[127] He was convinced that Sandwich, the first lord, was ignoring qualified men, and he probably wanted the power to make dockyard appointments in the hands of the Navy Board so that he could administer them. Sandwich and the Admiralty Board resisted this "official encroachment" on their powers.[128] The result was predictable. Middleton's agitation failed.[129]

How could Middleton reconcile these apparent discrepancies between his professed principles and his activities in the fields of politics, patronage, nepotism, and ambition? Evidently, he regarded his actions as just, even though they conflicted with his statements, largely because, either consciously or unconsciously, he felt that as one of God's elect he must do all he could to rescue the navy from the hands of the irreligious and immoral men who were making the Admiralty "rotten."[130] He believed, as most good Evangelicals did, that religion had to form an integral part of the public life of any good servant of the king. As he pithily put it, "In short, where there is no religion there can be no public principle."[131] Many years later, he composed a fuller summary of what he felt were essential qualifications for a good royal official. Religion stands out as a prime requirement in this passage, too—"Honesty and application will go a great way in carrying on public business; if these are wanting, all the talents which we hear so much of, will prove vain: I say nothing of religion and virtue, but whoever throws them aside, must have little to expect from Him, who governs even the falling of a sparrow."[132]

This view, when added to the conscious Evangelical certainty of his own salvation, may have led Middleton to the typically Evangelical conclusion that people like himself could use methods not acceptable among the less pious.[133] He was not merely asserting personal prerogatives when he persuaded himself that what was best for him and his friends was also best for the nation and the navy. Other Evangelicals showed this tendency toward self-righteousness, too.[134] Middleton also imbibed political conservatism along with self-righteousness from the Evangelicals. Like others, he seemed to feel that the appearance of depravity, sin, and vice in men was due to their lack of "true religion."[135] Thus he had apparently come to the position of trusting only himself and his fellow Evangelicals, while he often distrusted or despised others' ideas and motives.[136]

Such attitudes and behavior on Middleton's part, however, should not be used as the basis for a charge of hypocrisy against him. While many of his reform endeavors foreshadowed subsequent developments, he was a man of his time, attached to the political and social system of his day. In his rationale for his actions, he differed from those around him principally in the strong emphasis he placed on morality and righteousness and his comparison of himself with those around him who were not "religious" in the Evangelical sense of the term. In essence, the same moral intensity which caused him to undertake his humanitarian work seems also to have insulated him from any feeling of unjustifiable behavior.

Both of these characteristics of Middleton's religious temperament, as well as the Evangelical motivation of his reform measures, must be considered in any effort to summarize the consequences of his religious activities and beliefs. These consequences fall into three categories: first, their impact on his naval reforms; second, their direction of his attention to Evangelical causes; and third, their effect on his personality. In the field of naval reform, his convictions seem to have contributed to the bettering of the ordinary sailor's health and to the beginning of a remarkable change of behavior on board British warships.[137] Despite many sailors' earlier aversion to the strict religious and moral discipline which Middleton and Gambier maintained, crews after 1800 appear to have become more amenable to their ideas when other officers enforced them.

One illustration of the success of these disciplinary procedures was recorded by Private William Wheeler, a soldier in the British army who traveled aboard a British man-of-war in 1811. He wrote to his family that

the Captain [of the ship] goes by the name of "Father." Cursing and swearing is not allowed. The good feeling existing between the captain and the sailors was fully displayed last Sunday morning, when the ship's company assembled for the Captain's inspection. It was truly pleasing to see the good old man . . . walking through the ranks of sailors, who all appeared as clean as possible, with health and contentment glowing on their faces. . . .

. . . After inspection all hands were piped to church. . . . This day

the spirit of the fourth Commandment was put into force far beyond
anything I could have expected, nothing was done but what was
absolutely necessary. . . .[138]

The beneficial results of this discipline, fostered by officers who subscribed
to Middleton's opinions, helped to spread it to many ships of the British
fleet.[139] Indeed, after 1800 these Evangelical ideas advanced so rapidly in
the navy that some felt it was a special object of Evangelical attention.[140]
It may well be that Middleton played an important role in helping to further
the careers of the men who brought this reformation in naval discipline and
manners to pass.[141]

Middleton's efforts on behalf of Evangelical causes outside the navy were
also significant. As we have seen, he took part in the anti-slave trade agitation, and he provided part of the impetus which eventually brought William
Wilberforce into the movement. In fact, his early relationship with Wilberforce turned into a lifelong friendship which helped to draw Middleton into
the work of many Evangelical organizations.[142]

Middleton gained another even closer friend, Hannah More, as a consequence of his participation in the campaign against the slave traffic. He and
Lady Middleton strongly affected her development, and they fortified her
religious resolve and her opposition to the slave trade during the first years
after her conversion.[143] As time passed, Middleton carried on an extensive
correspondence with her. In addition, he sent money to support many of her
charitable schemes.[144] In return, Miss More praised him for his interest. She
revealed the intimacy of their friendship when she wrote in 1793, ". . . I
never name . . . [my humanitarian schemes to others] except in my letters
to Teston or Clapham . . . ."[145] This acknowledgment, together with Middleton's efforts in helping to convert Wilberforce, his labors in the anti-slave
trade work, and his activities in Evangelical societies, suggests the many
fruitful ways in which his religious convictions channeled his energies into
religiously connected undertakings.

From the evidence presented here, it is clear that religion influenced all
phases of Middleton's life. Historians who wish to understand his actions
and his personality will therefore have to emphasize this facet of his psyche
to a greater extent than they have yet done. Perhaps Hannah More made
the most fitting statements on the role of religion in his public and private
life. In a letter to Gambier in 1807, she wrote as follows: "It has pleased
God eminently to bless the undertakings of Lord Barham and yourself, and
I hope religion will no longer appear so formidable a thing to our great men,
when they see that, so far from disqualifying persons from executing high
and perilous offices properly, it inspires them with greater vigour and superior energy."[146] As for the significance of religion in Middleton's private

life, Miss More again summarized it well when she stated, "I know you are interested in the meanest attempt to spread Christianity. . . ."[147]

Although the indications of spiritual influences on Middleton's personality are not so plain and positive as they are in his naval reforms and in his Evangelical work, their effects still seem to have been considerable. There is little doubt that his religious convictions at least partially prompted his overweening self-righteousness which made it so difficult for him to work well with others in the navy.[148] They also seem to have caused him to assume an anomalous position with regard to the issues of politics, patronage, and nepotism in the navy, and to the fulfillment of personal ambition. On the other hand, this self-righteousness may have given him the confidence and fortitude he needed to push his naval work toward completion in the face of political and professional opposition.[149] Moreover, his religious ideas probably led him to help many serious young officers with Evangelical feelings to rise in the navy.[150]

Taking all of these elements as a whole, the impact of religion on the life of Charles Middleton seems to have been beneficial both to the Evangelicals and to the country. His religiously motivated naval reforms, his activities in the anti-slave trade crusade, and his contributions to the Evangelical movement all yielded constructive results. Even the flaws in his character which religion probably intensified may have proved productive in the end.

NOTES

* The author wishes to thank Professor Theodore R. Crane and Professor John C. Livingston of the University of Denver for their counsel and encouragement in the preparation of this essay.
1. John H. Overton, *The Evangelical Revival in the Eighteenth Century*, Epochs of Church History, ed. Mandell Creighton, vol. 4 (London: Longmans, Green, and Co., 1900), 45-46 and 187-188.
2. John R. H. Moorman, *A History of the Church in England* (London: Adam and Charles Black, 1953), 302.
3. *Ibid.*, 302-303.
4. Stephen C. Neill, *Anglicanism*, 3rd ed. (Baltimore: Penguin Books, 1965), 190.
5. Bernard Pool, "Lord Barham: A Great Naval Administrator," *History Today* 15, no. 5 (May 1965): 354. This is the only historical work that deals solely with Middleton except for volumes 32, 38, and 39 of the Naval Records Society series which contain his private naval papers. No published biography of Middleton exists. Piers Mackesy, however, gives a good account of some aspects of Middleton's character in his book entitled *The War for America 1775-1783*. See Piers Mackesy, *The War for America 1775-1783* (Cambridge, Mass.: Harvard University Press, 1964), 163-165,

398, and 484. See also Sir John Laughton, ed., *Letters and Papers of Charles, Lord Barham, Admiral of the Red Squadron, 1758-1813,* 3 vols., Publications of the Naval Records Society, vols. 32, 38, and 39 (London: Naval Records Society, 1907-1911). Hereafter cited as *Barham Pap.,* vol. 1, 2, or 3: page.

6. Ford K. Brown, *Fathers of the Victorians: The Age of Wilberforce* (Cambridge: Cambridge University Press, 1961), 101. Brown wrote that Middleton was "the first of a long line of Evangelical senior [naval] officers." See Brown, 101. See also John Norris, *Shelburne and Reform* (London: Macmillan and Co., 1963), 208.

7. *Barham Pap.,* 1: ix. It is probable that Middleton's wife, whose family had originally been Huguenot refugees from France when the Edict of Nantes was revoked, strongly influenced him in later life. See *Barham Pap.,* 1: xxiii. Middleton, however, was vigorously enforcing naval regulations regarding religious services, drinking, swearing, and immorality when he commanded naval vessels from 1757 to 1778. He was thus showing religious tendencies before he married his wife on 22 December 1761. See Sir William H. Dillon, *A Narrative of My Professional Adventures, (1790-1839),* ed. Michael A. Lewis, 2 vols., Publications of the Naval Records Society, vols. 93 and 97 (London: Naval Records Society, 1953-1956), 1: 94-99. Hereafter cited as *Dillon's Narrative,* vol. 1 or 2: page. See also Middleton's memorandum "Duty of Captains in the Navy," 1783, in *Barham Pap.,* 2: 161-165. Hereafter cited as "Duty of Captains." It is therefore likely that he received strict religious training early in his life, probably from his parents.

8. Robert Wilberforce and Samuel Wilberforce, *The Life of William Wilberforce,* 2nd ed., 5 vols. (London: John Murray, 1839), 1: 234. Hereafter cited as *Life of Wilberforce,* vol. 1, 2, 3, 4, or 5: page. Wilberforce's diary for 18 July 1789, reads as follows: "Came off to Teston, to see the Middletons and Mrs. Bouverie. How much better is this society! I will endeavour to confine myself more to those who fear God." See *Life of Wilberforce,* 1: 234. This quotation furnishes proof that Middleton was an Evangelical, for Ford K. Brown observed that "the expression 'those who feared God' . . . [is] one of the [Robert and Samuel] Wilberforces' favorite pseudonyms for the Evangelicals." These authors used pseudonyms instead of the term "Evangelical" because they wished to disguise their father's role in the Evangelical group within the Church of England. See Brown, 494 and 487-506. Brown went on to state that "from an early point . . . [in the Evangelical movement] the words 'religious', 'sincere', and 'pious' were used by the Evangelicals to designate Evangelicals only." When Evangelicals spoke of "those who fear God," "religious men," "true religion," or "serious men," they also referred solely to other Evangelicals. See Brown, 64.

9. Overton, 187-188.

10. Brown, 63 and 62-66.

11. *Ibid.,* 68-69.

12. *Ibid.,* 1-6.

13. *Ibid.,* 9 and 44.

14. *Ibid.,* 5-6. To the Evangelicals, making England "truly religious" would involve converting the Church of England, and through it the people of Britain, to Evangelical beliefs. See Brown, 5-6, 64, and note 8 above.

15. *Ibid.*, 3-4, 69-72, 266-269, and 526-529.
16. Leonard E. Elliott-Binns, *The Early Evangelicals: A Religious and Social Study* (London: Lutterworth Press, 1953), 420; and Brown, 106-115, 372-375, and 378-382.
17. Brown, 10-11.
18. Elliott-Binns, 420-423.
19. Brown, 261-262.
20. *Ibid.*, 9-11.
21. *Ibid.*, 390-392.
22. *Ibid.*, 475.
23. *Ibid.*, 391.
24. See *Barham Pap.*, 1: i-xxvi.
25. *Dictionary of National Biography*, reissue (1908-1909), s. v. "Middleton, Charles, First Baron Barham." Hereafter cited as *D. N. B.*, "Middleton."
26. Pool, 348; and Henry Dundas to Lord Spenser, 14 December 1794, Julian S. Corbett and H. W. Richmond, eds., *Private Papers of George, Second Earl Spenser, First Lord of the Admiralty, 1794-1801*, 4 vols., Publications of the Naval Records Society, vols. 46, 48, 58, and 59 (London: Naval Records Society, 1913-1924), 1: 5-7. Hereafter cited as *Spenser Pap.*, vol. 1, 2, 3, or 4: page.
27. *Barham Pap.*, 1: viii.
28. Mackesy, 164.
29. *Barham Pap.*, 1: viii-ix.
30. *Ibid.*, ix.
31. *Ibid.*, x.
32. *Ibid.*
33. *D. N. B.*, "Middleton."
34. *Barham Pap.*, 1: xiv-xv.
35. *D. N. B.*, "Middleton"; and *Barham Pap.*, 1: x.
36. See *Barham Pap.*, 1: x for the exact list of ships and dates that Middleton commanded them.
37. *Ibid.*
38. *Ibid.*, xviii-xix.
39. "Duty of Captains," in *Barham Pap.*, 2: 161.
40. *Ibid.*, 161-162; and *Dillon's Narrative*, 1: 96-97.
41. "Duty of Captains," in *Barham Pap.*, 2: 162-164. For information about chaplains in the navy during this period, see Michael A. Lewis, *A Social History of the Navy 1793-1815* (London: George Allen and Unwin, 1960), 250-255. Hereafter cited as Lewis, *A Social History*.
42. "Autograph Minute" by Middleton, undated, in *Barham Pap.*, 2: 10.
43. "Duty of Captains," in *Barham Pap.*, 2: 151-165.
44. *Ibid.*, 163.
45. *Ibid.*, 164.
46. Middleton's "Captain's Order Book [of H. M. Ship *Ardent*]," 1 August 1775, in *Barham Pap.*, 1: 41. Hereafter cited as "Order Book." The effect of all this new discipline, to which the crews of the ships Middleton commanded from 1757 to 1778 were not accustomed, is hard to evaluate. Middleton reported that it caused his men to become "as regular as any private family." See "Duty of Captains," in *Barham Pap.*, 2: 164. Sir William Dillon disagreed. He served on the *Defence* during 1793-1794 when James

Gambier, Middleton's nephew, enforced similar discipline. Dillon related that "these regulations caused much discontent and murmuring among the Ship's Company, who deserted when they could." See *Dillon's Narrative*, 1: 97. In any event, the general tendency of this discipline was probably beneficial in the long run. It became more and more widespread in the fleet until, by about 1821, its combination with other Evangelical schemes to promote religion and morality in the navy was probably largely responsible for the "remarkable change of manners on board [naval ships]." See W. G. Perrin and Christopher Lloyd, eds., *The Keith Papers, Selected from the Papers of Admiral Viscount Keith*, 3 vols., Publications of the Naval Records Society, vols. 62, 90, and 96 (London: Naval Records Society, 1927-1955), 3: 314. Hereafter cited as *Keith Pap.*, vol. 1, 2, or 3: page.

47. Brown, 141-144. See also note 19 above.

48. "Order Book," in *Barham Pap.*, 1: 39-45.

49. *Ibid.*, 40.

50. *Ibid.*, 39-40 and 45. This regulation seems unusual since the pursers on many naval ships sold clothes and other goods to seamen at outrageous prices during the eighteenth century. The officers on many British naval vessels seem to have done little to stop this practice. Middleton, however, forbade it, at least on paper. See Lewis, *A Social History*, 246-250; and *Barham Pap.*, 1: 40 and 43.

51. "Order Book," in *Barham Pap.*, 1: 41.

52. *Ibid.*, 42. The brackets in this quotation indicate editorial abstracting of the material in the *Barham Pap.* The parentheses are my own.

53. *Ibid.*, xxii-xxiii.

54. *Ibid.*, xxiii-xxiv.

55. Mary A. Hopkins, *Hannah More and Her Circle* (New York: Longmans, Green and Co., 1947), 146.

56. Georgiana, Lady Chatterton, ed., *Memorials, Personal and Historical of Admiral Lord Gambier, G. C. B.*, 2nd ed., 2 vols. (London: Hurst and Blackett, 1861), 1: 139. Hereafter cited as Chatterton, vol. 1 or 2; page. See also *Barham Pap.*, 1: xxiii-xxiv.

57. *Barham Pap.*, 1: xxiv.

58. Brown, 2.

59. *Ibid.*

60. Christian Latrobe to his daughter, 5 December 1815, *Life of Wilberforce*, 1: 142-144; and Hopkins, 154.

61. *Dictionary of National Biography*, reissue (1908-1909), s. v. "Ramsey, James." Hereafter cited as *D. N. B.*, "Ramsey."

62. *Ibid.*

63. *Ibid.*

64. Latrobe to his daughter, 5 December 1815, *Life of Wilberforce*, 1: 143; and Middleton to the younger Pitt, 7 August 1787, enclosure 2, "Statement of Public Services Performed by the Reverend James Ramsey, Vicar of Teston, in Kent" by P. Mitchell, in *Barham Pap.*, 2: 254.

65. Sir Reginald Coupland, *Wilberforce*, 2nd ed. (London: Collins Press, 1945), 78.

66. Latrobe to his daughter, 5 December 1815, *Life of Wilberforce*, 1: 142-144; and Coupland, 78.

67. Latrobe to his daughter, 5 December 1815, *Life of Wilberforce*, 1: 144.

Middleton had been elected M. P. for the Admiralty borough of Rochester in 1784. See *Barham Pap.*, 1: xix.

68. Latrobe to his daughter, 5 December 1815, in *Life of Wilberforce*, 1: 144-145. Latrobe is not wholly right on this point. Middleton had made two brief statements in Parliament during early 1786. See [William Cobbett and John Wright, eds.], *Parliamentary History of England from the Earliest Period to the Year 1803*, 36 vols. (London: T. C. Hansard, 1815), 25: 1122 and 1336.

69. Latrobe to his daughter, 5 December 1815, *Life of Wilberforce*, 1: 145-146.

70. *Dictionary of National Biography*, reissue (1908-1909), s. v. "Wilberforce, William." Hereafter cited as *D. N. B.*, "Wilberforce."

71. *Life of Wilberforce*, 1: 142-155; *D. N. B.*, "Wilberforce"; and Coupland, 78-79.

72. Brown, 106-115.

73. Hopkins, 146 and 154.

74. *Life of Wilberforce*, 1: 234 and 371; and 3: 459-460.

75. *Ibid.*, 1: 150; and Latrobe to his daughter, 5 December 1815. *Life of Wilberforce*, 1: 145-146. The most important of these people were Christian Latrobe and James Ramsay.

76. Hopkins, 146 and 154.

77. Coupland, 270-271 and 284.

78. *Ibid.*, 250, 282, and 377.

79. Brown, 355.

80. ["Obituary of Charles Middleton, First Baron Barham,"] *Gentlemen's Magazine* 83, pt. 1 (June 1813): 597-598; and Brown, 270, 349, and 359-360. Wilberforce's Proclamation Society (founded in 1788) tried to "diminish full-grown crimes by insuring certainty of punishment for the smaller ones, whenever reformatory prevention should fail." See Chatterton, 1: 165; and *Life of Wilberforce*, 1: 394. The Philanthropic Society (founded 1788) tried to stop crime by reforming criminal poor children. See Brown, 89, 241, and 333.

81. *Barham Pap.*, 1: x and xix.

82. Mackesy, 16 and 163-165.

83. Lord Sandwich to Middleton, 24 January 1781, G. R. Barnes and J. H. Owen, eds., *The Private Papers of John, Fourth Earl of Sandwich, First Lord of the Admiralty, 1771-1782*, 4 vols., Publications of the Naval Records Society, vols. 69, 71, 75, and 78 (London: Naval Records Society, 1932-1938), 4: 376-377. Hereafter cited as *Sandwich Pap.*, vol. 1, 2, 3, or 4: page.

84. Mackesy, 163-165. See also the correspondence between Middleton and Lord Sandwich in *Barham Pap.*, 2: 1-43.

85. "Duty of Captains," in *Barham Pap.*, 2: 161-165.

86. *Ibid.*

87. *Dillon's Narrative*, 1: 92-112; Private William Wheeler to his family, 9 February 1811, B. H. Liddell Hart, ed., *The Letters of Private Wheeler* (Boston: Houghton Mifflin Co., 1951), 41-43. See also [Sidney Smith], "[Review of] *Causes of the Increase of Methodism, and Dissension*, by Robert Acklem Ingram, B. D.," *Edinburgh Review* 11, no. 22 (January 1808): 352-355.

88. Dr. Gilbert Blane, "On the Comparative Health of the British Navy, from the Year 1779 to the Year 1814 with Proposals for Its Farther Improvement," in Christopher Lloyd, ed., *The Health of Seamen*, Publications of the Naval Records Society, vol. 107 (London: Naval Records Society, 1965), 181. Hereafter cited as *Health of Seamen*. Middleton was always an enemy of the impressment system. See *Life of Wilberforce*, 2: 211-212. He sent a memorandum to Lord Shelburne in 1782 outlining a method for procuring men by enlistment for a three-year term of service. Middleton proposed this procedure to replace the old impressment system which often merely consisted of kidnapping men for indefinite periods. See Middleton to Lord Shelburne, November 1782, Shelburne Papers, William L. Clements Library, University of Michigan, Ann Arbor, Michigan, vol. 151, item 37. Hereafter cited as Shelburne Pap., vol., item.

89. *Health of Seamen*, 181.

90. *Ibid.*

91. *Ibid.*, 181-182.

92. *Ibid.*, 155 and 182.

93. See notes 21, 22, and 23 above.

94. Middleton to Lord Shelburne, 26 September 1782, Shelburne Pap, vol. 151, item 41; Middleton to (?) Pitt, 27 December 1805, *Barham Pap.*, 3: 298; Middleton's endorsement, January 1786, on a letter intended for Lord Sandwich and never sent, [February 1781 (?)], *Barham Pap.*, 2: 30; and Mackesy, 163-165.

95. *Barham Pap.*, 3: xx.

96. Norris, 208. Bernard Pool seems to share the same view. See Pool, 354.

97. Henry Dundas to Lord Spenser, 14 December 1794, *Spenser Pap.*, 1: 6. Cf. Mackesy, 164 for Middleton's statement about his constant attention to business as the reason for his invariable "correctness" on matters of public concern.

98. *Barham Pap.*, 2: xi. See also Mackesy, 164.

99. *Dillon's Narrative*, 1: 5-6. See also note 109 below.

100. Lewis, *A Social History*, 202-227. See also *Dillon's Narrative*, 1: 93-96.

101. Middleton to Lord Shelburne, 14 October 1782, *Barham Pap.*, 2: 71-72. See also David Mathew, *The Naval Heritage* (London: Collins Press, 1945), 74. For the divisive and detrimental effect of politics on the navy from 1778 to 1782, see J. H. Broomfield, "The Keppel-Palliser Affair, 1778-1779," *Mariner's Mirror* 47, no. 3 (August 1961): 195-206.

102. Middleton to Lord Sandwich, 12 March 1780, *Sandwich Pap.*, 4: 415; Middleton's endorsement, January 1786, on a letter intended for Lord Sandwich and never sent, [February 1781 (?)], *Barham Pap.*, 2: 30; "Autograph Minute" by Middleton, undated, in *Barham Pap.*, 2: 10; Middleton to Lord Sandwich, 21 January 1781, *Barham Pap.*, 2: 17-19. See also other letters from Middleton to Lord Sandwich for details of this dispute in *Barham Pap.*, 2: 1-43.

103. Middleton's endorsement, January 1786, on a letter intended for Lord Sandwich and never sent, [February 1781 (?)], *Barham Pap.*, 2: 30.

104. Sir Oswyn A. R. Murray, "The Admiralty, VI," *Mariner's Mirror* 24, no. 3 (July 1938): 347.

105. Middleton to Pitt, 24 September 1789, *Barham Pap.*, 2: 328-330.

106. Lewis B. Namier, *The Structure of Politics at the Accession of George III*,

2nd ed. (London: The Macmillan Co., 1960), 78-79 footnote 3, and 124. Middleton had twice previously been offered a seat in the House of Commons representing either the borough of Scarborough or the borough of Callington with the government paying election expenses. See Middleton to Lord Shelburne, 26 September 1782, Shelburne Pap., vol. 151, item 41. It seems that much the same arrangement was worked out when he accepted the Rochester seat in 1784.

107. "Disbursements for Secret Service [1784]," in George III, *The Later Correspondence of George III*, ed. A. Aspinall, 5 vols. (Cambridge: Cambridge University Press, 1962-1970), vol. 1, *December 1783-January 1793*, (1962), 116.

108. *Barham Pap.*, 1: xix. Middleton wanted to stand for election from the borough of Poole in the election of 1790. He also said he would accept nomination from the borough of Portsmouth, but his plans evidently miscarried in both cases, for he was not elected again. See Middleton to Pitt, 24 September 1789, *Barham Pap.*, 2: 328-330; and Pitt to Middleton, 3 October 1789, *Barham Pap.*, 2: 332.

109. See note 101 above; and Middleton to Lord Shelburne, 9 September 1782, Shelburne Pap., vol. 151, item 40.

110. Middleton to Admiral Cornwallis, 7 November 1805, *Barham Pap.*, 3: 283-284. See also Middleton to Lord Shelburne, 26 September 1782, Shelburne Pap., vol. 151, item 41; Middleton to Lord Shelburne, 16 September 1782, Shelburne Pap., vol. 151, item 39; and Mackesy, 164.

111. *Life of Wilberforce*, 2: 212. The original word that Pitt used was "*Methodist*," but the confusion of these two names by non-Evangelicals in the eighteenth century and the circumstantial evidence offered in this paper seem to indicate that the term "Evangelical" is more appropriate here. See Overton, 45-46 and 187-188; and Brown, 2, 65, and 273-274.

112. For examples of the religious family connections of some of the many recipients of Middleton's patronage favors, see Sir Samuel Hood to Middleton, 13 December 1781, *Barham Pap.*, 1: 131; *Dillon's Narrative*, 1: 99; Middleton to Lord Sandwich, [1781 (?)], *Barham Pap.*, 2: 36-37; Captain Richard Kempenfelt to Middleton, 28 December [1779 (?)], *Barham Pap.*, 1: 308; Middleton to Lord Collingwood, [undated], *Barham Pap.*, 3: 339; and cf. names mentioned in correspondence in Chatterton, vols. 1 and 2. The religious feelings and affiliations of many of Middleton's patronage recipients have yet to be completely examined, but the indications of research already done seem to agree with a modified form of Pitt's statement. Pitt was, after all, Middleton's good friend and distant relative by marriage. See Pool, 354; Henry Dundas to Lord Spenser, 14 December 1794, *Spenser Pap.*, 1: 5-6; and *Barham Pap.*, 1: xxiii. Personal and family obligations, as well as recognition of merit, no doubt also entered into Middleton's thinking here to some extent, but religion seems to have played a large, if not dominant, role in this area.

113. Middleton to Lord Melville (Henry Dundas), "Memoranda of Advice," [May 1804], in *Barham Pap.*, 3: 32. See also Mackesy, 164-165.

114. Chatterton, 1: 5; and *Dillon's Narrative*, 1: xxxii and 96-97.

115. Captain Walter Young to Middleton, 8 February 1781, *Barham Pap.*, 1: 93; Young to Middleton, 3 March 1781, *Barham Pap.*, 1: 96.

116. J[ames] Ralfe, *The Naval Biography of Great Britain: Consisting of His-*

torical Memoirs of Those Officers of the British Navy Who Distinguished Themselves During the Reign of His Majesty George III, 4 vols. (London: Whitmore and Fenn, 1828), 2: 82.

117. *Dillon's Narrative*, 1: 93, 96-97, and 178.

118. *Ibid.*, xxxii, 96-97, and 107-108; and Oliver Warner, *The Glorious First of June* (New York: The Macmillan Co., 1961), 75.

119. *Dillon's Narrative*, 2: 122 and 126; and *Dictionary of National Biography*, reissue (1908-1909), s. v. "Gambier, James, Baron Gambier."

120. Wilberforce to Gambier, 6 August 1809, Chatterton, 2: 329.

121. Middleton to Lord Shelburne, 26 September 1782, Shelburne Pap., vol. 151, item 41. See also Middleton to Lord Sandwich, [February 1781 (?)], *Barham Pap.*, 2: 28-30; and Mackesy, 164.

122. Mackesy, 164; and Middleton to Lord Shelburne, 26 September 1782, Shelburne Pap., vol. 151, item 41.

123. Mackesy, 164.

124. *Ibid.*

125. Middleton to Lord Sandwich, [No date: 1781 or 1782], *Sandwich Pap.*, 4: 418-419.

126. Middleton to Lord Shelburne, 16 September 1782, Shelburne Pap., vol. 151, item 39; and Mackesy, 163-165.

127. For letters on this subject, see *Barham Pap.*, 2: 11-43. Middleton dominated the Navy Board almost entirely by the force of his personality. See Mackesy, 163.

128. Lord Sandwich to Middleton, 22 January 1781, *Barham Pap.*, 2: 19-20; Middleton to Lord Sandwich, 19 January 1781, *Barham Pap.*, 2: 17; and Middleton to Lord Sandwich, [undated], *Barham Pap.*, 2: 7.

129. Middleton's endorsement, January 1786, on a letter intended for Lord Sandwich and never sent, [February 1781 (?)], *Barham Pap.*, 2: 30. See also R. J. B. Knight, "Sandwich, Middleton and Dockyard Appointments," *Mariner's Mirror* 57, no. 2 (May 1971): 175-192.

130. Middleton to Lord Sandwich, 1779, *Barham Pap.*, 2: 2-6.

131. "Autograph Minute" by Middleton, undated, in *Barham Pap.*, 2: 10.

132. Middleton to Hannah More, 1811, William Roberts, *Memoirs of the Life and Correspondence of Mrs. Hannah More*, 2nd ed., 4 vols. (London: R. B. Seeley and W. Burnside, 1834), 3: 334.

133. Brown, 475.

134. *Ibid.*

135. *Ibid.*, 61-67.

136. *Ibid.*, 475.

137. *Keith Pap.*, 3: 314. See also note 88 above.

138. Private Wheeler to his family, 9 February 1811, Liddell Hart, 42.

139. [Smith], 353.

140. *Ibid.*; and Brown, 401-402.

141. See note 112 above.

142. *Life of Wilberforce*, 1: 142-152, and 393; 3: 459-460; 4: 122.

143. Hopkins, 146.

144. More to Middleton, 26 May 1803, Chatterton, 1: 391.

145. More to Middleton, 5 December 1793, Chatterton, 1: 234.

146. More to Gambier, 14 November 1807, Chatterton, 2: 88. This statement

is probably more valid with respect to Middleton than to Gambier because of Gambier's failings. See also notes 118, 119, and 120 above.

147. More to Middleton, 5 December 1793, Chatterton, 1: 234.
148. Henry Dundas to Lord Spenser, 14 December 1794, *Spenser Pap.*, 1: 6; Mackesy, 165; and Pool, 354.
149. See Middleton's letters to Lord Sandwich and to Pitt in vols. 2 and 3 of the *Barham Pap.*; See also Mackesy, 163-165.
150. See note 112 above.

PART II

The Tudor Governments and Dissident Religious Books*

FREDERIC A. YOUNGS, JR.
Louisiana State University

BOOKS WERE AT THE HEART of many Tudor religious controversies, and thus have a special fascination for anyone who would study that formative period in English ecclesiastical history. In them we see the rationale for the authors' positions, discover what plans and means they proposed, and discern which arguments they felt would best influence men to come over to their position, or which would demolish their opponents' reasoning. From those books we can get a deeper insight into the true meaning of their beliefs, for in them we can trace in successive books how, under the relentless attack of a protagonist, they clarified and even modified what they had originally asserted. We can often come to know an author in a less impersonal way, when occasionally the spirit and fire of his convictions leap from the pages of his arguments. But if we look at the very same books through the eyes of those Tudors who were charged with the affairs of state, we see a different and more sinister picture: all too often those books challenged, attacked, denounced, lampooned, and controverted the fruits of their statecraft, especially their religious policies. What a favorable press might do to convince, a hostile press could undo and even surpass. All who played a part in the complex world of Tudor ecclesiastical affairs, regardless of their beliefs, knew and understood the power of the printed word.

Many aspects of the books of the Tudor period are already well known: we have specialized studies on the technical details of book production, on the roles books played in the efforts of certain religious groups, on the control over printers and booksellers, and on controversies of unusual importance. With so many studies illuminating many different facets of books, and of religious books in particular, we should now be in a position to draw back from specific controversies and problems, and to attempt to view the question of religious books as a whole, with the goal of trying to develop a context in which the topic can be viewed over the eighty formative years of the English reformation in the Tudor period. It is time to concentrate on the specific topic of books, and not let it be always a part of a larger whole.

One cannot seek a unifying aspect from a consideration of the "production" side, that is to say, from considering the motivations, opinions, and writings of the religious challengers and champions, because the situations which elicited their books and the plans which they wished to see adopted varied so enormously. It seems to me that it is in the efforts of the "controlling" side that we can find the aspect under which the religious books can be studied and the uniform context provided. Those who wrote knew that they did so in a milieu of control, and that if they opposed the official religious policy, that they were in danger of suppression and punishment. By using the study of the actions of Tudor governments to control religious books, we create no artificial unifying pattern which did not exist, but rather attempt to re-create the conditions which those authors knew all too well. Furthermore, the successive actions of Tudor governments moved the realm farther and farther toward a complete secularization of the control of books, and the role of ecclesiastics and the use of devices proper to them receded accordingly, so that by the end of the reign of Elizabeth, the decision to take up the challenge which dissident books offered and the means to punish those responsible rested totally with the government. It is in such a context of governmental control that one can place and study those books which nominally are alike but differ so much: the champion of the Henrician settlement Bishop Stephen Gardiner who published *De Vera Obedientia* in 1535, and the expositor of the mature Anglican position, Richard Hooker, in his *Of the laws of ecclesiastical policy*; such diverse protestant challengers as William Tyndale and his Lutheran circle in the 1520s and 1530s, and those who sought a guide in Calvin in the 1570s and 1580s; such catholic champions and challengers as Sir Thomas More and Bishop John Fisher in Henry VIII's reign, and Cardinal Allen and the Jesuit Father Persons in Elizabeth's.

The roles of the Tudor governments in using propaganda actively to justify and persuade men to accept their religious and secular policies have been the objects of special studies, more numerous for the earlier than the later periods. Whether to use books in such efforts was, of course, an important decision, but one which is diffuse in that it can hardly be considered apart from the policies set forth in the books.[1] When one turns to the negative aspect of countering books which stood in opposition to the governmental religious policies, however, the problem finds a sharp focus, and it is with the aspect of control over dissident books that this study will be concerned.

Four ingredients of control can be isolated. Prevention attempted to keep dissident books from being printed within the realm, or from circulating there if imported from abroad. The other elements of control dealt with books which had eluded the preventative net, and were already a threat: the will to act against the books and suppress or answer them, the refutations of the opposing opinions through officially sanctioned books taking up the challenge, and the efforts to suppress the books and punish those who wrote, printed, distributed or read them.

Until 1520, all the efforts which were directed against dissident books were based on ecclesiastical authority and on the provisions in statute law, both of which had been framed in the first decade of the fifteenth century against the spread of the Lollard heresy. The statutory provisions were primarily enactments of the common law procedure which had reserved the trial of the offense to the ecclesiastical courts, and the punishment of burning to the secular arm;[2] the ecclesiastical precedents lay in the constitutions of the then Archbishop of Canterbury which had prohibited writing or favoring heretical books, and which imposed a censorship of books at the universities.[3] These procedures provided all that was needed to cope with the recurrence of Lollardy in the early Tudor period, and a large portion of the heresy trials of the Lollards included charges that they had spread their beliefs through books.[4]

After 1520, the vigilance against the Lollards continued unabated, but the focus of ecclesiastical efforts began to shift when Lutheran books from abroad began to circulate in England. The pope had condemned Luther's writings in a bull in 1520, and it was partly on this authority that book burnings were held in 1521 and in 1526.[5] From 1525 it became increasingly evident that the threat was not merely from abroad: the activities of an indigenous Lutheran circle based in Cambridge became notorious, and the extent of the participation of native English writers became known when it was discovered that William Tyndale's and William Roy's translation of the *New Testament* was being printed in Cologne. In spite of various efforts to prevent the completion of the printing, the *New Testament* reached England by March 1526, followed later that year by Tyndale's *Introduction to the Epistle to the Romans*. Roy's translation of *A Brief Dialogue* in 1527 swelled the number of distinctly English productions, as did his *Read Me* and Tyndale's *The Obedience of a Christian Man* and *Parable of the Wicked Mammon*, all produced in 1528.[6] Given this stepped-up pace of activity by English Lutherans, distinctly English remedies were framed. Bishop Tunstall of London took preventative steps when in 1524 he forbade importing Lutheran books and when in 1526 he forbade the circulation of the *New Testa-*

ment; Fisher and More continued their writings in answer to the books; and the first measures of suppression appeared in lists of condemned authors and writings, the first *Indexes* of prohibited books.[7]

Until 1530, the regulatory measures against the books had been distinctly ecclesiastical—heresy was the objection to all of them—but in that year the first secular provisions were framed against the books in two royal proclamations. These should be viewed as supplementary to the ecclesiastical provisions, for as long as Henry was king, the books were always "heretical," when measured against some norm of orthodoxy.[8] Yet these first provisions of secular procedures and the first definitions of secular offenses were important precedents, since, when the test of heresy was no longer available (as in Edward VI's reign when all heresy statutes had been repealed), or no longer used (as in Elizabeth's[9]), secularization would triumph.

The earlier of the two proclamations of 1530, the fruit of the urgings of Sir Thomas More who was extraordinarily zealous in hunting out heretics,[10] is a rather unimaginative recounting of the long-established spheres of activities of the secular and ecclesiastical arms in matters of heresy, doubtless in the hope that this reiteration would spur officials to diligence. To the existing provisions it added little except a list of fifteen prohibited Lutheran books, the requirement that any of these be turned in to the ordinaries, and a general command not to import, sell, receive, or take any of the books.[11] The second proclamation was sharper and more practical, commanding that any one caught possessing such books or any translations of Scripture should be sent before the king and his council, where exemplary punishment would be inflicted.[12] The supplementary nature of these proclamations is clear: it is not against the writers or publishers of the books that they were framed, but against those who were in the distribution net, or who retained any of the books—areas in which the existing law was insufficient.[13]

These proclamations were enforced both in the secular court of Star Chamber and in the ecclesiastical courts, and the differences in the two are instructive indeed. There were convictions in both 1530 and 1531 in the Star Chamber for having books contrary to the proclamation, and from different scraps of information about the trials, it can be seen that the defendants had been distributing Lutheran books and the *New Testament*, and that one of their number was John Tyndale, William's brother. Their punishment was to pay fines and to walk in procession wearing papers which announced their offenses to a bonfire at the cross at Cheapside in London, where they had to cast the offending books into the fire.[14] This "exemplary" punishment pales into insignificance when compared with what was meted out in the church courts. Most of those charged with offenses submitted— Foxe provides details of nineteen from the diocese of London, three from Lincoln and one from Norwich—but several of the flower of early English protestantism paid the ultimate price for offenses related to books, including John Bayfield, John Tewkesbury, James Bainham, Thomas Harrison, and Thomas Bilney.[15]

These procedures were not destined to last. The coming of the protestantly inclined Thomas Cromwell and Anne Boleyn, the passing of the staunchly orthodox Fisher and More, the sensed necessity of a rapprochement with German forces, and the enlistment of all manner of men into the task of justifying and implanting the new settlements of the 1530s supplanted what had never been lacking until that time—the will to suppress the books. Once the break from Rome was made and the supremacy of the state over the church established, there then remained the question of the direction which the *Ecclesia Anglicana* would take. A proclamation in 1538 which dealt with the books was important in a general sense, as an indication of which faction was dominant in the strife over the course of reform (it has been judged as "marking a retreat from a reformed position" and as "a victory for the conservative faction"[16]), and important in a more restricted sense in that it first introduced the secular licensing of books, that element of control over the press which was to be reintroduced by every succeeding Tudor monarch and on beyond (although Mary's requirement was for ecclesiastical licensing); furthermore, importing books was also regulated.[17]

There were additional measures against books and additional persecutions during the remainder of Henry's reign, but the former were mainly reiterations of previously adopted measures, and the latter occurred only fitfully. The one advance was made in a statute enacted in 1543 which dealt with offenders other than authors and printers: it made retaining a book which had been forbidden in one of the king's proclamations an offense punishable by a fine of £5, a severe scaling down of the penalties of the proclamation of 1538 which had threatened not only the usual "high displeasure and indignation," but also the loss of all goods and chattels, and imprisonment at the king's will. But the main import of that statute was with heresy, and it perished when Edward's first parliament repealed all previous legislation on heresy, and the proclamation, according to English law, died along with the king.[18] Once again, the writing, printing, distribution and retention of dissident religious matter was an open matter, to be resolved anew.[19]

Edward's government had little need or desire of regulations against heresy generally or against books in particular, since there was no real campaign by catholic forces abroad to send a stream of books into England to help retard the relentless movement toward a protestant establishment. The two persons who were burned in that rather tolerant reign were as pitiable and solitary as their religious opinions were extreme, and books played no part.[20] In 1551 the government issued a proclamation which reintroduced licensing and imposed controls over importing books, but although one can find some concern over a few catholic books immediately preceeding the issue of the proclamation, the provisions dealing with books were only a small part of an omnibus call for measures to restrict any occasion of disorder. The entire proclamation is an expression of the prevalent attitude in governmental circles; to use Professor Jordan's words, it was the "obsessive fear of public disorders" by a "government of fearful men."[21]

Though the six-year reign of Edward VI produced no comprehensive scheme for dealing with dissident religious books, the nearly five-and-a-half year rule of his half-sister Mary produced as full a set of provisions as could be devised. The main emphasis of the Marian regulations and of the persecution based on them was ecclesiastical: the heresy legislation originally devised against the Lollards and their books which had been used in Henry's reign and repealed in Edward's was revised; the Marian religious injunctions set forth procedures relating to books; increasingly stringent ecclesiastical commissions were issued which included specific authority for searching out and suppressing heretical books; and Cardinal Pole not only invoked the ecclesiastical requirement for licensing books which had been promulgated in a general council in 1515 but also included charges to inquire about heretical books among the visitation articles which he issued for his diocese.[22] Yet when one searches through the pages of Foxe's "Book of Martyrs," one finds that the dissident religious books played a very small part in the persecution, even though protestants in exile were much more active in sending books back into the realm than had been the case in the reversed conditions of Edward's reign. The charge of keeping and distributing heretical books was made against only one martyr, and then as one of many charges; another man was scourged for possessing a hidden book, and some of the underground protestant congregation in London were charged for the statutory offense of using the proscribed Edwardian *Book of Common Prayer*—but in all of this, as was the case in the reign of Henry VIII when the charge was heresy, it was for deviation in *opinion* rather than for the offense of dealing in books *per se* that persecution occurred.[23]

Yet as marked as was the ecclesiastical tenor of all that, the Marian government did not hesitate to seek and use secular means as well.[24] A proclamation issued in June, 1555, after the heresy statutes had been revived, not only ordered their enforcement, but reverted to Henry's tactics in providing a list of twenty-four forbidden authors and two forbidden books (Hall's *Chronicles* and the *Book of Common Prayer*) and in assessing the secular penalty of "high indignation and displeasure" as well.[25] But however strongly the danger from heretical books was felt, it became obvious that a new category had to be prohibited as well, "seditious books." The earliest prohibition was made in a proclamation in 1554 which complained of writings which defamed "noblemen and other personages of good worth, credit, and fame," at a time when pamphlets against Mary's future husband Philip of Spain and in favor of the princess Elizabeth were being circulated. Any who would be found "to have kept or to have published or declared to any others the effect or contents of any such seditious bill or writing" were to suffer exemplary punishment due "to the first authors and devisers of the same."[26] But the meaningful and enforceable definition of "seditous books" was framed in legislation of the parliament of 1554-1555: seditious books were those which contained "any false matter, clause or sentence of slander, reproach and dishonor" to the king or queen, or which encouraged any insurrection, when the writings did not fall within the scope of the basic treason statute of 1352. The penalty for the first offense was to be loss of the right hand; for subsequent offenses, life imprisonment and the loss of goods.[27]

The scope of this new category can best be illustrated by examining one of the more famous libels against Philip, *A Warning for England*. This book of anonymous authorship was probably written before Mary's marriage to Philip on July 25, 1554, because it warned of "the present misery that hangs this day over the noble realm of England." Its message was that Spain would take over England just as it did Naples, which "came into the hands of the Spaniards by a pretended title of marriage." The thirty-nine year old half-Spanish queen can hardly have liked the warnings for her: avoid the marriage, for when the Spanish took Naples and its princess, the Spaniard "would suffer none to come at her but himself alone and a keeper by him appointed. Unhappy is that honest woman that comes to the keeping of a Spaniard"; avoid the Emperor, who would not put the kingdoms "into the hands of one of whom his son can have no issue," and who would see her dispatched once the Spanish were in control, and her place taken by a younger woman provided for Philip.[28] The warnings for the realm were also pointed, though based strongly on economic arguments: it was alleged that all the taxations of the Neapolitans hitherto did not equal the extraordinary taxations of the Spanish; a table of Spanish-imposed customs was printed, complete with a conversion table into English values; and the ultimate warning was given by showing how all who would not obey the recent papal edict ordering the return of abbey lands (proved by the author to apply to England alone) already stood excommunicate. "The faggots be already prepared in that they all stand already by the Pope's sentence excommunicate and accursed. Nothing wants but a day to kindle the fire."[29]

No heresy here—but a threat to the Queen and her government of no small intensity. Yet although one can find many instances of enforcing the part of the statute which dealt with seditious rumors, there has been no evidence as yet of any enforcement in regard to books.[30] One author was in-

dicted in a London court, but those records went with the fire of the following century, so we cannot know the authority; the offender was never tried,
and was even released![31] The Stationers' Company was chartered during
Mary's reign, and could be pressed into service to help detect the printers
of dissident books, but in Mary's reign as in Elizabeth's, the company's primary interest was in protecting its own members' economic position.[32]

Elizabeth's reign is the most instructive in considering governmental activity against dissident books, because many groups wished something other
than her religious settlement, and wrote accordingly—catholic, puritan,
separatist, and on one occasion, Anabaptist. As markedly different as each
group could be, there were certain common traits in the government's activities against each. The role of prevention grew in importance: exceptional vigilance at the ports to prevent books coming from abroad, and extraordinary efforts to ferret out secret presses used within the realm. The system
of requiring licenses for printing was reintroduced, first in the royal injunctions of 1559, then later in more detail in both 1566 and 1586 in conciliar
orders from Star Chamber.[33] Almost every challenge in a dissident book was
answered, although these officially sanctioned responses were almost invariably entrusted to the clergy, doubtless so that a learned response might
be forthcoming, but with the equally effective if perhaps unwitting (one
wonders) result that later books in any controversy tended to become so
obtuse and long-winded that whatever fire there might have been in the challenge was snuffed out under the length and weight of erudition.[34]

The most important ingredients of repression in Elizabeth's reign were
the will to prosecute and the choice of legal means once the decision was
made. The reluctance to prosecute puritans on the part of many in the government is well known and well documented—Robert Browne, for example,
escaped much wrath due to the protection of his kinsman, Lord Burghley,
and the Earl of Leicester intervened on behalf of many a puritan. Yet a situation could become so acute that action was clearly needed, so that secular
and ecclesiastical measures were devised and punishment meted out. The
legal basis on which most who produced or distributed dissident books suffered was the Marian statute against seditious books, made to apply to
Elizabeth by the first parliament of her reign, and reshaped by the parliament of 1581 so that the offense became a felony.[35] Just how these measures
and punishments were worked out can be seen from a consideration of the
different groups, protestant first, then catholic.

In the last days of June, 1572, John Field and Thomas Wilcox published
their *Admonition to the Parliament*, a milestone in the puritan efforts in that
the book was aimed not at the parliamentarians concluding the present session, but rather at public opinion, taking to the realm the puritan cause which
had fared so unsuccessfully in the parliaments of 1566, 1571, and 1572.

Field and Wilcox were soon captured and in October, 1572, were convicted of offending against the Act of Uniformity; meanwhile, Thomas Cartwright had begun a series of defenses of the *Admonition*, and his former nemesis at Cambridge, John Whitgift, was pressed into service to reply, while the bishops sought vainly for a public condemnation.[36] That condemnation was issued in a royal proclamation dated fifty weeks after the *Admonition*, not because of a lingering indignation over that book, but because Cartwright in his *Reply* to Whitgift which was published in May, 1573, did what was extraordinarily unwise—he lectured the queen and her council on their religious duty. He wrote "And therefore if this book shall come into the hands of any that have access unto her majesty, the head of the common wealth, or unto her most honorable council, the shoulders thereof, my humble suit and hearty request in the presence of God is that according as their callings will suffer them, they will put them in remembrance of these things . . . ," and then Cartwright offered a veritable litany of Scriptural lessons, including that of Moses who not only brought the people out of Egypt but also sought to lead them into the promised land, and of David who was not content with reforming the abuses of Saul, but also built a temple to the Lord.[37] When a second impression of Cartwright's *Reply* was made soon after, the title page excused its appearance "notwithstanding our most gracious prince's late-published proclamation, procured rather by the bishops than willingly sought for by her majesty, whose mildness is such that she were easier led to yield to the proclamation of the Highest than drawn to proclaim anything against him, were it not for the subtle practices and wicked dealings of this horned generation. . . ."[38] However poorly he read the queen's earlier intentions, he read her later one properly, and soon afterwards left England, not to return until 1585, when only the Earl of Leicester's patronage protected him from Whitgift, then Archbishop.

My interpretation that the proclamation was issued to protect the queen's honor and not as a first step toward persecution is also suggested by its contents: there were no administrative procedures which might have been invoked to set in motion a full-scale search, and the penalty of "indignation" was the least that could be provided. The situation worsened through the summer while the royal court was away, even to the point that Field and Wilcox were treated more as celebrities than prisoners, and Cartwright's books were even praised from the pulpit at Paul's Cross.[39] Had not Peter Birchet, a more fanatic member of the movement, made an attempt to kill John Hawkins that autumn, thinking him to be Sir Christopher Hatton who was a known despiser of puritanism and a favorite of the queen, little might have come of that first expression of dissatisfaction in the proclamation of June, 1583; instead, new proclamations were issued announcing the issue of commissions to enforce the Act of Uniformity.[40]

In 1579, the advanced stage of the marriage negotiations between Elizabeth and the French duke, Alençon, a Catholic, alarmed the puritan John Stubbs enough that he published his *Discovery of a Gaping Gulf* which sought to dissuade Elizabeth from the marriage in order that true religion might be served (did he realize the parallel to the Marian *Warning to England*, now that the tables were turned?). Stubbs warned the second reigning Tudor queen "to keep this sin far from you" and "to deny some of your delights also, and enter with the whole Church into judgment of ourselves that we be not judged of the Lord." Again the queen's honor was at stake; again a royal proclamation was issued to protect her reputation, although in this sole instance a proclamation refuted a dissident book's arguments; again the secular magistrates were pressed into action; again secular punishments were enforced. The statute was that against seditious books, and accordingly Stubbs lost his right hand.[41]

In 1580, for the first and only time, the Elizabethan government branded some dissident religious books as heretical. The definition of heresy in the act of 1559 was negative: nothing was to be judged heretical unless it was so judged in Scripture, or by one of the first four general councils, or by a later council when the decision was based on the express words of Scripture.[42] But to the Elizabethan government, the Family of Love was an anabaptist sect, and so its writings were manifestly heretical. The sect had risen up in the Low Countries, and when the books of its leader Heinrich Niclas were translated into English in 1574 and groups of Familists detected in the eastern part of England, the English government took alarm. Whatever comfort there might have been when several anabaptists recanted and two others were burned in 1575 soon evaporated when, in 1578, five Yeomen of the Guard were suspected of being of the Family, and when the English leader Christopher Vitellis engaged in a controversy in print with several Anglican divines. I cannot find the occasion for the issue of the proclamation in 1580, nor has anyone found evidence of its effectiveness, or indeed much evidence of the sect itself until the seventeenth century.[43]

The early 1580s also witnessed the first distribution of separatist books, and in 1583 the first condemnation of them in the open forum of a royal proclamation when the books of Robert Browne and Richard Harrison were branded as seditious. In his earlier puritan days, Browne had been protected by Burghley, but he had progressed in his beliefs to a separatist position, had organized a congregation in Norwich, and then in late 1581 had taken them abroad into the Low Countries.[44] By the next summer the English government had learned that more than 1,000 Brownist tracts were being printed abroad, and in 1583 officials in Suffolk not only discovered the printed sheets which had been brought over, but seized them before they were bound into books and arrested the distributors as well.[45] At the assize at Bury St. Edmunds, three men who had been in trouble with the authorities in that county before were charged with denying the queen's supremacy and with dispersing the books of Browne and Harrison. All three were convicted, but the suspected printer, Thomas Gibson, submitted and was released; Elias Thacker was hanged at Bury on June 4, 1583, and John Copping on June 6, while a third man, William Dennis, was convicted of the same offense and hanged a few days later at Thetford. The books which had been found were publicly burned on those occasions.[46]

The double charge against the men precludes our knowing what might have befallen them had they been charged solely with dispersing the books—a thing doubly to be regretted since the case would have been against distributors of books whereas heretofore it had been against principals that charges were made, and since this was the first instance of a trial following the offense for seditious books having been made a felony. The proclamation which was issued against the books followed the cases at Bury and Thetford by four weeks, and was probably intended to call in any books which might have escaped; it commanded that those who printed or dispersed the books should be punished "as persons maintaining such seditious actions."[47]

Since this is the first separatist case, it will be useful to look at one of the books and see how it fit the definition of seditious. Browne's principal work was *A Treatise of Reformation without Tarrying for Any*, a continual and relentless condemnation generally of the secular involvement in what he considered to be strictly ecclesiastical affairs: woe to those who "pull down the head Christ Jesus, to set up the throne of the Magistrates," "who lift up the throne of the Magistrates to thrust out the kingdom of Christ."[48] On the contrary, the magistrate should be subject to the church, so that true reform will be delayed no longer, and so that the toleration of unreformed elements will be stopped: "How then dare these men teach us, that any evil thing is tolerable in the Church, as though the church government could not remedy it: yea and so tolerable, that all men should be brought into bondage thereby: yea into so foolish [a] bondage, that they should protest a thing to be evil, and so think they are excused to practice the same."[49]

No evidence of any success or failure in suppressing these books is to be found. Harrison died soon after, and Browne began a checkered career in Scotland and later in England. The fear of the spread of these books remained, however, probably leading to the reissue of conciliar decrees against unlicensed printing in 1586, an action that may have been intended as early as 1584.[50] The proclamation had condemned not only the Brownist books, but also "such like seditious books or libels," and hence will reappear shortly.

The years 1587-1593 were the climax of governmental activity against the dissident protestant books. Three separate streams of literary activity were damned in those years: the individualistic puritan efforts which found expression in the writings of John Penry and of Job Throkmorton in the Marprelate tracts; the separatist writings of Penry who had moved to that position in 1592, and of Henry Barrow and John Greenwood; and the movement against the surreptitiously organized presbyterian movement, for which the *Book of Discipline* served as an organizational manual.

John Penry published his *Aequity* in 1586, ostensibly a description of the deplorable state of religion in his native Wales, but in reality an attack on the episcopacy. For this he was imprisoned by the High Commission, but within a month he was freed.[51] The following year he was deeply involved in the major *cause célèbre* of puritan printing, the series of writings published under the pseudonym Martin Marprelate. Penry owned the press on which the tracts were printed and served as the business manager for the project, but the often asserted claim that he was the author·has been refuted by Professor Leland Carlson who conclusively shows that Job Throkmorton, a Member of Parliament, was the real author.[52] These brilliantly satirical pamphlets held up to ridicule the worldliness and foibles of the bishops, which not only set the government on a furious and relentless attempt to stop the printing and to arrest those involved, but also scandalized many puritans as well. Again, a proclamation was issued, this time after the third work of the series was printed, the *Minerals*; again, there were searches by secular officials; again, the capture of some who were involved, including Sir Richard Knightley in whose home some of the books had been printed; again, trials in secular courts. The magnitude of the scandal and the high social rank of Knightley seem to be reason enough why they should be tried in the prestigious Star Chamber, but at issue also might have been the question of the authority on which the case was to be based. The defendants were charged with offenses against the proclamation of February 13, 1589, and of June 30, 1583: against the former, Knightley *et al* had a defense, since it had been issued after the *Minerals*, and thus after their participation had ceased; against the latter which was the proclamation against the Brownist and "such like seditious books or libels" they had no defense, and so Knightley was fined £2,000 and committed to prison at the queen's pleasure, and the others were assessed lesser punishments in accordance with their rank.[53] It is interesting to speculate that their trial in Star Chamber may have occurred because their activities were that of accessories and not of principals: the proclamations covered the former, and the statute the latter. Throkmorton was indicted at the assize in Warwick in 1590, and even though he submitted and it never went to trial, the fact of indictment at an assize implies a statutory basis which would have been appropriate since he, unlike Knightley and the others, was a principal.[54]

The full scope of governmental actions against those involved with dissident protestant books was now developed. There is a real irony in the fact that an old Marian statute against seditious books had become the basis for proceeding against the books of protestant reformers, puritan and separatist alike, who would go farther than Elizabeth's settlement, since the inception of the statute of 1555 lay in remedies against men of a protestant persuasion who in many cases might have found a close kinship with the Elizabethan protestants whose writings were now branded seditious. That irony was not lost on the parliamentarians who in 1581 attempted to strike the antecedents of the bill of 1555 by repealing it entirely, while retaining the offenses of seditious words and seditious books.[55] The reworked statute of 1581 was the basis of the indictments in 1587 against two leaders of the separatist cause, Henry Barrow and John Greenwood; in 1593, the original charges against the puritan-turned-separatist John Penry were dropped in favor of a new charge based on his writings.[56] All three were executed in 1593, Barrow and Greenwood on April 6, seemingly as an act of spite when it began to be feared that the proposed extension of "recusancy" in legislation under consideration might not be limited to sectaries (the official explanation), but might become yet another weapon in Whitgift's arsenal against puritans generally, and Penry on May 29.[57]

The years 1589-1593 were noteworthy in the puritan movement also because "the quest for Martin Marprelate merged into a hunt for further traces of the clandestine presbyterian movement of which even an absorbed observer like [the acute hunter of puritans, Richard] Bancroft had hitherto enjoyed only a blurred impression."[58] The *Book of Discipline* of the 1580s was used as an organizational manual "to set up a godly discipline outside the law,"[59] because all attempts to enact such a program in the parliaments of the 1580s had failed. On the basis of evidence painstakingly gathered from the government's increasing awareness of the problem, a series of hearings and trials was held, first in the High Commission, then in Star Chamber to which the case was transferred in 1591. Professor Collinson has detailed the vicissitudes of this series of trials which led to an inconclusive result in 1593,[60] but the cases are of interest to us as a further example of how situations in which a book was a contributory, even an initial, part could be subsumed into a major case and the issue of books then recede in deference to the more important cause—in Henry's and Mary's reigns, into cases of heresy, and here in Elizabeth's, into a charge of conspiracy to subvert the religion of the realm.

When we turn our attention to the dissident Elizabethan Catholic books, some notable changes in emphasis can be discerned. Firstly, the books were of much more importance to the catholic cause, since they alone provided information and counsel to the English catholic laity who were left virtually leaderless from the time of the submission of nearly all the clergy in 1559 until the arrival of the first "missionary" priests from the continental English seminaries in 1574; even after the trickle of clergy began to form an underground movement, the role of books was scarcely diminished. The corollary of this is that the government had to devote a great deal of attention to the aspect of preventative control, especially to trying to seal up the routes through the ports by which the books were smuggled from abroad.[61] Secondly, the government's concern was almost always for those who were active in the distribution net (legally, aiders and abetters), since the authors were almost invariably abroad, and only a few of the approximately 250 Elizabethan catholic books were printed secretly in England.[62] Thirdly, the refutation of the Catholic books by the Anglican clergy came to be the only response in the open forum, when after 1570 the catholic books were never condemned in royal proclamations except when the honor of a privy councillor was at stake, or when the government could turn the books into effective counter-propaganda.[63] Finally, when proclamations were involved, they were primarily administrative documents in which intricate procedures for detecting and confiscating the books were provided.

The earliest of the controversies was provoked when, in 1559, Bishop John Jewel preached his famous "Challenge Sermon" at Paul's Cross, defying anyone to prove the existence in the primitive church of many practices such as private masses or communion in one kind only. An extraordinary flurry of activity followed, so that by the time in late 1568 when the government felt that something beyond controversy was necessary, the total number of catholic contributions from the English in exile in the Low Countries and of protestant responses numbered sixty-two.[64] The government's concern was clearly with those who spread the catholic books in England, and what it sought adds a new and yet paradoxical element to the study of dissident religious books.

Sir Nicholas Bacon, Lord Keeper of the Great Seal and as such the titular head of the legal system, set out the government's concern in a speech delivered in December, 1568, in the Star Chamber before the lords of the Privy Council. His concern that the existing law did not cover those who distributed the books is evident, and in admitting this Bacon made one of those explicit appeals to the necessity of bending the law in the name of higher "reasons of state" which one can rarely find, even though one may suspect it as having played a part in some important decision. Having begun his speech generally by referring to the dangers from religious factions, he then turned to the particular danger of books from abroad, saying that "albeit [the offenders] could not be brought within the compass of the laws, yet at all hands it must be confessed that thus to breed or continue factions is a very great and universal evil and for the dangers of it, necessarily to be reformed." He then set about expounding a statute which had been passed in

1563, which defined it as treason to extol the pope's authority, and asked for a constructive interpretation which would embrace the distributors of the books. That in itself is noteworthy, for to construe a penal law, making its scope wider than in the explicit words, was not a normal legal practice— an objection which Bacon anticipated by saying that "admitting it to be penal, then this question would be whether he that expounds a penal law to the correction of a few and saving of great numbers, or he that expounds a law to the destruction of a great number and saving of a few, does more cruelly expound the law."[65] That Bacon spoke not merely rhetorically is clear from the fact that the same question was submitted to the chief justices of the principal royal courts, who at a meeting at Serjeant's Inn on February 9, 1569 gave their reply to the question "Whether they that conveyed those books [written overseas against the queen or extolling the pope's authority] and they that have read them have offended against the statute Anno 5⁰ Reginae nunc or not."[66]

The judges divided their answers into parts: conveying the books from abroad, receiving them, obtaining, receiving, reading, conferring, and favoring them. The opinion was that all fell within the scope of the law except those who received or read the books with no discussion or sign of favoring them. Clearly their decision gave the government the tool it needed for proceeding against most catholic books, not as seditious, not as heretical, nor under pain for possessing them as devised by the temporary law of a proclamation, but as falling within the scope of the highest secular offense, treason. Thus, early in 1569, before the rebellion of the northern earls later that year and before the pope's bull of excommunication of Elizabeth in 1570, the twin pillars which supported the brunt of the government's argument that catholics were persecuted for "treason, not religion," the government had a decision which allowed it to proceed on the basis of treason.[67]

The paradox is that this decision was not used. Bacon had alleged in his speech before the Star Chamber that he spoke with warrant from the queen, but whether he stretched his interpretation of what she had in mind, or whether she was too lenient to use the decision, or whether there were other pressing reasons of statecraft to eclipse what this earlier effort had wrought, the decision never seems to have been applied. Earlier in the Hilary term which ended on the day of the judge's pronouncement, nine men had been tried in Star Chamber "for their contempt in receiving, buying, reading, keeping, commending, and sending abroad seditious books set forth beyond [the] seas in the name of Harding, Dorman, Staphilus, Stapleton, Sanders, Smith, Rastell, and others, enemies to God's truth and the quiet government of the Queen, in maintenance of the usurped jurisdiction of the Papistical See of Rome. Not receiving the Communion since the Queen's reign, and hearing of Mass contrary to the Laws," for which offenses they were sequestered from office and fined for their contempt, all penalties far short of what the judges would deem to be assessable at the end of the term.[68] Furthermore, a proclamation issued on March 1, 1569, warned of catholic books as seditious, but made no mention of treason, nor did the proclamations of the 1570s and 1580s which protected the honor of councillors and which suppressed books extolling the title to the English crown of Mary Queen of Scots.[69]

The first half of the 1580s was a time of exceptional challenge from the catholic forces. The entry of the Jesuit priests Robert Persons and Edmund Campion into England gave a psychological impetus to the mission all out of proportion to their numbers. There had been few catholic books in the last half of the 1570s, but now the number and matter posed a serious threat: Persons wrote on why catholics should not attend the Anglican services, Campion asserted his *Decem Rationes* for the truth of his cause, both books printed secretly in England as were others; and from Rheims William Allen wrote to deny the charges made in a royal proclamation of 1581 that the seminaries abroad were nurseries of treason and sedition. When Campion was executed, the first martyrological book appeared in the priest Thomas Alfield's eyewitness account of his death. Clearly these threats demanded a proportionate response, and a number of remedies were framed, some on parliamentary authority and some on the royal prerogative alone.[70]

Some of these actions were grounded on the questions of books alone. Alfield's printer, Stephen Vallenger, was tried in Star Chamber in May, 1582. The judges noted that he could be shown to have abetted traitors, yet they would punish his contempt first which they did by fining him £100 and by ordering him to be pilloried at Westminster Palace and at the cross at Cheapside (with loss of an ear at each location), and to be imprisoned at the queen's pleasure.[71] The printer William Carter was tried, convicted, and hanged, drawn, and quartered in January, 1584, for having printed Gregory Martin's *The Treatise of Schisme*.[72] Alfield himself was the defendant in a third trial, of special interest since he and a co-defendant were indicted and convicted as *distributors* of William Allen's *True, Sincere and Modest Defense*—not on the basis of the judges' opinion of 1569, but on the act of 1581 which had expanded on the original act of 1555, the very same authority used against the principals in the protestant cases which we have seen. For this offense which ironically had been first defined in a catholic reign, Alfield and Thomas Webley were hanged on July 6, 1585.[73]

The final controversy in the catholic cause was over the control of the mission. There had been a jurisdictional feud between the Jesuits and the secular priests, a quarrel with political overtones as well since the former had long since turned to foreign powers as the only hope of re-catholicizing

England, while the latter looked to a native solution of the problem. The seculars seemed to have won when one of their numbers was appointed Archpriest by the pope, but the first appointee was deeply influenced by the Jesuits, and the terms of his appointment ordered him to consult with them on matters of moment. The government was happy to support the dissension in the enemy's ranks and to assist the seculars even by allowing them leave to go to Rome to press their case against the Jesuits.[74] The acrimonious dispute broke into print as well, and the government even went to the length of allowing the seculars to have their books printed in England by well-established printers, although this was covered up.[75] There could hardly be a more pointed reminder of the supremacy of the decision whether to prosecute dissident books or not.

Thus, in spite of the enormous differences between the parties in the Elizabethan religious controversies, a uniform means of action had been worked out. The leaders in the church could take alarm at the appearance of certain books and petition that they be suppressed, but the decision whether to persecute, the allocation of roles in answering the books and in suppressing them, and the choice of the law on which the action would be based, were all secular decisions. This *modus operandi* had been worked out by the end of the first half of the 1580s—perhaps as a result of some grand scheme such as the parliamentary puritans of 1581 feared, but more probably because the government had gained enough experience from the rather infrequent controversies to guide its choice of effective means to deal with all types of religious dissent. We have seen how early in Elizabeth's reign the personal disrespect shown her in the literature had prompted the government to action, and that later more general repressions against dissent seem to have been the norm.

In retrospect we can see that arriving at a secular procedure against "sedition" was almost inevitable, since once the principle of secular headship over the church was established, any call for a change in the church's structure or practices could be construed as reflecting on the monarch at the church's head—the most temperate argument could be considered "reproach," and the more intemperate clamors as "slander" or "dishonor." As in so many other aspects of sixteenth-century life in England, political considerations choked off expressions of religious argumentation, no matter how well intentioned. Occasionally some other measure would indirectly handle a major part of the problem, as happened when legislation of 1585 made the mere presence of a priest in the realm treason *ipso facto*, and thus provided measures against the group of people who had been the main cogs in the distribution network for the catholic cause.

The Tudors as a whole had considered four rationales for dealing with dissident religious books:[76] heresy, sedition, treason, and the offenses for distributing books as defined in various proclamations. The first had been discarded; the advance obtained in the third category was not implemented. The triumph of secularization was complete.

NOTES

* I would like to express my appreciation to Professor Walter C. Richardson who read this article and made several useful suggestions.

1. G. R. Elton succinctly distinguishes between those historians of the earlier Tudor period who are more interested in the arguments put forward in official writings, and those interested in the propaganda campaign itself; for this and critiques of the various efforts, see his *Policy and Police. The Enforcement of the Reformation in the Age of Thomas Cromwell* (Cambridge: Cambridge University Press, 1972), 151 ff. For surveys of Elizabethan propaganda efforts, see Conyers Read, "William Cecil and Elizabethan Public Relations," *Elizabethan Government and Society*, ed. S. T. Bindoff *et al.* (London: Athlone Press, 1961), 21 ff, and Gladys Jenkins, "Ways and Means in Elizabethan Propaganda," *History*, new series, 26 (September, 1941), 105-114.

2. 2 Richard II, s. 2, c. 2; 2 Henry IV, c. 15; 2 Henry V, c. 7; *see* also Sir William Holdsworth, *A History of English Law*, vol. I, ed. A. L. Goodhart and H. G. Hanbury (7th ed., rev.; London: Methuen & Co., 1956), 616-617.

3. Arthur W. Reed, "The Regulation of the Book Trade Before the Proclamation of 1538," *Library*, 15 (1920), 158-159.

4. A. G. Dickens, *Lollards and Protestants in the Diocese of York 1509-1558* (London: Oxford University Press, 1959); John Fines, "Heresy Trials in the Diocese of Coventry and Lichfield, 1511-12," *Journal of Ecclesiastical History*, 14 (October, 1963), 160-174.

5. Carl S. Meyer, "Henry VIII Burns Luther's Books, 12 May 1521," *Journal of Ecclesiastical History*, 9 (October, 1958), 173-187; William A. Clebsch, *England's Earliest Protestants, 1520-1535* (New Haven: Yale University Press, 1964), 11-12; Reed, "Regulation of the Book Trade," 165-166; A. G. Dickens, *The English Reformation* (London: Batsford, 1964), 68 ff.

6. See Clebsch, *England's Earliest Protestants*, 24-27, 258 ff., for the importance of 1525; dates for the books are to be found in *ibid*. and in J. F. Mozeley, *William Tyndale* (New York: The Macmillan Co., 1937).

7. The best guide through the chronology of the indexes is in Clebsch, *England's Earliest Protestants*, 262-269, which corrects earlier source collections: Heinrich Reusch, *Die Indices Librorum Prohibitorum des Sechzenten Jahrhunderts* ("Bibliothek des Literarischen Vereins in Stuttgart," vol. 176; Tübingen: Literarischer Verein, 1886), 5-22, and Robert Steele, "Notes on English Books Printed Abroad, 1525-48," *Library*, 11 (1912), 189-236. The first papal index occurred in 1559.

8. The norm changed from time to time; in the statute of 1543 on heresy, it was "that doctrine which since the year of our Lord a thousand five hun-

dred and forty is or [during the king's life] shall be set forth by his Highness." 34 & 35 Henry VIII, c. 1.

9. For the one exception to this, *see* 176.

10. On More as the animating force in the persecution, see Clebsch, *England's Earliest Protestants*, 277-304, and E. G. Rupp, *Studies in the Making of the English Protestant Tradition (Mainly in the Reign of Henry VIII)* (Cambridge: Cambridge University Press, 1947), 23-26.

11. Paul L. Hughes and James F. Larkin (eds.), *Tudor Royal Proclamations*, vol. I: *The Early Tudors (1485-1553)* (New Haven: Yale University Press, 1964), no. 122, vol. I, 181-186 [hereafter, *Hughes and Larkin*]. For the correct date of this proclamation and More's role in it, see Elton, *Policy and Police*, 218-219.

12. *Hughes and Larkin*, no. 129, vol. I, 193-197. This proclamation elaborated on an ecclesiastical list of a few days earlier. *See* Clebsch, 263.

13. In legal terms, the problem was one of dealing with aiders and abetters; for an example of the like problem in relation to those who aided and abetted priests in Elizabeth's reign, *see* Frederic A. Youngs, Jr., "Definitions of Treason in an Elizabethan Proclamation," *Historical Journal*, 14 (December, 1971), 675-691.

14. The case of October 25, 1530, involved "Semen, Tyndall & all" according to Huntington Library. Ellesmere MS 6100, "John Parsecke, Semen, & al" according to Ellesmere MS 2652, fo. 15, and "John Borstick" as in Ellesmere MS 436 (which last source was cited by *Hughes and Larkin*, I, 181), so there is no way out of the problem of variant spellings. The Spanish ambassador in London identified these as "Lutheran merchants"; see Pascual de Gayangos (ed.), *Calendars of Letters, Despatches, and State Papers, Relating to the Negotiations between England and Spain, Preserved in the Archives at Simancas and Elsewhere*, vol. 4, part 1: *Henry VIII. 1529-30* (London: Longman and Co., 1879), 820-821, 847-848; Mozeley, *William Tyndale*, 171, following Strype added the name of Thomas Patmore and "a young man dwelling near London Bridge." On October 14, 1531, "John Coke" as in Ellesmere MS 2652, fo. 15, or Crocke, as Ellesmere MS 6100, or Croker as Ellesmere MS 436 (*Hughes and Larkin*, I, 193) was convicted for having a *New Testament* contrary to the proclamation.

15. John Foxe, *Actes and Monuments*, ed. Stephen Reed Cattley (8 vols.; London: R. B. Seeley and W. Burnside, 1824-1829), vol. 5, 29-39 (London submissions), vol. 4, 583-584 (Lincoln), 679-680 (Norwich); John Tyndale is included in the first list, but with no comments about books. The martyrdoms are noted in *ibid.*, vol. 4, 580-581, 619-656, 680-706.

16. Elton, *Policy and Police*, 221, 255-257.

17. *Hughes and Larkin*, no. 186, vol. I, 270-276. Elton notes that Henry's intended censorship could not stop heretical books "because the machinery did not yet exist for enforcing it. More's system, had it endured, could easily have been more formidable," in *Policy and Police*, 221. On the identification of approbation, see W. W. Greg, "Ad Imprimendum Solum," *Library*, 5th series, vol. 9, (December 1954), 242-247; on clandestine printing occasioned by the proclamation, see Colin Clair, "On the Printing of Certain Reformation Books," *Library*, 5th series, 18 (December, 1963), 275-287.

18. 34 & 35 Henry VIII, c. 1 [see note 8], repealed by 1 Edward VI, c. 12.

19. There were other proclamations dealing with books, but in specific, *ad hoc* instances not relevant to the above, such as calling in Fisher's books and sermons after his execution (*Hughes and Larkin*, no. 161, I, 235-237), or ordering the Great Bible to be placed in every church (*ibid.*, no. 200, 296-298).

20. On the burning of Joan Bocher in 1550 and George van Parris in 1551, see W. K. Jordan, *Edward VI: The Young King* (Cambridge, Mass.: Harvard University Press, 1964), 228-229, 330.

21. *Hughes and Larkin*, no. 371, vol. I, 514-518; W. K. Jordan, *Edward VI: The Threshold of Power* (Cambridge, Mass.: Harvard University Press, 1970), titles of sections beginning at pp. 44 and 56. For other Edwardian action on books, see D. M. Loades, "The Press under the Early Tudors. A Study in Censorship and Sedition," *Transactions of the Cambridge Bibliographical Society*, 4 (1964), 34-35.

22. Revival of heresy legislation by 1 & 2 Philip and Mary, c. 6; injunctions, printed in *Hughes and Larkin*, vol. 2: *The Later Tudors (1553-1587)*, [publ. 1969], 35-38 (but they are not a proclamation); the commission of February 8, 1557, authorized impaneling juries to discover a wide range of offenses, prominent among them heretical and seditious books, printed in Foxe, *Acts and Monuments*, vol. 8, 300-303; Leo X's bull "Super impressione librorum" promulgated in the tenth session of the Fifth Lateran Council, in G. D. Mansi (ed.), *Sacrorum Conciliorum Nova et Amplissima Collectio* (Paris, 1902), vol. 32, cols. 912-913; Pole's articles for Canterbury in 1556 and 1557 are in Walter Howard Frere and William McClure Kennedy (eds.), *Visitation Articles and Injunctions of the Period of the Reformation*, vol. 2: *1563-1558* ("Alcuin Club Collections," XV; London: A. R. Mowbray & Co. Ltd., 1910), 388, 425.

23. The martyr, Ralph Allerton, Foxe, *Acts and Monuments*, vol. 8, 405-420, especially p. 417; the man scourged, Thomas Green, *ibid.*, 520-525; the London community, *ibid.*, 443 ff.

24. On Mary's political approach to the settlement, see D. M. Loades, "The Enforcement of Reaction, 1553-1558," *Journal of Ecclesiastical History*, 16 (April, 1965), 54-55.

25. *Hughes and Larkin*, no. 422, vol. II, 57-60.

26. *Ibid.*, no. 410, 41-42. On the circulation of a libel against Philip and an examination on the matter, see John Strype, *Ecclesiastical Memorials, Relating Chiefly to Religion, and the Reformation of It, and the Emergencies of England, under King Henry VIII, Edward VI, and Queen Mary I.* (3 vols.; Oxford: Clarendon Press, 1822), vol. 3, part 1, 156-157; see Loades, "The Press under the Early Tudors," 44, for a critique of the theory that there was an organized campaign to send books into England, set forth by Christina Hallowell Garrett, *The Marian Exiles. A Study in the Origins of Elizabethan Puritanism* (Cambridge: Cambridge University Press, 1938).

27. 1 & 2 Philip and Mary, c. 3.

28. *A Warnyng for Englande Conteyning the horrible practises of the Kyng of Spayne in the Kyngdome of Naples. . . . Whereby all Englishe men may vnderstand the plage that shall light vpon them yf the Kyng of Spayn obtyne the Dominion in England* (n.p., 1555), sigs, A3, [A6ᵛ]. Foxe, *Acts and Monuments*, vol. 7, 127-128, thought this was the occasion for the proclamation in 1555 (note 25 above) and in this he was followed by

Raphael Holinshed, *Holinshed's Chronicle of England, Scotland, and Ireland*, ed. Henry Ellis (6 vols.; London: J. Johnson *et al.*, 1808), vol. 4, 83, by Strype, *Ecclesiastical Memorials*, vol. 3, part 1, 197-200, and hence by many modern commentators. A more likely occasion would have been the capture by the Lord Mayor of London in May, 1555, of 1000 copies of a now lost book identified as the "Dialogue," described as full of seditious and scandalous things against the religion and government," Garrett, *The Marian Exiles*, 117.

29. *A Warnyng for Englande*, sigs. [A4ᵛ], A5[-A5ᵛ], [A7ᵛ-A8].
30. For an example of action of seditious rumors, Norfolk and Norwich Record Office, Norwich Mayor's Court Book 6, fo. [294]. Loades tells of his fruitless search in the most likely place, the records of King's Bench, in his "The Press under the Early Tudors," 44.
31. *Ibid.*
32. Charter printed in Edward Arber (ed.), *A Transcript of the Registers of the Company of Stationers of London; 1554-1640 A.D.* (5 vols; vols. 1-4 London: Privately Printed, 1875-1877; vol. 5 Birmingham: Privately Printed, 1894), vol. 1, xxvii-xxxiii.
33. The injunctions are printed in Hughes and Larkin, no. 460, vol. 2, 117-132 (but are not a proclamation); the contemporary copy of the decree of 1566 is printed by Cyprian Blagden, "Book Trade Control in 1566," *Library*, 5th series, 8 (December, 1958), 287-292; for 1586, *see* p. 177.
34. A. C. Southern, *Elizabethan Recusant Prose 1559-1582* (London: Sands & Co., 1950), prints as an appendix (537-538) a compilation of three lists of popish books made by the controversialist William Fulke, the third of which was "A Catalogue of all such Popish Books either answered, or to be answered, which have been written . . . since the beginning of the Queen's Majesty's reign."
35. 1 Elizabeth I, c. 5; 23 Elizabeth I, c. 2; on the debate over the latter, see J. E. Neale, *Elizabeth I and her Parliaments, 1559-1581* (London: Jonathan Cape, 1953), 393-398.
36. Patrick Collinson, *The Elizabethan Puritan Movement* (London: Jonathan Cape, 1967), 118 ff; W. H. Frere and C. E. Douglas (eds.), *Puritan Manifestoes. A Study of the Origin of the Puritan Revolt* (London: Society for the Promotion of Christian Knowledge, 1907); Donald Joseph McGinn, *The Admonition Controversy* (New Brunswick: Rutgers University Press, 1949).
37. *Hughes and Larkin*, no. 597, vol. 2, 375-376; T. C. [Thomas Cartwright], *A Replye to an Ansvvere made of M. Doctor VVhitgifte, Agaynste the Admonition to the Parliament* (n.p., [May, 1573]), sig. [A.ii.ᵛ].
38. Printed by John Ayre (ed.), *The Works of John Whitgift, D.D.* . . . ("Parker Society," [vol. 40]; Cambridge: Cambridge University Press), vol. 1, 13-14.
39. John Strype, *Annals of the Reformation and Establishment of Religion and Other Various Occurrences in the Church of England During Queen Elizabeth's Happy Reign* (3 vols.; Oxford: Clarendon Press, 1824), vol. 2, part 1, 426-429.
40. *Ibid.*; *Hughes and Larkin*, no. 599, vol. 2, 379-381.
41. The best recent summary of the controversy as well as the text of the book is to be found in *John Stubb's Gaping Gulf with Letters and Other Relevant*

Documents, ed. Lloyd E. Berry ("Folger Documents of Tudor and Stuart Civilization"; Charlottesville: The University Press of Virginia, 1968); the proclamation is in *Hughes and Larkin,* no. 642, vol. 2, 445-449.

42. 1 Elizabeth I, c. 1.

43. The best recent summary on the sect is that by Julia G. Ebel, "The Family of Love: Sources of Its History in England," *Huntington Library Quarterly,* 30 (August, 1967), 331-343. *See* also Champlin Burrage, *The Early English Dissenters in the Light of Recent Research (1550-1641)* (2 vols; Cambridge: Cambridge University Press, 1912), vol. 1, 209-214, and C. E. Whiting, *Studies in English Puritanism from the Restoration to the Revolution* (London: Society for the Promotion of Christian Knowledge, 1931), 283-290. The proclamation is in *Hughes and Larkin,* no. 652, vol. 2, 474-475.

44. Burrage, *Early English Dissenters,* 94-103; Champlin Burrage, *The True Story of Robert Browne* (London: Henry Frowde, 1906); the works are in *The Writings of Robert Harrison and Robert Browne,* ed. Albert Peel and Leland H. Carlson, "Elizabethan Nonconformist Texts," vol. 2 (London: George Allen and Unwin Ltd., 1953); *see* especially the introduction and the chronologies at pp. 1-25.

45. Dwight C. Smith, "Robert Browne, Independent," *Church History,* 6 (December, 1937), 304-305.

46. Whiting, *Studies in English Puritanism,* 310; Albert Peel, *The Noble Army of Congregational Martyrs* ("International Congregational Council Publications, vol. I; London: Independent Press, 1948), 30-32. Thacker and Copping only are mentioned in *Holinshed's Chronicle,* vol. 4, 505, and in John Stow, *The Annales of England* (London, 1605), 1174; Gibson's name is also in Strype, *Annals of the Reformation,* vol. 3, part 1, 268-269. Two others may have been handed at Bury in July, 1584; *see* Huntington Library. Ellesmere MS 2076 C and 2066, printed by Albert Peel, "Congregational Martyrs at Bury St. Edmunds. How Many?", *Transactions of the Congregational Historical Society,* 15 (April, 1946), 64-67.

47. *Hughes and Larkin,* no. 667, vol. 2, 501-502.

48. Printed in *The Writings of Robert Harrison and Robert Browne,* 153, 154.

49. *Ibid.,* 170.

50. W. W. Greg, Letter to the Editor, *Library,* 5th series, vol. 11 (March, 1956), 53.

51. Donald Joseph McGinn, *John Penry and the Marprelate Controversy* (New Brunswick: Rutgers University Press, 1966), v-viii.

52. Leland H. Carlson, "Martin Marprelate: His Identity and His Satire," in *English Satire, Papers Read at a Clark Library Seminar January 15, 1972* (Los Angeles: William Andrews Clark Memorial Library, 1972), 3-53; Carlson gives complete references to other writers on the Marprelate controversy.

53. The proclamation is in *Hughes and Larkin,* no. 709, 3 [Vol. 3: *The Later Tudors (1588-1603),* publ. 1969], 34-35; the references to the trial are in Carlson, "Martin Marprelate," p. 45, note 20.

54. Carlson, "Martin Marprelate," 33-34.

55. Note 35, before.

56. McGinn, *John Penry and the Marprelate Controversy,* v-vi.

57. J. E. Neale, *Elizabeth I and her Parliaments, 1584-1601* (London: Jonathan Cape, 1957), 280 ff.
58. Collinson, *Elizabethan Puritan Movement*, 404.
59. *Ibid.*, 292.
60. *Ibid.*, 403-431.
61. Southern, *Elizabethan Recusant Prose*, 34-43.
62. The standard catalogue is A. F. Allison and D. M. Rogers (eds.), *A Catalogue of Catholic Books in English Printed Abroad or Secretly in England 1558-1640* (London: Wm. Dawson & Sons Ltd., 1964 [reprint from the 1956 appearance in the journal now known as *Recusant History*]).
63. Burghley's reputation defended in 1570 and in 1573, *Hughes and Larkin*, nos. 577 and 598, vol. 2, 341-343 and 376-379, respectively; the Earl of Leicester's, in *Hughes and Larkin*, no. 672, vol. 2, 506-508. For counter-propaganda, *see* p. 183.
64. Southern, *Elizabethan Recusant Prose*, 60 ff.
65. Huntington Library, Ellesmere MS 2573, fos. 10ᵛ-14. There are many other collections of his speeches with this one included, e.g., Folger Shakespeare Library MS X.d.377. Foxe, *Acts and Monuments*, vol. 8, 740-742, prints a version, with the year wrongly converted from the notation of the regnal year.
66. Bodleian Library, Tanner MS 50, fo. 136.
67. The most forceful presentation of the "treason, not religion" case was Burghley's *The Execution of Justice in England* of 1583, answered by Cardinal Allen (see Alfield's case for distributing the latter on p. 182).
68. Huntington Library, Ellesmere MS 2768, fo. [23], cited also in *Hughes and Larkin*, no. 561, vol. 2, 312-313. Case noted in British Library, Harleian MS 2143, fo. 24.
69. *Hughes and Larkin*, no. 561, vol. 2, 312-313. For an argument that it was part of the government's covert campaign against Mary Queen of Scots, see James Philips, *Images of a Queen: Mary Stuart in Sixteenth-Century Literature* (Berkeley: University of California Press, 1964), 56.
70. Youngs, "Definition of Treason in an Elizabethan Proclamation," *passim*.
71. Full account of the case in Folger Shakespeare Library MS X.d.338; decision noted in British Library, Harleian MS 2143, fo. 24. *See* Anthony Petti, "Stephen Vallenger (1541-1591)," *Recusant History*, 6 (October, 1962), 248-264.
72. Southern, *Elizabethan Recusant Prose*, 352-353.
73. Alfield's indictment is printed in *Unpublished Documents Relating to the English Martyrs*, vol. I: *1584-1603*, ed. John Hungerford Pollen ("Catholic Record Society," 5; London: Privately Printed, 1908), 112-117; his trial, 117 ff. *See* also J. N. Langston, "Robert Alfield, Schoolmaster, at Glocester; and his Sons," *Transactions of the Bristol and Gloucestershire Archaeological Society*, 56 (1935), 141-163.
74. Thomas G. Law, *A Historical Sketch of the Conflicts between Jesuits and Seculars in the Reign of Queen Elizabeth* (London: D. Nutt, 1889) is a standard account.
75. That many of the books were printed in England is demonstrated in Gladys Jenkins, "The Archpriest Controversy and the Printers, 1601-1603," *Library*, 5th series, 2 (September-December, 1947), 180-186. The end to this brief partnership was signaled in a proclamation of November 5, 1602,

banishing all priests, with only slightly less rigorous procedures for the seculars, *Hughes and Larkin*, no. 817, vol. 3, 250-255.

76. Once in Mary's reign, and once in Elizabeth's, the procedures of martial law were threatened in connection with books, but both cases seem to me to be war measures, with the issue of books subsumed into the question of countering a foreign enemy, and not new measures arising from the problem of books as such. The Marian measures were stated in a proclamation of June 6, 1558 (*Hughes and Larkin*, no. 443, vol. 2, 90-91) during the war with France which led to the loss of Calais; the Elizabethan, on July 1, 1588 (*Hughes and Larkin*, no. 699, vol. 3, 13-17), when the Armada was on the way.

Gerrard Winstanley: A Critical Retrospect

C. H. GEORGE

Northern Illinois University

GERRARD WINSTANLEY has long seemed to me the first secular saint of the modern world; I have, therefore, long been annoyed by the unimaginative and mistaken scholarship that has obscured his life and work. In this essay I hope somewhat to redress the balance that has tipped the scale of his historical reputation toward the limbo of antiquarian inconsequence. Although justice has been done him in this century by George Sabine's competent editing, the thrust of the rather modish interpretive monographs has been to leave his major achievements unrecognized.

Winstanley studies are a very special part of the historiography of the English Revolution. There is, after all, something a bit exotic about discovering the world's first communist amid the anarchic rhetorical and political debris of the crisis years (1647-1653) in the civil wars. To be sure, we are by now rather used to finding communists in modern revolutions; but that the first should have been perhaps the greatest is an exciting discovery. The other revolutionary leaders, the Army Grandees, Regicides, and Levellers, are not a terribly attractive group—at least most of those we know much about are the usual irresolute, hypocritical, dissimulating, and self-serving public men of any revolutionary (or otherwise) epoch. Cromwell, Fairfax, Rainborough, and Lilburne about exhaust the list of the heroes to be found among the galaxy of revolutionary activists in high councils. And Winstanley makes even them look corrupt.

For a meteoric moment in the history of that great revolution, Winstanley illuminated the dark corners and left candles at many a rude door. He lived and wrote with a brilliance and purity of heart that exploded the new radical morality and its social policy as effectively as it exposed that of the Council of State. At the very height of Leveller agitation and success following the

Army *coup d'etat* and the execution of the king, with "corresponding" cells springing up in and about London and *The Moderate* adding its powerful voice to the swell of Leveller pamphlets, in that flood tide of radical advance and revolutionary fervor, Winstanley began to dig on the Commons with his little band in Surrey. He planted beans and preached encouragement to his poor following, and months before the crucial betrayal and cowardice which lost both Cromwell's and Lilburne's causes, Winstanley wrote his great, angry, masterfully rational pamphlets condemning all of the interlocked manipulators of promises that had been made to the English people—Council of State, Parliament, Levellers, Army, gentry, ranting sectaries, all the conspiracy of defeat were incisively labeled and eloquently excoriated.

In the course of that extraordinary performance on St. George's Hill and its aftermath, Winstanley's underground genius completed itself and left to us the first rational statement of socialist idealism and programmatic ambition. And all of it happened so rapidly, unexpectedly, briefly.

Thus the most enduring excitement for the student of Winstanley is this knowledge that he is the *original* socialist. Socialism did not spring, as most recently George Lichtheim has argued in *The Origins of Socialism*, newly hatched by the social conflicts of the French Revolution. Nor did it originate with Plato, early Christianity, the medieval sects; nor even with the Taborites and their ideological followers in 16th Century Germany. The only other conceivable claim is that of Thomas More's *Utopia*, a claim built upon profound ambiguity and ambivalence in the author, and forfeited by his perverse intellectualism. No, it all began with Gerrard Winstanley, freeman of the City of London, in the year of our Lord, 1649.

I

The events that constitute what we know of Winstanley and the Diggers are by now probably as well reconstructed as luck and the existing sources will ever permit. The corpus of his published work is established, and there will be no private papers except for the chance of an occasional letter like that uncovered by Professor Hardacre.[1] To the basic collection edited by George Sabine in 1941, which printed everything of importance after the first millenarian tracts and corrected the earlier attributions of the *Light Shining in Buckingham-shire* pamphlets to Winstanley, nothing of much importance has been discovered. Professor G. E. Aylmer recently published a previously unknown dialogue, *Englands Spirit Unfolded*, from the Clarke Papers at Worcester College, Oxford.[2] Winstanley's authorship (in 1650) is almost certain, and the value of this short pamphlet is primarily to settle further the debate over the curious dating of Winstanley's longer, apocalyptic piece, *Fire in the Bush*.

The issue involved in the disputed dating of *Fire in the Bush* is a significant one in the context of Winstanley's intellectual development. As will be clear later, there is a central controversy over the existence, nature, and chronological genesis of Winstanley's secular rationalism. The pattern of development from apocalypticism to rationalism was accelerated throughout 1649 to its climax in the publication of *The Law of Freedom* in 1652. In the remarkable *True Leveller's Standard Advanced* of (April) 1649, Winstanley moved for the first time decisively, without backsliding, away from religious toward secular perceptions and articulation. But *Fire in the Bush* was dated by the printer, Giles Calvert, 1650 (New Style)—months after all other evidence of Winstanley's development indicated that his former religious vision had been supplanted by a consistent strengthening rationality.

Fire in the Bush, if indeed written in 1650, after his Digger experience and the great analytic tracts that followed hard upon it, would be a puzzling anomaly in the Winstanley canon, a return (or retreat) to at least the millenarianism of *The New Law of Righteousness*, if not to the outright hysteria of *The Mysterie of God*. Presumably, if this were the fact, it could only be explained as the effect of despair over the collapse of the Digger movement in the Summer of 1650. But, at the latest, it antedated that trauma, and, further, we know Winstanley was very soon at work on *The New Law of Freedom*, the masterwork of his reasoning imagination.

I think the problem is a false one based upon an unreasonably mechanistic view of the printing evidence. I rather like the solution of Lewis Berens, probably the first scholar to see the tract: he simply changed the date of his copy (from the Bodleian) to 1649, apparently on the assumption that the printer had made a simple mistake with a piece that in any case Berens viewed as no more than an appendage to *The New Law of Righteousness*.[3] Sabine thought the pamphlet belonged (from internal evidence) to February or March of 1649, but felt it "credible that, after the failure of his movement," Winstanley should have reverted to an address directed to the churches.[4] Most scholars, however, have favored the post-Digger dating because they can see no basic conflict in Winstanley's work before and after April, 1649. Recently Keith Thomas has given them reassurance ("put a close to these speculations," he says) by discovering a copy of the tract which Thomason dated "Mar. 19. 1649" (that is, New Style, 1650).[5] Professor Thomas thinks the substance of *Fire* not inconsistent with Winstanley's position in 1650. But, in the context of what I shall argue later, the pamphlet is substantively almost impossible to reconcile with a post-Digger date.[6] Professor Aylmer concludes, more sensibly, that the most likely explanation is the one suggested to him by Christopher Hill, that "it may have been written early in 1649, laid aside, then taken up again and published—as dated—in 1650."[7]

The important point about this mini-controversy is the revelation it affords of the "Puritanization" of Winstanley's mind by contemporary scholarship. Even such distinguished Marxists as Professor M. A. Barg have been seduced by the convenience of Puritanizing problems with the result that nearly everyone has failed to observe one of the most sensational metamorphoses in modern intellectual history: the transformation of a religious mystic into the first rational, analytic socialist. That is, the misplaced pamphlet is not perceived as a serious interpretive problem because Winstanley is viewed as essentially a religious thinker throughout his life.[8] I can just imagine Winstanley, for some unknown strategic reason, turning for a moment to his old way with the churches—though I think it improbable. But the failure to see the anomalous *intrinsic* nature of this otherwise slight tract, is a mark of the failure of most scholarship to understand what happened to Winstanley in 1649. In any case, except for the *Fire* problem, we have a reliable canon of Winstanley's published thought.

II

There are not any major problems with reconstructing the outlines of the few years of Winstanley's life which the sparse data permit. An error in the dating and interpretation of a pamphlet in the catalogue of the Thomason collection earlier led both Eduard Bernstein and G. P. Gooch into the false assumption that Winstanley ended the decade of the fifties as a Quaker.[9] But everyone recognizes the mistake now.

Recently Paul Hardacre has enriched our meager information about Winstanley's activities by uncovering a letter written by him to "never so mad" Lady Eleanor Douglas in the year 1650.[10] The letter illuminates the state of Winstanley's mind after the Digging failure, and it proves that he experienced firsthand the most humiliating form of the capitalist revolution on the land—wage labor.

However, there is a special feature of the historiography of Winstanley's life which deserves more notice than it has received. Winstanley is one of the very few historical figures about whom a good novel has been written. David Caute is the talented historian who has performed this rare and valuable feat in a novel entitled *Comrade Jacob*, which was published in 1961 in a single, much too limited English edition. Although I confess it has long been a complaint of mine that historians who teach stupidly ignore the value of good historical fiction, this Caute novel is special, in some ways the only significant effort to get inside Winstanley.

Much of the strength and historical value of Caute's novel is that he is not lured into an effort to tell the whole story of Winstanley's life; except for a few fugitive flashback sequences, he concentrates the story on the months of

Digging for which reliable sources exist. He doesn't even attempt to take Winstanley to the publication of his major work in 1652; since virtually nothing is in fact known of him after 1650, Caute ends there.

One of the theses which Caute does with both fidelity to the record and evocative power, is that of Winstanley's confrontation with the Council of State over the Digging on St. George's Hill. The dialogue between Fairfax and Winstanley is a masterly construction of the character of the challenge which the Diggers represented to the best of the revolutionary leadership. At the other end of the political scale, Caute has some marvelous scenes of the local worthies—like the following recreation of a gathering in Cobham with the purpose of trying once more to resolve the threat of the community on the Hill:

"Well, it's got to stop," declared Parson Platt, slamming his tankard down on the table. "Once and for all." And was met by a chorus of alcoholic assent.

It was rarely that Herley the sexagenarian keeper of the White Lion Tavern could boast such a distinguished bunch of patrons. The parson himself presided, pulling on a clay pipe and putting back his pints as rapidly as the rest. In a shaded corner slouched a rare bird, Sir Francis Vincent, Baronet, the largest landowner in the district, remote, superior, complaining of Herley's Burgundy.

"Deuced cat's piss," he grumbled.

Scattered round the room in various postures were Mr Francis Drake, newly arrived from Amersham, Mr Gilders, Attorney of the Kingston court, Mr Worthy, a timid lecturer called in from the Guildford Classis to preach down the colonists, Captain Gladman and several smaller fry who contrived to place at least one foot, their right foot, in the establishment, including Ned Sutton and John Taylor.

Mr. Worthy had been instructed to give an account of his activities and was busily justifying his existence to an audience whose expressions ranged from the sardonic smile of Vincent to the contemptuous scowl of Gladman, an audience who found Mr Worthy's existence to be of no consequence at all.

"Gentlemen," he pleaded, small and alert like a bird in the mating season, "I have spread the word of the Lord as revealed to us in the Scriptures and to the limits of my meagre capacity. I have made it very clear that the ranters offend all of God's laws."

"All of them?" drawled Vincent. "Must be deuced remarkable chaps."

"Quite so," said Platt sharply, "yet my pews grow emptier by the week and the numbers on the hill swell daily, and not entirely with strangers."

"Intolerable," piped Mr Worthy, as if the matter were beyond his control. Platt was an important man at the Classis and he feared his displeasure.

"Perhaps less words and more deeds," said Vincent.

"I don't think anyone will accuse *me* of inactivity," growled Platt.

Vincent thrust his silver-buckled shoes onto the table. "You've got a damned troop of horse here under Gladman. That should do the trick."

Platt reflected darkly on the life Vincent had been leading among the flesh pots of London. With his long, oiled hair, his lace collar and cuffs, his stylish satin coat tagged with silk, the aristocrat looked too much the cavalier for Platt's taste. As a mere landowner he would have quailed before so powerful a man, so ancient a lineage. But as parson, as keeper of the public morals, he found a new dimension of courage, heavily laced with contempt.

"Gladman," he said curtly, "has orders to proceed no further unless there is rioting or a positive danger to the peace."

"Who on earth would give such an order?"

"The Lord General," said Platt, finding the words tasting good on his own tongue.

"The fellah must be out of his mind."

"The point is this. Force is ruled out of the question."

"What about the trading ban?" drawled Vincent, who had only just heard about it, but spoke of it possessively, as if it were his own brain-child.

"That is totally effective," declared Mr Worthy, anxious to get at least one pat on the back. "No shop in Cobham will now sell to the ranters. I am personally very pleased with the ban."

"Is that true?" said Platt to Ned Sutton.

Causing his bailiff to grunt.

"Well, don't these damned fellahs eat up there or something?" inquired Vincent.

"They eat all right," said Platt. "They buy and sell at Walton and even at Kingston. A trading ban here in Cobham is one thing, but the whole county is a different kettle of fish."

Sir Francis Vincent stirred himself. Already he had put back too much "cat's piss."

"Well look here, I mean damn it, are we sure there's a deuced lot of harm in these fellahs? No, really, I mean to say we've had a deuced lot of bad harvests and there's a good deal of poverty round the parish. I mean charity and all that. Fair's fair. I mean really."

Silence.

"I mean live and let live, what. Don't you think?"

"It may be, sir, that your attitude would change if they planted themselves on your land," said Platt. "I suppose you know they've been cutting your own wood."

Vincent's lethargy left him. "The deuce they have. They have, eh? Get the vermin out, that's what I say."

"And I suppose you know their doctrines," said Platt, following up his advantage.

"Do they have those as well, old fellah? I thought you kept that side of life pretty well tied up, parson." Vincent had recovered his composure.

For a moment Gladman was almost in sympathy with Platt. They shared a common antipathy to inherited ease and grace: and both desired them. In some ways Gladman was reminded of Fairfax, leaving him cooped up in this hole, with Cromwell just off to Ireland. Honours and promotion were to be won across the sea, chopping down papist Irish like the swine they were. He wanted to smash this tavern out of its provincial complacency . . .

. . . and lay a girl on the counter. Any girl.

"They've got a lot of money," said Ned Sutton out of the silence.

"And that's another thing," pressed Platt. "They're extending their acreage and planting every day. They've got barns up there full of hay, they've got cattle up there and fowl. They're buying and selling, they're printing pamphlets in London, making us the laughing stock of the whole Commonwealth. Where do they get all the money? That's what I'd like to know."

But though the reconstruction of social interaction in Surrey is what he does best, Caute makes a fine, original effort to penetrate the mysteries of Winstanley's political personality (based very perceptively on the bits of autobiography scattered throughout Winstanley's work). One brilliant scene is that of a great meeting of colonists and sympathizers called on St. George's Hill following a brutal invasion of the Common. After drinking free beer and singing Digger songs, the company wait in disciplined rows for Winstanley to speak:

Tom Haydon, squatting on the ground in the front rank, beside the Coultons, with the sun warm and comforting on his neck, was rapt in admiration, yet kept a calm head, aware of the devices his leader used. On several occasions Gerrard had spoken freely to him about the art of preaching. All teaching, he had said, whether by word of mouth, or through the pen, is an art. In this there is nothing despicable, so long as the teacher is honest. Man, as an audience, is naturally lethargic. Common folk especially are usually fatigued from hard labour in the fields, and in any case unused to strenuous mental exercise. Thus the preacher resorts to art. Judge him, Gerrard had pleaded, by what he says, and by that alone.

"Now hear me," called Winstanley, his soft voice carrying

effortlessly across their ranks. "Generations ago our land was stolen. Even the commons and waste land, two-thirds of the acreage of England, is denied to us. *They* own the land (he thrust an accusing finger over his shoulder towards Cobham), *they* sit in a parliament of their own making, concocting foul laws to enforce their robbery. *They* hire lawyers to plead their cause. *They* sit themselves as judges and jurymen. This is not the first time I have said it, brethren, and I will say it till the day I die or till the day when Jacob our comrade walks the world supreme. Now you have seen the process before your eyes. A most perfect example of what I have preached, was it not, the way they dragged us to their court at Kingston, not suffering us to plead our case or know the charges against us, with Platt, Taylor, Sutton and that lot on the jury?

"Well, am I right?"

"Yes, yes, yes, yes," shouted the Diggers.

"Very well then. They have flung poor Henry Bickerstaffe, a cripple, and Henry Longhurst, a most peace-loving man, into prison. They have hunted down Will Starr, our dear comrade, and intend to hang him for some miserable theft. They will hang him as a lesson to us all, to try and shake our faith and resolution And I ask you this: "is it reasonable to hang a man who steals a little bread because he is starving? If such thefts are punishable by death, then our lords and masters should have been swinging from trees these many centuries past!"

A tide of anger swept the company like a purge. Calm, detached, inwardly possessed, Winstanley watched the uproar, gauging his moment.

Finally, an excerpt from the end, when all is lost, the gallant effort in Surrey crushed, and we are treated to a look at Winstanley, sick and feverish and battling back mystical visions, always returning to the calm pride of his masterful rationalism:

Christmas comes, on dry bread and a stolen chicken.

I wrote *A New Year's Gift for the Parliament and Army*, my longest work for some months, filling one hundred and fifty pages of my own script, sixty pages as printed by Giles Calvert. The money from this source was miserable enough, but not to be scorned, in our condition. I'm sure this work will change the world, oh yes, all the Parliament men will resign their seats and all the officers their commissions, we'll have so many great men begging to join us on the hill we don't know where to lodge them. Writing, scribbling all useless . . . delirium . . .

—Gerrard, you are ill.

—Yes, Judith, I had a fever a year ago, in January, and I dream of the colony. Judith, brush the hair from my eyes.

—There is no hair in your eyes, Gerrard.

—Has the colony been according to my dream? Is the fire burning in the bush? Can you see?

—Fire in the bush? I don't understand. He's feverish (her voice fading as she turns away).

—Go and look at the bush. The fire will spread.

—He's feverish.

—Who's that?

—It's me, Gerrard, John Coulton. You've a fever. It'll pass. They threw old Nell and Bobby Webb on the heath last night, leaving them in the snow.

—They what?

—Gladman came in the night. They made the two old people climb out of bed and then took their hut to pieces, setting fire to the lot. They were drunk, I'd wager. Poor old Bobby and Nell, being over seventy, lay down in the snow, shaking of shock. We found them this morning clasped together.

—It doesn't bear thinking of, cried the girl, breaking into tears.

—This is murder, murder, murder . . .

—Hold him down, Judith, he's delirious.

—There's nothing they won't stop at. Look evil in the face, my brethren, naked evil. Platt, Gladman, Vincent, Drake, in their fine houses, pulling down the calf-cribs of old people and leaving them in the snow to die. Murderers!

John Coulton's voice, calm as ever. —We buried them decently.

—Thank you, John.

Judith's hand is on my brow. I will cry it abroad, how cruelly they treat us, regarding us as less than human. This is the end of an epoch. We are finished and cannot rise again. Centuries of darkness are closing in. There's snow coming through the roof.

—Help me move the bed, said Judith.

I moved in space. The snow was no longer falling on my face.

—We must patch that ceiling, I heard John Coulton say.

—No tools, grunted Tom Haydon, who had scarcely opened his mouth all winter. Silently he toiled, bowed down with remorse.

The centuries of private ownership are closing in. Some may look back on us as mere ignorant peasants, which is true enough, but we were more than that, we were the pioneers of a great movement, a great ideal, which will one day come to fruit, not when God wills it, but when man wills it. If I did not believe that, I would take my own life. Man's essence, after all, lies in man's existence, not in God's existence. Let the poor and the exploited find a way of coming together. Then, my masters, there will be rivers of blood. . . .

*   *   *

January, February, March. I recovered. Tom Haydon and Adam Knight have been on the road these last two months, tramping around the counties of England, collecting money for our enterprise. In short—begging. A little forthcoming, some from a mad visionary woman called Lady Eleanor Douglas of Pirton in Hertfordshire who had no sooner given than she wanted it back, but our clever boys were well away with many blessings, promising the lady a prominent place in our prayers, which she shall have. Tom Haydon, who spoke to me briefly before starting once again on his travels, reported this lady to be an identical twin to Mrs Platt, calling herself the prophetess Melchisedecke also. We may have to gather all the Melchisedeckes together and draw lots to settle the issue. Or perhaps a rain-making competition. So we lived a bit on this money, and on cutting wood. Nobody would graze their cows on my pasture these days, Platt had seen to that. I lost all sense of time and space. I could write no more, being underfed, my mind refusing to function. My clothes hung loose on my emaciated body, and you could have pinched my arm to find bare bone. It was the same case with us all. It was quite impossible to sow crops. We had no sooner built a house than Gladman searched us out and flattened it, usually drunk, cursing us for keeping him bottled up in this part of the world.

Happiness began to steal in on me, and a great peace. Often I thought of our departed friends, those who died, those killed by Gladman, and those who wandered away. Where they have reached I may never know.

*   *   *

The week before Easter, and Mr Platt is active in the pulpit. Live in peace with all men, and love your enemies, he preaches. . . . He hires three mercenaries to reside on the common by day and night, not suffering us even to dig caves in the earth. We are men: yet we may not live above or below the ground, like the humble mole.

Judith, my dear creature, fell into a faint with hunger, and Robert Coster went out, pocketing his pride, to beg a little food. It being Easter, and a time of Christian love, they had him publicly whipped in the White Lion, so that he could hardly walk. And the people, common folk like ourselves, stood by and laughed, as if he were a bear in a circus.

Oh, my poet.

A year ago we were full of hope, Will Everard and I. Then we believed in oppression, but also in God's power to right all. Now I know nothing of Will Everard, and less of God. Man must fend for himself, and the poor perhaps have centuries to go before they are strong enough to rise as one man and destroy their oppressors.

There is really only one caveat to observe in using Caute's Winstanley: The power and originality of Gerrard's intellect are insufficiently portrayed. But any quarrel seems ungrateful; David Caute has made a unique and permanent contribution to the history of the Diggers. *Comrade Jacob* should be read by all students of English radicalism, and it should be reprinted for a much wider audience.

I might conclude my comments on the "life" of Winstanley by noting some of the important facts missing—and likely never to be recovered. Most unfortunate, because fundamental to our understanding of his intellectual development, is our virtually complete ignorance of his education, travel, and reading. We can cull from the evidence of his published pamphlets only such obvious items read as the Bible and the Leveller literature—his only explicit references are to the Bible. Winstanley expressly shunned learned marginalia and any other appearance of book-sense (except for scripture) because he considered such learning to have been corrupted into instruments of oppression. His writing makes clear that he had read some history, probably some law. But how we should like to know his reactions to the books that David Caute has Robert Coster taking from his bulging pack! (*Comrade Jacob*, p. 166) It is very possible that he felt it politically necessary in leading his unlettered constituency to conceal what I suspect was his knowledge of More, Bacon and Coke.

The other principal unknowns concern such things as his relation to and the fate of his wife Susan, the possibility of his having children; all the questions of his own earlier family relations with parents, siblings, and relatives. We don't even know anything of his friendships. Did Winstanley have any intellectual compatriots beside Robert Coster? Was there a cadre of leadership in the counties where the Diggers were active? And, of course, what of his activities after 1650? How did he manage to get from 1650 to the firm optimism of 1652? From the lists of Diggers we may get a few tentative answers to some of the latter queries, but even that is unlikely.

III

Perhaps the most perplexing set of problems relating to Winstanley and the Diggers are those concerning the extent of the movement and the nature of its influence. George Sabine, Margaret James, and David Petegorsky have argued with various degrees of probability for evidence of Digger colonies spreading from the base in Surrey to Kent, Buckinghamshire, Northamptonshire, Gloucestershire, Staffordshire, and even as far north as Cumberland.[11] Digger agents looking for money and recruits were very active in 1650 in London and some thirty-five other towns, and in some six counties in addition to Surrey (Berkshire, Buckinghamshire, Hertfordshire, Huntingdonshire, Middlesex, and Northamptonshire).[12]

Recently Professor Keith Thomas has discovered a Buckinghamshire broadside published in 1650 by Diggers from the Parish of Iver which adds five more locations of colonies going north to Nottinghamshire.[13] The ten signatures on this latest manifesto brings to ninety the number of known Digger names—reminding us again that further research (or more likely, a sharp eye for incidental disclosure) might conceivably reveal something of the social details of the movement in the 1650s. Soviet scholars have insisted—without any new data—that the Digger movement was much more widespread than bourgeois historians have allowed.[14]

But though evidence mounts of the widespread activities of Digger groups and agitators, there is only a single piece of evidence that the colonies of 1649-1650 and the leadership of Winstanley lasted any longer than the prototype on St. George's Hill. That evidence is from Enfield Chase in Middlesex, some nine miles from London. The Iver broadside named a colony at Enfield in 1650; in 1659 rioting broke out there over property rights between monied "Intruders" upon the Chase and the "Inhabitants" who defended their feudal rights. From the social war waged between the purchasers (such new men of new wealth as the famous Colonel Joyce) and the local oligarchs (who had earlier ejected the local Diggers from the Commons), one gets an impression of a community fighting battles in a familiar context of Digger agitation. In any case, out of that bitter struggle came one of the major radical proposals of the revolution.[15]

William Covell, preacher and landowner, proposed a solution for the problems at Enfield which might owe something to Winstanley—though far less than has been alleged.[16] Basically, since he had no theory of history or right, Covell simply proposed ending the conflict by a paternalistic scheme to soften the harsher effects of capitalist predation through the establishment of co-operative family units under the control of the rich.[17] He denied being a Leveller, but his scheme came to nothing anyway.[18] He seems to me a forerunner of John Bellers and the philanthropic utopians.

Among the Levellers themselves, except perhaps in the intriguing complexity of Buckinghamshire radicalism, Winstanley appears to have had little positive influence. His major work, *The Law of Freedom*, went into two printings and was pirated and excerpted in the 1650s, but no one can be found who acknowledges even reading it. The greatest Leveller, John Lilburne, explicitly abjured any connection with

this silly conceit of Levelling of propriety and magistracie . . .
because it would, if practised, destroy not only all industry in the
world and raze the very foundation of generation and subsistence or
being of one man by another. For . . . who will take paines for that
which when he hath gotten it is not his owne but must equally be
shared in by every lazy, simple, dronish sot?[19]

Richard Overton was the only Leveller who had any conception of Winstanley's style of analysis.[20] There was interestingly, one other work contemporaneous with Winstanley which was informed by powerful sympathy for the poor, hatred of the hypocrisy and greed of the clergy and the rich, and by a primitivistic communist idealism. This was the anonymous *Tyranipocrit*, published at Rotterdam in 1649—a vintage year, 1649! However, all other political radicals frantically denied the label, "Leveller," with all its social implications. As Margaret James put it, "The political Levellers hated their offspring as a Radical father hates a Socialist son, and their schemes included specific precautions against the levelling of estates."[21]

About the only positive trace of the impact of Winstanley's cometic genius after 1650 is that intrinsically possible in the work of the Dutchman, Peter Cornelius Plockhoy. He was more sophisticated than Covell, a friend of Cromwell's, and an imaginative philanthropist. But he too insisted that alleviation of the misery of the poor was not inconsistent with the principle that "every one may keep his propriety".[22] After Plockhoy, the evidence for a "Winstanley effect" is even thinner. It is commonplace among socialist historians to see the Quakers taking from the "quiver" of his early writing their most pointed arrows, and to see his influence on John Bellers.[23] They are almost certainly mistaken, especially when they then argue a transmission of his work from Bellers to Robert Owen or Henry George![24]

Indeed, tragically, but, of course, inevitably, Winstanley's genius and Digger courage were the triumph of a moment. No tradition emerged to enshrine either the colonized enclaves of their brave efforts or the broader world touched by his printed thought.

IV

The history of the scholarship devoted to Winstanley and the Diggers is a predictable bag of tricks played on those troublesome dead.[25] The major contemporary historian of the revolution, Lord Clarendon, lost the Diggers among the amorphous unpleasantness of those whom he saw as responsible, from 1647 on, for the "many propositions to their officers and to the Parliament to introduce an equality into all conditions, and a parity amongst all men; from whence they had the appellation of Levellers; which appeared a great party."[25] Sober, perceptive Clarendon was at his weakest trying to explain the fanaticism of the revolution—all those more radical than Cromwell tended to blur for him into a faceless mob.[27] Agitators and Diggers were particularly indistinguishable in their dangerous unreasonableness. I suspect Clarendon never got through a Leveller or Digger pamphlet; his disgust and impatience would have made the effort too painful.

Once the English got beyond the Glorious Revolution, past what Olivier Lutaud calls their *"mauvais souvenir,"* some interesting reactions set in. With the triumph of a distinctly bourgeois culture, the greatest intellectuals of the next century looked upon the radical republicanism (a rubric that included social revolutionaries) of the civil wars with relaxed contempt. Blackstone thought even Locke advocated a levelling of property![28] Samuel Johnson found it necessary to explain to the Whig intellectual, Catherine Macaulay, the error of her sympathy for republicanism: "I thus, Sir, showed her the absurdity of the levelling doctrine. . . ."[29] And David Hume lumped all "levellers" together with the religious sectaries as simply a gaggle of madmen.[30]

On the other hand, although silence, and, eventually total ignorance, engulfed the Digger experiments, the Levellers proper fared much better in some corners of the 18th century. The few exceptions are noteworthy. Apart from the Vicar of Wakefield's now famous tribute to those "honest men who were called Levellers [who] tried to erect themselves into a community where all should be equally free," there were in England two major bits of evidence of the survival of some memory of revolutionary radicalism. The most astonishing of these is the very long article on Lilburne in the *Biographia Britannica*, the publisher's effort to produce an English version of Bayle's *Dictionnaire Historique et Critique*. Lilburne is given three times as many pages as Laud, and almost as many as Oliver Cromwell! Moreover, though clearly the author(s) of the piece are horrified by the Great Rebellion, Lilburne, "the coryphaeus of the Levellers," is viewed as a major figure in opposing the despotism of Cromwell.[31] Then there was the important *History of England* written by Catherine Macaulay in which she praised the republicans who had been "in derision styled Levellers".[32]

The virtual loss to England of both the Leveller and True Leveller traditions from the revolution was tragic, but understandable enough. What is harder to comprehend is the apparent ignorance of English radicalism demonstrated by the intellectual ferment which became a crucial part of the French and American revolutions of the next century. We know that a French translation of the *Agreement of the People* appeared as early as 1653, in French translation, as a manifesto of the *Ormée* revolution at Bordeaux; it was also well known to Mirabeau.[33] Christopher Hill has told me that hard work might well turn up more evidence of English radical thought in France for the years between *l'Ormée* and the great revolution. But so far there is amazingly little such evidence for France. Even more surprising is the lack of any sort of Leveller tradition in the most radical English-speaking society after the passing of Cromwell's England—the North American colonies. The American Revolution was intellectually nourished by the relatively conservative likes of Algernon Sidney, James Harrington, John Trenchard, and Thomas Gordon.[34]

Nineteenth-Century historiography contrived much fuller accounts of the Leveller years while continuing to confuse Levellers with Diggers (repeating, for the most part, the propaganda line of the royalists, i.e., that "levelling" was a social doctrine). François Guizot thought Everard the leader of the "band of rough men" in Surrey whose doctrines came from Lilburne and his "little anarchical associations, civil or military. . . ."[35] William Godwin, broke and fast losing the passion and insight of the *Political Justice* years, wrote at sour length of Lilburne and the Levellers in *History of the Commonwealth* (1824-28). Carlyle treated Lilburne and Winstanley as co-captains of "a whole submarine world of Calvinistic Sansculottism, Five-point Charter and the Rights of Man, threatening to emerge almost two centuries before its time!"[36] Predictably, Carlyle treated Lilburne and his "five small Beagles" (the Leveller cadre!) with more contempt than he reserved for Everard and Winstanley "and the poor Brotherhood, seemingly Saxon, but properly of the race of the Jews, who were found dibbling beans on St. George's Hill, under the clear April skies in 1649, and hastily bringing in a new era in that manner."[37] Ranke saw Winstanley's letter to Fairfax in the Harleian Miscellany, and the anti-property drift of *The Moderate*, and concluded that Lilburne and the Levellers were social revolutionaries.[38]

Samuel Rawson Gardiner was, of course, more on target than anyone before him. He had done the research and saw much of the radical history accurately in spite of his conservative prejudices. In particular Gardiner knew Lilburne had heatedly denied any social levelling just two weeks after Winstanley began Digging.[39] He concluded his account of the Diggers, "communism had no root in the England of the seventeenth century. The political Levellers had followers enough."[40] Gardiner was also, I believe, the first historian to note the "socialist effusion" of *The Law of Freedom*, "too far removed from the actual world to move Cromwell either to approval or indignation. It was otherwise with Lilburne and the political Levellers."[41]

And what of Marx on the subject of levellerism in the English Revolution? Most disappointing in this regard is the circumstance that neither he nor Engels ever discovered Winstanley (I would love to have had Marx's view of Winstanley's "utopianism"—certainly True Levellerism would not have been equated with True Socialism!). Marx was very impressed with the far less exciting essays of John Bellers. Why Marx failed to come across Winstanley from the accounts in Guizot's histories of the English Revolution which he read will remain a mystery.

At any rate, in 1847 Marx did write an article for the *Deutsche-Brüssler-Zeitung* in which he declared that

socialism and communism did not originate in Germany, but in England, France, and North America. The first appearance of a really active communist party may be placed within the period of the middle-class revolution, the moment when constitutional monarchy was abolished. The most consistent republicans in England, the Levellers, in France Babeuf, Buonarotti, etc., were the first to proclaim these "social questions."[42]

The Levellers as the first "really active communist party" ("wirklich agieren-den kommunistischen Partei")! Obviously Marx had not done his home-work in the *Biographia Britannica*, or Godwin. Yet Christopher Hill has noted that Marx considered the 17th Century and 18th Century proletarians did not constitute "independent evolved classes or sub-classes."[43] They were simply part of the revolutionary bourgeoisie. Rare analytical inconsistency from the master! Unhappily, when he was later installed among the Thoma-son pamphlets in the British Museum, Marx did not return to the subject of 17th Century English radicalism.

Engels in various places developed a similarly mistaken analytical con-text in which to place the Levellers. The clearest example of his confusion is in the introduction to the *Anti-Dühring*:

And although, on the whole, the bourgeoisie in their struggle with the nobility could claim to represent at the same time the interests of the different sections of workers of that period, yet in every great bourgeois movement there were independent outbursts of that class which was the more or less developed forerunner of the modern proletariat. For example, the Thomas Münzer tendency in the period of the reformation and peasant war in Germany; the Levellers in the great English revolution; in the great French revolution, Babeuf. Alongside of these revolutionary armed uprisings of a class which was as yet undeveloped, the corresponding theoretical manifestations made their appearance; in the sixteenth and seventeenth centuries, utopian portrayals of ideal social conditions; in the eighteenth century, actual communistic theories (Morelly and Mably). The demand for equality was no longer limited to political rights, but was extended also to the social conditions of individuals; it was not merely class privileges that were to be abolished, but class distinctions themselves.[44]

But if Marx and Engels did nothing for Winstanley, and little for the his-tory of levellerism, an able Marxist, Eduard Bernstein, was the one who finally began the first serious study of Winstanley and his movement before the end of the century. Bernstein's *Sozialismus und Demokratie in der gros-sen englischen Revolution* was unquestionably the turning point in the mod-ern scholarship of English revolutionary thought. Bernstein did, unaccount-ably, repeat serious errors for one who had seen the major sources (he has the Levellers championing "with vigour the political interests of the contemporary and future working class"[45]); but he also provided the first appreciation and a lengthy summary of *The Law of Freedom*, which he correctly described as "an important and interesting document in the history of Socialism. Dropping all mysticism and paraphrase, the author propounds a complete social system based on communistic principles."[46] Bernstein concluded that, indeed, Winstanley represents the most advanced ideas of his time; "in his Utopia we find coalesced all the popular aspirations engendered and fertilized by the Revolution."[47]

The 20th Century can celebrate the fact that the best thing that has happened to Winstanley since his death has been the editorial labors of George Sabine, who in 1941 published very nearly the whole corpus of Winstanley's work. The year before Sabine's edition appeared, the Marxist scholar, David Petegorsky, published the best monograph that has been done on the Diggers (its defects, curiously, are typical of those of the non-Marxist scholars whose work I shall comment on subsequently). Although there has since been a steady flow of literature on Levellers and True Levellers, and more good editing of the body of Leveller tracts, I find only the work of Hill, Brailsford, and Macpherson to have added anything of much value to the interpretation of that canon of radicalism.[48]

Finally, in this historiographical overview, it is worth observing that in textbooks, general histories, and encyclopedias, the problem is not so much that they have the contours of Leveller history wrong (which they have); it is that the movement and its people are almost totally ignored! I can't possibly illustrate this dreary point at any length, so just let me note a few typical examples of the magnitude of incompetence.

In D. H. Willson's *History of England*, one of the most recent of such textbooks by a specialist in Stuart history, the "Levelers" get three sentences of attention—one of which tells us simply that Lilburne was "a restless and unreasonable man"; the "religious mystic," Winstanley, and the Diggers are accorded all of six sentences which begin, "Cromwell was wise enough to ignore a small harmless group who called themselves True Levellers and were known as Diggers." Is that any advance over Clarendon! Even worse is the effort of the most popular and otherwise best *History of the Modern World* by my erstwhile teacher Robert Palmer, in which neither Lilburne nor Winstanley is mentioned (!) and the "Levellers, Diggers, or Fifth Monarchy Men" are equated as favoring a leveling "between rich and poor"! If one is obliged then to turn to a standard reference work, the most recent edition of the Encyclopedia Britannica will provide no less than Christopher Hill—but with some twenty lines to explain Winstanley to the world. The editors allotted a third more space to the minor royalist poet, John Cleveland!

V

Thus, although I guess I must presume the subject of the Levellers, let alone Winstanley, to be a very esoteric one, I will stubbornly attempt to identify what seems to me the greatest obstacle to a modern estimate of Winstanley. To do that I must first characterize and illustrate the interpretive approach of perhaps twenty monographs, written over the past thirty years, which share a basic preconception—after which I will suggest an alternative understanding.

In my view, the fault with recent Winstanley studies is the same as that which distorts most other scholarship devoted to exploring the 17th Century cultural landscape in England. It is the error in the prevailing definition of and obsession with Puritanism, the effort to make this reified monster of Weber's imagination into the causative or conditioning factor in the explanation of virtually all innovation and change in the modern world.[49] Everything from "the spirit of capitalism" to the new science has been attributed to Puritan culture. It is hardly surprising that the Weberian incubus has also fastened itself about Winstanley's neck. There are two principal errors that result from the dead weight of the Puritan hypostasis within the complex relations both of Winstanley's thought and its relation to a modern cultural sea-change. For Winstanley is not only the first communist; he is also a major and very nearly unique representative (sharply focused within a few years of crisis in his own life) of the change from religious to secular perceptions and terms of social analysis.

The errors I refer to are perfectly illustrated by the piece published in 1946 by Professor Winthrop Hudson which propounds the incredible question, ". . . Gerrard Winstanley: Was He a Seventeenth-Century Marxist?", and opens,

Unfortunately, from the point of view of a balanced appreciation of Winstanley, his initial resurrection from the limbo of forgotten men was accomplished by one who was a better Marxist than historian. Eduard Bernstein found Winstanley interesting as an early exponent of the class struggle and as a class-conscious agitator in behalf of "a complete social system based on communistic principles." This is the pattern of interpretation that has been followed by most of those who have given attention to the Digger movement since that time. Indeed, much of the current interest in Winstanley is due to a desire to demonstrate that left-wing socialism is indigenous to the British Isles and has its roots in "the native British tradition." [Hill][50]

Following a summary misstatement of previous Marxist work, Professor Hudson makes his first thesis statement:

Except for the peculiarity of "digging," there is little in
Winstanley's basic philosophy to distinguish him from the other
religious radicals produced by the Puritan revolution who, as the
representatives of the dispossessed, gave voice to the social discontent
of the time and looked forward to a day of retribution when God
would intervene and mete out justice to the oppressors. The
similarities of the Diggers, the Quakers, the more enthusiastic
Baptists, and the Fifth Monarchy men, with regard to both their
theological points of view and their social attitudes, are more
significant than their differences. They were cut off the same piece,
according to much the same pattern, and in large measure preached
a common message of social redemption. They all believed in
visions and dreams, in direct illumination and guidance by the
Spirit.[51]

Further argumentation professes to establish that Winstanley drew his
"ideational pattern and program" from the (thirty-sixth chapter of the)
Book of Ezekiel. In fact, Ezekiel is cited throughout Winstanley's work
about once for every five citations from Acts, John, Isaiah, and Revelations,
and there is no evidence at all that Ezekiel was of any special importance to
Winstanley—let alone a well of intellectual inspiration. Not surprisingly,
Hudson uses *Fire in the Bush* as evidence of Winstanley's enduring apocalypticism while dating its composition, without any explanation, in the *summer* of 1650!

Most outrageous and yet basically typical of the conclusions which flow
from this kind of hypothesized reconstruction of Winstanley's mind and
work, is that which sees the Digger colonies and *The Law of Freedom* as no
more than "eschatological signs", fulfillments of scriptural prophecy with
no intended impact on the real world, simply chiliastic statements of belief
in divine interference in the future of man:

The Diggers, we may conclude, did not conceive of their venture
as a means of effecting social change or as a way of gaining desired
ends. They did not think of the practice of Christian love as a
method for the achievement of the good society; rather, their
intention was to live now as all will live after the restoration. They
were bearing witness to the new life to come. Having done that,
they waited for God to act. "I . . . . have declared . . . . the whole light
of that truth revealed to me by the word of the Lord," wrote
Winstanley. "I shall now wait to see his hand, to do his own work
in what time, and by what instruments he pleases." Elsewhere he
declares: "I have Writ, I have Acted, I have Peace: and now I must
wait to see the Spirit do his own work in the hearts of others, and
whether England shall be the first Land, or some other, wherein
Truth shall sit down in triumph."

The peace they experienced in their hearts was the final
justification of the digging.[52]

So resolved is Hudson to see Winstanley as another religious radical, that
he baldly insists *The Law of Freedom* is "a clear indication that he had been
converted to the Fifth Monarchy point of view" (!) and that his utopia was
conceived as merely another eschatological symbol. Thus one of the most
interestingly secularized social treatises in all history becomes a tract that
could have been conceived by any Baptist or Ranter of talent! The painful
political experiences of 1649-50, which led Winstanley to turn for a final
appeal to Cromwell for support against the depredations of clergy, lawyers,
and landlords, is seen by Hudson to prove Winstanley's reliance upon Fifth
Monarchist thought on unreformed magistracy! He has not one shred of
proof of such influence; but anything is better than admitting the importance
of Winstanley's own rational thought about his particular social experience.
Thus Hudson concludes:

In spite of the limitations imposed upon him by his environment,
Winstanley discharged successfully and effectively one of the most
important functions of any true preacher of the gospel of Christ . . .
a preacher he was, not an economist. And if his writings have been
correctly interpreted, modern historians interested in Marxist
parallels in English thought have superimposed upon Winstanley
their own preconceptions. He was not interested primarily in a
practical program of social reform but in the approaching reign of
God, and it was that impending cataclysm which he proclaimed.
The digging, therefore, had less significance as a communistic
program than as a "sign" demanding attention to a message from
the Lord. Winstanley stood in the succession of prophets who have
measured men and their society with the plumb-line of God and
found them wanting. And, like the prophets, he had great faith in
the power of God to redeem the world from bondage, injustice, and
oppression.[53]

One other illustration of the neo-Puritan folly—this from Wilhelm
Schenk's monograph, published in 1958:

It would seem then that the kind of spiritual religion represented
by Winstanley was one of the factors changing the climate of
opinion at a crucial period of European history. Some of its doctrines
—notably the possibility of perfection in this life and the
immanence of God in the world—were likely to support a tendency,
widespread for many other reasons, towards secularisation.
However that may be, Winstanley evidently stands "betwixt and

between"— a religious fanatic of the Puritan Revolution, yet anticipating something of a later intellectual atmosphere. But it is important to bear in mind that even those of his views which strike us as characteristically modern were not unconnected with his religious beliefs, which were, indeed, as far as we can gather from his writings, the mainspring of all his thought. Any interpretation tending to minimise the importance of his religious beliefs must remain unhistorical.

It would be a truism to say that Winstanley had a one-track mind; all fanatics have, and this is at the same time their weakness and their strength. When one believes oneself to have been favoured with a revelation one does not pause to consider much besides. And Winstanley's chief claim to our attention does, in fact, rest on his compelling vision of a brotherly community of peace and goodwill, on that very message which he felt to have received from the Spirit.[54]

VI

Before I examine in some detail the evidence of Winstanley's rationalism and secularism, I must clear away some of the underbrush that has obscured the character of Winstanley's religious thought. Years of reading theology, sermons, and varieties of religious tracts have made me skeptical about even categorizing such mental gymnastics as "thought" in any serious, rational sense. In 17th Century England, in particular, the frequent lapses of clerical writers into anagogical musings over Scripture, added to the "literal" school which is never literal, and the allegorical commonplaces which defy reasonable imagination, make it very difficult to judge the rational content of most religious writing. Mystics, of course, compound all these problems with the solipsism of their relation to God. Thus Winstanley's early writing, from *The Mysterie of God* through *The New Law of Righteousness* is undistinguished genre literature of this sort. It is interesting *only* because the same antinomian, chiliastic, apocalyptic—that is, totally irrational—man was subsequently transformed by some miracle of his time and genius into a rational, secularized observer of English society. That process is as baffling as it is momentous; but before it can be at all appreciated it is necessary to understand the continuing use of biblical references and rhetoric in Winstanley's mature, secular writing.

The matter of biblical rhetoric in rational prose is easily dealt with: R. H. Tawney was just yesterday brilliantly deploying many of the same rich scriptural metaphors in his battles with capitalism and other enemies he shared with Winstanley. English bibles have long been storehouses (Winstanley, incidentally, used the King James rather than the "Puritan" Geneva Bible) of magnificent language.

The only significant question relates to the use Winstanley made of the conceptual substance of biblical rhetoric. Is the Bible a source of *ideas* for Winstanley?

In the pre-Digger tracts, the intoxication of biblical moods, the evocation of the prophets, the textured majesty of the stories, and, above all, the extraordinary verses of the Book of Revelation, certainly moved Winstanley to a passionate, messianic involvement with the destiny of God's Englishmen. But even in his first published uses of scriptural citation, Winstanley was cavalier to careless. If one traces the references to discover the possible sources of his thought in the texts, he will find little relation (even anagogical) of text to exhortation. But I don't want to strain the connections in this early apocalyptic literature—I could miss some of the mystical reading Winstanley intended very easily; the wild flow of his religious imagination is autonomous frenzy. The closest Winstanley comes to revolutionary thought before 1649 is in the antinomian zeal he shares with a Dell or Saltmarsh.

Very different and much more important is the question of the function of his biblical learning in Winstanley's post-Digger thought. An investigation reveals some interesting facts about the uses of the Bible and the surprises in Winstanley's intellectual development from *The True Levellers Standard Advanced* through *The Law of Freedom*. Let me illustrate. In *The True Levellers Standard*, his first revolutionary tract, Winstanley's head was spinning with the effort to conceptualize the drama in which he was caught— the confrontation in Surrey with class solidarity, hypocrisy, and injustice. Ideas that would become basic to his revolutionary perceptions, like those of the Law of Creation, the Common Treasury, the spirit of Universal Liberty, and the Norman Yoke, he had seized and developed from a variety of contemporary pamphlets (Winstanley never complains of the secularism of Leveller literature which modern scholars do admit), his own (unknown to us) more basic reading, and the crowded private thoughts hammered into shape by the events of April, 1649. Here is a look into this intellectual volcano:

And that this Civil Propriety is the Curse, is manifest thus, Those that Buy and Sell Land, and are landlords, have got it either by Oppression, or Murther, or Theft; and all landlords live in the breach of the Seventh and Eighth Commandements, *Thou shalt not steal, nor kill.*
First by their Oppression. They have by their subtle imaginary and covetous wit, got the plain-hearted poor, or younger Brethren, to work for them, for small wages, and by their work have got a great increase; for the poor by their labour lift up Tyrants to rule over them; or else by their covetous wit, they have out-reached the

plain-hearted in Buying and Selling, and thereby inriched themselves, but impoverished others: or else by their subtile wit, having been a lifter up into places of Trust, have inforced people to pay Money for a Publick use, but have divided much of it into their private purses; and so have got it by Oppression.

Then Secondly for Murther; They have by subtile wit and power, pretended to preserve a people in safety by the power of the Sword; and what by large Pay, much Free-quarter, and other Booties, which they call their own, they get much Monies, and with this they buy Land, and become landlords; and if once Landlords, then they rise to Justices, Rulers, and State Governours, as experience shewes: But all this is but a bloudy and subtile Theevery, countenanced by a Law that Covetousness made; and is a breach of the Seventh Commandement, *Thou shalt not kill.*

And likewise Thirdly a breach of the Eighth Commandement, *Thou shalt not steal*; but these landlords have thus stoln the Earth from their fellow Creatures, that have an equal share with them, by the Law of Reason and Creation, as well as they.

And such as these rise up to be rich in the objects of the Earth; then by their plausible words of flattery to the plain-hearted people, whom they deceive, and that lies under confusion and blindness: They are lifted up to be Teachers, Rulers, and Law makers over them that lifted them up; as if the Earth were made peculiarly for them, and not for others weal: ... For what are all those Binding and Restraining Laws that have been made from one Age to another since that Conquest, and are still upheld by Furie over the People? I say, What are they? but the Cords, Bands, Manacles, and Yokes that the enslaved *English*, like *Newgate* Prisoners, wear upon their hands and legs as they walk the streets; by which those *Norman* Oppressors, and these their Successors from Age to Age have enslaved the poor People by, killed their younger Brother, and would not suffer *Iacob* to arise.

O what mighty Delusion, do you, who are the powers of *England*, live in! That while you pretend to throw down that *Norman* yoke, and *Babylonish* power, and have promised to make the groaning people of *England* a Free People; yet you still lift up that *Norman* yoke, and slavish Tyranny, and hold the People as much in bondage as the Bastard Conquerour himself, and his Councel of War.

Take notice, That *England* is not a Free People, till the Poor that have no Land, have a free allowance to dig and labour the Commons, and so live as Comfortably as the Landlords that live in their Inclosures. For the People have not laid out their Monies, and shed their Bloud, that their Landlords, the *Norman* power, should still have its liberty and freedom to rule in Tyranny in his Lords, landlords, Judges, Justices, Bayliffs, and State Servants; but that the Oppressed might be set Free, Prison doors opened, and the

Poore peoples hearts comforted by an universal Consent of making
the Earth a Common Treasury, that they may live together as one
House of Israel, united in brotherly love into one Spirit; and having
a comfortable livelihood in the Community of one Earth their
Mother.

If you look through the Earth, you shall see, That the landlords,
Teachers and Rulers, are Oppressors, Murtherers, and Theeves in
this manner; But it was not thus from the Beginning. And this is one
Reason of our digging and labouring the Earth one with another. . . .
And that not only this Common, or Heath should be taken in and
Manured by the People, but all the Commons and waste Ground in
England, and in the whole World, shall be taken in by the People
in righteousness, not owning any Propriety; but taking the Earth to
be a Common Treasury, as it was first made for all. . . . It shewed
us, That all the Prophecies, Visions, and Revelations of Scriptures,
of Prophets, and Apostles, concerning the calling of the Jews, the
Restauration of Israel; and making of that People, the Inheritors of
the whole Earth; doth all seat themselves in this Work of making
the Earth a Common Treasury; as you may read, *Ezek*. 24. 26, & c.
Jer. 33. 7. to 12. *Esay*. 49. 17, 18, & c. *Zach*. 8. from 4. to 12. *Dan*.
2, 44, 45. *Dan*. 7. 27. *Hos*. 14. 5, 6, 7. *Joel* 2. 26, 27. *Amos* 9. from
8. to the end. *Obad*. 17. 18. 21. *Mic*. 5, from 7 to the end. *Hab*. 2.
6, 7, 8, 13, 14. *Gen*. 18. 18. *Rom*. II. 15. *Zeph*. 3. & c. *Zach*. 14. 9.[55]

The list of some sixteen scriptural references contains perfect evidence
of the almost ornamental, certainly at best tangential, relation of the Bible
to Winstanley's thought.[56] Twelve of the references are simply to various
versions of promises that the tribal exiles will be returned to Palestine; the
Habakkuk verses cry woe on "him that *increaseth* that which is *not his*";
the verses from Ezekiel declare that upon receiving news of the fall of Jeru-
salem, he will be no longer dumb; Romans is a prophesy that Israel will be
converted *before the Day of Resurrection*; Zachariah speaks of the *bounty*
to come to God's people with the restoration of Israel (emphasis mine).
Thus there is no possible rational support (let alone ideational source) in
any of this barrage of citation for the key arguments in Winstanley's text:
civil property as a curse, the oppression of wage labor, the injustice of a
money economy, the symbiotic relation of landlordism and magistracy, the
law of Reason, the Norman Yoke, the spirit of Universal Liberty, the earth
as a Common Treasury. Aside from a vague allegorical comfort that might
be derived, there was simply nothing in the verses cited to help solve the
problems Winstanley and his Diggers faced as they launched their struggle
against squires and parson in Cobham.

From a hundred possible examples, let me choose a few more to establish
my point. Here from *The Law of Freedom* is the way Winstanley uses the
important text of First Samuel:

The use or work of a fighting Army in a Commonwealth

Is to beat down all that arise to endeavor to destroy the Liberties
of the Commonwealth: For as in the days of Monarchy, an Army
was used to subdue all who rebelled against Kingly Propriety; so in
the days of a free Commonwealth, an Army is to be made use of
to resist and destroy all who endeavor to keep up or bring in Kingly
Bondage again.

The work of this fighting Army is twofold.

The first is to withstand the Invasion, or coming in of a forraign
Enemy, whose Invasion is for no other end, but to take away our
Land and Earth from us, to deny us the free use thereof, to become
Kings and Landlords over us, and to make us their slaves.

As *William* the Conqueror, when he had conquered *England*, he
gave not only the Land in parcels to his Souldiers, but he gave all
men, their wives and children, within such a Lordship, to his Lords
of Manors, to do with them as they pleased: And for this cause
now doth an Army arise to keep out an Invasion of a Forraigner,
that by the defence of our Army, who is part of our selves, the rest
of our brethren in the Commonwealth may plow, sow, and reap,
and enjoy the fruits of their labours, and so live in peace in their own
Land.

Or secondly, If a Land be conquered, and so enslaved as *England*
was, under the Kings and conquering Laws, then an Army is to be
raised with as much secrecy as may be, to restore the Land again,
and set it free, that the Earth may become a Common Treasury to
all her children, without respecting persons, as it was before Kingly
Bondage came in, as you may read, I *Sam.* 8.

This latter is called Civil Wars, and this is the Wars of the
Commoners of *England* against King *Charls* now cast out, for he
and his Laws were the successive Power of that *Norman* Conquest
over *England*.

And now the Commoners of *England* in this age of the World are
rise up in an Army, and have cast out that Invasion of the Duke of
Normandy, and have won their Land and Liberties again by the
Sword, if they do not suffer their Councels to befool them into
slavery again upon a new accompt. . . . Therefore you Army of
Englands Commonwealth look to it; the Enemy could not beat you
in the field, but they may be too hard for you by policy in Councel,
if you do not stick close to see Common Freedom established.

For it so be that Kingly Authority be set up in your Laws again,
King *Charls* hath conquered you and your posterity by policy, and
won the field of you, though you seemingly have cut off His Head.

For the strength of a King lies not in the visible appearance of his
body, but in his Will, Laws and Authority, which is called
Monarchial Government.

But if you remove Kingly Government, and set up true and free

Commonwealths Government, then you gain your Crown, and
keep it, and leave peace to your posterity, otherwise not.
     And thus doing makes a War either lawful or unlawful.[57]

Not only is there no picture in Samuel of a Common Treasury before Kingly
Bondage, but Winstanley uses the text as proof of God's condemnation of
monarchy *per se*! Interestingly enough, First Samuel had been the major text
used to sanction monarchy since the 10th Century. It concludes "and the
Lord said to Samuel, Hearken unto their voice [i.e., the people of Israel]
and make them a king." Hardly an endorsement of republicanism, this demand from the people of God—sealed by the command of Yahweh himself
—to deliver Israel from the corrupt judges of Samuel's loins! Why, then,
so ridiculous a citation to support all alone so important an argument? I
think the answer is simply that Winstanley never lost a kind of reflex urge
to believe there must be scriptural support for that truth which he increasingly arrived at by reasoning from the logic and evidence of his experience
interpreted by his considerable fund of knowledge. If no verses could be
found which fit a specific argument, he cites anything on the subject and
relies on ambiguity and intellectual lethargy to carry it off.

     But an uneasy sense that his truth was often not really even *supported*
by the Bible became strikingly apparent in *The Law of Freedom*: although
dedicated to Cromwell, and quite self-consciously his major statement, Winstanley chose to all but eliminate even the mechanics of biblical reference.
The formal scriptural structure of authority for his arguments was suddenly
abandoned for a kind of common-sense reasoning based on egalitarian moral
imperatives combined with a few historical myths. The imperatives were derived from his unique conscience; the myths he believed to be sound history;
the arguments rested upon his radical assumption of the intellectual competence of Everyman.

     The biblical etiology of Winstanley's thought aside, there remains the basic
Weberian incubus to foul the understanding of the special historical character of his post-Digger writing. The general learned opinion is that Winstanley's social analysis was a logical extension of his religious views, that *The
Law of Freedom* was the intellectual successor to *The New Law of Righteousness*. The orthodox view is one which puts Winstanley's thought in the
same mold as that of Thomas Müntzer. Just recently Professor M. A. Barg
of the Soviet Union has restated this orthodoxy; however I tend to agree
with the conclusion of Gordon Rupp that it is quite wrong "to try to read a
sociological ideology" into Müntzer's professions.[58] And I certainly think
one important test of Winstanley's innovative genius is precisely his intellectual distance from the medieval and 16th Century religious radicals. But
Norman Cohn sees Winstanley as just another pamphleteer of "a primitivist

Millennium";[59] to Rufus Jones he is one of the miscellany of sectarians of the civil wars;[60] and William Lamont is persuaded by Hudson that Winstanley owed more to "*Revolution* than to Karl Marx" [sic]![61]

The major editors of Leveller literature stress the continuity of religious radicalism, the whole cloth from which all manner of Leveller is cut. In the view of Professor Woodhouse, Winstanley belongs to a "Puritan party" and his utopianism, along with others, "takes its rise in the Puritan mind and temper. . . ."[62] Professor Don Wolfe believes Winstanley's utopia "represented the rebellious response of idealists to the dogmatic, mothering Calvinism" of their youth (though he does see rationalism dissipating his "theological emphasis").[63] William Haller, on the other hand, while characterizing the Leveller *leaders* as religious, considered the *movement* to be secular![64] This prevailing line of argument seems to me analogous to maintaining that La Flèche and Father Dinet are the essential factors in producing Descartes' *Discours*!

There is another far more important background to Winstanley's intellectual transformation than "mothering Calvinism," but we at present know not nearly enough about it. I refer to the revolutionary subculture of rationality. Christopher Hill has done a brilliant reconnaissance of the progressive development in 17th Century English culture of "reason and reasonableness," from which survey he concludes that Winstanley was a pioneer of enlightenment.[65] Recently Hill has further shown that Winstanley also developed "the most consistent and rational version of the radical and internationalist Antichrist myth."[66] Still more recently, one of Brian Manning's students has explored the interesting identification of nature and grace in Leveller theory: the equating of justice with both Christian and natural law.[67] The truth that is emerging is that for advanced thinkers of the Century of Genius—Winstanley prominent among them—God became a deity, a principle of Reason, the prototype of 18th Century Deism.

I cannot hope satisfactorily to demonstrate in this essay the fascinating metamorphosis of Winstanley's mind from the chrysalis of mysticism to the organically mutated, winged splendor of rational socialism, but I can indicate the major elements in that transformation by reference to the rational qualities of his last and greatest work.

The Law of Freedom was separated in time from *The New Law of Righteousness* by only some two years, in life by the events of Digging and colonizing; but in intellectual substance by an unfathomable gulf. The Digging, organizing, struggling, recruiting, losing, forced Winstanley to test his eschatological fantasies in the real world of conflict and contradiction. He found Parson Platt, Sir Francis, and General Fairfax to be no abstract, eternal principles of Antichrist, and the struggle for life and a small equity to reveal no immanence of the Godhead. Somehow, mysteriously, in irrecoverable moments of lucidity and intellectual daring, this very special English mystic, living with his eyes and pores open through a very special time, began to see everything differently, experienced a unique kind of conversion. The author of *The Saints Paradice* suddenly was thinking in terms of landlords who were also members of Parliament, of ministers who were hirelings of landlords who were members of Parliament, of tithes, rents, wages, copyhold indentures, and of laws that served only privilege and power.

In those embattled months in Surrey and other places around London, Winstanley foreswore eschatology and apocalyptic frenzy for social action through political agitation, confrontation, organization, propaganda, and recruiting drives. He wanted desperately and planned intelligently to *change* the world radically; but he soon learned that was impossible unless he could come to and share a more reliable *understanding* of that world. Winstanley was through with the symbols of fantasy victories crowning chimerical battles defined by the spirit world; his powerful, untrained intellect turned to social facts for data, and to rational analysis as method. Some indication of the results follows.

Winstanley opened *The Law of Freedom* with a marvelously muscular dedication to Cromwell:

And now I have set the candle at your door, for you have power in your hand, in this other added opportunity, to Act for Common Freedome if you will; I have no power.

It may be here are some things inserted which you may not like, yet other things you may like, therefore I pray you read it, and be as the industrious Bee, suck out the honey and cast away the weeds.

Though this Platform be like a peece of Timber rough hewd, yet the discreet workmen may take it, and frame a handsome building out of it.

It is like a poor man that comes cloathed to your door in a torn country garment, who is unacquainted with the learned Citizens unsettled forms and fashions; take of the clownish language, for under that you may see beauty.

It may be you will say, If Tythes be taken from the Priests and Impropriators, and Copy-hold Services from Lords of Mannors, how shal they be provided for again; for it is not unrighteous to take their estates from them?

I Answer, when Tythes were first enacted, and Lordly power drawn over the backs of the oppressed, the Kings and Conquerors made no scruple of Conscience to take it, though the people lived in sore bondage of poverty for want of it; and can there be scruple of conscience to make restitution of this which hath been so long stoln goods? It is no scruple arising from the Righteous Law, but from covetousness, who goes away sorrowfull to heare he must part with all to follow Righteousness and Peace.

But though you do take away Tythes, and the Power of Lords of
Mannors, yet there will be no want to them, for they have the
freedome of the Common stock, they may send to the Storehouses
for what they want, and live more free then now they do, for now
they are in care and vexation by servants, by casualties, by being
cheated in buying and selling, and many other incumbrances, but
then they will be free from all, for the common Storehouses is
every mans riches, not any ones.

Is not buying and selling a righteous Law? No, It is the Law of the
Conqueror, but not the righteous Law of Creation: how can that
be righteous which is a cheat? for is not this a common practise,
when he hath a bad Horse or Cow, or any bad commodity, he will
send it to the Market, to cheat some simple plain-hearted man or
other, and when he comes home, will laugh at his neighbours hurt,
and much more &c.

When Mankinde began to buy and sell, then did he fall from his
Innocency; for then they began to oppress and cozen one another
of their Creation Birth-right: As for example; If the Land belong to
three persons, and two of them buy and sell the Earth, and the
third give no consent, his Right is taken from him, and his posterity is
engaged in a War.

When the Earth was first bought and sold, many gave no consent:
As when our Crown Lands, and Bishops Lands were sold, some
foolish Soldiers yeelded, and covetous Officers were active in it, to
advance themselves above their Brethren: but many who payd
Taxes and Freequarter for the purchase of it, gave no consent, but
declared against it, as an unrighteous thing, depriving posterity of
their Birth-rights and Freedoms.

Therefore this buying and selling did bring in, and still doth bring
in, discontents and wars, which have plagued Mankinde sufficiently
for so doing. And the Nations of the world will never learn to beat
their swords into plowshares, and their spears into pruning hooks,
and leave of warring, until this cheating device of buying and selling
be cast out among the rubbish of Kingly power. . . .[68]

Throughout the ensuing treatise Winstanley developed a penetrating,
original and very rational theory of political economy. I am inclined to agree
with Professor Max Patrick that no direct evidence is needed to affirm that
Winstanley was powerfully influenced by More's *Utopia*; also that he is likely to have read Bacon's *New Atlantis*.[69] But whatever its sources, he drew
from his critical theory a plan of rational social organization, of which the
following is a sample:

Some hearing of this Common Freedom, think there must be a
Community of all the fruits of the Earth whether they work or no,
therefore strive to live idle upon other mens labours.

Others, through the same unreasonable beastly ignorance, think there must be a Community of all men and women for Copulation, and so strive to live a bestial life.

Others think there will be no Law, but that every thing will run into confusion for want of Government; but this Platform proves the contrary.

Therefore because that transgression doth and may arise from ignorant and rude fancy in man, is the Law added.

That which true Righteousness in my Judgment calls Community, is this, To have the Earth set free from all Kingly Bondage of Lords of Manors, and oppressing Landlords, which came in by Conquest; as a Thief takes a true mans purse upon the high-way, being stronger than he.

An that neither the Earth, nor any fruits thereof, should be bought or sold by the Inhabitants one among another, which is a slavery the Kingly Conquerors have brought in, therefore he set his stamp upon silver, that every one should buy and sell in his name.

And though this be, yet shall not men live idle; for the Earth shall be planted and reaped, and the fruits carried into Barns and Storehouses by the assistance of every family, according as is shewed hereafter in order.

Every man shall be brought up in Trades and labours, and all Trades shall be maintained with more improvement, to the inriching of the Commonwealth, more than now they be under Kingly Power.

Every Tradesman shall fetch Materials, as Leather, Wool, Flax, Corn, and the like, from the publike Store-houses to work upon without buying and selling; and when particular works are made, as Cloth, Shooes, Hats, and the like, the Tradesmen shall bring these particular works to particular shops, as it is now in practise, without buying and selling. And every family as they want such things as they cannot make, they shall go to these shops, and fetch without money, even as now they fetch with money, as hereafter is shewed how in order.

If any say, This will nurse Idleness; I answer, This Platform proves the contrary, for idle persons and beggers will be made to work.

If any say, This will make some men to take goods from others by violence, and call it theirs, because the Earth and fruits are a Common Stock; I answer, The Laws or Rules following prevents that ignorance: For though the Store-houses and publike Shops be commonly furnished by every families assistance, and for every families use, as is shewed hereafter how: yet every mans house is proper to himself, and all the furniture therein, and provision which he hath fetched from the Store-houses is proper to himself; every mans wife and every womans husband proper to themselves, and so are their children at their dispose till they come to age.

And if any other man endeavor to take away his house, furniture,

food, wife, or children, saying, every thing is common, and so
abusing the Law of Peace, such a one is a Transgressor, and shall
suffer punishment, as by the Government and Laws following is
expressed.

For though the publike Store-houses be a common Treasury, yet
every mans particular dwelling is not common, but by his consent,
and the Commonwealths Laws are to preserve a mans peace in his
person, and in his person, and in his private dwelling, against the
rudeness and ignorance that may arise in Mankind.

If· any man do force or abuse women in folly, pleading
Community, the Laws following do punish such ignorant and
unrational practise; for the Laws of a Commonwealth are Laws of
moderate diligence, and purity of Manners.

Therefore I desire a patient reading of what hereafter follows;
and when you have heard the extent of Commonwealths Government
or Freedom, then weigh it in the ballance with Kingly Government
or Bondage, and see whether brings most Peace to the Land, and
establish that for Government. . . .[70]

The richness of secularist and radically rational social commentary cannot be very adequately conveyed within the compass of any possible essay,
so I invite skeptics to a rereading of, for instance, Winstanley's "political
science," which displays qualities of shrewdness and imagination worthy of
Aristotle or Harrington, and depicts a commonwealth that would have been
no more a theocracy for Fifth Monarchist Saints than it was a polity for the
rich.[71]

Finally, one should emphasize the consistency of Winstanley's anticlericalism, a deeply alienated rejection of the new-style ranters as much as the
old-style priests.[72] Here is an excerpt from one argument:

This devining Doctrine, which you call spiritual and heavenly
things, is the thief and the robber; he comes to spoile the Vinyard
of a mans peace, and does not enter in at the door, but he climbes up
another way: And this Doctrine is two fold.

First he takes upon him to tell you the meaning of other mens
words, and writing by his studying or imagining what another mans
knowledge might be, and by thus doing darkens knowledge, and
wrongs the spirit of the Authors who did write and speak those
things which he takes upon him to interpret.

Secondly he takes upon him, to foretell what shall befall a man
after he is dead, and what that world is beyond the Sun, and beyond
the Moon, &c. And if any man tell him there is no reason for what
you say, he answers you must not judge of heavenly and spiritual
things by reason, but you must believe what is told you, whether it
be reason or no. . . .[73]

Winstanley on law, on education, on war, on the family, was similarly involved in challenging his society by precept and example. His "inner light" had been utterly transformed by the events on St. George's Hill from the whispering imperatives of an immanent God to the equally imperative but far more complex demands of common sense and a revolutionary socialist ethic. The importance and honor of that moment demand recognition.

NOTES

1. Paul Hardacre, "Gerrard Winstanley in 1650," *Huntington Library Quarterly*, 22 (1959), 345-350.
2. *Past and Present*, No. 40 (1958), 3-15.
3. *The Digger Movement in the Days of the Commonwealth* (London, 1961), 78, 255.
4. George H. Sabine (ed.), *The Works of Gerrard Winstanley* (Ithaca, 1941), 443.
5. Keith Thomas, "The Date of Gerrard Winstanley's *Fire in the Bush*," *Past and Present*, No. 42 (1969), 160-162.
6. On this *see* chapter X of the unpublished doctoral dissertation of my former student, George Juretic, *The Mind of Gerrard Winstanley: From Millenarian to Socialist* (DeKalb, Northern Illinois University, 1972).
7. Aylmer, *op. cit.*, 7.
8. For example, Winthrop Hudson, "Economic and Social Thought of Gerrard Winstanley: Was He a Seventeenth-Century Marxist?", *The Journal of Modern History*, 18 (1946), 1-21; Wilhem Schenk, *The Concern for Social Justice in the Puritan Revolution* (London, 1948); M. A. Barg, *Narodye nizy v Angliiskoi revoliutsii XVII v. Dvizhenie i ideologiia istinnykh levellerov* (Moscow, 1967): roughly, *The Lower Classes in the 17th Century English Revolution: the Movement and Ideology of the True Levellers*; David Petegorsky, *Left-wing Democracy in the English Civil War* (London, 1940), knew Winstanley became a convert to "progressive rationalism," but he is murky on the religious etiology of the change.
9. Bernstein, *Sozialismus und Demokratie in der grossen englischen Revolution* (Stuttgart, 1895), trans, H. J. Stenning as *Cromwell and Communism*, (New York, 1963), 132; G. P. Gooch, *English Democratic Ideas in the Seventeenth Century* (Cambridge, 1927), 190; recently Richard Vann has adduced some very shaky evidence to reopen the possibility that Winstanley became a Quaker. "The Later Life of Gerrard Winstanley," *Journal of the History of Ideas*, 26 (1965) 133-136.
10. Hardacre, *op. cit.*, 346.
11. Sabine, *op. cit.*, 439-441, 641-651; Margaret James, *Social Problems and Policy During the Puritan Revolution* (London, 1966), 101; Petegorsky, *op. cit.*, 163; 173-174.
12. Sabine, *op. cit.*, 440-441.
13. Thomas, "Another Digger Broadside," *Past and Present*, No. 42 (1969), 57-68.

14. See Professor S. I. Arkhangelsgiy's chapters in the most beautifully produced of all histories of the English Revolution, *Angliyskaya Burzhaznaya Revolyutziya XVII Veka* (Moscow, 1954), I, 200-407; and Barg, *op. cit.*, chapters IV and VII. What I know of Soviet historical opinion I owe to Christopher Hill's reviews and the kindness of my friend and student, Robert-Georges Paradis, who offered translations.

15. *See* J. Max Patrick, "William Covell and the Troubles at Enfield in 1559: a Sequel of the Digger Movement," *The University of Toronto Quarterly*, 14 (1944), 45-57.

16. *Ibid.*, 49-57.

17. *Ibid.*, 55-56.

18. *Ibid.*

19. Petegorsky, *op. cit.*, 232; *see* also the April, 1649 *Manifestation* of the chief Levellers printed in *Leveller Manifestoes*, edited by Don Wolfe (London, 1944), 388-396; and Lilburne's *Legall Fundamentall Liberties*, in *The Leveller Tracts, 1647-1653*, edited by William Haller (New York, 1944), 449.

20. *See An Appeale From the degenerate Representative Body of Commons* (London, 1647) in Wolfe, *op. cit.*, 157-195.

21. *Ibid.*, 105.

22. Plockhoy, *A Way Propounded to Make the Poor in these and other Nations happy* (London, 1659); see Christopher Hill, *The World Turned Upside Down* (London, 1972), 279; Bernstein, *op. cit.*, 213ff.; Barg, *op. cit.*, 368ff.

23. *See* Margaret James, "Contemporary Materialist Interpretations of Society in the English Revolution," in *The English Revolution: 1640*, edited by Christopher Hill (London, 1940), 100; Bernstein, *op. cit.*, 132; 259ff.

24. Berens, *op. cit.*, 233; James, *loc. cit.*

25. *See* the excellent historiographical essay on all the Levellers by Olivier Lutaud in the *Revue Historique*, 227 (1962), 77-114; 377-414; Professor Lutaud is currently engaged in writing a study of Winstanley which I look forward to reading.

26. Edward, Earl of Clarendon, *The History of the Rebellion*, ed. W. D. Macray (Oxford, 1888) vol. 4, 276.

27. The best appreciation of Clarendon as historian is the essay by Christopher Hill, "Lord Clarendon and the Puritan Revolution," in *Puritanism and Revolution* (London, 1958), 199-214.

28. *Commentaries on the Laws of England* (Oxford, 1766), I, 213.

29. Lutaud, *op, cit.*, 97.

30. *The History of England* (London, 1825), vol. 7, 151.

31. *Biographia Britannica* (London, 1747-66), vol. 5, 2937-2961.

32. *History of England from the accession of James I to the elevation of the House of Hanover* (London, 1768), vol. 4, 355.

33. *See* H. N. Brailsford, *The Levellers and the English Revolution*, ed. Christopher Hill (Stanford, Cal.; 1961), 685-692.

34. *See* Caroline Robbins, *The Eighteenth-Century Commonwealthmen* (New York, 1968).

35. The basic work, revised many times in later editions, is *Historie de la Révolution d'Angleterre depuis Charles 1er a Charles II*, 2t. (Paris, 1826-27). *See A Popular History of England*, trans, M. M. Ripley (Boston, 1876), vol. 2, 125-126.

36. *Oliver Cromwell's Letters and Speeches* (London, 1888), vol. 2, 27-29.

37. *Ibid.*, 28.
38. Leopold von Ranke, *A History of England Principally in the Seventeenth Century* (Oxford, 1875), vol. 3, 19-21.
39. *History of the Commonwealth and Protectorate, 1649-1656* (London, 1903), I, 42.
40. *Ibid.*, 43-44.
41. *Ibid.*, II, 79.
42. "Die moralisierende Kritik und die kritisierende Moral: Beitrag zur Deutschen Kulturgeschichte gegen Karl Heinzen von Karl Marx," *MEW* (Berlin, 1964), vol. 4, 341: trans, H. J. Stenning in *Selected Essays* (London, 1926), 140-141.
43. "The English Civil War Interpreted by Marx and Engels," *Science and Society*, 12 (1948), 145.
44. *Herr Eugen Dühring's Revolution in Science*, trans. Emile Burns (New York, 1939), 24.
45. *Cromwell and Communism*, 86.
46. *Ibid.*, 114-115.
47. *Ibid.*, 131.
48. For Hill on Winstanley, *see The World Turned Upside Down* (London, 1972), *passim*; his introduction to his edition of *Winstanley: the Law of Freedom and Other Writings* (London, 1973); Brailsford, *op. cit.*; C. B. Macpherson, *The Political Theory of Possessive Individualism* (Oxford, 1962) doesn't deal with Winstanley, but it clears up some basic problems related to levellerism; Perez Zagorin, *A History of Political Thought in the English Revolution* (London, 1954), 43-57, has some interesting things to say; George Juretic, *op. cit.*, and in a forthcoming article in the *Journal of the History of Ideas*, "Digger No Millenarian: the Revolutionizing of Gerrard Winstanley," is well worth reading.

   I should probably add that there is one major fund of scholarship on the English Revolution and its radicals which I know something about from bibliographies which a generous colleague supplies: the Japanese are doing a great deal of work in their own language which I can neither read nor afford to get translated!
49. *See* my "Puritanism as History and Historiography," *Past and Present*, No. 41 (1968), 77-104.
50. Hudson, *op. cit.*, 2-3.
51. *Ibid.*, 2.
52. *Ibid.*, 11.
53. *Ibid.*, 21.
54. Schenk, *op. cit.*, 110-111.
55. Sabine, 258-260.
56. For Winstanley's critical attitude toward the Bible, *see* Hill, *The World Turned Upside Down*, 114ff.; Paul Elmen's "The Theological Basis of Digger Communism," *Church History*, 23 (1954), unfortunately has nothing to do with theology!
57. Sabine, 573-574.
58. *Patterns of Reformation* (Philadelphia, 1969), 298ff.; *cf.* Barg, *op. cit.*, 172ff.; Von Thomas Nipperdey, "Theologie und Revolution bei Thomas Müntzer," *Archiv für Reformationsgeschichte*, 54 (1963); Hans-Jürgen Goertz, *Innere und Äussere Ordnung in der Theologie Thomas Müntzers* (Leiden, 1967).

59. *The Pursuit of the Millennium* (New York, 1961), 322.
60. *Studies in Mystical Religion* (London, 1908).
61. *Godly Rule: Politics and Religion, 1603-60* (London, 1969), 8.
62. A. S. P. Woodhouse, (ed.) *Puritanism and Liberty* (Chicago, 1951), 48; see also Max Patrick, "The Literature of the Diggers," *The University of Toronto Quarterly*, 12 (1942), 95-110.
63. *Milton in the Puritan Revolution* (New York, 1941), 39.
64. *Ibid.*, 7.
65. " 'Reason' and 'Reasonableness' in seventeenth-century England," *The British Journal of Sociology*, 20 (1969), 244-245; *cf.* Olivier Lutaud, "Entre Rationalisme et Millénarisme au cours de la Révolution d'Angleterre" in *Hérésies et Sociétés* (Paris, 1968), 343-366.
66. *Antichrist in Seventeenth-Century England* (London, 1971) 116-117.
67. J. C. Davis, "The Levellers and Christianity" in *Politics, Religion and the English Civil War*, (ed.) Brian Manning.
68. Sabine, 510-511.
69. Patrick, *op. cit.*, 110.
70. Sabine, 526-527.
71. *See*, for example, Sabine, 540-544.
72. *See* Sabine, 401, 539.
73. Sabine, 567.

"Hope Without Illusion":
A. J. P. Taylor's Dissent, 1955-1961

C. ROBERT COLE
Utah State University

TO BE A DISSENTER once required only refusal to accept the lawful communion of the established church. Baptists, Congregationalists, Quakers, even Catholics—though the term Recusant was reserved specifically for them—were by their nature practitioners of dissent. But this narrow application hardly describes the secular experience of more recent times. A legion of issues with little if any religious connection has raised argument and repudiation that is characteristic of the Nonconformist values behind the religious dissent of earlier centuries. This has been true of social reform, economic organization, taxation, foreign relations and a hundred other issues. The common feature is twofold: first, as its basic premise, dissent disputes established policy on moral grounds; and second, its efficacy stems from the victories won for the freedom of conscience by religious Nonconformists. Regardless of political, social, intellectual, or other preferences, dissenters have been motivated first and last by the conviction that they were Right, and that conforming to any policy regarded as Wrong was to acquiesce in the forfeiture of their inherent right as Englishmen. Upon this foundation rested the edifice of dissent as it translated from religious to secular application in the twentieth century—a carry-over perhaps of the certainty felt by many early sectarians that they were God's Elect. The burden of this essay is to examine the example of the historian and polemicist A. J. P. Taylor, a contemporary dissenter, in whose writings from 1955 through 1961 may be observed in full array some of the clearest expressions of that moralistic, individualistic, and humanitarian system of values that may be termed the Dissenting Tradition.

226

I

Secular dissenters have above all desired to avoid commitment to any orthodoxy, and to repudiate the policies put forth by those whose views represent orthodoxy. The reasoning is simple: liberty, the essence of Nonconformity, means freedom. In the "mass-age," ideological orthodoxy and the techniques of policy making have flowed more and more frequently from the "scientific" analysis of society identified with behaviorism—that is from the assumption that men's actions are determined for them by external factors, economic, political, intellectual, psychological, or technological. From the beginning, Taylor's *cause célèbre* as a dissenter was repudiation of the influence of this view. He sought always liberation of the people, by revolution at first, which as a young Marxist he regarded as necessary. An unspoken concept of *vox populi* ran through his writings, as his controversies, whatever the specific subject, defended popular liberty and rights, the capacity of the people to achieve complete self-fulfillment in government and society, and recognition of the people as individuals. Doctrinaire views on politics, social change, and foreign policy, manifested in established political parties and ideologies, were anathema to him. Intellectuals seemed to be the carriers of the antidemocratic spirit in the present century, just as aristocrats had been in early times. Both had seen the freedom of the masses as a threat to order and stability. Taylor vigorously opposed the paternalistic yet coercive Establishment as the illiberal framework within which intellectuals, elitists, and their servants, the party men, worked against the fundamental interests of the people. As an Oxford undergraduate he had belonged to the Communist Party and supported the General Strike of 1926 in expectation that it was the beginning of the English working-class revolution. This lasted until, beginning with the General Strike and ending with Trotsky's expulsion from the Soviet Union, he observed the Marxist's lack of humanitarian as opposed to doctrinal interest in the liberation of the people. He became convinced that ideological purity served mainly the interest of the ideologue, just as he saw policy making as a service primarily to policy makers. Thus disillusioned by finding that more often than not great men—and what youth does not yearn for heroes?—have feet of clay, he based his socialism on a libertarian radical doctrine with dissent as its methodology.

In the 1930s Taylor came to practice dissent mainly in the area of foreign relations. His fascination with foreign policy, foreign policy making, and statesmen has several explanations: his social background and his place in academic society worked against any immediate sensitivity to the social deprivation of the working class; an academic grounding in diplomatic history made international politics a natural area of concern; and the failure of the intellectuals to whom he was akin to establish a reasonable and libertarian approach to domestic policy in the 1920s and 1930s left a vacuum which he and others tended to fill by opposing fascism. Fascism was a problem of international significance, an enemy clearly defined, and a target for dissent which required no particular party or doctrinal affiliations—only devotion to liberty and human dignity. Such is the sense, derived from the collected fragments of explanation Taylor has provided, behind his preoccupation as a radical and dissenter with international relations. It has been borne out by what he said at length in academic as well as polemical writings, especially in the later 1950s, on the foreign policy of the European powers and their representatives.

Taylor believed always that the great value of foreign policy dissent was its ability in the long run to produce change. If you want to know the future foreign policy of Great Britain, he wrote in *The Troublemakers: Dissent Over Foreign Policy, 1792-1939*, (1957) pay attention to what foreign policy dissenters are saying now. *Troublemakers* was the published version of his 1956 Ford Lectures at Oxford, in which he defined dissent as repudiation of the *status quo* on moral and patriotic grounds. The thesis was that the only constant thing in British foreign policy was the controversy it generated. The motivation was: "These lectures are a gesture of repentance for having written recently a substantial volume of what I may venture to call 'respectable' diplomatic history."[1] A curious justification for a series of lectures that Professor Richard Pares called "the highest honour, in my opinion, which an English historian can receive." By respectable diplomatic history Taylor meant his major work *The Struggle for Mastery in Europe, 1848-1918* (1954) an effort which, though not universally acclaimed, was nonetheless widely recognized as a major contribution to diplomatic historiography, and may be presumed to have been at least a factor in his nomination to the Ford Lectureship. Indeed *Struggle for Mastery* was his last "respectable" book, in the academic sense, until he published *English History, 1914-1945* in 1965.

In *Troublemakers*, Taylor examined the personalities and philosophies behind foreign policy opposition from Charles James Fox to the anti-appeasers of the 1930s, and clarified his emotional and intellectual kinship with agitation in international relations. He used the term "dissent" because none other depicted so well the complete mood of repudiation and moral certitude that attended those who decried government policy. He wrote:

A conforming member of the church of England can disagree with
the Bishop and, I understand, often does. A Dissenter believes that
Bishops should not exist. And so it is with foreign policy, in this
country. . . . The Dissenter repudiates its aims, its methods, its
principles. What is more, he claims to know better and to promote
higher concerns; he asserts a superiority, moral and intellectual.[2]

Foreign policy dissenters crossed party, religious, ideological, and social lines: Fox was a Whig scoundrel and profligate; William Cobbett was a Tory populist and rustic; John Bright was a Quaker and Free Trade Radical; David Urquehart was a Tory Radical and pro-Turk; William Gladstone opposed the Turks and was a Victorian Liberal and Highchurchman; J. T. Walton Newbold was a Quaker and the first communist elected to parliament; E. D. Morel was an intellectual socialist and impractical visionary; and Keir Hardie was the "man in the cloth cap," a miner, parliament member, and socialist Labour leader. (This has continued: opposition to Britain's entry into the Common Market has included left-wing socialists, radical trades unionists, and reactionary back-benchers.) Creeds, political or otherwise, were not so important here as were the characteristics common to both the English Nonconformist heritage and dissent over foreign policy: contempt for authority, dedication to the cause of Right, loyalty to England, concern with principles above party or doctrine, and a radical temperament. Taylor shared these characteristics. As he put it: ". . . this book deals with the Englishmen whom I most revere. I hope that, had I been their contemporary, I should have shared their outlook. I should not have been ashamed to make their mistakes."[3]

Foreign relations remained Taylor's chief concern throughout his career as a dissenter, but his criticism of them stemmed from his sensitivity to domestic political and social relationships—a sensitivity which began with his libertarian view that most institutions and forms of authority treat the liberty of the people as a threat to their own position. There were many factors of a social, intellectual, economic, political, or other nature affecting the development of foreign policy perspectives which he thought required treatment as issues in themselves. It is possible to extrapolate them from his "London Diary," a series of notes written on commission for *The New Statesman and Nation* beginning in 1955. In attacking the House of Lords, commercialized Christmas, British Railways, National Service (since abolished), public schools, the lowering of university standards, the motivations behind various forms of dictatorship, and Labour Party leadership he was commenting on the class system, the loss of principle in politics, the lack of concern for human values, the cheapening of human resources, and the regimenting of human life. Foreshadowing the style of his more extensive editorializing in *The Sunday Express*, "Diary" showed Taylor's repudiation of conformity, uniformity, orthodoxy, and authority, and his commitment to freedom from all forms of oppression and to improvement in the human condition. That this should come through total democratization of economic and social resources revealed that his socialism, repeatedly a projected avenue for eliminating these problems, was principally an expression of egalitarian radicalism. Here as elsewhere he rejected profound social analysis, dealing rather with society as an organization for living, the nature of which is taken for granted. Only in foreign policy was he more thorough in delineating structural systems and cause and effect relationships. His technique as expressed in "Diary" reflected that which he described in *Troublemakers*: simplistic solutions to complex problems, and only the most nebulous alternative programs to offer against existing ones. The point was simply to "bring down the mighty"; all that was needed was to equalize wealth, eliminate privilege, maintain leadership on a high moral plain, defend liberty, encourage toleration at all levels, and trust in the wisdom of the people. "Diary" epitomized this approach, and provided examples of the cryptic and epigrammatic style that distinguished Taylor throughout his career. For example, when Krushchev beat the anti-imperialist drum in condemning western policy, Taylor liked his style, but questioned its ideological pretensions: "Fine, old-fashioned radicalism, but not, I think, anything to do with Marxism." Krushchev would be better for sharing Taylor's own dissenting version of anti-imperialism: "I am against colonies because I think colonies morally wrong and imperialism wicked."[4] On the continuing debate over appeasement, he wrote: "The hard truth about the situation before 1939 is that whatever we did was wrong. There was no right course. The choice was not between the wise and the unwise, but between the honourable and dishonourable. The men in power chose the second."[5] Of the conflict between commercial and public communications he wrote: "From now on whatever the BBC tries to do, commercial radio can do better. . . . I am beginning to think that I shall see the end of the BBC before I die. This will be the biggest knock at The Thing since the abdication."[6] The basis of these remarks was Taylor's repertory of common-sense maxims, illustrated perfectly by two examples from his discussion of personal political, social, and intellectual philosophy: "I believe in pure socialism. Take the money from the rich and give it to the poor." And: "I am no better than anyone else, and no one else is better than me."[7]

II

Taylor was a lifelong dissenter, partly by conviction and partly by family tradition. Even in primary school in an educational game called "Cavaliers and Roundheads" he had taken always the side of parliament, assuming that all wrongs were accountable to "landlords and gentlemen." "Diary" revealed his determination and dedication to remain vigorous in opposition to the Establishment. In 1955, he was forty-nine. Hugh Gaitskell had become leader of the Labour Party, and was thought of now as "the old man." Taylor found this depressing, because "Gaitskell is younger than me by a few weeks. Until now I have been 'one of our promising historians,' casually sowing wild oats and accepting the assurances of others that years of discretion lay ahead of me. Overnight I have become an elder statesman."[8] It might now appear, he went on, that he should confine himself to elderly interest in the doings of younger men. But Taylor's wit and energy were undimmed. Rather: "A radical spirit, I fear, does not diminish with age. Start off with the desire to pull down the mighty from their seats and it is with you to the end of the chapter. It is all very disappointing. I shall never be knighted; nor even sink into the easy somnolence of a university chair."[9]

"Pulling down the mighty" was the view that stressed Nonconformity, and was Taylor's legacy from the chapel tradition of his family whose roots were deep in radical, industrial Manchester. Radicalism was a frame of mind as much as a doctrine, and could encompass diverse creeds. Taylor recalled: "My parents were ordinary radicals before the first world war and became socialists under the impact of war."[10] Their socialism varied widely on matters of dogma and organization: yet both remained radical in approach. Constance, A.J.P.'s mother, was an orthodox socialist. Percy, his father, opposed dogma, remaining devoted to the libertarian views of the radical tradition. But together they shared liberal friends from the Manchester commercial world when they lived in Birkdale, where A.J.P. was born in 1906, and Labour friends after moving to Preston during the war. Percy, a Manchester cotton merchant, retired after selling out profitably at the top of the 1920 cotton boom, and spent the remainder of his life involved in local working-class politics as an unorthodox member of the Labour Party. Party politics did not interest him; nor did ideology, especially after exposure to the I.L.P. and Third International just at the end of the war. He remained unmoved by intellectual Marxism, and continued to regard the Communist Party as a nuisance. He represented Labour, however, on the Preston Town Council, as a member of the General and Municiple Workers' Union, and as chairman of the Preston Strike Committee in 1926. But as a leader of the Preston unemployed, party was of no concern. Through this latter experience he became, in spirit at least, a "true working man." There is every probability that the chapel association, Quaker on his mother's side, contributed to Percy's adherence to common-sense populism rather than party orthodoxy. Constance was the political intellectual in the Taylor family, who subscribed to Marxist theory from 1917 on, after she had become a hard-line supporter of Conscientious Objector absolutists. A.J.P. flirted with her outlook until the disillusionment of his university years brought him back to the perspectives of his father. By the 1950s Percy's radicalism and populist socialism were standard features of A.J.P.'s dissent.

The Taylors were Mancunians, and the world of commercial Manchester became to A.J.P. the symbol of the egalitarian, individualistic spirit with which he believed the people were endowed. Such was the burden of a ro-

epitomized the right to dissent; it had been the nineteenth-century arena for the expression in both religious and secular terms of a great tradition.

III

Taylor has been charged with being anti-intellectual. In a curious way this both is and is not warranted. To attack scientific analysis in arguing that men are capable of self-motivated thought is an affirmation of intellectuality; to claim that intellectuals are responsible for this analysis, which in their hands becomes an expression of intellectualism, is anti-intellectual. This confused pattern of interpretation was an important element in Taylor's attacks on system-making during the 1950s.

As a historian he had seen what he believed to be the fallacy of extrapolating absolute and theoretical systems from real situations, criticism of which had been a subtle but significant theme in *Troublemakers*. *Troublemakers* also coincided with his agitation against the Suez invasion of 1956 and against the nuclear arms race, both of which he regarded as major efforts by statesmen to operate on the basis of systematic foreign policy rationalization. Believing himself to be a rationalist, he resented what he regarded as a methodology based on the reasoning of the Age of Reason, but perverted in modern times into a form of irrationality. He argued that reducing everything to a system flies in the face of reason itself. For example, he wrote, it is unreasonable to imagine that endowed with independent minds men are incapable of using them independently, that decisions are always based on *a priori* assumptions concerning the behavior of men, societies, and nations. He blamed historians above others for helping, as intellectuals, to perpetuate the fallacy through their application of irresponsible behaviorism or intellectualized methodology to historical situations. The fault lay in "new" historiographical disciplines, chief of which then was historical psychoanalysis. Taylor claimed that, in fact, seeing the thinking of political leaders and statesmen as reactions to external stimuli was as misguided as seeing them in the control of "profound" historical forces—perhaps an expression of the same thing.

Taylor showed here a notable lack of understanding for the uses that reasonably can be made in historiography of behavioral disciplines. What he offered was typical of his humanistic mentality: men willfully accept a cause, a policy, or an ideology as their own and give it unexpected twists, he wrote, whether in politics, foreign policy or revolution. He went on to charge that theorizing systematic behavior on the part of men and institutions runs the risk of giving politicians the excuse they need to build systems of their own, ever more elaborate and absolute. As shown by the post-war foreign-policy planners in the Labour Party, by nuclear technologists, and by neo-Metternichian statesmen in general the result could be disastrous. Taylor warned that imagining the existence of constant, predictable, and exploitable patterns of behavior leads simply to ever more elaborate and sophisticated schemes for extinguishing choice. Of all men, he wrote, historians should resist this: they should stand aside from the system-makers, "deriving only malicious pleasure from the efforts of present-day politicians to enlist their great predecessors in contemporary disputes."[16] This was the theme which he developed in great detail when he approached the problem of European diplomacy in the cold war.

System-making had become particularly manifest in foreign policy theory since the Second World War as paranoia spread regarding communism and the Soviet Union. In Taylor's view, contemporary "cold warriors" such as Hans Morganthau of the University of Chicago, were instrumental in playing the systems "game." That game, as he understood it, was to resurrect the ghost of Metternich, the greatest system-maker of them all, as a guide to creating an anti-revolutionary international front, ideologically and diplomatically aligned against the Soviet Union. In 1951 Taylor had devastated Morganthau's *The National Interest* specifically on these grounds. Typically, he seemed pleased by Morganthau's subsequent animosity: "I once tore apart a book by Hans Morganthau, so naturally he does not love me."[17] The present conflict repeated the confrontation of Metternich's age, Taylor went on. In 1848 all the struggles of revolutionaries were directed against Metternich in defense of freedom. It was so again. Nowadays: "It is the fashion of historians to go wandering about the past regretting what has happened. I do not share this contemporary taste. . . . It is hard enough to find out about it without trying to alter it. Least of all can we put it back. So-called restorations simply create new systems and institutions with old names."[18] As Metternich had believed that Austria was a European necessity, the great powers now believed that, in the same way, so was its equivalent in NATO or some other supra-national organism directed against the communist world. "And they agreed upon it because the Austrian Empire, the empire of Metternich, had ceased to exist." Reveling in this irony, Taylor added cryptically: "Yes, he is dead all right."[19]

Military realities in the nuclear age were the key to the dangers of foreign policy system-making. Taylor argued that systems require rational control of military as well as political factors. But the truth is that wars happen when conditions are out of control, when for example, a given state believes: "I can win if I fight now; I shall lose if I fight later."[20] In 1959 a technological balance existed which prevented war, but which, Taylor argued, would also be its future cause. He laid out a simple timetable. Russia would pull ahead in long-range missiles by 1961; but, underestimating American scientists, would soon fall behind in ICBMs and anti-missile missiles. That would be the logical moment for World War III, when America would have a momentary advantage—around 1965. The reality was that whoever believes in weapons, as western, especially American, leadership seemed to, must be prepared to use them; and given the excuse, willy-nilly would. He went on to reiterate the error in American nuclear thinking: that assuming superiority in weapons precludes the possibility of war. In the past powerful nations made war only when threatened by the rise of other great powers. He saw America's fear of Soviet power in this light. He warned that "we will have war in six or eight years. Unless one power manages, with or without war, to dominate the world."[21] This warning characterized the motivation for Taylor's participation in the Campaign for Nuclear Disarmament. That he proved off-base in detail was no guarantee that he was wrong in assessing long-range possibilities. His most valid point was implied: that the awful reality of nuclear and related forms of military technology had not entered the mentality of statesmen responsible for foreign policy decision-making sufficiently to alter their adherence to traditional great-power modes of analysis . Ironically, that this charge is no longer entirely valid is partly to the credit of students tutored first or secondhand by Hans Morganthau.

Foreign policy in every modern phase of history had come to rest on ideological consideration more than in the past, both in terms of objective and practice. Taylor had written earlier about foreign policy in the "new democracies," and had once even defended the virtues of the "old diplomacy"—if properly understood, still a manifestation of his dissent. In Taylor's own experience, fascism and socialism had had the greatest impact on the bases of foreign relations.

Fascism was the darker side of democratic politics, a mass-party under the control of a body of disciplined men drawn from the disgruntled elements within industrial society following a few self-chosen leaders.[22] Adhering to a creed of hatred and emotion, fascists parodied other ideologies, and had as their sole purpose plunder on a large scale. Fascism was nothing more than the vocalization of psychopathic irrationality: ugly resentments and emotional hatreds combined with elitism produced the fascist mentality. The memory of the British Union of Fascists in the 1930s, attractive temporarily to so many intellectuals and others who harbored elitist sympathies, lingered as evidence. Taylor recalled that between 1945 and 1960 a pro-Russian could not get a hearing except in a few leftist journals, (he seemed to have forgotten in making this comment his appearances on the BBC, and his writing for *The Sunday Express* owned by the Conservative, Lord Beaverbrook.) while during the 1930s a pro-German had no such problem.[23] In large part, he concluded, foreign policy failures between the wars had been due to reluctance among members of the Establishment to oppose fascism by force, the only language fascists understood.

Socialism was of greater interest, however, because a socialist himself, Taylor believed in the impact of the left more than that of the right. But socialism, holding the potential for a truly enlightened and pacific foreign policy, all too often betrayed it to the quest for organization, power, and success. This was the fallacy of the left which pervaded socialist activities equally in foreign and domestic affairs. Between the wars, the free-wheeling socialism of early twentieth-century Labour had ended, and the planners took charge. Systematic, unsympathetic, and pragmatic, they took the liberty out of socialism. When leadership fell out of working-class hands, humanitarianism gave way to bureaucracy and administration, to party, office, and function—in short, to the socialist version of the Establishment, middle class in outlook if not in origin, intellectual and rigid. In part, this was an accidental by-product of the socialists' eternal dilemma: the problem of gaining office and achieving change, but without sacrificing freedom. It was the problem of socialism without revolution. In Russia the Bolsheviks who had no experience with freedom had been willing to abandon it for power. In the West at the same time, socialists had preached freedom and practiced democracy, deluding themselves that they would get power once they got a majority. In fact they had achieved neither. It was only when socialist leaders succumbed to Bolshevik technique as they had in Spain in 1936, or to that of the Establishment as they had in England under Macdonald in 1929, that the mandate came. And it came at the expense of fundamental libertarian beliefs. As Taylor saw it, western socialism's fatal disease was its leaders' frustration at not being better Bolsheviks. He remembered his boyhood enthusiasm for the ILP when, with James Maxton and Clifford Allen as leaders, it only mattered that you stuck to your guns: "Who cares about success. Right is Right though the heavens fall."[24]

The present Labour Party was the case in point. As a historian, Taylor saw that idealists often are men of high principle and low political acumen. This was the sense of his observation that no man more than ILP founder Keir Hardie had "better instincts or a weaker head." The leadership of such men was a good example of the socialist paradox: the early left had failed to get power because it did not divorce itself from the libertarian socialist outlook; the later left failed to get socialism because it got power—and with it, the Establishment. The first Labour socialists knew nothing about power and bureaucracy, Taylor went on, and very little about systematic planning. They learned the hard way that politics is a tough game, that Arthur Greenwood crying "it's not fair!" did not win elections. In spite of George V's remark at the kissing of hands on January 22, 1924: "We are all socialists now, . . ." Labour soon discovered that it was a hollow victory; a year later in defeat Labour was not even treated as the official opposition. Nonetheless, it expected to profit by the swing of the pendulum as a matter of course: "They would come into office on the great British principle of Buggin's turn.

The left became frivolous: gay young things of intellectualism."[25] And the turn did come again in 1929. But Labour was no better prepared and made an even worse showing than in 1924. Labour, Taylor believed, was responsible by virtue of its weakness in the face of Establishment perfidy for the economic crises of 1929-1931, and for appeasement by virtue of its unrealistic foreign policy—noble, for all of that, but unrealistic—in the 1920s. However, he reflected, outside of Labour Party leadership, the left made a better showing by far than the right:

The left were asserting the great principles of freedom and
democracy, however unsuccessfully. They were seeking to resist
the systems of dictatorship which plunged the world into war . . .
What were Baldwin and the so-called governing classes doing during
this great crisis? They were fussing over the question of whether a
middle-aged man should marry a woman who had two previous
husbands, both living.[26]

The Labour Party won its first absolute parliamentary majority in 1945, and made "the great leap forward" as a result: national health, nationalized utilities, railroads and coal, and comprehensive welfare assistance programs. Socialism seemed to have arrived. But the reforms of 1945-1951 exacted a high price. Socialism, Taylor believed, was kept healthy by argument, conflict, and dissent. But in gaining power and achieving the outlines essentially of the Beveridge package of 1942, it had lost its edge within the limits of the Labour Party. A disgruntled Taylor declared in 1969 that the Labour Party no longer had any socialism. In the later 1950s he had begun to recognize the factors from which he drew this conclusion, and placed responsibility for them on Labour politicians who thirsted for power and prestige, and especially on socialist intellectuals who, following Namierist historians, proclaimed the end of ideas: "Contemporary philosophers say that the difference between tyranny and freedom, wrong and right, is, like red and white wine, a matter of taste. Universities study machinery not principles. Administration has replaced government."[27] This was wrong, he countered. Ideas were not outmoded; the problem was an apathy similar to that which settled in after the Reform Act of 1832. Labour had achieved, apparently, so much reform that there was nothing left to do. Even conservatives now accepted "welfare socialism." Only false issues raised hopefully at election time were in question. He concluded:

The moral seems to be that politics will come to life all right when
there is something worth fighting over. Until that time it is useless
conjuring up artificial issues in the hope that the electorate will be
taken in. Passion in politics is a good thing; but the price is high. For

the virtuous can triumph only if provoked by wickedness. Do we
really want Tories to be as wicked as they were in Chamberlain's
day or Disraeli's so as to arouse a new Gladstone or a new Lloyd
George?[28]

This is among the most ambiguous of Taylor's political arguments. He
appears to warn against both apathy and political "excitement." Was his
reluctance in this passage an aberration,—many would say merely another
Taylorian contradiction—or a hint that middle age had in fact caught up
with "Peck's Bad Boy"? Had he found confronting wickedness too exciting,
and the socialist dilemma too perplexing? To achieve socialism remained
his ultimate hope for England; but how to do it was unresolved. After the
war, Labour appeared to have secured at least the outlines of a society plac-
ing domestic improvement first. Did he now hope that Labour's efforts
would inspire the final realization of socialism, even if the party was no
longer socialist itself? I would suggest two, interrelated, solutions. The nature
of Taylor's dissent was to provoke his readers by contrary, or paradoxical,
allusions. Hence the apparent contradictions here. But also, he never ceased
believing in Tory wickedness, or in socialism as predicated upon dissent.
Dissent required valid causes and the reforms of 1945-1951 had, for the
time being at least, rendered innocuous the reactionary qualities within the
conservative party, even in foreign affairs. Until they reopened the struggle
with a serious challenge to what progress had been made and until Labour
challenged them with a truly internationalist rather than nationalist foreign
policy, issues would remain phoney, more apparent than real in terms of
political disputation. Of course, foreign policy was a key disappointment for
dissenters: determination to "not go naked to the conference table" was
backed by Labour's commitment of 30% of the budget to armaments.

However, the right was not defeated. Labour did not stay long in office.
At the time Taylor was reflecting on what Labor had achieved, he was living under a Conservative government which was, as always, tied to the Establishment system of politics. Sooner or later it would reassert its old powers
and prejudices—as in fact it did, he believed, in Suez in 1956 and in nuclear
foreign policy. Antipathy towards the Establishment was the longest thread
in the fabric of Taylor's dissent, reaching back in his intellectual heritage
to the earliest Nonconformists' opposing the established church. Even though
his Magdalen College fellowship, membership in the British Academy, and
other symbols of social and academic respectability made him a part of its
external structure, Taylor's most vituperative writings were aimed at this
all-pervasive manifestation of Britain's ancient class system. Traditionally,
the Establishment belonged to the Tories, whom Taylor described as opponents of popular sovereignty, as paternalistic reformers, and in general as

the enemies of freedom. They would always hedge on liberty, he wrote, no matter how benevolent their aims might appear. The Establishment considered those who defend liberty as disruptors of stability, security, and good order. However, being paternalists and philosophic pragmatists, its members sought to absorb all social progresses that had been consummated. Such were the implications of a book by two Tory M.P.s, Angus Maude and Enoch Powell. As Taylor described their thesis: "Democracy for our authors means social reforms; and the Welfare State is its culmination. . . . A very satisfactory and a very comforting history for the company directors who now seem to determine the character of the Conservative Party."[29] The great danger remained the fluid nature of the Establishment mentality, which accepted the Labour Party for exactly the reasons it accepted social change: in order to absorb and disarm it. Liberty was the sacrificial lamb; without liberty socialism was useless. Taylor charged that Tory welfare was nothing more than a condescending paternalism, a sort of velvet prison.

From William Cobbett, an early nineteenth-century populist whose political personality was similar to his own, Taylor adopted the term "The Thing" in describing the Establishment. A truly democratic society, he began, would choose its rulers by lot for short stretches. Not in Britain: there the rulers were a select group who passed through a given set of tests, of which ambition and ability were not necessarily a part, that, once met, ensured permanence. Democracy in Britain was merely a process by which members of The Thing were periodically endorsed by the public. The Thing was tolerant, exclusive, and dominating. To belong one must be white, willing to wear a uniform of collar, tie, and dark suit, stay indoors at a desk, have a reasonable command of grammatical English, and the ability to read from typescript. Gaining entrance was easier than in the past. Almost anyone could join providing he could conform to these requirements. Only the most wretched were permanently excluded—the sons of agricultural laborers and blacks, for instance. The right parents—the nobility or professional people, preferably— were always an asset. Having the wrong parents could be overcome by attending the right schools: Eton for the upper classes, Winchester for the Labour Party. Running away to sea, Taylor observed wryly, was preferable to a secondary modern. The distinguishing mark was still religion; if not Anglicanism at least a code of morality befitting "liberal" christianity. Even adherents of the Free Churches were now junior members.

Why did the Establishment succeed? Taylor took another page from Cobbett's book and wrote ". . . the very word, so plummy, so ponderous, so respectable, tempts us to acknowledge the moral superiority of 'The Establishment.' It conjures up benign, upholstered virtues, calm, steady, reliable. They would never pass a dud cheque or cheat at cards. Not intellectually dazzling, perhaps, but patient, understanding, and tolerant—above all tolerant."[30] But it was only the Establishment itself that benefited from all of this: "They look upholstered because they are well fed. Their air of moral superiority is really an assumption that someone else will always cook their dinner—and a very good dinner at that."[31] Establishment hypocrisy was underlined, Taylor felt, by the example of Lloyd George's experience in the war years. Intellectually at odds with The Thing, he had nonetheless saved it in 1916, only to be hunted from power by it, and kept from power once the crisis was past.

The Establishment would always be the radical's enemy, partly because of its conservatism and partly because the radical is, intellectually and emotionally, a sectarian dissenter. No Anglican could ever be a complete radical: George Lansbury had come the closest, Taylor believed, but even he had never quite lost his Anglican sense of superiority. The most disillusioning fact of leftist politics in the 1950s was that this Church of England syndrome seemed to have become part of the official Labour Party attitude also. Inclusion in high Labour circles was based on a proprietarian mentality, even if egalitarian principles were still proclaimed at annual party conferences. (Any photograph of T.U.C. leaders provides documentary evidence of Labour's upholstered look.) Clearly, the Thing ought to be gotten rid of. "The country would be more alert, more receptive to new ideas, more capable of holding its own in the world. The Thing is on the surface a system of public morals. Underneath it is a system of public plunder." To end it was simply a matter of economics: "The time is coming when the average reader of The Daily Mirror will get more than the average reader of The Times. Who will then care if the readers of The Times go on imagining that they are the Top People?"[32]

In the meantime, the Establishment remained in control, limiting, coercing, controlling. Taylor believed this was the cause each time he was denied access to certain classifications of official papers. He believed this so much that a striking portion of his dissent was devoted to criticizing government policy on archival research. Archival secrets disturbed him deeply, as their very existence seemed to deny the citizen's right to know the affairs of his nation and government. Government secrets are not in the public interest, he wrote. They limit the making of intelligent decisions by the people, and into the bargain add to public expense. Documents are kept locked up and guarded, requiring the hiring of Keepers, until the moment when the government hires a historian—or a group of historians—to publish large collections. The official archivist was the perfect Establishment type, carrying out his secretive duties with zealous devotion. He possessed a classic bureaucratic mind, and fitted all the requirements for membership. His vanity was flattered by handling documents prohibited to others, and all readers who would naturally disturb the neat arrangements on his shelves, and sometimes mishandle the precious hoard, were his enemies. However, some English documents had been carried off to North America, there to be used by American researchers who often published in England—a fine irony. Taylor wrote: "American historians who are ransacking the papers of Roosevelt and Truman would have the true nature of British freedom brought home to them if they were sent to prison for quoting the papers of Lloyd George."[33] Taylor was intellectually curious, a quality he believed was an expression of the freedom that is essential to democracy. Secrecy limited both curiosity and freedom, meanwhile performing no service to anybody:

It is not even a service to governments or to ministers. It thwarts the spirit of democracy, which is, no doubt, why officials seek to maintain it. It will go in time, if democracy survives at all. The American rule is to have no secrets; the Russian is to keep everything secret. I am on America's side in this as in nearly everything else. Our rulers follow their usual practice; American in talk, Russian in practice. Meanwhile, the contemporary historian should tell the public that he cannot do his job properly.[34]

In *The Troublemakers* he did just that, writing with a fine sense of indignation:

Things have come to a pretty pass when we cannot consult Gladstone's "cabinet papers," really private jottings, without the permission of the Cabinet Office—an organization created many years after his death. . . . The secrecy is imposed solely to bolster up the self-importance of the civil servants who insist on it. I regard every official as my enemy; and it puzzles me that other historians do not feel the same way.[35]

There was an interesting history behind this. Official secrets, excepting military ones and those pertaining to the contents of certain international agreements, were a twentieth-century phenomenon, at least as a matter of law. An act of parliament in 1911 began it by limiting the publication of political and foreign policy papers. As time passed, this Official Secrets Act was widely interpreted, joining after 1916 with the newly created Cabinet Secretariat in demanding that all ministerial papers be placed under official control. Ministers who refused to hand over their personal minutes, official correspondence, etc., found they could be threatened by the OSA. Thus a climate was created which in Taylor's opinion had dangerous implications. In 1952 a storm broke around the Cabinet Secretariat, and Taylor leaped into the fray. Aneurin Bevan had published cabinet minutes in defense of his resignation from the cabinet. In response, Clement Attlee, prime minister at the time of Bevan's revolt, charged that he had violated the 1916 Act. Taylor saw this as an attack primarily on political freedom, and only secondarily as a matter of legality. Attlee was technically correct; but, the rule ought not to exist in the first place. In *The Times* Taylor wrote: "The unity of a political party can surely be maintained by other means than the manufacture of a precedent designed to keep the people, and even posterity, in ignorance."[36] These kinds of restrictions were debilitating to politicians, the public, and especially to historians who were thus denied access to materials necessary to their work. From their position, at least, there was a logical alternative: "Publish nothing, but allow scholars unrestricted use of the records. Editorial susceptibility will be upheld; and the historical story will be made known."[37] Taylor continued this line throughout the decade. When a law was passed in 1958 determining that a fifty-year moratorium would be observed on the opening of official papers, Taylor wrote cryptically: "How can generals learn how to lose the next war unless they know what happened 'last time'?" And more seriously: "No harm would be done to states or individuals if the records were open without restrictions. . . . But this would destroy the prestige of diplomacy and of the archives themselves. It is more impressive to appear to be protecting guilty secrets than to confess that there are few secrets to defend."[38] As he wrote years later: "The rule is in fact an unworthy survival from the time when government was a 'mysterie,' reserved for the Crown and its servants. Such rigmarole has no place in a community which claims to be democratic."[39]

From Taylor's perspective, the Establishment was a benevolent despotism predicated upon distrust of the people, indifference to democracy, doubt regarding the common sense of ordinary men, and susceptibility to the attractions of power, wealth, and privilege. His constant argument was that the people have the right to decide their own fate, and are sufficiently wise to do so. As one indication, he wrote, one need look only at the difference between capitalist and worker:

The worker is by nature less imaginative, more level-headed than
the capitalist. This is what prevents him becoming one. He is content
with small gains. Trade union officials think about the petty cash;
the employer speculates in millions. You can see the difference in
their representative institutions. There is no scheme too wild, no
rumour too absurd, to be without repercussions on the stock
exchange. The Public House is the home of common sense.[40]

The key to the Establishment was class, an implicit elitism found throughout European society. Using history to make his point, Taylor noted certain nineteenth-century liberal intellectuals who, like Alexis de Tocqueville, were shocked at rudeness on the part of their servants, or who, like François

Guizot, limited liberty to men of the "rich and enlightened classes." Jacob Burckhardt, the eminent historian of Renaissance culture was another. He had once refused Ranke's Chair at Berlin in protest against Prussian philistinism and authoritarianism. But he expressed hatred for the "loud mouthed masses," and claimed that the only possible tyranny would be the despotism of their rule. "This sounds impressive," Taylor wrote, "until one discovers that he regarded the Health Insurance Act as 'the despotism of the State over the private lives of individuals in its most extreme form.' "[41] The elitist principle was common to all opponents of democracy, Taylor believed, including leaders of ideological mass movements. He had argued this in terms of both right and left, and applauded the British for having thwarted the efforts of communists to gain power in the name of the people. This, Taylor claimed, was one of the English people's great achievements. Even among historians arguing that the emergence of the power of the people is the key to modern civilization could be found those who spurned the people, abhorring, in the case of Arnold Toynbee, their lack of "culture." Of Toynbee he wrote: "He never sees people. Ruins and museums are all very well in their way; but I prefer the example of that great historian Marc Bloc, who in a foreign city made straight for the music hall."[42]

That the individual supersedes class, ideology, or political loyalties is assumed in Taylor's arguments. Such was the essence of his epigrammatic observation on a number of historical characters whose lives seemed to underscore courage and high mindedness, but who were in no particulars necessarily alike in other ways. Among others there was Keir Hardie, "that rare character a truly independent working man." Hardie united a vision of the future with political action in the present, and based both on a firm belief in the virtues of the common man. Often he stood alone against threats and harassment; against severe opposition from mine owners in the 1880s and 1890s, and no less from "patriots" during the First World War when he was bitterly castigated for his pacifism. Hardie was Taylor's representative dissenter: moral, straightforward, dedicated to principle, and above all, independent-minded. In 1956 Taylor wrote: "Now . . . any Labour Party member eager to fight for the Suez Canal must be relieved that Keir Hardie lies a-mouldering in his grave. But perhaps his soul goes marching on."[43]

Others included Charles James Fox, Madame de Staël, Lord Northcliffe, and General de Gaulle, each of whom had made a stand for what appeared to be right in the context of given situations.[44] Parliamentary opposition in late eighteenth-century England would have been poorer without Fox, Taylor wrote: indeed, it would be, today. A profligate with loose morals but an incomparable political heretic, he immeasurably enriched secular dissent. Those who protested British oppression in Cyprus—a problem spot for declining British imperialism in the 1950s—belonged to his "party," and Irish and Indian independence stood as his memorials. It was Fox's spirit that shadowed Britain whenever Britain stood behind freedom, Taylor proclaimed. For similar reasons, he was drawn to Madame de Staël, courtesan, spy, intellectual and intimate of intellectuals, crowned heads, and statesmen, in the exciting time of the Napoleonic Empire. Alone among her French contemporaries she stood up to Napoleon: the first to confront totalitarian dictatorship with liberty. Napoleon could deal with her only through brutality. No less admirable in his own way was Lord Northcliffe. Proprietor of *The Times* early in the twentieth century, he sought to impose his own foreign policy on the nation, a policy which he believed was morally and practically superior to that pursued by the government. Like Taylor's great friend Lord Beaverbrook, he was a typically energetic press lord, indeed the prototype of this English phenomenon from Beaverbrook to Lord Thomson of Fleet. Northcliffe was, Taylor noted, a journalist of fire, passion, and energy, who fought off the cloying traditions of that venerable Establishment paper and made it a paying concern, instituting meanwhile the freedom of the press as no other English publisher had done. Contrasting him with his editors, Wickham Steed and Geoffrey Dawson, Taylor described Northcliffe as a radical individualist, the editors as uninspired and uninspiring bureaucrats. Likewise, General de Gaulle stood against lesser men and, during the war years, pursued a vision that transcended the mundane. His was a story of romantic dimensions in which will triumphed over circumstance. In large part, de Gaulle's work was a wasted effort; yet from exile he performed a service for France of Churchillian proportions. His sole purpose in going to London after the fall of Paris had been to emerge as the living symbol of the French people. It was, Taylor believed, a task which only a man of de Gaulle's stature and qualities could have accomplished. The result was an inspiration to mankind: ". . . an individual defying the world and succeeding in his defiance however briefly, will always inspire admiration until the rule of the masses submerges us. The story of de Gaulle has, maybe, little to do with the Second World War, but it is magnificent all the same."[45]

These examples of Taylor's "heroes," as in their particular way they may be regarded, underline the point that he believed the individual's version of the truth and his willingness to stand by it to be the essence of dissent. He felt the weight of his burden personally and bore it well. Two events produced by the cold war provided most dramatic and appealing opportunities for him. The first was the Eden government's decision in 1956 to join the French and Israelis in seizing the Suez canal. At that time, Taylor was appearing regularly on a panel show for Independent Television called "Free Speech." He was morally outraged when the news of British intervention broke. At the panelists' customary pre-broadcast luncheon, he and the other leftists could hardly speak to their conservative colleagues. Almost at once large-scale demonstrations against government policy began, in which Taylor took part. For most eventualities he advocated politics by argument; but this time, he said, had the government not backed down, he would have been prepared to "raise the banner of revolt."[46] His attitude at this critical moment reflected perfectly his radical mentality, his advocacy of dissent as a weapon of democratic politics, and his intellectual willingness to pay the price. Taylor demonstrating in 1956 and his choice of topics for the Ford Lectures may have influenced an important academic appointment made the following year. As an expression of his relationship to contemporary British radicalism, the circumstances of this appointment warrant some attention.

The Regius Chair of Modern History is among the premier appointments at Oxford University. In theory, its holders are scholars and lecturers of the first rank who devote their time and energies to the task of leading and encouraging historical studies. In 1957, Professor V. H. Galbraith stepped down, and Taylor's name was among those raised as a possible successor; indeed he was the choice of Galbraith himself, and of two other prominent Oxford historians, Sir George Clark and A. L. Poole.[47] The Regius Chair is a government appointment (once, as a graduate student, I mistakenly called it a "sinecure," and was properly chastised by my professor, an old Oxonian) established by royal command during the reign of George II. There was considerable reservation among some historians, including, it has been suggested with some authority, Sir Lewis Namier, then the *doyen* of English historians, regarding Taylor's scholarly qualifications for the Chair. Possibly Taylor's loud criticism of Anthony Eden and Harold Macmillan in the Suez affair added considerably to their doubts. Earlier he had asserted in his "London Diary" that he would never gain a Chair. Was this only a dissenter's certainty that he will always be an outsider or evidence for his claim to intuitive capabilities?[48] In any event, there were other outstanding candidates available, among whom was the ultimate choice, Hugh Trevor-Roper. A modern history lecturer and Fellow of Christ Church, Trevor-Roper was considered to be a supurb lecturer and, at least by some, a superior scholar. Curiously, he too had a reputation for controversy, almost the equal of Taylor's. But he had once said: "When radicals scream that victory is indubitably theirs, sensible conservatives knock them on the nose."[49] It is more likely that Trevor-Roper's conservatism got him the chair than that Taylor was passed over because of his dissent over Suez—at least one Oxford undergraduate from the period has since urged that such a factor would raise too much resentment and opposition among the dons. It is more probable simply that his Ford lectures, capping an increasingly widespread notoriety as a "performer" on radio and television, were too "popular"—they also were delivered on television for the BBC's Third Programme. It is probable also that despite his later objections that he was not put out by his failure, Taylor took being by-passed first as political discrimination and then as an academic slight. This sheds light on his "outsider" personality, carefully nurtured throughout his years as a don, and on his self-identity as a dissenter. Shortly after the appointment was made, he wrote that "the historian needs influence to get himself into the academic world, and greater influence to ascend the academic ladder. He avoids commitment to a cause or creed, and finds it difficult to imagine that anyone would jeopardize promotion for principle."[50] This remark would appear inspired by a combination of pique and moral righteousness, and must be taken in the light of his dissent over the Suez policy. It may well be taken also in light of his advocacy of dissent in the Ford Lectures as a method for political, and by implication, for academic, action. Other clues followed: in 1963, upon giving up unwillingly his university lectureship in international history, he made reference to having been "sent" to Oxford from Manchester in 1938 to get started on acquiring a Chair, and having, of course, failed; and in the preface to *English History, 1914-1945* (1965) he thanked Sir George Clark for having "sustained me when I was slighted in my profession."[51] The substance and place of these remarks is compelling—they could hardly have been coincidence. But in time, the highmindedness overcame the pique, at least publicly, and he asserted that: "I should have refused the Regius Chair if it had been offered me. Macmillan was then Prime Minister, and his hands were still red from the bloodshed of Suez."[52] The Regius Chair appointment makes more interesting David Marquand's observation in 1966 that: "Taylor . . . unsettles his academic colleagues because they suspect, quite rightly, that his conception of history is not merely irreverent, but seditious."[53]

The second event came soon after the Regius appointment. In the late 1950s dissent against nuclear weapons was a primary activist concern involving many among England's most prominent intellectuals. Leadership in the Campaign for Nuclear Disarmament included such as Taylor, Canon and Mrs. J. L. Collins, J. B. Priestley, and Bertrand Russell. In popular parlance the issue was whether it was better to be Red or Dead. Lacking formal discipline and relying upon argument as well as demonstration, the movement was made to order for Taylor. He claimed to have spoken in more halls against nuclear weapons than had John Bright against the Crimean War. Disagreement with Russell's attempts to make the movement hard-core and doctrinaire caused him to disassociate with it in the end. In the meantime, he resorted to the kind of attack illustrated by this letter to *The Times* in 1958:

A number of your correspondents announce that they would prefer suicide to life under communism. So would I. Our wish can be met simply and cheaply by issuing a phial of poison to every registered anti-Communist. But why should we insist that the rest of the population accompany us on this death ride; that many millions of Russians may also be obliterated; and that the atmosphere be polluted so that future generations will be born maimed or monsters?[54]

As always, he enjoyed intellectual—or perhaps, more properly, emotional—battles, reveling in paradox and irony as well as in moral assertion. The satiric tone of this letter paralleled his satisfaction when the police discovered on one occasion that the crowd he was haranguing before 10 Downing Street was middle class; he noted with obvious relish that they had to be polite in breaking it up. With that conviction peculiar to the radical mind, he added that a crowd of students would have been attacked and roughed up. The kind of commentary Taylor made before CND crowds also paralleled the letter, at least in moral certitude. Speaking to a crowd of demonstrators on February 18, 1958, he pleaded for people to "stand by humanity." Typical was this line: "Is there anyone here who would want to do this to another human being? (Pause—no answer). Then why are we making the damned thing? (Applause and uproar)."[55]

Taylor was not always pleased with the CND, however. In a "Campaign Report" for *The New Statesman*, he wrote: "I often detect restlessness in the audience when I develop the practical, even cynical, arguments that we should be more secure from a military point of view without the H-bomb."[56] This situation, he feared, resulted from the fact that only the committed really listened, and they did not see the morality inherent in such practical arguments. In part, "Report" was a warning against the Russellian type of intellectual extremist that the movement was adopting. In Taylor's mind morality was the key to the campaign, and the more practical the better. It was wrong to use nuclear bombs, nothing more, nothing less, and this should be expressed through free debates. The problem was that in age the audiences were over fifty or under twenty-five. The older generation wanted moral arguments while the younger demanded action. The young must be won back to morality, he argued, and the way to do this was to dissipate the campaign's intellectualism—as always, workers were more enthusiastic for morality than were egg-heads! "The H-bomb is morally wrong," he concluded, "and it is idiotic into the bargain. It took the Anti-Corn Law League eight years to argue its way to victory. I doubt whether we have that long. But whatever the time, we must go on arguing."[57] In March, 1959 Taylor's participation in the CND reached a dramatic peak when he joined 16,000 protesters, marching from Aldermaston to Trafalgar Square—though Taylor did not walk the entire fifty miles. It was a moment of great excitement, a triumph of belief in both the methods and principles of dissent. Ecstatic, he proclaimed: "In all its long history, Trafalgar Square had never seen a demonstration of this size. In all of its long history Trafalgar Square had never seen a demonstration of this intensity."[58]

IV

Taylor's dissent was an intellectual exercise shaded over by emotional rhetoric. At its best, the emotion added effect to sound knowledge and logical arguments, however controversial or seemingly contradictory the result might appear. This analysis has thus far been largely in terms of the values expressed in his dissent over contemporary issues. His most significant and often explosive critiques were within the confines of historical investigation, critiques based, however, on the same values. Taylor was not merely a revisionist as he has often been called. In spite of "provocative" interpretations and judgments, his work frequently only reaffirmed earlier judgments and in spite of appearances was not aimed at proving any contemporary point. In his eyes, there were eternal truths in history as in politics, and if the scholar did his job properly and in the right frame of mind, they would emerge of themselves. Indeed, as Taylor defined him, the historian ought to be always dissenting over old arguments, with an eye towards arriving at a purer understanding of what had happened. As he put it in *Englishmen and Others*: "I write to clear my mind, to discover how things happened and how men behaved. If the result is shocking or provocative, this is not from intent, but solely because I try to judge from the evidence without being influenced by the judgment of others."[59] Here is almost verbatim Ranke's famous dictum: "Wie es eigentlich gewesen." To see what actually happened was the object of historiography: seeking to discover the truth about the past, whether or not it proved in aid of contemporary disputes. Often, of course, it did—or seemed to—even though Taylor persistently disclaimed presentist values in history.

His writings on German history and European diplomacy provide the best examples in this regard in the later 1950s. On the one hand, he was convinced as always that the basic problem of Germany was its flirtation with wickedness; but on the other, he developed more completely than before an idea that had been hinted at as early as *The Italian Problem in European Diplomacy, 1847-1849* (1934), that historical causation was not produced by conscious determination and plan but by accident and opportunism. And he placed the responsibility for success and failure squarely, as he had always believed it should lie, with the people. In 1945 he published *The Course of*

German History, an uncompromising denunciation of the historical German nation. His arguments did not substantively alter in the 1950s. He continued to argue, for example, that Nazism was a disease born out of the German people's failure historically to cope with their political institutions, particularly those of a popular nature thrust upon them full blown after 1918. German history from Martin Luther on had prepared the Germans to obey authority without question, a philosophy obviously inconsistent with democracy. At the same time, they tried to escape from authority through the fantasy that authority and freedom could be part of the same fabric. In one instance, Taylor wrote tongue-in-cheek that the trouble with the Germans was their ability to read; this would be no problem except that they also inclined to take what they read seriously. They had not recovered in the twentieth from their nineteenth-century romantic *Sehnsucht*: "The Germans have prolonged their Romanticism into the twentieth century," he wrote. "People talk nonsense in every country, but only the Germans take it seriously."[60] The "aggrieved man" in German romanticism symbolized the selfishness germane to their national character, and inspired them to accept Hitler. By 1961 this picture of the Germans had changed only with regard to Taylor's view of their future. Where in 1945 he urged Germany's destruction as the only way to ensure European stability, he now believed that there were hopeful signs of maturation. A peaceful Germany seemed to be developing out of the two small states set up in 1945, which would last as long as reunification was forgotten. Perhaps, he concluded, if we ignore the Germans they will go away. Time might do what war and forced re-education had failed to accomplish.

The accidental causation theme applied throughout German history. The German problem had been most on historians' minds in the postwar decade, and had gotten in the way of that essentially radical objectivity every historian should possess. Germany more than any other European state since 1848 had produced statesmen to whom were attributed by convention the choices and deeds that had caused two world wars. Nazi barbarism raised frightening questions for men who had firmly believed in "enlightened" western civilization. However, the Germans, Taylor wrote, were much like people elsewhere; no more or less wicked, but equally a product of their own history. It may be inferred from this that he regarded acceptance of Hitler by the Germans to be as logical as acceptance of political and social progress by the British. In diplomacy, German statesmen mirrored their counterparts in other nations. There was no wicked Hitlerian duplicity beyond that which might be expected in any practitioners of statecraft, nor was Nazism the end product of the policies, domestic or foreign, which German statesmen had pursued. For instance, Taylor wrote, it is easy to denounce interwar German diplomats for equivocation; but, like others, they were only looking after national interest. In the pre-1914 era there was Holstein, for example, the "hidden hand" at the *Wilhelmstrasse*. Contrary to consensus scholarship, Taylor argued that he was only another hard-working policy maker concerned about German security, dealing with situations as they arose with the materials at hand. His main problem was serving Wilhelm II, a king whose foreign policy in many respects did foreshadow Hitler's. The published Holstein papers finally proved, to Taylor's satisfaction, that he had been right. There was nothing sinister or unexpected to be revealed.[61]

Hitler, too was no different from other Germans, though Taylor found him more complex. Through Hitler, and through Bismarck whom many postwar diehards had interpreted as part of the German plot leading up to the Nazi revolution, Taylor began to develop more fully his chance and accident theory. Statesmen do not plan, they react. In *Origins of the Second World War* (1961) he described Hitler's policies as the full manifestation of views that were acceptable and consciously a part of the German mentality: "The unique quality in Hitler was the gift of translating commonplace thought into action;" and, "Everything which Hitler did against the Jews followed logically from the racial doctrines in which most Germans vaguely believed. It was the same with foreign policy." And finally: "In principle and doctrine, Hitler was no more wicked and unscrupulous than many other contemporary statesmen. In wicked acts he outdid them all."[62] Hitler remained an evil man. What he was not, in Taylor's view, was a diabolical genius who designed the European situations that led to war.

However, this was the conclusion of a long process of research and writing. Hitler was too complicated to be clarified all at once. In 1957, for example, Taylor wrote that no peaceful overtures would have satisfied Hitler in 1939: "In 1939 Hitler was relentlessly set on war with Poland and ignored the diplomatic turmoil." In 1958 he observed that appeasement "remains the noblest word in the diplomatist's vocabulary;" but Hitler, bent on war from the start, was the wrong man to try it on.[63] But, however applicable this was to Hitler at Munich, was it also to the Hitler of the early thirties who had just acquired power domestically and was busy consolidating it? Like others, Hitler was not a static but an organic figure, moving with the tides that carried events along. Some of the determined postwar advocates of the "good German" theory—that is, Hitler and the Nazis had seduced and misled the Germans, none of whom knew about Buchenwald or Dachau, nor really wanted the war which revised the Versailles Treaty—such as Elizabeth Wiskman, insisted that Hitler had planned the war from the start: rearmament, political rhetoric, economic planning, and Nazi ideology were offered as proof.[64] But Taylor was growing in the conviction that prior to the moment when a situation for successful military adventure was apparent, and then only against a minor state, Hitler was playing a purely opportunistic game. He did not, after all, ignore the diplomatic maneuver of Munich. Czechoslovakia was attacked only for what remained of it after the Munich Pact, in which England, France, and Italy agreed to German expansion, and Poland only when Colonel Beck had in effect declared war on Germany. Taylor never portrayed Hitler as a pacific ruler opposed to planned aggression; but then neither did the Germans fit this category as a nation. His argument was more clearly that Hitler could be seen as an expansionist who, in the final analysis, was able only to profit by others' mistakes. "Foreign policy on the cheap" comes close to capturing Taylor's point. To some extent he did echo the then prevalent judgment that Hitler's role in Germany was diabolical; at the same time, however, he saw Hitler as being only vaguely aware of what he wanted in the long run or how it might be obtained. One gets the idea, Taylor wrote, that he took up the conquest of Russia in 1941 "merely for the sake of having something to do. Anything was better than planning the empire he had acquired so unexpectedly."[65] So, too, were the Germans only vaguely aware of their desires once Versailles had been overturned. In this way, Hitler was a democratic leader, following the "lead" of his people.

The Origins of the Second World War, Taylor's most controversial example of scholarly dissent and which had been foreshadowed by these and other writings on Germany and European diplomacy, clarified his position on Hitlerian opportunism and thus on chance as historical causation. Even if the nazis were wicked, Hitler's diplomacy was traditional. Though he believed in war and was able to translate latent German aggression into totalitarian rule at home and conquest abroad, his success surprised him. Historians, Taylor argued, had simply credited German fascism with too much intelligence. This was the theme of "Who Burnt the Reichstag?" (1960). Once, he noted, historians, himself included, accepted the nazis' responsibility. But when the facts were in, it was clear that they were innocent: their guilt was part of a communist myth useful as a propaganda device. Nor, as the nazis had claimed, were the communists guilty: this too was a myth, to justify totalitarian rule on a legal basis. There had been no conspiracy at all. Van der Lubbe set the fire by himself, as he claimed, simply an individual, implicitly heroic, protesting the nazi regime. To Taylor the entire affair proved that the core of German policy under Nazism was catch-as-catch-can, and that historical causation included personal principles and self-motivation. The nazis were not acquitted of being evil men, however. The point was simply that they were mainly evil opportunists. He concluded of Hitler: "He was far from being the far-sighted planner that he is usually made to appear. He had a genius for improvisation; and his behavior over the *Reichstag* fire was a wonderful example of it. When he became Chancellor, he had no idea how he would translate his constitutional position into a dictatorship."[66] Drawn after at least the thinking out of *Origins* was underway, this conclusion shared its point of view. In both writings, Taylor was asserting a "common sense" historiographical and intellectual position, and in the process played the part of the dissenter by debunking not only Hitler but many of his historians.

Bismarck was equally important in Taylor's historical work. The theme was similar in scope: if overestimating Hitler could give credence to dangerously irrational "devil" theories of history and politics, was raising Bismarck's ghost not giving equally dangerous credence to the systems fallacy that often was placed in opposition to revolutionary personalities and ideologies? Bismarck had been the more successful—and conservative—statesman; yet, Taylor urged, he had been no more prescient, and for modern statesmen to judge him as a system-maker of profound vision was to parallel the historians who judged Hitler as the profound manipulator of modern European history. *Bismarck: The Man and the Statesman* (1955) was Taylor's basic view of a gifted but not prophetic figure. Bismarck played his cards as they came up, never knowing in advance what was in them. That he played successfully only marked his skill at maneuvering and the general state of diplomatic anxiety among the European powers during his era. The fact of Bismarck's entire existence, Taylor concluded, was that he never was what he tried to be, nor able to accomplish exactly what he envisioned. His accomplishments were the result of flexibility. More often, and this was the thrust of Bismarck's *Reminiscences*, he took credit for developments that he had not planned but which in retrospect appeared successful. Clever at seizing opportunities, he seldom saw beyond them until afterward. He went to war with Austria in 1866 because he thought Austria planned war against Prussia; yet it was his counselors, not the Iron Chancellor himself, who had so divined Austria's supposed intentions. Bismarck had no clear aim after the victory of 1866, either in foreign policy or in the victory it gave him over the Prussian parliament. Almost on the eve of war with France in 1870 he was seeking accomodations with Napoleon III. The French war was an accident, neither planned nor forseen, but claimed as his own device once it had become inevitable. This was in order to present himself as the creator of the empire he had never wanted. Bismarck imagined that his duty was to build a German state that would be Prussian. That Germany after 1870 became greater than Prussia went beyond his goal and opened the door for Wilhelm's *Weltpolitik*, a policy he disapproved and always fought against. Such was Taylor's view of Bismarck.

He was concerned also to contrast Bismarckian national interest with Hitlerian *Weltanschauung*, out of which came another repudiation of the cold-war system-makers. Bismarck was no better able than Hitler to eliminate opposition to his policies or to create a one-dimensional order domestically and internationally that would serve his interests. This was Taylor's warning against seeking historical precedents by which the door could be closed to communism and fascism alike. His admonitions against neo-Bismarckianism lay in what happened to the Bismarckians, that is, the conservatives and old army men, in Germany after the First World War. After 1919 Bismarck's achievements became more appealing: the diplomacy of *Realpolitik* rather than a visionary League of Nations, and national interest rather than *Weltanschauung*. (The obvious fallacy in this comparison is that world views since 1815 have usually asserted national interest). Between the world wars they were successful in emulating Bismarck. Versailles was overturned, reparations were ended, and the German army was restored. "Then the Bismarckians discovered to their horror that, while they had got everything that they wanted they had also lost everything that they prized. The *Rechtstaat*, the rule of law, had vanished. The Nazi barbarians ruled. The Bismarckians were helpless."[67] Hitler was wicked and megalomaniac into the bargain, and the Bismarckian legend was no defense against him. The army hierarchy, Bismarckian to a fault, attempted to resist in 1944—tardily, hesitantly, and futilely. They wanted to combine militarism and the rule of law, to find an "authority" that from its own decency would be moderate. They had no contact with the German people nor faith in democracy; they epitomized all that for centuries had been missing in German history. It was a mistake, Taylor concluded, to see in Bismarckian Germany either the forerunner of Nazism or an anti-revolutionary solution to present difficulties. Yet, he urged, this was what Bismarck's present-day emulators did. The true measure of his view that Bismarck's role in German and European history was historiographically paradoxical emerged when he concluded: "Bismarck would be content that his name is still a symbol of policy and he himself a subject of controversy."[68] In this respect, he observed wryly, Bismarck, and Hitler, had indeed determined the course of history, or at least its interpretation.

V

In many respects Taylor's was the mentality of the 1950s, at once cynical and hopeful: a mentality which supported dissent when it counted, and which had begun to rely on its historic qualities of faith in common sense and fundamental human intelligence. This was the theme of his comment on Hugh Trevor-Roper's *The Last Days of Hitler*. Reason and Virtue would somehow triumph again, as they had done in the past. Taylor wrote that: "Fools and lunatics may govern the world, but later on, in some future century, a rational man will rediscover *The Last Days of Hitler* and realize that there were men of his sort still alive."[69] The 1950s, Taylor claimed, faced the problems of today, not those of yesterday—in itself a rational viewpoint. He might have been speaking of himself when he wrote: "Centuries, like human beings, take half a lifetime to reach maturity. They acquire confidence and character in the fifties."[70] Since 1945 much had been done to rebuild England, and much had happened to relieve its leaders of the inspiration to follow old paths to power. As the withdrawal from Suez indicated, domination by the old order was gasping its last. Englishmen no longer cared about being reduced in international stature. Loss of empire in fact ushered in greater domestic prosperity, which was more than enough to alleviate remorse for all but a few diehards. Even the cold war was winding down; Taylor thought that President Eisenhower had unwittingly indicated the reason when he had said that the people wanted peace and meant to have it— the handwriting on the wall for both statesmen and commentators on world affairs. Communism, Taylor continued, had not overrun the world as it was supposed to do, and Russia appeared to be taking her place as a traditional power in world affairs—becoming more like America. World conquerors are now out of fashion, and sensible countries are coming into their own. "We are entering Utopia backwards, constantly surprised that the future turns out so much better than we expected."[71] The true revolution in modern society was neither social nor political. It was, Taylor noted, intellectual: the overthrow of belief in God, national greatness, world conquest, and dogma about individual behavior. The young of the 1950s left principle to their elders, among other things making love because they wanted to, not because it shocked their parents. They conducted their lives on the basis of common sense. Lucky Jim was their symbol; not rebellious, not even angry: "He was the modern Everyman—more fortunate than the original and more attractive too; no longer trailing his soul among imaginary evils, but lucky to be alive when mankind was coming to its senses."[72] This seems surprising, because here Taylor is heard treating as encouraging the very indifference to morality that in the CND he had found alarming. Perhaps in 1960 he saw that nuclear warfare was further off than he had imagined a year before, and was prepared to accept that the earlier attitudes of the young activists in the campaign had been more realistic than his generation's "old-fashioned" morality. In any event, he noted that, as Lucky Jim made clear, seriousness had vanished—and why not, when the Archbishop of Canterbury could produce theological justifications for the H-bomb and then declare that adultery was a crime. The 1950s had won a victory for democracy in other ways as well. Now greater care was taken for popular tastes in journals and on television. Man had found that he could conquer the world of motor cars and refrigerators with less pain than he had that of political greatness. Would it last, Taylor wondered? "We have the world at our feet; and someone may be tempted to give it a kick. Such doubts suggest that I am growing old. Maybe the young will win out. At any rate, if the next ten years do anything like as well as the last they will do very well indeed."[73] Of course, Taylor had not yet seen the next round of crises: the war in Vietnam, the student revolutions, pollution, compounded in the early 1970s by a world-wide energy shortage, and renewed violence to human rights in quarters where, in the afterglow of this new "enlightenment," it might not have been expected.

VI

Although it has not been the thrust of this essay to dispute Taylor, it would be incomplete without noting what may be called the dissenting fallacy in his work: the tendency toward contradiction and confusion of hard analysis and general assumption. First, with regard to the quality and depth of the thinking and scholarship upon which his dissenting and historical reputations rest, a point of separation must be noted. Contrary to some opinions, while Taylor's historiography and polemics come together on matters of style, attitude, and criticism, they are separate in the degree to which he did his homework: in international history his reputation for nineteenth-century scholarship is rejected only by a few diehards who, as in the case of Hans Morganthau, have been burnt by his rejection of their views on contemporary power politics; but the polemical pieces have been overly simplistic, creating as often as not the image of a foolish, muddleheaded thinker —or non-thinker—whose purpose is to shock or entertain, rather than to enlighten. It is no surprise that critics have had difficulty in "seeing him as a whole," and subsequently have refused to "take him seriously." As a polemicist, his arguments in the 1950s, as later, were often shallow, and philosophically if not factually contradictory. From the very beginning, for example, he was never able to decide if he regarded the United States as the villain or the hero of the democratic century. Another problem was the basis of his attack on pomposity and elitism: "No one is better than I am, and I am better than no one else." Yet again he pointed to the superiority of moral righteousness especially in foreign policy dissent. Also, he argued strongly against systems and system-makers, and against intellectualism manifest as systematic philosophic or behavioral theories; yet as diplomatic historian he treated thoroughly, rationally, and logically, European diplomacy as a system, and the actions of European statesmen as a part of its structure. Also his study of Bismarck, historically interesting and, I think, refreshingly realistic, relied heavily upon a quasi-behavioral format. Further, his anti-intellectualism, thinly disguised as advocacy of "common sense," was presented throughout as an expression of the right of men to think freely and to be able to think absolutely. This was a curious way to deal with intellect, since anti-intellectualism was then becoming the viewpoint of academic behavioralists and, in England, had often been that of reactionary parliament backbenchers though for quite different reasons. Of singular importance was the historiographical theory of accidental causation, which argued against profound conceptions of history. But in dealing with historical events he relied upon various philosophic precepts: he saw repetition of alignments, and often used historical analogy with the present in explaining them. This would seem to constitute a watered-down cyclical view of history, no doubt unwittingly construed, but clear enough to indicate a shallow sensitivity to many of the implications of his observations. And last, the accident theory contradicted his most basis belief in freedom. Determinism in history eliminates freedom of choice when it is assumed that men are manipulated by profound forces. In this Taylor was consistent, for he denied the existence of such forces. But history as accident no less denied historical actors freedom of choice, except in the very limited sense of being able to act according to opportunity. But as he explained events, choices again and again were determined by opportunity, and men seemed to have little control over either.

Understanding these weaknesses is useful in assessing secular dissent and Taylor's contribution to it. The key point is the nature of dissent as method, and radicalism as outlook. Bryan Magee was not thinking of Taylor specifically—though his name did appear—in *The New Radicalism* (1962). But his definition of radicalism suited Taylor perfectly. It pursues, he wrote, "not a programme, but *a way of looking at things*, from which follows a way of doing things."[74] And as Taylor made clear, believing one is right on a given issue is fully as important as being right, since the latter is in any case almost always a matter of opinion. Taylor's dissent rested no less on his implicit agreement with John W. Derry's description of radicalism as "belief in the goodness of man, the bright confidence in human reason. . . ."[75] Taylor's writings in the later 1950s bear witness to the continuity of this viewpoint. As he put it together, dissent elaborated the radical mentality which was simply the certainty that reason is efficacious and truth is virtuous. Scholarship and dissent became part of a single intellectual fabric, in this regard, an effort to combine objectivity with criticism. When he stayed within familiar areas, the result was often brilliant. He was no more a victim of prejudices there than were others. Two features emerged in Taylor's writings between 1955 and 1961. First, they reflected constantly the personal sense of virtue dissenters seem to derive from opposition, the assumption that from reducing issues to their essential qualities must come more rational actions, and the determined belief in the wisdom of the people. Second, they indicate his utilization of historical subjects as the material from which dissent could draw substance. Frequently he denied connections between his history and criticism, claiming a refusal to use history for political purposes. He wrote in 1952: ". . . I am only curious to know what happened in Europe in the second half of the nineteenth century without worrying anymore about the outcome."[76] On one level, as has been shown in these pages, this was correct. But on others, as *Troublemakers* made clear, history contained inspirations, examples, and personalities from which dissent could legitimately profit. If not always characteristic of dissenters, analogies with the past, especially in the era of sectarian Nonconformity, were never far from dissenting minds. Certainly this has been true of Taylor as a secular dissenter as well.

Taylor remains one of England's most important dissenting intellectuals, perhaps in a sense, the last of a kind. His image rests upon style, forms of expression, and a scintillating wit that has left few indifferent to his presence, even if they have sought to disregard it. His appeal in the late 1950s as a radio, television, and journalistic personality, as well as a historian, was his epigrammatic approach to history and to polemics that sometimes inspired, uplifted, and encouraged, and sometimes irritated and outraged. But his point was always to take the side of the people: as a historian to tell the truth in terms the common man could understand; as a polemicist to rouse them to their public duty, the exercise of democratic responsibilities. The lesson Taylor sought to teach, and which he himself sought to live, was simple and purely contemporary: "to take the world as it is and improve it; to have faith without a creed, hope without illusion, love without God."[77] Whether it was learned will not be seen for a long time; perhaps not until the twenty-first century when Taylor may have become, as Cobbett once was, the Grand Old Man of dissent.

NOTES

1. A. J. P. Taylor, *The Troublemakers: Dissent Over Foreign Policy, 1792-1939.* (London: Hamish Hamilton, 1957): 12. Cited hereafter as *Troublemakers.*
2. *Ibid.*, 13.
3. *Ibid.*, 9.
4. Taylor, "London Diary." *The New Statesman*, 51 (January 7, 1956), 6. Cited hereafter as "Diary" with appropriate date.
5. "Diary." 54 (July 6, 1957), 6.
6. "Diary." 54 (July 27, 1957), 106.
7. Taylor, interview with the author, London, September 23, 1969; letter to the author, July 2, 1973, 2.
8. "Diary." 50 (December 25, 1955), 849.
9. *Ibid.* Fifteen years later he was no more willing to slow down: "It seems unnecessary to remember birthdays," he wrote, "when advancing years

bring me more work instead of the retired ease which others apparently expect and enjoy. I should hate it." Letter to the author, March 23, 1970.

10. Taylor, letter, July 2, 1973, 2.
11. Taylor, "Manchester: The World's Cities." *Encounter*, 8 (March, 1957), 3. Cited hereafter as "Manchester."
12. Taylor, letter, July 2, 1973, 2. I have found it amusing that Taylor here admitted to a class-conscious reaction for which he once criticized Alexis de Tocqueville. When de Tocqueville first noticed August Blanqui, the republican, he was shocked that Blanqui "wore no visible linen"—an oblique reference to urine stains on his trousers. Taylor regarded this reaction, typical of an aristocrat, as a shameful opinion for one who has been for years regarded as the father of libertarian political thinking.
13. "Manchester.", 7.
14. *Ibid.*, 3.
15. *Ibid.*, 9.
16. Taylor, "Books in General." *The New Statesman and Nation*, 49 (January 22, 1955), 108.
17. Taylor, letter, July 2, 1973, 2. When I raised this point in a letter to Morganthau, he responded with this comment on Taylor: "I met Taylor once and found him charming and articulate, but generally unimpressive." Letter, May 8, 1973.
18. Taylor, "Metternich and His 'System' for Europe." *The Listener*, 62 (July 30, 1959), 167.
19. *Ibid.*, 168.
20. Taylor, "How Near is World War III?" *The Manchester Guardian Weekly*, September 3, 1959, 5.
21. *Ibid.*
22. Taylor, "The Isms in 1957: Fascism." *The Saturday Review of Literature*, 60 (June 8, 1957), 9.
23. Taylor, interview, September 23, 1969.
24. Taylor, "Hope No More." *The New Statesman*, 51 (April 14, 1956), 392; *See* also: "A Wasted Life." *The Observer*, May 15, 1955, 16; and Taylor, letter to Lady Allen of Hurtwood, June 13, 1955 (From the Lord Allen of Hurtwood Papers, The University of South Carolina, Columbia).
25. Taylor, "Confusion on the Left." *The Baldwin Age*, John Raymond, ed., (London: Eyre and Spottiswood, 1960), 73. He made the same point in "A Look Back at British Socialism, 1922-1937." *Encounter*, 10 (March, 1958), 31. Cited hereafter as "British Socialism." Then again, he wrote to me that "I am intellectually frivolous, partly by character, partly because this is what we were all like in the mid-twenties." Letter, May 13, 1967.
26. "British Socialism.", 33.
27. Taylor, "Nothing Left to Reform: The Political Consequences of 1945-1950." *The Manchester Guardian Weekly*, February 27, 1958, 7.
28. *Ibid.*
29. Taylor, "Without Tears." *The Manchester Guardian Weekly*, August 4, 1955, 10.
30. Taylor, "The Thing." *20th Century*, 162 (October, 1957), 295.
31. *Ibid.*
32. *Ibid.*, 297.
33. Taylor, "Keeping it Dark." *Encounter*, 13 (August, 1959), 42. Cited here-

after as "Keeping it Dark." And, Review of *i Documenti diplomatici Italliani*, 9th Series, Vol. I. *The English Historical Review*, 70 (October, 1955), 654.

34. "Keeping it Dark," 44.

35. *Troublemakers*, 22.

36. Taylor, "Handicap for the Historian." *The Times*, August 6, 1952, 5e.

37. Taylor, "Aid to Historical Perspective." *The Times*, August 19, 1954, 7e.

38. "Keeping it Dark," 42.

39. Taylor, *English History, 1914-1945*, (Oxford: The Oxford University Press, 1965), 602-603. Cited hereafter as *English History*.

40. *Troublemakers*, 55.

41. Taylor, "Burckhardt's Life and Letters." *The Manchester Guardian Weekly*, April 7, 1955, 11.

42. Taylor, "Dr. Toynbee's Roundtrip." *The Observer*, October 9, 1958, 10.

43. Taylor, "The Socialism of Keir Hardie." *The Manchester Guardian Weekly*, August 23, 1956, 12.

44. Taylor, "Charles James Fox: Champion of Liberty." *The Manchester Guardian Weekly*, September 20, 1956, 11; "A Most Impossible Person." *The Observer*, May 10, 1959, 25; "The Chief." *The New Statesman*, 57 (June 27, 1959), 896-897.

45. Taylor, "Man of an Idea." *The New Statesman*. 57 (October 29, 1959), 547.

46. Taylor, interview, September 23, 1969.

47. V. H. Galbraith, interview with the author, Oxford, December 18, 1969. A persistent rumor of the time had it that Namier himself, Taylor's great friend from Manchester University, queered his appointment.

48. Taylor, letter to Lady Allen of Hurtwood, June 13, 1955.

49. Hugh Trevor-Roper, quoted in Ved Mehta, *The Fly and the Fly Bottle: Encounters With British Intellectuals*, Penguin edition. (Baltimore: Penguin Books, 1961), 111.

50. Taylor, "Another Version of the Same." *The New Statesman*, 54 (November 30, 1957), 747.

51. Taylor, "On Satan's Side." *The New Statesman*, 65 (May 31, 1963), 826; *English History*, vii.

52. Taylor, letter, May 13, 1967.

53. David Marquand, "Historian of the 1990's." *The Manchester Guardian Weekly*, Air Edition. May 1, 1966, 10.

54. Taylor, "Letter to the Editor." *The Times*, March 11, 1958, 11.

55. Taylor quoted in Charles W. Lomas and Michael Taylor, eds., *The Rhetoric of the British Peace Movement*, (New York: Random House, Inc., 1971), 77.

56. Taylor, "Campaign Report." *The New Statesman*, 55 (June 1958), 799.

57. *Ibid.*, 800.

58. Taylor, quoted in *The Times*, March 31, 1959, 4.

59. Taylor, *Englishmen and Others*, (London: Hamish Hamilton, 1956), vii. Cited hereafter as *Englishmen*.

60. Taylor, "German Riddles." *The New Statesman*, 52 (October 6, 1956), 247.

61. Taylor, "The Problem of German Diplomacy." *The Manchester Guardian Weekly*. March 24, 1959, 11; "Evil Genius of the Wilhelmstrasse." *The Listener*, 54 (July 21, 1955), 104.

62. Taylor, *The Origins of the Second World War*, Premier Edition. (New York:Fawcett World Library, 1963), 72.
63. Taylor, "How Hitler Went to War." *The Manchester Guardian Weekly*, February 28, 1957, 11; "Munich Twenty Years After." *The Manchester Guardian Weekly*, October 2, 1958, 7.
64. *See* also, C. Robert Cole, "Critics of the Taylor View of History," *The Wiener Library Bulletin*, 22 (Summer, 1968), 29-35. This essay contains a summary and interpretation of attacks on Taylor's position in *Origins*.
65. Taylor, "When Germany Ruled Europe." *The Manchester Guardian Weekly*, August 15, 1957, 10.
66. Taylor, "Who Burnt the Reichstag?" *History Today*, 10 (August, 1960), 522.
67. Taylor, *Bismarck: the Man and the Statesman*, (New York: Alfred A. Knopf, Inc., 1955), 271.
68. *Ibid.*, 274.
69. *Englishmen*, 183.
70. Taylor, "Look Backwards to Utopia." *The New Statesman*, 59 (January 2, 1960), 5.
71. *Ibid.*
72. *Ibid.*
73. *Ibid.*, 6.
74. Bryan Magee, *The New Radicalism*, (New York: St. Martin's Press, 1962), 67. The italics are Magee's.
75. John W. Derry, *The Radical Tradition*, (London: The Macmillan Company, 1967), 403.
76. Taylor, *Rumors of War*, (London: Hamish Hamilton, 1952), 52.
77. Taylor, "Up From Utopia: How Two Generations Survived Their Wars." *The New Republic*, 123 (October 30, 1950), 16.

The Historian as Dissenter:
The Function of Criticism in Lord Acton's
"Inaugural Lecture on the Study of History"

RICHARD J. SCHOECK
The University of Colorado

THE FULL STORY of the context and reception of Lord Acton's "Inaugural Lecture on the Study of History," delivered at Cambridge on June 11, 1895, and reprinted in his *Lectures on Modern History*,[1] is yet to be told.[2] The lecture has become a classic, though like many classics it has often been misunderstood. This essay will attempt to shed light on only one of its many aspects: as a text in which Acton offered his credo as a dissenting historian.

We are of course generally accustomed to the word *dissenter* as a purely religious term, understood in a religious context; and even here we tend too much to restrict the signification to one who separates himself from the established Church of England. But as the O.E.D. observes, it was occasionally distinguished from *nonconformist* and restricted to those who not only dissented from the national church as actually constituted, but disagreed with the very principle of national or state churches. It is well, therefore, to note at the outset the earlier meanings of the word dissent. In Middle English, *Dissenten*—despite the force of *dissencioun* and its pointing of disagreement towards quarreling or strife—meant simply to express disagreement or to withhold consent. Much of the sense of withholding consent has carried into Modern English. In Acton's own times, it is important to note the O.E.D. citation from Swinburne's *Essays and Studies* which refers to the intellectual stimulation emanating from Mathew Arnold: "Mr. Arnold, with whose clear and critical spirit it is always good to come in contact, as disciple or as dissenter."[3] Here there is the sense implied of neutrality, of being either a disciple or a dissenter. In this usage a dissenter, then, is one who withholds consent and does not become a disciple. In Acton's view the dissenter is thus disinterested; chiefly he is a critic.

In this lecture which obviously meant so much to him, speaking as he was at a university where because of his religion he had been denied admission as a youth, Acton offers this credo for the dissenting historian: "For our purpose, the main thing to learn is not the art of accumulating material, but the sublimer art of investigating it, of discerning truth from falsehood, and certainty from doubt. It is by solidity of criticism more than by the plenitude of erudition, that the study of history strengthens, and straightens, and extends the mind."[4] Much has been made of the erudition shown in Acton's Inaugural Lecture, and too much of its polylingual aspects: it is true that the authorities cited would daunt any other historian, then or now, and it is true that the languages range from English to German, French, Latin, Italian and Spanish. But too little has been made of the lecture's emphasis upon method: the title, in fact, is "Inaugural Lecture on the Study of History," and Acton began by addressing his audience as "Fellow Students." It is clearly criticism more than erudition that matters to him, that operates to strengthen the mind.

Here is the heart of Acton's essay on the study of history, the fulcrum about which the complex structure and even more weighty superstructure of citation and allusion turns: "And the accession of the critic in the place of the indefatigable compiler, of the artist in coloured narrative, the skilled limner of character, the persuasive advocate of good, or other causes, amounts to a transfer of government, to a change of dynasty, in the historic realm."[5] It is a simple point, really, but without seeing it clearly the reader founders in a sea of one hundred and five footnotes, six languages, citations from history, memoirs, literature, philosophy, religion, and all that. Should we not recognize that in this crucial section of his lecture the erudition is largely to be found in the footnotes (as distinguished from the wisdom, which is in the main text), and stress the point that in the main text—and for nearly an entire page at this stretch there is not a single footnote—Acton sets about enunciating the three operations of the critical mind, of the dissenter in the scholarly process. These operations are the key to the historian's version of the "higher criticism," his essence as a dissenter.

How do we recognize the critic, and how does the dissenter-critic function, we may well ask, as no doubt did Acton's audience in 1895? He provided a complex answer, beginning thus: "For the critic is one who, when he lights on an interesting statement, begins by suspecting it. He remains in suspense until he has subjected his authority to three operations. First, he asks whether he has read the passage as the author wrote it."[6] And the critical faculty is turned several ways, not least upon the student himself, the observer—an anticipation, or at least an analogue of Heisenberg's Uncertainty Principle: we must consider the variables of the observer.[7] Acton explains further:

For the transcriber, and the editor, and the official or officious censor
on the top of the editor, have played strange tricks, and have much
to answer for. And if they are not to blame, it may turn out that
the author wrote his book twice over, that you can discover the first
jet, the progressive variations, things added, and things struck out.[8]

Acton, as I have commented elsewhere,[9] had a marvelous acumen in literature, having anticipated the twentieth-century fascination with the persona of Thackeray. This strong sense of the importance of studying the writer at work, the variations of thought in the process of "technique as discovery," to use Mark Schorer's fine and heuristic phrase, is characteristic of his analysis everywhere.

The next operation concerns the author's sources, the nature of which must be closely examined:

Next is the question where the writer got his information. If from a
previous writer, it can be ascertained, and the inquiry has to be
repeated. If from unpublished papers, they must be traced, and when
the fountainhead is reached, or the track disappears, the question
of veracity arises. The responsible writer's character, his position,
antecedents, and probable motives have to be examined into; and
this is what, in a different and adapted sense of the word, may be
called the higher criticism,[10] in comparison with the servile and often
mechanical work of pursuing statements to their roots. For a
historian has to be treated as a witness, and not believed unless his
sincerity is established.[11]

The footnote citation at the end of this last sentence (fn.61) reads: "The only case in which such extraneous matters can be fairly called in is when facts are stated resting on testimony; then it is not only just, but it is necessary for the sake of truth, to inquire into the habits of mind of him by whom they are adduced. Charles Babbage, *Ninth Bridgewater Treatise*, (1837), p. xiv." Acton is stressing the point that the historian himself is like a witness; what is remarkable is that Acton should cite so obscure a work as that of Babbage, published sixty years earlier. But Babbage was a figure of some interest in the nineteenth century for his writings on method, and it may well be that there is a special interest in Babbage on the part of Acton—an hypothesis which may be confirmed by further examination of his library and notes at Cambridge. The notion that the historian is a witness is not unique at this time, and one thinks indeed of an effort like Browning's in *The Ring and the Book* (1868), in which the murder story is told from several points of view to the effect, as Robert Langbaum has suggested,[12] that we have a relativist poem.

Acton concludes the paragraph with the statement that "the maxim that a man must be presumed to be innocent until his guilt is proved, was not made for him." That maxim is, of course, a maxim or principle from the Anglo-American legal tradition, and therefore did not need to be annotated. In the next paragraph Acton returns to the question of weighing authorities and how this can best be taught to the student of modern history: "For us, then, the estimate of authorities, the weighing of testimony, is more meritorious than the potential discovery of new matter."[13] Here his citation of John Stuart Mill simply reinforces the statement.[14] He goes on:

And modern history, which is the widest field of application, is not
the best to learn our business in; for it is too wide, and the harvest
has not been winnowed as in antiquity, and further on to the
Crusades. It is better to examine what has been done for questions
that are compact and circumscribed, such as the sources of Plutarch's
Pericles, the two tracts on *Athenian Government*, the origin of the
Epistle to Diognetus, the date of the *Life of St. Antony*; and to learn
from Schwegler how this analytical work began.[15]

Acton's breadth of knowledge is notable here. The range of examples moves from classical to patristic and medieval. Schwegler, not footnoted, was Friedrich Carl Albert Schwegler, the learned editor of Aristotle, Clement, and Eusebius, who wrote a celebrated *Geschichte der griechischen Philosophie*, as well as a Roman history, and was editor of a *Jahrbuch der Gegenwart*: this all reflects Acton's thorough grounding under Dollinger in ecclesiastical and classical history.

After praising two recent Cambridge scholars, Lightfoot and Hort, both theologians and Scripture scholars, for their critical faculty, Acton takes up the third operation of the critical faculty: "The third distinctive note of the generation of writers who dug so deep a trench between history as known to our grandfathers and as it appears to us, is their dogma of impartiality. . . . History, to be above evasion or dispute, must stand on documents, not on opinions."[16] The range of supporting citations is interesting,[17] but I want to move on to the example which Acton brings forward, for he always believed in the study of great examples:

Ranke is the representative of the age which instituted the modern
study of history. He taught it to be critical, to be colourless, and to
be new. We meet him at every step, and he has done more for us
than any other man. . . . He was the first eminent writer who

exhibited what Michelet calls *le désintéressement des morts*. It was
a moral triumph for him when he could refrain from judging, show
that much might be said on both sides, and leave the rest to
Providence.[18]

As Acton goes on to say, "We who have to learn [these fundamental techni-
calities], must immerse ourselves in the study of the great examples." The
point, of course, is that: "Apart from what is technical, method is only the
reduplication of common sense, and is best acquired by observing its use
by the ablest men in every variety of intellectual employment."[19] And the
authorities range from Papillon and Cournot to Ruskin, Coleridge, Descartes,
Laplace, Pasteur, and Dumas. For students of history can learn from the
men of science much that is essential: "For they can show how to test proof;
how to secure fulness and soundness in induction, how to restrain and to
employ with safety hypothesis and analogy. . . . Theirs is the logic of discovery. . . ."[20]

I should like to go on, to do a fuller analysis of this celebrated lecture-
essay, for there is God's plenty here, particularly when Acton moves to
"those shining precepts which are the registered property of every school"[21]
such as having no favorites, and being more severe to ideas than to actions,
or judging talent at its best and character at its worst—or that superb precept
for departments and interdisciplinary programs: ". . . study problems in
preference to periods." But all of these lead to his major exhortation:
". . . never to debase the moral currency or to lower the standard of recti-
tude, but to try others by the final maxim that governs your own lives, and
to suffer no man and no cause to escape the undying penalty which history
has the power to inflict on wrong." Among other authorities in Acton's rather
brief footnote at this point, note 90, there is this dictum from a treatise on
natural law: "Pour juger ce qui est bon et juste dans la vie actuelle ou passée,
il faut posséder un criterium qui ne soit pas tiré du passé ou du présent, mais
de la nature humaine." It is a vital point in the structure of Acton's thought
that there was no compartmentalizing of the past from present life, and that
the criterion for judgment was drawn from human nature and the natural
law.

The entire section which follows deals with the concept that morality is
not ambulatory (to follow Sir Thomas Browne) and that the principles of
true politics and history are those of morality enlarged (to follow Burke).
And so Acton ends on a note which nearly all in the dissenting tradition
which preceded him (and which he knew and understood so richly) would
have applauded. That conclusion is the capstone of this lecture on the study
of history which has presented his credo of the dissenter as historian:

The historians of former ages, unapproachable for us in knowledge
and in talent, cannot be our limit. We have the power to be more
rigidly impersonal, disinterested and just than they; and to learn from
undisguised and genuine records to look with remorse upon the
past, and to the future with assured hope of better things; bearing
this in mind, that if we lower our standard in history, we cannot
uphold it in Church or State.[22]

And that standard was liberty, understood as free and critical inquiry.

There are, as indicated at the outset, other contexts in which this inaugural
lecture must be placed, and they are, among others, the history of higher
education in the United Kingdom and the admissibility of nonconformists
and Roman Catholics to the universities, the discussion of methodology in
the study of history (and Acton's massive essay in the first volume of the
English Historical Review on "German Schools of History" must be a part
of our continuing discussion of that methodology), and not least the milieu
of Acton's complex study and thought—but that is all a larger task that I
cannot assume here. I have tried simply to emphasize that the fulcrum of
Acton's argument in this lecture rests upon a sense of the critical mind in its
work, a sense ultimately no less important in the history of nineteenth-century thought and the history of scholarship than Matthew Arnold's more
celebrated disinterestedness of the critic. And I would add that in his much
observed and widely read inaugural lecture at Cambridge, Acton seized a
precious opportunity: "I shall never again enjoy the opportunity of speaking
my thoughts to such an audience as this," he said; "on so privileged an occasion a lecturer may well be tempted to bethink himself whether he knows of
any neglected truth, any cardinal proposition, that might serve as his selected
epigraph, as a last signal, perhaps even as a target." That neglected truth
and target was the centrality of the moral sense in history; it was a cardinal
proposition to all in the long English tradition of dissenters.

NOTES

1. Printed at Cambridge University Press in 1895 (with a 2nd edition of 1896,
   from which quotations are drawn), the lecture was reprinted in *Lectures on
   Modern History* (London: Macmillan Co., 1906), 1-30, with footnotes
   given on 319-342. (Ed.n.: It has been more recently reprinted in *Lord Acton: Essays in the Liberal Interpretation of History*, ed. W. H. McNeill
   (Chicago: University of Chicago Press, 1967).
2. Something of the story of the reception of Acton's inaugural lecture has
   been told recently by Alan Bell (in *TLS* February 8, 1974). Lord Russell
   of Killowen described the lecture to Roseberry as "one of the most sugges-

tive and condensed utterances I've read for a long time: I only wish my reading were wide eno' fully to appreciate it." And the young G. M. Trevelyan has been identified by Bell as the source of Sir George Trevelyan's bulletin to Roseberry in November:

> You may care to know, what perhaps you may have heard from other quarters, what an immense success Acton is at Cambridge. At least 200 people came to his first lecture, and quite as many attend every one of them since. . . . He is regarded distinctly as a *great* man, and the young people pay him the unusual compliment of thinking him a great deal younger than he is. The feeling is that the lectures which he is delivering are literature of a very high order. Altogether, it has been a tremendous hit.

3. The O.E.D. under the date of 1869 cites Swinburne's *Essays and Studies* (1875) 213. For the Middle English I am indebted to the *Middle English Dictionary*, ed. Hans Kurath, *et. al.* (Ann Arbor: University of Michigan Press, 1962), part D.4.

4. *Inaugural Lecture*, 40.

5. *Ibid.*

6. *Ibid.*

7. On the Renaissance discovery that the observer may be moved, see my "Note on Copernicus and Thomas More," *Moreana* 38 (1973), 58. Heisenberg's Uncertainty Principle that "the product of the uncertainties in the values of certain related variables, as of the position and momentum of a particle, is greater than or equal to Plack's constant"—and that the position of the observer is a variable—was of course enunciated well after the publication of Acton's lecture.

8. *Inaugural Lecture*, 41.

9. *See* my "Lord Acton as a Literary Critic." *Revista di Letterature Moderne e Comparate*, xx.1 (Manzo 1967), 53-61.

10. Acton on the Higher Criticism is a separate study in itself, but it may be noted that Acton thought George Eliot one of the fine spirits of the age and that he quoted Mark Pattison and Benjamin Jowett frequently.

11. *Inaugural Lecture*, 41-42. The question of sincerity has recently moved once again to the foreground of literary studies: long an issue with Catholic writers (there is much periodical literature on Joyce, Graham Greene and others), it is the subject of a recent series of lectures by Lionel Trilling at Harvard, *Sincerity and Authenticity* (Harvard University Press, 1972).

    The question of conscience is intimately related to that of sincerity, and Acton speaks frequently enough about conscience. I anticipate dealing with Acton and conscience in a volume on the European conscience which has grown out of a Folger conference held in November, 1973, "The European Conscience from Erasmus to Pascal."

12. Cf. Langbaum's reading of Browning's *Ring and the Book* as a "relativist poem," in *The Poetry of Experience* (New York, 1957), 109-136.

13. *Inaugural Lecture*, 42.

14. The footnote here is number 62, which quotes two comments by Mill: "There is no part of our knowledge which is more useful to obtain at first hand—to go to the fountain-head for—than our knowledge of history."— J. S. Mill, *Inaugural Address*, 34. And, "The only sound intellects are those which, in the first instance, set their standards of proof high."—J. S. Mill, *Examination of Hamilton's Philosophy*, 525.

15. *Inaugural Lecture*, 42-3.
16. *Ibid.*, 44-45.
17. Footnote 63 cites Greg, Lavaleye, Scherer, Michelet, and Jowett. Of these, perhaps the most interesting is from W. R. Greg's *Political Problems for our Age and Country* (1870): "There are so few men mentally capable of seeing both sides of a question; so few with consciences sensitively alive to the obligation of seeing both sides; so few placed under conditions either of circumstance or temper, which admit of their seeing both sides."
18. *Inaugural Lecture*, 48-51.
19. *Ibid.*, 53.
20. *Ibid.*, 55.
21. *Ibid.*, 62.
22. *Ibid.*, 74.

The Contributors and Editors

W. D. J. Cargill Thompson, Lecturer in Ecclesiastical History, University of London Kings College. He has held the posts of Fellow of King's College, Cambridge, and Lecturer in History, University of Sussex. Publications include "The Philosopher of the 'Politic Society': Richard Hooker as a Political Thinker." In W. Speed Hill, ed., *Studies in Richard Hooker*. Also, he has authored numerous articles on Luther and sixteenth-century English church history for *Journal of Ecclesiastical History, Journal of Theological Studies,* and *Harvard Theological Review.*

Vernon Carner, Instructor in American Church History, Loma Linda University. He is co-editor with Ray Billington of *People of the Plains and Mountains: Essays in the History of the West Dedicated to Everett Dick,* and is publisher of *Adventist Heritage: A Magazine of Adventist History.*

C. Robert Cole, Assistant Professor of History, Utah State University. He has held instructorships at Pomona College, and Whittier College. Publications include articles and reviews for *The Wiener Library Bulletin, The Rocky Mountain Social Science Journal, The Journal of Modern History,* and *Bulletin of Bibliography.* Forthcoming is a book *A. J. P. Taylor: A Radical Historian of Foreign Policy.*

Patrick Collinson, Professor of History and Head of the Department of History, University of Sydney. He has held academic posts at the University of London. Publications include *The Elizabethan Puritan Movement,* an edition of *Letters of Thomas Wood, Puritan, 1566-1577,* and *A Mirror of Elizabethan Puritanism: The Life and Letters of 'Godly Master Dering.' "* Forthcoming is a biography of Edmund Grindal, Elizabethan Archbishop of York and Canterbury.

270

MARK H. CURTIS, President and Professor of History, Scripps College. He has held posts at Williams College, University of California at Los Angeles, and the Pacific School of Religion. Publications include *Oxford and Cambridge in Transition, 1558-1642*, "Education and Apprenticeship" in *Shakespeare in His Own Age*, and articles for *History* and *The Library*.

C. H. GEORGE, Professor of History, Northern Illinois University. Publications include *The Protestant Mind of the English Reformation* with Katherine George, *Revolution: European Radicals from Hus to Lenin*, and articles in *Past and Present* and *Science and Society*.

MICHAEL E. MOODY, Instructor in History, Denver University. He has been a teaching fellow at Pitzer College. Forthcoming publications include a critical edition with Leland H. Carlson of George Johnson's *A Discourse of Some Troubles in the Banished Church at Amsterdam*. He is joint editor with Leland Carlson and Frederick J. Youngs of the "British Commonwealth and Ireland" section of the *American Historical Review* bibliographical section on journal articles.

J. MAX PATRICK, Professor of English, University of Wisconsin-Milwaukee. He has held posts at the University of Manhattan, Buffalo University, Princeton University, Emory University, the University of Florida, Queens College of the City University of New York, the Claremont Graduate School, and New York University. Publications include *Hugh Peters, The Quest for Utopia*, and *The Pioneer Theater in Savannah*. He has edited works on Milton, Herrick, Bacon, and W. H. Mallock. In progress is an edition of the poetry of George Herbert.

RICHARD J. SCHOECK, Professor of English, the University of Colorado, and until recently, Director of Research Activities, Folger Shakespeare Library. He has held positions at Cornell University, the University of Notre Dame, St. Michael's College of the University of Toronto, and the University of Maryland. Publications include editorship of Ascham's *Scholemaster*, Delehaye's *Legends of the Saints, Editing Sixteenth-Century Texts*, and general editor of the 3-volume Yale edition of *The Confutation*.

FRANKLIN D. SCOTT, Professor Emeritus in History, Northwestern University. He is presently curator of the Nordic Collections in the Honnold Library, Claremont. Publications include *The United States and Scandinavia, World Migration in Modern Times*, and *The Peopling of America*.

JOHN W. WILKES, Professor of History, New York University. He has held posts at Pomona College, Claremont, and Northwestern University. Publications include *A Whig in Power: A Political Biography of Henry Pelham*, and essays in *The Huntington Library Quarterly*. Forthcoming is a book *Essays on Eighteenth Century England*.

FREDERICK J. YOUNGS, Associate Professor of History, Louisiana State University. He has been at California State University, Long Beach. Publications include several articles on Tudor history, editorship of *The History Teacher*, and editorship with Leland Carlson and Michael E. Moody of the "British Commonwealth and Ireland" section of the *American Historical Review* bibliographical section on journal articles.

CECILE ZINBERG, Associate Professor of History, California State University, Fullerton. She has been at Ohio State University, Brooklyn College and York College of the City University of New York, and C. W. Post College of Long Island University. Publications include articles and reviews in *Notes and Queries*, *American Historical Review*, and *British Studies Monitor*. In progress is *John Strype and the Sixteenth Century: Portrait of an Anglican Historian*, and *University Law Degrees in England, Their Pursuit and Application, 1540-1640: A Study of a Professional Class*.